The
Comforts
of Home

The
Comforts
of Home

Prostitution in Colonial Nairobi

LUISE WHITE

The University of Chicago Press
Chicago and London

LUISE WHITE is assistant professor of history at the University of Minnesota.

The University of Chicago Press, Chicago 60637
The University of Chicago Press, Ltd., London
© 1990 by The University of Chicago
All rights reserved. Published 1990
Printed in the United States of America
99 98 97 96 95 94 93 92 91 90   5 4 3 2 1

Library of Congress Cataloging-in-Publication Data

White, Luise.
    The comforts of home : prostitution in Colonial Nairobi / Luise
White.
       p.   cm.
    Includes bibliographical references.
    ISBN 0–226–89506–8 (alk. paper).—ISBN 0–226–89507–6
(pbk : alk. paper)
    1. Prostitution—Kenya—Nairobi—History.   2. Kenya—Colonial
influence.   3. Women—Kenya—Social conditions.   4. Working class
women—Kenya—Social conditions.   5. Kenya—Social conditions.
I. Title
HQ260.5.N35W45   1990
306.74′2′0967625—dc20   90–34266
                                                        CIP

Contents

Maps

Acknowledgments

This project began, many years ago, as a way to study the history of women exclusively, to privilege women's experiences and not turn the discussion back onto men. The more I learned, however, the more I became aware that prostitutes could not be studied in isolation from the men who visited them, nor could they be studied through the generalizations of exploitation or degradation. Nairobi prostitutes described a world of hard work and opportunity in which prostitution was not evidence of social pathology or moral decay or male dominance, but a complex relationship between men and women and their respective families. In colonial cities built by male migrants, prostitution was a specific relationship between men and women, their families, and private employers. Research that began as a way to study women's work became a way to study the workings of a colonial society from its most intimate moments—the interaction of the work of daughters, the makeshift arrangements of male migrants, and the long-term strategies of rural lineages and urban employers. The colonial state forms a backdrop in this book; when it did have impact on women's private lives, it did not have it for very long. Thus the weakness and later the unwillingness of colonialists to enter the terrain of domesticity meant, very simply, that domesticity and its situation were controlled by the people who provided it.

A number of institutions, archives, and friends have supported this research over the years. The Office of the President in Kenya gave me permission to do research. Research in Kenya was funded by the Jan Smuts Memorial Commonwealth Fellowship of Cambridge University and later by the Division of the Humanities at Rice University, where I am especially grateful to Allan Matusow and Albert van Helden for their support; uncompleted research in Tanzania was funded by the Social Science Research Council. In Kenya the staff at the National Archives—particularly Richard Ambani and Musila Musembe—made my research possible; I am also indebted to the staffs of the Public Records Office, Rhodes House, Oxford, and the Church of Scotland Missionary Society Archives in Edinburgh. Home comforts were often provided by my hosts in these places: Erica Flegg in London, Helen and Robert Irwin in St. Andrews and later in London, Sidney Westley and Judith Geist in Nairobi, and Birgitta and Per Larsson in Bukoba. During my years in Kenya, I have been grateful for the camaraderie of members of the Department of History at the University of Nairobi, especially James de V. Allen, Mwangi wa Githumo, Karim Janmohammed, Benjamin Kipkorir, Godfrey Muriuki, Atieno Odhiambo, B. A. Ogot, Ahmed Salim, and Gideon Were, and Tabitha Kanogo and Henry Mwanzi of Kenyatta University, and William Ochieng' and Mathias Ogutu of Moi University. None of this research would have been possible without my assistants, Margaret Makuna and Paul Kakaire, and the friends, colleagues, and neighbors in Nairobi who provided leads, contacts, and fresh insights: Judith Butterman, Clement and Pheobe Cottingham, Alice Gold, Edith Miguda, Odhiambo Opiyo, Carl Rosberg, and the women I lived with in Westlands. Janet Bujra, Marshall Clough, Michael Cowen, Major Ernest Christian Lanning, Birgitta Larsson, Scott MacWilliam, Jeremy Newman, Richard Waller, and Roger van Zwanenberg all generously loaned me unpublished material. Copies of my interviews are deposited in the Institute for African Studies, University of Nairobi. The names of all informants have been changed but are consistent with the women's ethnic and religious affiliations.

Half of this book was written when I was an Izaak Walton Killam Postdoctoral Fellow at Dalhousie University in Halifax, Nova Scotia, where Jane Parpart provided exemplary collegiality and encouragement. The book was completed at the University of Minnesota, with support from the Graduate School. Frederick Cooper, Sara Evans, Laura Fair, Susan Geiger, Margaret Jean Hay, Allen Isaacman, and Saulo Busolo Wanambisi read all or part of this manuscript. Phil Schwartzberg of the University of Minnesota Cartography Lab did the maps. This book was written in the wider community of the feminist scholars who write on women, especially women in Africa. Naming them would leave me with no reviewers, but they have provided a vision and an example of African social history that is engaged with and by the voices of ordinary women.

No one can write African labor history in the 1990s without acknowl-

edging the influence of Frederick Cooper. In my case, however, his stal-
wart friendship and support, and his exceptionally clear insights about
work in general and work in Kenya's cities in particular, have empowered
my work and the task of being an African historian. My greatest intellec-
tual debt is to John Lonsdale. I was his student for much longer than most
people need to be tutored—it takes a special kind of person to supervise a
doctoral thesis on the history of prostitution—but his knowledge of state,
society, and social process in Kenya has informed this study in more ways
than I can ever fully acknowledge. He knew what the major issues of this
study were long before I did, and if any parts of this work seem insightful
or wise, it is because of what he has taught me.

A Note on Currencies

The units of currency employed here are rupees, pounds sterling (£), or shillings (/). From the early days of the protectorate to 1920, rupees were used, with a standard exchange rate of fifteen rupees one pound. With the suspension of the gold standard the value of the silver rupee rose and fell, and in 1920 ten rupees equalled one pound (see chapter 3, note 13). In 1921 Kenya made its currency pounds, shillings, and cents, converting at a rate of twenty shillings to one pound, with two shillings being equal to one rupee, and one hundred cents to the shilling. After much debate the size of the smaller coins were to be fifty cents, ten cents, five cents, and one cent; a twenty-five-cent coin was replaced by the fifty-cent coin. A few years after independence, in 1967, Kenya went off the sterling standard, and until the mid-1970s the value of the Kenya shilling was between seven and nine shillings to the United States dollar.

1

Introduction: Prostitution in Comparative Perspective; or, Casual Sex and Casual Labor

This book is about the history of prostitution in a city in British colonial Africa. Nairobi, the capital of Kenya, was founded in 1899 in the middle of a region that had barely recovered from epidemic and famine. From its earliest years Nairobi had a special relationship to people in the countryside who were trying to recoup their loses. Unlike other capitals in settler societies, Nairobi had no industrial base—the wealth of Kenya was kept in the agricultural sector—and hence no need for a permanent labor force. While the British colonialists sought to make the capital a city of male migrants, the permanent African population clustered in the service sector: servants, prostitutes, and householders. Indeed, prostitutes often became landlords and many landlords were prostitutes: this was not because illicit and respectable roles were indistinct in cities in British colonial Africa, but because women, in the absence of formal employment opportunities, earned the money with which to acquire property through prostitution, and landlords, however rapacious their rents, had a degree of legitimacy because of the years they had spent in these communities as good neighbors and valuable, peace-keeping tenants. The illicit often supported the respectable. There were no pimps at any time in Kenya's history, so that prostitutes were able to retain control over their earnings—when they so desired—and have intimate and stable relations with the laboring men who were their customers.

Not all Nairobi prostitutes acquired urban property. Some subsidized their families' farms, others bought livestock (precapitalist wealth in East Africa), while others—fewer in the past than today—just managed to get by. Even women who never managed to acquire real property spoke of the value of self-reliance and having a few material possessions; women saw

1

prostitution as a reliable means of capital accumulation, not as a despica-
ble fate or a temporary strategy. Indeed, whether a woman invested in urban real estate for herself or bought goats for her father did not seem to
have been a personal or a cultural decision. The work of prostitutes was
family labor. Prostitutes' patterns of reinvestment reproduced families:
either with themselves as heads of household, as in the case of women who
bought property for themselves, or for their families of origin, as daughters' revenues restored the shattered fortunes of agriculturalists. Nairobi's
situation is ideal for studying the interaction of town and countryside, so
that the place of prostitution in cash crop production, and the place of pastoral economies in prostitution, can be not only ascertained but also put
into a historical context.

Some of these insights about peasant production, housing, and prostitution contradict prevailing notions about the place of prostitution, and
the exploitation of prostitutes, in capitalist societies. Is this because prostitution in Nairobi is unique—and thus could never be compared to anything in the West—or is it because the way that scholars have looked at
prostitution in Europe and America has been determined by specific attempts to control prostitution? Are my findings different because Africa
is so different, or because interviews with former prostitutes revealed another picture altogether? If this book challenges any of the conventional
assumptions about prostitutes' degradation and victimization, is it because
Nairobi is unlike anywhere else on earth, or because those assumptions
are flawed and based on information generated by attacks on prostitutes?

Regulation, Reform, and the Construction of Historical Data

Modern studies of prostitution began with the influential work of the
early-nineteenth-century Parisian public health official, Parent-Duchatelet. His detailed research, his specialized vision, and his access to police
records enabled him to catalogue prostitutes' weight, eye color, place of origin, years of schooling, and father's occupation. He concluded that prostitutes were not biologically different from other women and that they
became prostitutes for short periods of time because of economic need.
But whatever their motivations, they were "the most dangerous people in
society" not just because they were diseased; "they destroy one's fortune as
well as one's health." "Prostitution, as I have already said several times, is
similar to a torrent that one cannot stop," but with the proper legislation
and medical controls, it could be contained. In this way Parent-Duchatelet

reduced prostitutes to a noxious part of the environment, identifiable and controllable, not unlike sewers or decaying meat.[1]

Parent-Duchatelet's study was immediately influential in England, where he was called the "Newton of harlotry." Although British investigators were unable to duplicate the precision and scope of Parent-Duchatelet's study, they took certain generalizations from it: that prostitutes could be studied and classified much like biological specimens, and that prostitution emerged, full-blown and irreversibly, from a degenerate and impoverished environment. By the 1850s and 1860s British reformers replaced the economic causes of prostitution with sanitary ones and suggested that prostitution was inevitable and possibly even beneficial, given the differential sexual appetites of men and women, if prostitutes could be made healthy and were under official control. In 1857 William Acton wrote an influential tract suggesting that since prostitution was a phase of poor women's lives, the state should register a prostitute "to pass through this stage of her existence with as little permanent damage to herself and as little mischief to society as possible."[2] These ideas were taken up in Europe and the British Empire. Italian criminologists of the 1890s praised the registration of prostitutes; without it "an enormous number of young men would be thrown into desperation."[3] An 1897 Johannesburg newspaper editorial put it more bluntly: "the virtue of the *monde* is assured by the *demi-monde*."[4] Although feminist critics of the registration of prostitutes challenged these beliefs and claimed that prostitutes were victims of men and poverty,[5] the metaphors and categories of Parent-Duchatelet and Acton, the language of sickness, scrutiny, and sanitation, have dominated most discussions of prostitution, both inside and outside the academy.

Most of what is known about prostitution in the nineteenth and twentieth centuries comes not from prostitutes but from this conjunction of ideas about prostitutes' function and pollution: the registration of prostitutes to keep them healthy while making them available to middle-class men. Much of the data available to historians comes from the files of police forces concerned with tallying prostitutes' previous employment, marital status, medical history, and fathers' occupation. While the actual data are excellent, their use by historians has been problematic; these categories were the information required for registration, and taken together they made prostitutes—and prostitutes alone—a distinctive group. Moreover, registration criminalized unregistered prostitutes, thus criminalizing poor women's occasional labor and creating an illegal population of streetwise, community-minded prostitutes who privileged the bonds of place and privacy over the clientele—and the medical examinations—registration offered them.[6]

Although registration raised such severe protests that it was eventually abandoned everywhere, the implementation of registration had made prostitutes' working conditions so difficult that the structure and the organization of their labor had changed. As it became increasingly illegal for women to be self-employed on the streets or to rent rooms for themselves, prostitutes entered into relationships with men to provide the protections that the new laws required—men solicited customers, or posed as husbands in furnished rooms, or bribed the police—"so that almost every prostitute is under the control of some bully," wrote a London magistrate in 1895.[7]

The English Contagious Diseases legislation brought men into prostitution in a way that they had never been before. The Contagious Diseases Acts made casual labor calculated; they made it a crime and involved it in a series of social relations that courted dependency. The American 1910 White Slave Traffic Act (the Mann Act), which made it a felony to entice a woman to cross state lines for "the purpose of prostitution or debauchery," also institutionalized and certified the role of men in prostitution.[8] Both the Contagious Diseases laws and the Mann Act were designed to curtail women's mobility. The differences between the legislations are greater than the similarities, but for my purposes it is necessary to understand that men and male control enter prostitution only *after* the state does. Studies that show the male domination and violence behind women's participation in prostitution may well reverse this particular chronology of criminalization and control. Moreover, they shift the focus away from women and onto men, and away from the initiatives of women and their families. In most of the world, it would seem that prostitution became a social problem when impoverished peasantries and urban work forces sent their daughters onto the streets in increasing numbers, and when the monies those daughters remitted to their families slowed down the rate of proletarianization of the peasantry or entrance of casual laborers into the order and discipline of wage labor. When states legislated against prostitution, ostensibly to protect middle-class men, the men in prostitutes' lives began to provide a structure and an infrastructure for their work. The assault on prostitution in nineteenth-century England, for example, was part of a larger assault on casual labor, not just because prostitution was casual labor, but because urban prostitution subsidized casual labor. No wonder men in the 1890s began to "bully" the prostitutes with whom they lived: the criminalization of prostitution brought about its decasualization. "A husband or a lover drifted into being a 'bully . . . much as women . . . drift into prostitution.'"[9]

It was the criminalization of prostitution that created the conditions—the pimps, the apparent forcing of women onto the streets—that horrified reformers of the early twentieth century, who compiled vivid reports about the extent of prostitution in a variety of American cities. In this way much of the data available to scholars about prostitution was created and determined by the political efforts to regulate and reform it. The categories and constructs were in a direct line from Parent-Duchatelet and Acton, and did not reveal the place of women's work in women's families. Where there was no registration—Africa, or the American West—the data about prostitution have been more economic. This was not because the line between respectable and unrespectable was so thin in Nairobi or Mombasa or Elko or Helena but because census manuscripts, tax records, and oral data revealed a very different picture of prostitutes' lives—and prostitutes' earnings—than police records did.[10]

In the rhetoric of reform, the middle-class men whose needs and energies required a population of registered prostitutes were replaced by pimps as the source of prostitutes' exploitation. The idea that women were forced into and then trapped in prostitution was well suited to the turn-of-the-century American ambivalence about urbanization, immigration, and the mobility of young men and women,[11] but it also implied that women were more passive and dependent than they had ever been in regulationist ideology. American vice commissions reported that pimps "maintained tyrannical and brutal control" over women on the streets; neither social reformers nor their historians could find evidence of women's resistance and subversion.[12] The temporary nature of prostitution, women's ability to move in and out of it, were all erased by the con- ceptualization of the pimp. Indeed, the very idea of a pimp—with all the violence and expropriation the word conjures up—is one that separates prostitutes from their own accumulation. Before World War I pimps were a convenient way to blame boyfriends and lovers and dependents for exploiting prostitutes. No less an authority on the expropriation of prostitutes' earnings than American madam Nell Kimball, who had operated brothels in New Orleans and San Francisco, complained "that most of her girls had pimps who mooched off them."[13] It is not that there is a fine line between a prostitute supporting a devoted, unemployed lover and a man violently taking the plurality of a woman's earnings, but the kinds of data available to historians blur such distinctions. For example, single Japanese women could not emigrate to late-nineteenth-century Hawaii, so most prostitutes arrived there as mail-order brides. Contemporary sources described prostitutes' husbands as their pimps, but individual prostitutes boasted that they sent $200 home to Japan each month.[14] It would seem that a pattern of male control, force, and expropriation did not apply to 1890s Hawaii. Elsewhere, the middle-class revulsion at men living off prostitutes' earnings—even if the couple were legally married—prompted scathing newspaper descriptions about "the thing that looked like a white man" who lived with a prostitute in Virginia City.[15] Reformers' horror at the working-class men and immigrants who avoided legitimate work through the proceeds of prostitution successfully shifted attention away from the middle-class patrons of prostitutes and also made male exploitation—in this case extended to include a construction of working-class or immigrant sexuality that was as violent as it was promiscuous—central to reformers' discussions of prostitution.

There is nothing inevitable about pimping. It is not a relationship that prostitution evolves into. There were no pimps in Nairobi or anywhere else in Africa, outside of Johannesburg in the 1890s. Nairobi prostitutes expressed some dismay at the concept of paying a man to help them in their work. These women were, if anything, mean-spirited about what to give any man—a taxi driver, or a friend—who occasionally brought men to them: they all believed that such remuneration was their customer's responsibility. Even wartime prostitutes who had European customers who did not speak an African language did not retain African men to solicit, translate, or negotiate for them: "there was no reason, if a white man came alone, he knew enough to help himself, if an African man brought him, he would help him."[16]

Ruth Rosen cautions us that denying male violence against women is "to hold women responsible for their own victimization."[17] But if women are not responsible for being on the streets, or for being victims of abusive customers or rapacious policemen, how can they be responsible for earning enough from streetwalking to set themselves up as milliners or brothel keepers, or to bring a dowry to a respectable marriage? There must be some middle ground between denying male violence and overestimating it to the extent that it makes women seem immobile.

Prostitution and Pollution

How did a literature that does not emphasize prostitutes' earnings come into being? How did it become a literature that speaks of women's victimiz-

ation and not women's actions? The continued use of metaphors of pollution and passivity in recent scholarship reveals how many of the categories
of Acton or Parent-Duchatelet have been taken to heart, and how often
even analytical studies of prostitution have identified with regulationists'
and reformers' values. Marion Goldman, for example, wrote of Nevada's
silver towns that "traces" of prostitution "were everywhere, just like the
chronic pollution from the mines and ore mills." Frances Finnegan
claimed that Victorian prostitutes emerged from the "moral degradation
of life in filthy overcrowded slums." Ruth Rosen called streetwalking "a
particularly formidable and degrading occupation." According to Anne
Butler all prostitutes' "interaction with their customers sank to the lowest
levels and depravity," while Barbara Hobson observed that most nineteenth-century prostitutes did not ply their trade long enough to have
been "rapidly transformed into the most down and out whores."[18]

Where do these words come from? Filth, degradation, depravity, even
"down and out whores"—these were the clichés of nineteenth-century
outrage and control; they have no specificity, no analytical use. Deployed
in contemporary scholarship, these terms have produced clichés of their
own. They have naturalized prostitutes in the language of biological processes, explaining women's labor in an idiom of inevitability, corruption,
and decay. In such scholarship, actions by and attitudes toward prostitutes
are not the result of specific historical and material conditions, let alone
specific interactions of reformers, casual laborers, and police, but biological and cultural absolutes.

The data on nineteenth- and twentieth-century prostitution reveal a
very different picture from the generalizations about degradation and
victimization. The image of the aging prostitute is a good example. Who,
after all, does not feel some discomfort at the idea of prostitutes between
the ages of thirty-five and fifty-five? It seems safe to assume that this discomfort is natural and is based on the tragic lives of such women. A
nineteenth-century Russian doctor, a follower of Parent-Duchatelet,
noted how "masculine" prostitutes looked as they aged.[19] Prostitutes, in
other words, became less womanly the longer they worked. Rosen likened
prostitutes to athletes dependent on their youth; "older and less attractive
women" walked the streets, as madams and pimps would not have them.[20]
But in late-nineteenth-century St. Paul, Minnesota, women on the streets
had the same average age as women in the better brothels.[21] Elsewhere,
older women walked the streets because it was advantageous for them to
do so. As early as 1973 Judith Walkowitz demonstrated that, as police surveillance increased in the south of England, so did the average age of pros-

titutes. More-experienced women had more survival skills, and this led to camaraderie between prostitutes and a sense of professional identity among them.[22] A similar situation developed elsewhere in England. In 1864, 58 percent of prostitutes applying to enter the workhouse at York were between fifteen and twenty, and 19 percent between twenty and twenty-five: clearly there was something to recommend entering the streets at a more advanced age. Many of the most-experienced American prostitutes did not end up on the streets at all, but in the mining camps of the American West; these women were sent there, by pimps or gangs or agents, because of their age—not as a punishment, but because they were less likely than younger women to elope with their customers. In Rocky Mountain mining camps, prostitutes over fifty were not uncommon; their earnings were high, and they were able to support adolescent children.[23] American nineteenth-century data suggest that women did not prostitute themselves for very long periods of time;[24] it is possible that some of the women who chose to work into middle age realized rewards that women of twenty-five did not earn. On the Comstock Lode, as the working male population dropped 30 percent between 1875 and 1880, the number of prostitutes halved; the percentage of prostitutes between the ages of thirty-five and fifty-nine dropped 30 percent as well, but the number of prostitutes over forty-five increased by 5 percent.[25] If supply and demand means anything at all, these older women must have done quite well for themselves.

Such generalizations come from a scholarship that privileges prostitutes' physical characteristics over their earnings. In this way, the generalization that women became prostitutes when family ties were weakened is frequently reproduced in the contemporary literature. While this sounds reasonable, is it supported by evidence? Rosen and Hobson provide excellent summaries of surveys, made by vice commissions, reformers, and rescue houses, of prostitutes' backgrounds, and they present fascinating, if dangling, hints about who these women were and why they prostituted themselves. They came from working-class families in which some of their mothers worked. They were seduced and abandoned, they were tired of work, they came from "bad home conditions," they were lonely and bored.[26] But data about a woman's home life reveal only the quality of her home life; how a woman spends her earnings explains something about why she became a prostitute. The emphasis on families of origin, not economics, reflected reformers' biases and their ideas about the ability of families to control and support their daughters.[27] Reformers' data indicated, however, that native-born American women frequently entered prostitution because of a husband's desertion or the death of a working-class parent; only in rural areas did women report prostituting themselves to support their husbands.[28] Such prostitution was women's response to the precarious position of unskilled young women and working men in late-nineteenth-century America, not the failure of families as an institution. The women who became prostitutes in order to support their families through hard times, or the abandoned wives who prostituted themselves to support themselves and their children, even the women thrown out of their homes because they were "ruined anyway,"[29] were not the victims of weak families; they were the victims of strong ones. The daughters whose prostitution subsidized recently indebted cash crop producers[30] or famine victims,[31] or even the ten women in Kansas who supported their husbands through prostitution, were living testimonies to a belief in families, that they should continue and prosper at any cost.

Sometimes daughters did not believe this, but their parents did. There was, for example, a strong correlation between opium addiction and prostitution in nineteenth-century China, but it was not the prostitutes' addiction. They were not addicted at any points in their careers but were sold to brothels and procurers to finance the addictions of fathers, brothers, and uncles.[32] The fate of daughters was frequently linked to the financial fortunes of their families. In the 1870s agents of San Francisco brothels scoured the Cantonese countryside, trying to purchase young girls from their parents; when they failed to find enough young girls this way, they kidnapped others.[33] But at the same time in the north of China there was famine, and daughters were systematically sold into prostitution, for two or three times more than they could have fetched had they been sold as servants.[34] Sometimes getting rid of older children could help a family make ends meet. An 1887 law allowed Guatemalan courts to send teenage girls who had been declared incorrigible to the debt servitude of licensed brothels, thus relieving the state and parents of the burden of support and the girls' "bad conduct."[35] Getting daughters back from brothels was somewhat more complicated and rested on a family's willingness to support a daughter or young wife: in Shanghai in the 1920s women who had been sold to brothels had no legal recourse, but those who had been tricked or kidnapped into prostitution could become free, providing they had a loyal family—"natal or marital"—to testify in court on their behalf.[36]

Less gothic examples reveal how prostitution enabled poor families to stay together. Finnegan illustrates her book with photographs of ten- and eleven-year-olds, abandoned by widowed mothers or jailed parents in Victorian York, who were rescued before they could fall into "moral danger" and trained as laundresses. The contrast could not be greater between these young girls and York's notorious families, such as the Varelys and the Bickerdikes, in which the aging prostitute mother "retired into the role of brothel-keeper, pickpocket, or procurer . . . leaving the main business of the house to her daughter . . . aided in their activities by a helpful brother."[37] Sometimes prostitution articulated the strength and support of blood ties that other relationships lacked: in 1878 a woman left her husband, who tried to force her into prostitution, and joined her sister in a St. Paul brothel.[38] Indeed, prostitution was sometimes a way for poor women to create families with themselves as household heads. Many propertied Nairobi prostitutes adopted younger women and designated them as their heirs; these women had contact with their own families but were forming units of descent and inheritance that successfully kept their property out of patrilineal control.[39]

Prostitution was a way for communities to maintain themselves in isolated respectability. In 1890s South Africa, Jewish pimps made only half-hearted efforts to recruit women locally but sent retired prostitutes and their husbands to Poland to return with teenage girls from Galicia to work in the brothels of Johannesburg; the same recruitment pattern obtained among the Hungarian, French, and Jewish communities in Argentina between 1877 and 1920.[40] Even as Jewish leaders blamed white slavery on "the spiritual poverty and decay of the family," Jewish prostitutes, pimps, and procurers in Buenos Aires founded their own synagogues and cemeteries.[41] Prostitution did not just subsidize other prostitutes, however. In 1976 the postal-order remittances daughters in Bangkok massage parlors and brothels sent to the village of Dok Kam Tai totalled $152,000.[42]

How do we reconcile these data with the assertions that women become prostitutes when family and community ties are weak? How is it that the language of reform has become the language of academic description a century or more later? The problem is not that scholars lack an accurate language with which to depict the specifics of prostitution. Such a language exists, as I shall show, but it is a very different language from that of reformist zeal. It is a language that comes from the work and experiences of prostitutes themselves.

Prostitution, Women's Work, and the Family

What do prostitutes and their customers do together? Men, for example, rarely visit prostitutes in order to subsidize peasant households, and

women hardly ever become prostitutes so that they can have sexual relations with men. Nevertheless, these and many other phenomena occur
when women become prostitutes and men visit them. How then do we explain what goes on between prostitutes and their customers? Is there a way
to study prostitution that does not draw a firm line between gender and
economics, women's work and men's work? Is there a way to show how
prostitution links formal and informal economies, casual and wage labor?
How do we write the history of prostitution without isolating women in the
categories of deviancy and subculture?

I want to begin by establishing what prostitution is and how it is done;
definitions of prostitution must come from the labor process of prostitution, not reformers' moralisms. Identifying prostitution as the occasional
work of poor women has gone a long way toward situating these women in
their communities as lovers, mothers, and wives, often in that order,[43] but
it only tells us the frequency with which the work is performed, nothing
about the work itself. But it is in the work of prostitutes that we can begin to
see the parallels between what prostitutes do for men and what they do for
their families. Prostitutes' work is reproductive—in fact, they sell that part
of themselves—of male labor power and family formations. Prostitutes
perform tasks that frequently include conversation, cooked food, and
bathwater that restore, flatter, and revive male energies: prostitutes sell
sexual intercourse in a relationship, whether abrupt or deferential. It is
possible that a part of the ambivalence toward prostitutes is that they sell as
transactions all that is legitimately available in marriage, and that they are
paid out of male wages. Thus, prostitution exists in a direct relationship to
wage labor and is domestic labor;[44] it is illegal marriage.

Prostitution is a capitalist social relationship not because capitalism
causes prostitution by commoditizing sexual relations but because wage
labor is a unique feature of capitalism: capitalism commoditized labor.
There have been some assertions that old, precapitalist forms of exchange
of women, polygyny, concubinage, or ritualized sex with strangers might
influence the local conduct of prostitution, or even its persistence.[45]
These activities are most correctly identified as multiple-partner mating
patterns, in which payment only occasionally changes hands;[46] most of
these assertions conflate a number of legal gradations of servility with
prostitution, and they reproduce nineteenth-century ideas about the uni-
versality of prostitution and promiscuity in non-western societies.[47] Medieval prostitution, in which municipalities received the profits from
regulated brothels, not only restrained male sexuality but prostitutes'
sexuality—and accumulation—as well.[48] Medieval records suggest, how-

ever, that all women entering prostitution and prostitutes themselves did not have the same legal rights as free adults—fifteenth-century mothers were said to force their daughters into prostitution to earn their dowries, Italian brothel keepers could strike prostitutes so long as they did not maim them,[49] the Muslim prostitutes in the royal brothels of medieval Valencia were usually slaves[50]—so that generalizing about the nature of their labor and the product of their labor is difficult at best.

In this book I am concerned with studying the labor processes of prostitution in a way that reveals the two sides of prostitution, what prostitutes do with their customers and what they do with their earnings. It is sex and money that interests me here. The reproduction of male energies, whether to make men more restrained husbands or more efficient wage laborers, is only part of what prostitutes do; they also work to reproduce themselves and their dependents. But both kinds of reproduction do not necessarily take place in the same context. Economic systems coexist and are often interdependent. The same women who make working life tolerable for wage laborers may use their earnings so that brothers and lovers can avoid wage labor. The same women who cater to the needs of working men may buy houses and rent rooms to wage laborers at rates that impoverish them.

But why do some women reproduce male labor power in the streets, while others do so in their own rooms? Much of the literature on prostitution contends that it is better—whatever that means in the study of prostitution—for a woman to be a call girl than a streetwalker, and indeed that the enormous differences between call girls and prostitutes have to do with status. Streetwalkers were "the group with the lowest prestige,"[51] who were "dissipated and unattractive," with "spoiled identities" that separated them from other prostitutes.[52] That such an emphasis on hierarchy should dominate feminist scholarship is unfortunate and, I think, erroneous: it has served as a forcible way to remove labor from discussions of prostitution. Moreover, such hierarchies cannot be attributed to women's earnings unless some time dimension is applied: it means nothing to say that streetwalkers earned less—or more—than brothel prostitutes unless we know how long a period we are talking about—a night in June, six months, or six years.

If prostitution is one of the forms domestic labor takes, then where it takes place merely describes the site of the reproduction of male labor power. Whether a woman is on the street or in her own room reflects her access to housing. The conduct of prostitution is determined by where the work takes place, not by a woman's personality, culture, or insecurities.

The site of reproduction determines the form of a woman's prostitution; this contradicts the idea of deviant street networks, which claims that women are incorporated or recruited into networks that place them where their prostitution is to occur. Much of the literature about deviant careers argues that becoming a deviant—breaking a law or a moral code—requires a redefinition of self in which deviant behavior is appropriate.[53]

The forms of prostitution have their own characteristics, behavior, rate of accumulation, and organization of labor time. My data indicate that women chose one form over another partly because of the availability of housing (and the cost of rent) and partly because of the rate of accumulation the form provided. Each labor form represents a specific organization of work and a specific rate of accumulation; labor forms reveal precisely what kind of rational economic choice prostitution is. Since most prostitutes have spent some time on the streets in their working lives—according to my data, in their youth, not their old age—most prostitutes have practiced more than one form but generally identified with one during their careers. This is not because of the status of the form, but because of how well the form suited their economic needs; a cultural content developed from that. Frequently, when a specific labor form failed to suit women's needs, they altered the form.[54] These forms do not represent "stages" in the life cycle of prostitutes nor do they constitute a hierarchy of respectability among prostitutes or anyone else. Of the three forms of prostitution in which women are not employees—excluding women with pimps who expropriate a plurality of their earnings, women who receive regular salaries from brothels, and generally, women who are paid as day laborers by escort agencies (all of whom seem to be engaged in independent, if slow, accumulation)—all are defined by the practitioner's relationship to her place of residence, providing, of course, that she has one. Nairobi prostitutes identified themselves—and other prostitutes—by the form they practiced. I have retained the Swahili names for the labor forms.

The *watembezi* form—from the Swahili verb, *kutemba*, "to walk"—is streetwalking. This includes all those women who solicit men in all the places the law calls public: bars, hotel lobbies, and of course streets. It is the form in which a woman seeks men somewhere other than her place of residence. Most prostitutes have spent some time streetwalking; it is the only form available to homeless women and those runaways who figured so strongly in both American and East African ideas about social breakdown. It is significant, however, that these women and many other women worldwide do not abandon the form once they are able to rent a room for themselves. Despite its popularity, academic studies of prostitution have condemned streetwalkers: their "income, blatant solicitation, promiscuity and impersonal sexuality combined to offer them little comfort"; their work was "at the bottom of the social scale."[55]

But was it? Did no women choose streetwalking for the specific advantages and financial rewards accruing from the form? My own and other data indicate that streetwalkers have greater control over their customers than do women practicing other forms, and that prostitutes themselves recognize this. Streetwalkers seem to have been physically safer than women who worked in other circumstances; the heinous crimes of Jack the Ripper—five murders of streetwalkers in ten weeks of 1888—were popularized by a journalistic vision of gender and class in Victorian London that reflected ideas about female passivity more than ideas about prostitutes' vulnerability.[56] In many places, streetwalking endangered men at least as much as it did women. Jill Harsin's study of police records from nineteenth-century Paris reveals that, while streetwalkers might be arrested regularly for drunkenness or theft, they were not the victims of violence the way women in their own rooms were.[57] Streetwalkers' solicitations in twentieth-century Shanghai "could shade into pickpocketing," but the women were not in any physical danger from their customers.[58] Women on the streets could refuse any man or run for safety with greater ease than they could in their own rooms or in a brothel. In a 1970s study of the social life in a Toronto hotel, most of the prostitutes who worked in the hotel bar—and were thus *watembezi*—had made careful and conscious decisions not to work as call girls because the risks were too great "taking dates to my apartment" and because of the difficulty in collecting payment.[59]

Streetwalkers cross-culturally were fond of contrasting their lot to that of wives: a successful Nairobi *watembezi* said that practitioners of the indoor, *malaya* form were just like married women; they had sex with whoever came to them; one American prostitute described "the gulf between the sheltered woman in her home and the streetwalker."[60] Both descriptions allude to the passivity of married women and the adventurousness of *watembezi*, probably with good reason: streetwalking has frequently been associated with relatively high earnings over fairly short periods of time (measured in months or years, depending on local conditions), and it involves less labor time than other forms of prostitution. The greatest risks streetwalkers faced seem to be from police harassment—including bribes—rather than customers' violence,[61] and their networks and mechanisms for evading the police may well have encouraged men to seek them out, thinking they too would be protected from arrests.[62] Watembezi prostitutes often shared rooms, and this, as well as the public nature of their work, inspired strong ties between women, who often paid each other's bail and helped each other through lean times.[63]

The conventional wisdom about streetwalking is that it was the most public and vulnerable kind of prostitution in which women had to have sex with anonymous strangers. But women on the streets, exactly like women in their own rooms, had regular customers and comported themselves in such a way as to develop repeat business.[64] The prevalence of the watembezi form makes it especially difficult to assess its economic motivations, but my data strongly suggest that women who worked the streets for any length of time were generally not involved in independent accumulation. Their prostitution was in financial support of their families, whether families or origin, or, after a certain decomposition of peasant agriculture was complete, husbands and children, or the men who had become dependent on them—including pimps.[65]

In the *malaya* form—taken from the proper, dictionary Swahili word for prostitute—the woman stayed inside her room and waited for the men to come to her. This form was predicated on the woman's having a room to which a man might also purchase access, and in Nairobi and elsewhere, malaya prostitutes provided the most extensive set of domestic services for sale, including food, bathwater, conversation, and, when a man spent the night, breakfast. The form seems to be very old: the vernacular word *bordel* meant "little house."[66] Although malaya women in Africa and most of the American practitioners of the form were self-employed, this was also the form of the elite courtesans of China—the girls purchased in rural China, usually before they turned six, and later sold to brothels or wealthy men—and the geishas of Japan. Practitioners of the malaya form and those close to it stressed the nonsexual services they sold: malaya women in Nairobi charged for each foodstuff provided and said that profits derived from their ability to convince a man of their financial need. On the colonial Zambian Copperbelt the slang term for prostitute was "a good friend" who, among other things, "could cook and wash."[67] On the Comstock Lode, two euphemisms for prostitute were "dressmaker" and "housekeeper."[68] A Japanese prostitute who worked out of her home in Hawaii in 1900 said of the monies she sent home, "Am I not a real patriot who enriches our country?"[69] In 1923, protesting an attempt to register, license and tax them at the same rate as teahouse and brothel prostitutes, the elite "singing girls" of Shanghai displayed banners that proclaimed, "We sell our voices, not our bodies."[70]

The malaya form demanded the greatest investment of women's time in cooking, cleaning, skilled entertainment (if any was offered), and simply being home and being available there. Malaya women in Nairobi claimed the form mimicked marriage. Being in their own rooms protected women from arrest—and the vigilance of reformers, who were nevertheless obsessed by the number of prostitutes who were not on the streets[71]—but they had no control over who came to them. Once they let a man inside their rooms, they could not always be sure of payment or safety. Indeed, since malaya women needed their rooms to do their work, in the highly competitive housing market of Nairobi women often tolerated abuse and refusals to pay rather than disturb their neighbors and alienate landlords; malaya prostitutes in nineteenth-century Paris bribed landlords to change the legal status of their rooms to avoid police raids.[72]

Nevertheless, malaya women were regarded as something "better" in much of the secondary literature. According to Goldman, "they did not have to disgrace themselves by flagrant solicitation or accept customers who were diseased, violent, or overly demanding."[73] They also conducted their prostitution "in secret," their work was clandestine, and in the absence of eyewitness accounts it is impossible to know who they allowed in their rooms, and how, and at what moment, they assessed violence. Except for a few women whose careers soared in exceptional times, the malaya form was characterized by slow and steady accumulation in which even the most modest practitioners could earn each month twice as much as what an unskilled man earned. As an accumulation strategy, the malaya form was a very long-term investment; it required its own work rhythms and financial planning. A young malaya woman in prerevolutionary Ethiopia complained that from the middle of the month until the next payday "I am lucky if I get three overnight customers."[74] On the whole, malaya prostitutes did not support their families with their earnings, other than their children, although they often gave their kin gifts. They tended instead to establish themselves as independent heads of households. They were women inaugurating the cycle of family and lineage formation in literal, concrete terms, and, taken in the aggregate, they were involved in class formation; they were joining the ranks of the urban petty bourgeoisie.

Malaya prostitutes invariably began their careers as urban tenants, an experience that gave many of them their values and a healthy respect for the value of real estate. The "capitalists with rooms" of Helena and the famous madams of nineteenth-century America all practiced the malaya form and invested their earnings in urban real estate with the same frequency that malaya women in Nairobi or in Katsina in Northern Nigeria did.[75] Nineteenth-century America offered a wide variety of madams: Ah Toy, a self-employed Chinese prostitute who arrived in San Francisco in 1848, had purchased a brothel there three years later; Nellie Sayers, Rose Benjamin, and Jessie Lester of Nevada; Pearl Miller of Calgary—these women crossed the boundaries of respectable and unrespectable, entered into popular memory and popular history without the baggage of reformers' scorn,[76] and left a record that is one of the only available glimpses into the malaya form in nineteenth- and twentieth-century America.

Although brothel keeping did not occur in Nairobi, madams and their employees are important to discuss; they have been mystified in the literature on prostitution. It is not always clear when a woman kept a brothel and when she owned property in which her tenants were independent malaya women; reformers recognized no such distinctions.[77] For example, Wanjira Ng'ang'a built a house in a squatter settlement near Nairobi in 1940; she rented her four rooms to prostitutes with whom she developed long-term, reciprocal relationships; she never claimed any part of their earnings other than rent. The classification of the range of brothels from "the high-priced brothel" to "a middle class whorehouse"[78] tells us little more than how much men paid to go to them—information in and of itself, but not necessarily an indication of how women worked and cooperated and resisted in them. Brothel residents exhibited both a loyalty to their workplace and a cynical view of their other employment options. During police raids on Shanghai brothels in the 1950s, prostitutes "often clung to their madams, . . . shouting 'Don't take me away from my 'mama,'"[79] while prostitutes in Peruvian brothels in the 1970s named sexual positions after women's legal occupations, such as *la secretaria*.[80] The data scholars have obtained from the use of madams' memoirs have not elicited the most reliable insights into employer-employee relationships but they are revealing. On the whole madams' words have been taken at face value in ways that ordinary prostitutes' words—or what can be inferred from their actions—never were: "most madams seem to have viewed their achievement with pride and satisfaction."[81]

And what did madams say? They did not speak of degradation and passivity. They spoke of the long-range planning, calculation, and investment their work required and of their ability to control and protect a labor force; they described the realities of urban real estate, the rate of profit

that could be obtained without the sale of sexuality, the need to avoid police surveillance, and the need to cater to specific segments of a given male
population. Sally Stanford claimed that women did not drift into becoming madams any more than someone drifted into "getting a battlefield
commission or becoming Dean of Women at Stanford University."[82]
Bolognese madams in the 1860s may have exploited the women who
worked for them, but they also successfully defended them against the
sexual harassment of police;[83] in the 1890s an El Paso madam paid her
employees a monthly salary: "on commission they were sometimes inclined to cheat."[84] A Guatemala City madam patiently explained that violence rarely broke out in brothels because "people generally don't want to
be seen or have it known that they go there." Nineteenth-century Parisian
madams made their greatest profits renting clothes to their employees.[85]
In St. Paul adolescent girls were frequently turned away when they tried
to enter brothels,[86] but Nellie Sayers of Virginia City, where there were no
age-of-consent laws, preferred to employ girls fifteen or younger,[87] while
teenage prostitutes in Bangkok massage parlors were allowed to be
"choosey" about who they would have sexual relations with.[88] All of this
reflects the practice, however atypically successful or rarified, of a labor
form that was anything but casual, that was much more a part of—and far
more attentive to the vicissitudes of—respectable society than it was part
of a subculture of deviance. The malaya form was the labor form of pro-
fessionals, of women whose social identity was that of malaya women. Malaya women did not see their work as a survival strategy; they saw it as a way
to prosper.

Malaya women were supported by the communities in which they
worked. Communities of migrants and transients approved of prostitution not because they themselves were not sufficiently well established to
define urban respectability, but because malaya prostitution subsidized
and supported them. This approval is often described as romanticization
or idealization in secondary sources, but it is approval and reflects the ambiguous position of prostitutes, who made homes for many men. Malaya
women "both epitomized and in effect caricatured the values of a commoditized, accumulating society"[89] at the same time those values were beginning slowly, and with considerable resistance, to dominate urban life.
Kansas's frontier towns used prostitution as a way to attract the Texas cattle trade and profit from cowboys' participation in casual labor. Throughout the boom years of the late 1870s and early 1880s, newspapers and
court records displayed only tolerance for brothel keepers and their employees.[90] Nairobi's World War II Municipal Native Affairs Officer said

that the malaya women of the 1920s and 1930s had a degree of approval and respect that wartime watembezi never had.[91] Among Muslim Hausa migrants in a southern Nigerian town in the 1960s, "the *karuwa* is idealized in the culture as a woman of strong character, intelligent, and highly entertaining." They were always sought after in marriage. But secluded Hausa wives had greater opportunities to earn money through trading in cooked food than did karuwa, who were forbidden to participate in any business other than prostitution. Divorced women became karuwa, married, divorced, became karuwa, and married again. Prostitutes and respectable women are not discrete categories, but both serve the needs of male migrants who go from migrancy to settlement to migration again.[92]

In the *wazi-wazi* form, women, sat outside the doors of their rooms, if they faced the street, or on the porches of the houses in which they rented rooms, or in the windows and waited for men to approach them there. They called out to men, but they could refuse any man before they went indoors with him. Wazi-wazi women had considerably more control over their clientele and their labor time than malaya women had. These women provided few, if any, services that were not sexual; in Nairobi, wazi-wazi women would only cook food for men with whom they had established relationships, and then only if the man brought it; they made no effort to reproduce prevailing notions of intimacy and privacy. They specialized in brief sexual encounters for which they charged a fixed price, usually maintained at a low, stable rate by the density of wazi-wazi women living nearby; in Katsina *akwato* prostitutes had their minimum price posted on the doors of their rooms.[93] This was the form of the women who inhabited the cribs of the American West; it was also the form of immigrants in crowded tenements. In 1900 two Jewish immigrant prostitutes rented a second-floor room on New York's Lower East Side and "most of the stoop," from which they would cry out, "Only fifty cents"; other women sat in chairs on the sidewalk on sunny days.[94] According to a wazi-wazi woman in Nairobi in the 1960s, such a dense population of prostitutes guaranteed protection: if there were problems with a customer, someone would hear her cries for help.[95] The rooms wazi-wazi women lived in were spare, usually furnished only with a bed and a chair, as small as four feet by eight feet in Nairobi during the acute housing shortage of the late 1930s, and about the same size in the cubicles of New Orleans or gold rush San Francisco, and as large as eight by eight in some Western towns.[96]

Wazi-wazi women were regarded as the most pitiable of American prostitutes, without much regard for why women might choose to work in those

conditions. My data from Nairobi indicate that, to a woman, wazi-wazi prostitutes worked intensively for relatively short periods—measured in years,
however—to revive the failing economies of their families of origin. These
women willingly accepted—indeed, many sought—the mean conditions
of wazi-wazi work because almost all the monies so earned could be fun-
nelled back to their parents. And monies were earned: in Boise, Idaho, in
1888 cribs rented for two and a half to three times more than rooms in more
sedate brothels, indicating something about the profitability of crib residence.[97] In Bukoba, Tanganyika, in the 1940s returning Haya women—
who had given the wazi-wazi form its name in Nairobi—were said to have
saved a generation of indebted cash crop producers.[98] This was the prostitution of daughters, women supporting their parents through prostitution, women who made no effort to invest in property where they lived; the
term *crib* may have been structurally descriptive in several ways. The small
rooms, the brief encounters—although in Nairobi, and presumably elsewhere, wazi-wazi prostitutes had men who visited them more than once—
signified the temporary work of daughters about to return home or to follow the labor supply once more before returning home; this was the prostitution that reestablished parents in smallholdings or in trade. Despite the
public nature of this prostitution, wazi-wazi women were rarely arrested;
once cribs were formally or informally zoned into their own areas, the police and the state seemed to tacitly approve of them.[99]

Conceptualizing prostitution through its labor forms tells us about
women's access to housing and property ownership. Labor forms tell us
that a prostitute's conduct is determined by strategies of reproduction, not
personality; they tell us that rural relationships extend into the back alleys
and lodging houses of the city; they tell us that kinship permeates a vast
number of the relationships we tend to think of as anonymous, furtive,
and sordid.

Labor forms tell us when prostitution is family labor, and what intensity
of family labor it is, and when it is not. Labor forms reveal the duality of
prostitution. It is of great importance that we understand that work performed one way in one place can have the opposite meaning in another
place, and that the most aggressive prostitution, conducted from windows
and stoops, was performed by the most dutiful of daughters. The women
who walked the streets were also working for their families. It was the
women who waited decorously and discretely in their rooms, peaceful and
isolated, deferential and polite, who were in fact entirely out for themselves, eager to disinherit fathers and brothers and to establish themselves
as independent heads of households. It was some of these women who

went so far as to solicit, hire, and exploit other prostitutes: they believed in independent accumulation. The contradictions present in a prostitute's behavior and her motivations are enormous, but they are not unknowable.

African History and Oral History

The main concerns of this book—the interaction of class and kin, family and farm, migrants and housing—are the concerns of any historian of twentieth-century Kenya. But here these concerns are articulated and illuminated by the oral interviews I conducted with seventy former prostitutes in Nairobi. They were the ones who pointed out in dozens of different ways that the most aggressive prostitution could not be studied in isolation from rural accumulation. They were the ones who insisted that I be aware that women's property inheritance was precarious but manageable, and they were the ones who alerted me to the presence of labor forms in prostitution. In this book I use these prostitutes' words to construct a picture of Africans defending their access to and control over land, labor, and cattle—the staples of East African historiography. If this picture looks somewhat different from earlier histories of Kenya, if for example it contains more women actors or different insights about urban economics or the colonial state, it is not necessarily because this is women's history. It is altogether possible that it is because this study is political economy written with women's words.

The use of oral sources in African history has been much more common for the precolonial period than for the colonial era. The presumption behind this has been that colonial historians had written records at their disposal and, even if literacy was parcelled out by white males to a very few African males, this was sufficient with which to write history. Such a presumption privileges written material over oral material. But colonialists did not do such a good job understanding African social life that we can safely rely on their writings. Feminist historians writing on Mombasa, Lagos, Accra, Nakuru, and Dar es Salaam used interviews to demonstrate that Islam, Christianity, and colonialism influenced people's lives somewhat differently than we had originally thought.[100] As more colonial historians discovered that they needed—and had at their disposal—oral data too, oral history has been turned into a higher art than perhaps it needs to be. To all the emphasis on precolonial methodologies was added controversies about how to interpret songs and dances and about the labor process of collecting life histories.[101] To be sure, such controversies reveal scholars' discomfort at establishing themselves as authorities separate from their subjects' vision, but they also reveal a distrust of oral sources that is disturbing. What is true and what is false, what is accurate and what is not, what is reliable information and what cannot be trusted have been, in Africanists' hands, subjects for debate and reflection. In 1967 Jan Vansina wrote that personal reminiscences were "preserved in the memory of the informant" and "are often astonishingly detailed . . . and very diverse." Indeed, "falsification rarely occurs."[102] Almost twenty years later he was more wary: "prodded by questions or not. . . . They are the image of oneself one cares to transmit to others . . . part of an organized whole of memories that tend to project a consistent image of the narrator and, in many cases, a justification for his or her life."[103] The excitement of the discovery of African memories had been muted by the discovery of African consciousness.

Where does this suspicion get us? How do we do research and stay on guard to ferret out the lies and distortions that are hurled at us in every interview? I suggest that it is not all that difficult, and possibly not all that necessary. Frederick Cooper's interviews with the descendants of slaves on the East African coast presented a different picture of slaves' daily labor requirements than the one told him by the descendants of slave owners.[104] Clearly one was a distortion, what people wanted Cooper to believe, and probably both were. But does it matter? Is it important to find out who is wrong, "to find the gap between the past as it may have been and its rendering,"[105] or is it important to understand that something as straightforward as the length of time it took to clear a specific amount of land was contested by slaves and slave owners alike? It is really necessary to find out how long it took to clear one *ngwe*? Or can we concentrate on what informants are indeed telling us, that labor time itself, even among peoples whose labor was owned, was contested terrain, and that the nature and limits of slaves' work loads were deeply ingrained in the society? These self-serving memories indicate that slave work loads were important enough to be passed on to children even after the legal statuses of slavery and slave ownership had been abolished.

It is perhaps the nature of the questions a researcher asks, rather than the nature of the answers an informant provides, that should be the subject of scrutiny. The idea that oral historians can be neutral and be simply the recipients of volunteered information from which they will then be able to select a statistically reliable account avoids a key fact: oral historians generate our own data. Our data usually come from our questions. We may ask questions that we believe are open-ended and value-free, but these questions reflect our own research agendas and our methodological biases. For example, I began my research with a long, rather pedantic questionnaire; it asked women about their fathers' polygyny, it asked who did the repairs where they first lived in Nairobi—it certainly was not a bad questionnaire, but it was not a terribly good one either. Questions like "Did you think it was dangerous to be a prostitute, that you could be arrested for it?" demonstrated an ethnocentrism that I did not know I had. These women did not become prostitutes to be safe, they became prostitutes to make money: they made that perfectly clear to me. More important, as chapters 3 and 4 show, these questions were extraneous to the working life of many Nairobi prostitutes and reflected my assumptions, not those of my informants. What was important to my informants was a concept I knew nothing about before I went to Kenya, *heshima,* "respect" or "dignity," accorded to rank and to the proper conduct. Nothing I had read had prepared me for the place of dignity in Nairobi prostitution, but respect and its absence informs this study. Listen to what Margaret Githeka, a Kikuyu prostitute born in Nairobi at the end of World War I, said about respect, its influence on prostitutes' relations with their customers and the wider society, and its decline among the young prostitutes of the mid-1970s.

> Today, when prostitutes greet some man who had cheated them they say right away "give me my money, why did you cheat me?" or "I want my money right now." But in the old days something like that would never happen. Even the prostitutes themselves would never want it to be known that they were prostitutes. That's why they asked men for gifts, even if they wanted money, because they did not want to be thought of as prostitutes. And those malaya women, they had a lot of respect in the old days and that is why the men loved them even though they were prostitutes.

I know enough now to say that in many ways this is a very idealized quotation; Githeka herself would have been hard pressed to tell me when "the old days" ended and "today" began; she had opinions about the role of cash in prostitution that most of her cohorts did not share. But this quotation also tells us how—and in what mediums—relations between prostitutes and their customers were conducted and how vivid the changes in Nairobi prostitution seemed to older women. The fact that it was idealized, or a justification, or part of Githeka's larger complaint about younger women hardly matters. The fact that she organized this brief tirade around the role of cash in prostitution revealed her belief that capital ac-

cumulation in prostitution should always be secondary to maintaining respect in the local community. Not only is this hard data, but it is hard data
of a dynamic sort: it describes prostitutes' relationships to their customers
and to the community in which they lived and worked.

But where does an informant's voice end and my own begin? What
about perceptions? How can I, or anyone else, be sure that I have not
made an abstract, academic category out of an isolated phrase, or worse,
taken as a historic observation something the informant realized only a
day or two before the interview? If a woman told me that prostitution
brought her "extra money," could I reasonably assume that she was talking about a surplus? Or was surplus my own construction, revealing my
intellectualized concerns and concealing an informant's reality? And if
she did mean surplus, how could I be sure *when* she realized it was a surplus? Extra money, however, is not an insight or an analytical category: it is
as hard and real as a brass pot; it has objective qualities regardless of
whether or not a recipient appreciates them at the time. Just as researchers have to be careful not to force our own interpretations into oral
data, we have to be mindful not to belittle informant's perceptions and
concepts: usually "extra money" means extra money.

What about data that are not subjective? What about the data about
work, and working conditions, and remuneration? How can I, or anyone
else, be sure that it is accurate and reliable? It seems to me that the nature
of the questions I was asking did not invite lies or exaggeration. I was asking women what they had done in their teens, and in their twenties, and in
their thirties; I was not asking them about prostitution as a social phenomenon, I was asking them about prostitution as their experience: there
seemed scant reason for women not to tell their own stories in order to
present a version of their lives that they had not lived. Nevertheless, I fully
expected women not to tell the truth about what men paid them. I thought
this would be exaggerated, either upward or downward: I could think of
several reasons why they might do one or the other. I was very surprised
when in the last few months of my research my assistant and I began interviewing men: the prices they reported were for the most part within fifty
cents Kenyan of the prices women reported. This is not to say that none of
my informants, male and female, ever lied, ever got anything wrong, or
ever were woefully misinformed. But what men paid prostitutes for which
services does not seem to have been something they lied about.

One possible way to correct for falsification in oral interviews is numbers: not a "representative" sample—whatever that might mean with oral
data—but enough so that interviews may be checked against each other.

But should we do fifty or sixty interviews only to guarantee that a few liars be identified? Having done that, would we have arrived at the whole truth? Ideally, scholars do fifty or sixty interviews to see the largest possible picture, to be able to generalize about as many varieties of African experience as possible. As in the case of Margaret Githeka, I know enough about the conduct of women who began prostitution in the mid- to late 1930s to know what was typical about her ideas and what was anomalous. Her opinions about the role of cash in prostitution were atypical of her generation—and I am not certain that she herself ever acted on these opinions—but not of the community in which she had been raised. I learned this by doing many interviews. I had a totally lopsided picture of Nairobi prostitution in the early months of my research when I had talked only to malaya women. But the more I interviewed successful watembezi and malaya women who had lived in other parts of Nairobi, the less particular and hegemonic the malaya view of the world appeared. The quotations for malaya prostitutes in chapter 3 show women who were exceptionally self-confident about how their world worked, and that was very appealing to me for a long time. I did not appreciate that these women saw themselves and their world as a mirror of coastal society that was outdated by 1929. The fact is, I did not realize that this was just their point of view until I had interviewed a number of other women, including cynical malaya women of the same era, who practiced other forms of prostitution elsewhere and who mocked—to me, in interviews—every self-satisfied aspect of the malaya form. I assumed, rightly or wrongly, that if these women felt so strongly about the malaya form more than forty years after they left the streets, they probably also condemned it while they were walking the streets. Their condemnation of the malaya form was of course inaccurate; it was biased; it was self-serving. But it also revealed another dimension to, and tension in, Nairobi prostitution that I had neither known about nor anticipated. Somewhat later on, I realized the extent to which I had internalized the values of the more conservative practitioners of the malaya form when I asked a younger malaya woman who had lived in Danguroni (see chapter 4) about its slang names, without any sense that these might offend her. She was rightfully insulted, which made me realize that one woman's pejorative appellation was another woman's idealized memory. There is no question of what is accurate or inaccurate here, of whether or not Danguroni was truly "shameful" or wonderful: both opinions are important. In fact, both opinions, especially when voiced forty years later, emphasized divisions and tensions within and about the conduct of Nairobi prostitution that were central to the repro-

duction of East African peasantries. It is not just that many interviews
leveled and explained the inconsistencies in my oral data, but that these
inconsistencies revealed commitments, concerns, and strategies that
might otherwise not be discernible to historians.

All of my informants had biases. Each woman had opinions, passions,
deeply held beliefs, scores to settle, and they involved me, sometimes, in
forty-year-old diatribes. Watembezi scorned the passivity of malaya
women, malaya women described their shock at the wazi-wazi form as if
1937 were last week, malaya women denied that forays into the watembezi
form made them streetwalkers, and postwar watembezi implored me to
understand the economic realities of their time. To have removed these
biases would have provided a bowdlerized history from which all conflict
had been excised; it would have presented a Nairobi in which people la-
bored and competed in harmony. It seems entirely reasonable to assume
that prostitutes would describe their choice of a labor form as the most
rational choice of all (although many of the women in this study were tolerant of other forms in ways that surprised me), or that they would describe the form that had once eroded their rate of profit as antisocial and
shameful. What is important, I think, is that women defended their choice
of labor form and complained about other ones thirty and forty years after they had last prostituted themselves; they may well have been justifying their own lives, but they did it in a way that brought home to me the
complex issues of identity involved in women's self-employment in the African communities of Nairobi.

There is a body of thought among oral historians that you cannot ask
informants leading questions, that you cannot come right out and ask if
the chief made rain, protected female fertility, and settled disputes about
land use. If you do, informants will agree with you; they will tell you what
they think you want to hear. I had never heard that before I went to
Kenya, so I asked dozens of leading questions, and for reasons that may
have to do with theories of interviewing, no one ever agreed with me. In
fact, my informants argued with me when I asked them why they did not
do what I had heard that dozens of other women did. Some of the quotations in this book include "don't you see," or "you don't understand" not
because I am proud of it, but because I want to make it perfectly clear that
the information presented here is information my informants cared
enough about to defend. This was indeed people justifying their own
lives: explaining and articulating motivations and choices was much more
important to my informants than ordinary politeness was.

The data on prostitutes' earnings in this book are more detailed and more comprehensive than any derived from written sources. These data came from what women, and some men, told me; the detail is contextualized in this study, however, because I was able to establish a fairly reliable chronology for prostitution in Nairobi. I was able to do this in two ways, through circumcision years and internal dating. Women who went to Nairobi during and after World War II generally knew the year of their birth and when they first went to Nairobi. But most of my older women informants did not "know years"; they might have known that something happened during the fighting of the Italians (World War II) or before Mau Mau (1946–52), but usually that was as definitive as they could be. However, most Bantu-speaking people in Kenya practice circumcision on both adolescent men and women; each circumcision year became an age grade named for a memorable event for which a fair number of District Officers or scholars have provided actual dates. Thus I could safely assume that a Kikuyu woman who was circumcised in Munoti (for "note," the year the first paper currency was introduced, 1922) was between fourteen and eighteen at the time. Such a fact alone was not always helpful: knowing how old a woman was in 1922 was problematic when the woman did not know how long after her circumcision she went to Nairobi. But the more interviews I did, the more I could get an accurate sense of when a woman arrived in Nairobi by asking her about other women who had been my informants. Here I found the concrete benefits of a number of interviews, most of them in one part of Nairobi, Pumwani. By the time I had done thirty interviews, I had a general sense of what Pumwani was like in the 1920s or 1930s and could ask a woman I was interviewing where any number of women were living when she first arrived. If she knew, and if I had some date for even one or two of those women, then I would know if she had first come to Nairobi in 1930 or 1936. I was fortunate that two women knew the year of their children's births, so sometimes I could ask informants how old the daughter or son of one of these women was when they first came—did the child crawl, or walk. I had hoped that informants' experience of events in Nairobi housing policy would provide exact dates, but this proved as approximate as the methods I was already using. For example, I often asked women to tell me what they were doing when Pangani village was demolished in 1939, but since Pangani was in the process of being demolished for several years, my informants did not make a hard-and-fast distinction among the year of the first evictions, the year when there were only fifty structures remaining, and the year when there were none. Nevertheless, I could eventually determine when a woman first arrived in Nairobi, particularly if she went to Pumwani or Pangani, to within a year or two; where I refer to dates as 1934/35, for example, it means that I do not know the exact year.

The chapters derived almost exclusively from oral data lend themselves to narrative history far better, with far greater attention to chronology, than does the chapter derived primarily from colonial sources. This is, I think, methodological; it is because the oral data from prostitutes revealed greater consistency, greater community, a greater degree of shared conceptions, vocabularies, and goals than did the data derived from colonial administrators' writing. The latters' tasks in urban Kenya were frequently so contradictory, so fraught with complications and contestations, and so often ignored, that even as straightforward a question as urban segregation in a settler society is difficult to put into a reliable chronological sequence and is almost impossible to study as an implemented policy. The origins and the development of the wazi-wazi form may lend themselves to narrative history with greater ease than does the history of British policy toward African landlords. As African historians are beginning to privilege participants' accounts over those of colonial rulers, the contradictions and ambiguities of colonial policies have become more apparent. It may be that writing colonial history from colonialist sources is far less revealing than writing colonial history from the words of the colonized.

2

Livestock, Labor, and Reproduction: Prostitution in Nairobi and the East African Protectorate, ca. 1900–1918

The British colonization of what is today Kenya[1] began at the end of a succession of ecological disasters. The changes brought about by these disasters were enormous, but they were absorbed within the even greater changes colonial capitalism brought to East African societies. Identifying the social transformations that came from catastrophe rather than colonialism is difficult; studying women's lives in this period is harder. Histories of precolonial East Africa have not as a rule been able to include women in their narratives beyond bland structural descriptions of what women represented, or how they were exchanged, rather than what they actually did ⨯ at specific times. This chapter is an attempt to correct this, and as such it does not add new research to the little evidence we have, but is a reinterpretation of that evidence. By placing women's work and sexuality at the center of this reinterpretation, the relationships within families, between communities, and between cattle keepers and agriculturalists may appear more dynamic than they have done previously.

In this chapter I argue that the events of the 1890s ruptured the established economics of African marriage systems by shifting wealth away from cattle owners and toward agriculturalists. Colonial capitalism and migrant labor provided the mechanisms through which cattle-owning elders, the wealthy of most precolonial societies, reasserted their dominance by the start of World War I. In the early years of this century, prostitution was for many women participation in the migrant labor economy, a phase in their youth. Indeed, the emergence of full-time, self-employed prostitutes in Nairobi during World War I—women who were clearly and, for a change, correctly identifiable as prostitutes, however

29

short-lived that identity might have been—marked the end of the reconstruction of East African peasant society.

Despite the characterization of precolonial East African societies as either "pastoralist" or "agriculturalist," most of the peoples the early European explorers and administrators described as one or the other in fact combined agricultural production with livestock accumulation. Only the Maasai were said to have been entirely pastoralist. In the nineteenth century they occupied the grazing lands from their present homelands in Kajiado and Narok to the Usan Gishu plains and the Laikipia plateau, where they had a long history of intermarriage and cooperation with the agriculturalist Kikuyu in Nyeri; in the west and south they became the military clients of Luhya and Chagga farming communities.[2] The pastoralist Nandi were in fact agriculturalist as well, as demonstrated by the number of crops destroyed and granaries emptied in the punitive expeditions of 1900–1906.[3] The Bantu-speaking Kikuyu and Kamba and the Nilotic-speaking Luo were all cultivators, but better-off members of those societies accumulated cattle and smaller stock (sheep and goats), which they

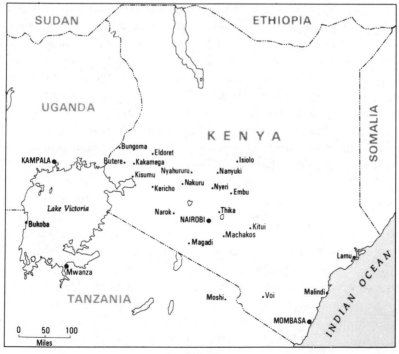

Kenya

exchanged for a wide variety of products, all of which were valued in terms of their exchange rates for livestock.

Livestock had exchange value in precolonial East African societies, with cattle having the highest value. Livestock reproduced, and thus female stock were uniquely suitable for bridewealth, exchanged by a husband to a woman's father for a woman's reproductive and labor power.[4] Thus the men who owned the most cattle were reckoned the wealthiest, and they had ample opportunities for acquiring many wives, who in turn could increase agricultural production, either for themselves or their sons, whose loyalty their fathers could insure, at least in theory, with the promise of cattle when they became adults. At the end of the nineteenth century most East African societies were composed of stratified agricultural producers among whom the agreed-upon elements of wealth, exchange, and status—women and cows—generated each other in a cycle of accumulation and family formation. In that cycle, wealth in women depended on men's access to land: men with many wives could trade the surplus produced by those wives to pastoralists for livestock.[5] Young men would provide labor and loyalty for their father so that they would eventually be given the livestock with which they could marry. Men with daughters could increase their herds with their daughters' bridewealth, some of the surplus from which went to pay for their sons' marriages. What happened to these societies, and the stratifications specific to them, when most of the livestock died?

Natural Disaster and Social Change, 1890–1900

Rinderpest first appeared in Africa in 1889. A highly contagious fever that killed cattle, game, and, in a somewhat mutated form, sheep, it swept through Kenya in the epidemics of 1890–91, 1894, and 1898. In some areas cattle losses were estimated as high as 90 percent; the Machakos Kamba lost fifty thousand head of cattle. Elsewhere, wealthy men were left with only a few cattle from their enormous herds.[6] In 1897 there was an outbreak of bovine pleuropneumonia, followed the next year by locusts, rinderpest, and the failure of the long rains. This caused a severe famine, in which Ukamba seems to have been the worst-hit area. Many Kamba travelled south and west, foraging for food. This spread smallpox, long endemic in Ukamba, to communities of Kikuyu and Embu and Meru already swollen with pastoralists, whose normal populations were too sparse to support infectious diseases and who had come to find food. It was estimated that twenty-five thousand died of disease and starvation in

Ukamba alone; mortality estimates for central Kenya ranged from 10 to 70 percent of the population.[7]

In this section I am more concerned with cattle deaths than with human deaths, since the loss of high-value stock altered the form of bridewealth, relations of exchange between elder and junior men, and the social life organized around those relations. "A time when everyone was forced to marry," even the youngest boys, all without bridewealth, was how Mbeere of the east central region described the extent of the crisis.[8] The loss of so many cattle inflated their value relative to that of grain and the exchange value of women. In the coastal hinterland, Giriama trade and agriculture expanded in the 1890s even while almost all the cattle died; this may have enabled many Giriama to purchase new livestock or use cash for bride-wealth, which may have diminished fathers' rights over their children.[9] Elsewhere, people took more desperate measures. Pawning, in which Maasai and after 1898 Kamba "loaned" women and children to Kikuyu and Embu households in exchange for grain, seems to have increased fairly steadily after the rinderpest epidemics of 1893.[10] Embu elders re-called, "The Kamba first brought livestock for exchanging for foodstuffs. Later they brought their wives and children."[11] About a thousand Maasai were taken into an Imperial British East Africa Company (IBEAC) settle-ment in Fort Smith at the end of 1893, and by the time they numbered five thousand they were moved to Ngong, where they farmed. Ngong became a refuge for pawned, captured, and runaway Maasai women until the end of the decade.[12]

What happened to marriage customs in the areas where women were not pawned, and where the IBEAC did not have stations? While there are not enough data to show any aggregate changes in property relations be-tween 1890 and 1900, informants recalled instances of a cash and luxury-commodities bride-price on the caravan routes and in Nairobi as late as 1905.[13] This would have favored men whose wealth was acquired outside the established hierarchies of precolonial society, caravan porters and the cultivators who sold crops to the caravans.[14] It would seem likely that many areas went onto a goat standard for bridewealth transactions,[15] which would have favored livestock owners.

The high mortality rate, especially among children and, perhaps almost as frequently, young men;[16] the loss of livestock; famine and foraging for food; an increased number of widows and orphans; a breakdown in leviratic marriages:[17] all removed a number of potential spouses from East African societies. Some of the mechanisms of generational control were eroded by disease: many young men, unable to acquire livestock from their fathers or in raids, left their homes and eventually settled and married among other peoples, changing ethnic affiliations.[18] But in areas where a goat bridewealth obtained, elders may have been able to maintain control over younger men. Women's travels in search of food, shelter, and protection took a similar form: they journeyed to new areas and married among other peoples and took on the ethnicity of their spouses, sometimes several times over: "a woman is a woman, there is no tribe."[19] One woman was born in Meru, journeyed to Ukambani, where she was married and widowed; then she went to Kikuyu, married, and "became a Kikuyu." The process seemed commonplace to her daughter: "I don't know how my mother became a Kikuyu, the Kikuyu are the ones who could tell you how she became one of them."[20] Customary marriages, as relations of exchange between a man and his wife's kin, were frequently ruptured in the 1890s. Nevertheless, marriage itself, control over female labor power, adoption of children and their socialization all took place, but in a context of women's having taken what Marcia Wright has called "the raw fact of negotiability"[21] into their own hands, and transferred their own labor and reproductive power as survival dictated. From this a heritage of women's mobility was forged.

The construction of the Uganda Railway from Mombasa to Lake Victoria between 1896 and 1901 created a new option for Africans in those years. Food was plentiful in the railway camps, since it was shipped up the line from the coast, and was often resold to Africans at exorbitant rates of exchange reckoned in livestock, as the scarcity of food made grain more valuable than cattle,[22] or was made available in exchange for services performed in the camps themselves. Sir Frederick Jackson, a senior IBEAC official, described the Indian laborers' camps on the Mau escarpment in western Kenya in about 1899: "Apart from the squalor, they were crowded with prostitutes, small boys, and other accessories to the bestial vices so commonly practiced by orientals. Complaints by Nandi and Lumbwa natives were frequent . . . on account of so many of their young women being inveigled away from their homes, and harbored in those sinks of iniquity."[23]

It is impossible to tell from the above the nature of the tasks these Kalenjin youth performed in the camps or how voluntarily they came to be there, but it is clear that new social relations had emerged from Africans seeking food at the railhead. By 1899 the movement of the younger generation, male and female, from spouse to spouse, from tribe to tribe, from rail camp to rail camp, had begun to people the *majengo* (literally "the buildings" in Swahili, but used to refer to any settlement of urban Africans) that surrounded the nascent townships and trading centers of the protectorate. According to Charles Ambler, "lacking the support or protection of family or lineage, numbers of men, women and children settled down permanently, becoming part of these small Muslim societies."[24]

By 1899 a proportion of Africans' social relations were carried out in new places and new contexts. Prostitution was one of these new relationships. In July of that year the leader of a geographical expedition wrote from Machakos, in Ukamba, that John Ainsworth (then of the IBEAC) taxed at the rate of one rupee per month the Maasai-owned huts, which "usually belong to loose women." Two months later he described Naivasha, then twenty-five miles from the railway, as a small village with "some thirty Masai prostitutes in it. The race is fast being ruined," he announced, and perhaps more important, "Rupees have completely driven out trading goods."[25]

Who were these "loose women"? They may have been Maasai women who had at one time been pawned, and it is hardly surprising that women who had been mediums of exchange should have established themselves as prostitutes, especially when there was no other livelihood available to them in the newborn colonial economy. In 1899 we can see prostitution as occasional labor, engaged in by women and men in need of food and shelter, or when they were between families, *and* prostitution as profession, as occupation, as capital accumulation that led rapidly to property ownership in urban centers by women who helped to usher in a money economy.

Both these prostitutions coexisted in the eyes of some observers and in the lives of some women, for a while at least. A dozen years later, Kamba minstrels were heard to sing, "When it rains very little, we are deprived of the wives," who went to nearby townships "to dig with the back."[26] In the next section we will see professional prostitution emerge as part of the cycle of family formation—a cycle beleaguered by the events of the 1890s—but it is important that we recognize working prostitutes as Kenya's urban pioneers, the first urban residents. While many men flocked to food relief stations and the railway camps, few remained for long periods. Janet Bujra's data from Nairobi show that the earliest African male householders lived in town for only part of the year, spending the remainder of their time in wage labor and on the family farm. Women householders, on the other hand, most of whose incomes were derived from prostitution (few women would have arrived in Nairobi solvent enough to establish themselves as full-time brewers), lived there year round.[27] This suggests that men used urban real estate to supplement the process of family formation, whereas women used their town properties to inaugurate the same cycle. In early Nairobi, then, the point at which class formation diverged from family formation was expressed in real estate.

By 1900, however, women's prostitution—as distinct from women's migrations toward marriage or other protection—became a source of capital accumulation at a time when East African societies were recovering from a shift in their economic hierarchies and were rife with potential for generational conflict: agriculturalists were profiting over cattle owners, and sons had married without the aid of their fathers. Whoever encouraged young women into prostitution, if indeed any encouragement was needed, the profits derived from that labor could be and often were returned to women's natal families at a time when money was sorely needed. Through prostitution women could provide their fathers with wealth as surely as they would have done had they married for cattle in their homes. Thus "the regular trade in . . . girls" between Maasai villages and Railway officials in Nairobi in 1902 helped to reconstruct the rights and responsibilities of pastoral family life and fathers' control over it. "If a man tires of his girl he goes to the village . . . and gets another one, or in several cases . . . three."[28]

Wage Labor, Marriage, and Prostitution, 1900–1914

European settlement, encouraged by the protectorate's second Commissioner, Sir Charles Eliot (1901–4), was conceived as a way to develop the country's resources and pay the debt accrued by the construction of the Uganda Railway. The number of settlers grew from just under six hundred in 1905 to about two thousand in 1911,[29] and the labor requirements of European-owned farms, as well as those of the new colony, increased accordingly. African agriculturalists, recovering from the events of the 1890s and entering into a boom era after 1900, had no strong interest in building the infrastructure of colonialism and had to be induced to work through taxation, a method that had already proved successful in southern Africa.[30]

A tax rate payable in coin (one to three rupees, depending on region), livestock (testimony of the low cash value of stock in the early years of this century), or government work obtained until 1905, when settlers pressured for taxes that would be payable only in coin, in order to stimulate a supply of labor. African agricultural production boomed, and by 1906 tax payments in livestock were observed to be dying out, as the value of livestock rose steadily after 1906.[31] The Hut Tax, first introduced in 1902, amounted to a tax on household heads, generally married men. In 1910 taxation was extended to include single men in the form of a Poll Tax on all males over sixteen. Testimony before the 1912–13 Native Labour Commission indicated that a large proportion of laborers before 1910 began their working lives as single men—usually sons working to pay their fathers' tax obligations, in the spirit of precolonial social relations—but that after they married they continued in wage labor.[32]

The abuses of the labor system were enormous—including forcible recruitment, unpaid wages, and near starvation—and are capably documented elsewhere.[33] One overall effect, however, of early labor inducement and recruitment in the protectorate was to increase young men's access to cash, with which the cultural symbols of wealth and status could then be purchased: wage labor meant that young men could buy the livestock they needed for bridewealth.[34] As a result, more and more men were marrying, and the cost of livestock, especially female stock, was rising rapidly, as was bridewealth, after the dramatic fluctuations of the 1890s. According to disparate colonial sources, none of which may be altogether trustworthy, bridewealth was reckoned as high as one hundred goats in Kiambu and eighteen cows in Gusii in about 1890, possibly because of the limitations on grazing land. It then dropped dramatically after the initial rinderpest epidemics and rose to thirty or forty goats in Nyeri by 1902, twenty-five in other Kikuyu areas, and ten in Ukamba. By 1912 the goat bride-price had increased to about thirty goats in Ukamba for men with no cattle; for men with cattle it was the equivalent of over fifty goats. In Ngong and Dagoretti, Maasai areas adjacent to Nairobi, bridewealth was said to be forty to seventy goats; in Kiambu between thirty and one hundred goats. Between 1910 and 1912 the price of a female goat had more than doubled from its 1903 levels to between six and ten rupees, while wages for skilled laborers ranged from between six and ten rupees per month.[35] Thus bridewealth and the cost of livestock seems to have increased, and whether or not it was paid in installments, its cash value was the equivalent of years of wage labor.

There were many reasons for this increase in livestock prices and bridewealth. The agriculturalist boom allowed cultivators to begin to reinvest in stock, and as the state sold off every living animal taken from Africans in punitive expeditions, the supply of and demand for stock increased.[36] There is scattered evidence from Kikuyu and Ukamba that bridewealth became the primary noncapitalist mechanism by which elders could reestablish their dominance and manipulate stock holdings, as well as keep livestock prices buoyant relative to the increases in cereal prices.[37] As a woman who went to Nairobi before 1910 complained, "My father sold me, as if I were a goat."[38] In the Kikuyu Central Province, especially Fort Hall District, fathers were beginning to marry their daughters outside their home districts in order to take advantage of a higher bridewealth elsewhere.[39] Christianity was beginning to inflate the bride-price in Kiambu even more, as missions supplemented livestock payments in cattle to insure parental blessings for Christian unions.[40] Only Islam tended to deflate bridewealth, as a number of disinherited converts' lawsuits in Ukamba and on the coast demonstrated.[41]

Given this evidence for the renewed value of livestock, what would dissuade a woman—and her family—from a proper marriage, and turn her toward prostitution? The inflation of bridewealth did not take place in a political or ecological vacuum. We have already seen that the predominantly pastoralist Maasai lost cattle in the rinderpest epidemics of the 1890s. The somewhat pastoral Kipsigis (then called Lumbwa) raided the railway lines with diminishing regularity from 1899 to 1903; the cattle-rich Nandi, better organized for raiding and substantially more aggressive, attacked the railway lines steadily from 1899 to 1906. In response to both, British-led, Maasai-manned punitive expeditions took cattle and goats. In 1905, with one year of fighting remaining, it was estimated that British forces had taken ten thousand head of cattle from the Nandi's total stock of eighteen thousand.[42] The Kajiado Maasai were able to replenish their herds and retreat from wage labor with the earnings of *askaris* who fought against the Nandi, and a healthy participation in early prostitution. But how did the Kipsigis and Nandi elders replenish their herds? We have already seen that acquiring bridewealth through the revenues from wage labor was a lengthy process. It seems to have been from these destocked societies that entrepreneurial prostitution emerged purposefully, as women used their earnings from the repeated sale of sexual relations to acquire livestock.

In 1909 Normal Leys, the Medical Officer in Nakuru, wrote an unsolicited appendix to his Annual Report, identifying prostitution and what was even by that year a colonial obsession, venereal disease,[43] as "inevitable by-products of certain social conditions." The report is as remarkable for its compassion as it is for its observations. The quotation below bears out with precise chronology a pattern of destocking, prostitution, and livestock accumulation.

> Every *boma* has some prostitutes. In some Stations they live in separate huts. Elsewhere they lodge with friends. They wander through settlers' farms often travelling by the "rail-

way landhies" which play the part of the travellers' rests to the
native of this country. They charge for their services as a rule
from one to three rupees and often make as much as an
artisan in Europe. They live and dress well and generally save
considerable sums which they invest in stock. Five to ten years
ago most of these women were Masai. Now more than half
are Lumbwa and the next most numerous are Nandi.[44]

Women and girls from pastoral societies figured prominently in descriptions of prostitution in early Nairobi. An anonymous, undated, and
I suspect imaginative account by a missionary from Sagala claimed that
the most expensive prostitutes were Somali and Maasai at the turn of the
century.[45] In 1907 a police officer reported that there were three to five
hundred prostitutes in Nairobi, mainly Nandi and Lumbwa, some of
whom he said were ten years old. Within a few months they were sent
home by train, but disembarked at Nakuru instead.[46] In 1909 the Chief
of Police reported the jocular roundup of almost three hundred prostitutes, "the Masai being greatly in the majority."[47] At about the same
time a traveller noted that Nandi "women were notorious from Mombasa to Kisumu," and that many were prostitutes in Nairobi. There is no
evidence that these women were alienated from their families or societies. On the contrary, they returned home when they wished. In 1911,
for example, Maasai prostitutes from Nairobi went to pay their respects
to the leader Ol Lenana at Ngong,[48] and in 1913 the District Officer in
Nandi proclaimed that "the most enlightened members of the tribe appear to be the prostitutes who have spent some time in Nairobi or
elsewhere."[49]

Although it seems unlikely that young girls, especially the ten-year-
olds, entered prostitution wholly of their own accord, the issue here is
not whether or not these women were ordered into prostitution by their
families. To say that they were coerced would misrepresent the complex
negotiations that led the daughters of recently impoverished families to
East African townships. Other women left home and did not become the
prostitutes colonial officials could readily identify. Leys detailed other
work relationships between women and laboring men in 1909, "connections of different degrees of permanence," which may well have been
preferred by those women whose goal was not the rapid acquisition of
livestock. The issue here is the vitality of the noncapitalist sector of East
African society as late as 1910—the primacy of wealth measured in livestock, and the exchange value of women's reproductive labor for
livestock—and the particular ability of women, through prostitution, to

enable that sector to replenish itself and to profit from the revenues obtained from the capitalist sector. Laboring sons may have done the same, but their revenues came back to their homes slowly—sometimes through the mediation of prostitutes—and in a form, whether goats or blankets or cash, that they themselves possessed, wealth that was not the property of their fathers. Indeed, late in 1912 Kikuyu elders in Dagoretti complained that "after returning from work in the towns and wearing clothes our young men are spoilt. They are different men."[50]

The women who arrived at Nakuru and Nairobi, or the women who ran off with young men to Kisumu "to escape tribal control" (as well as bridewealth payments),[51] were seen as casualties in a battle rural East African society was supposedly having, resisting the onslaught of the modern world. Then and now, these women were seen as unfortunate counterparts of laboring men, pushed and pulled out of their homes by forces they barely understood.[52] But Africans did comprehend these forces; in fact, they manipulated them. The evidence before the 1912–13 Native Labour Commission shows that young male wage laborers were working for their fathers in a new context; what helped to break down older, hierarchical bonds was the long-term nature of early colonial wage labor and the fact that the wages paid laborers could lessen a son's dependence on his father. Women, on the other hand, were performing labor for their families that strengthened the position of a generation of fathers: whether through marriage—at inflated rates of bridewealth—or prostitution, herds were replenished and livestock values maintained in relationship to the steadily rising values of agricultural produce. But in prostitution the sale of sexual relations came under the woman's own control.

That control was mediated by the needs of male migrants, however, and prostitution mirrored the material conditions in which it took place. Migrant laborers were removed from their own homes, in jobs that provided neither food nor someone to cook it, let alone a context in which meals might be truly replenishing. The only way a laborer could obtain that was to establish a family presence where he worked—a cost that was impossible. Prostitution divided and commercialized such services—a working man could buy, for a bit of his wage, a piece of the totality he could not possess while working. Prostitutes in and after 1909 performed tasks normally associated with domestic labor in advanced capitalist societies—the privatized maintenance of a home, sometimes for several men in succession. In Leys's words, "it is a mistake to imagine that sexual desire is the sole source of these conditions. . . . The fact that a boy who works outside all day wants someone to cook for him is of equal importance."

Prostitution in Nairobi, 1900–1914

In 1899 the railhead reached Nairobi. An unoccupied area thought by officials to be therefore free of interethnic violence, it was made the capital and grew rapidly. By 1901 the population was estimated at almost eight thousand, and by 1906 it was said to be over thirteen thousand. Both figures included Africans (about nine thousand of the 1906 figure), Indians, and Europeans. In the years before World War I Nairobi consisted of huts made of wattle and daub, or grass; government buildings; Railway Quarters; and a rebuilt Indian Bazaar, all laid out in a piecemeal fashion and surrounded by infant suburbs and five African villages separated by arable land.[53]

There was a large number of single men in the city, Africans and non-Africans alike, but the conditions under which prostitution developed in early Nairobi had more to do with Africans' access to arable land than with the social life engendered by an imbalanced sex ratio, the causal factor frequently cited in the literature on African prostitution.[54] The 1911 census revealed a sex ratio of six men to each adult woman, but many of these women were married; many were part of the numerous Maasai and non-Maasai couples who had come to Nairobi from Ngong to work.[55] Conditions for married life were considerably better in the African villages than they were to become later in Nairobi's housing estates. Moreover, it was fairly commonplace for settlers and officials to have African mistresses at this time,[56] and many Indian-African and indeed many unrecognized European-African marriages took place. In Nairobi it was largely Muslim Indians who married Muslim Africans, usually for a high cash bride-price.[57]

Because of the proximity of forest north and east of Nairobi and the availability of arable land within and around the city, Nairobi's pre–World War I prostitution was neither as entrepreneurial nor as professional as that observed in Nakuru. In Nairobi, prostitution was combined with other forms of women's work, usually cultivation and gathering, the products of which were usually sold for cash but were sometimes consumed by the women's household. Male observers, both African and European, seemed to have stressed the sale of sexuality as the crucial aspect of these women's work, but that sale was combined with petty trade, as an old Kikuyu man told a researcher in 1966.

I remember seeing Nandi women before the German War
[World War I]. They were cutting wood over near Muthiaga
and they took it to Mombasa Village to sell. Some of these girls
would go . . . with anybody, even white men and Indians. You
could give her anything you wanted—half a rupee, one
rupee—but some men gave a cow or some goats. You know, in
those days a very important African only made Rs. 4 or Rs. 5 a
month, and workers got even less. So those prostitutes really
made a lot of money—more than most men—and they even
raised their prices after the German War. That's how they
came to have so many houses in Pumwani.[58]

Amina Hali was born to a Maasai mother and a Nyamwezi father in
Ngong in about 1895. Her family moved to the Nairobi village of Kileleshwa
in about 1900. She described her prostitution with Europeans—called
Kibura, after Boers, a term that emerged in Nairobi after World War I—
between about 1909 and 1916 as having developed out of her and other
women's cultivation of the fields her village maintained in Nairobi.

When we went to pick beans, we sometimes found these Kibura
men, so it was extra money, we went to pick beans and had
a man in secret. Sometimes a woman would go there just for
the men, she would take a *gunnia* [gunny sack] so that no one
would be suspicious, it looked like she was going to pick beans
but she would use the gunnia as a blanket. . . . When they saw a
woman lying on her gunnia they would take out their money,
and she would motion for him to lie down with her. They paid
us and sometimes they gave us babies, so we were rich, we had
money and babies that way.

These quotations describe a form of prostitution that developed out of
women's work, agricultural production and petty trade, made possible by ✱
the fact of African cultivation within Nairobi. That work involved mobility,
as did the experience of women in the 1890s. This led to the emergence
of a mobile form of prostitution, the watembezi form, in which the
sale of sexual relations took place away from the woman's residence—
conduct necessitated, if not preferred, by the family life and scarce housing
in the gerontocratically controlled African villages of early Nairobi.
For those years there is no firm evidence of the sale of domestic services as
there had been in Nakuru in 1909. Instead, there was the sale of household
production and sexuality: Amina Hali said that sex with men was
"extra money," suggesting that some of the beans she picked were also
sold for cash.

Both these quotations stressed the interracial dealings of watembezi prostitution, historically the most-profitable transaction in Nairobi prostitution and the one to which watembezi women had easiest access. This emphasis may well have been the informants' way to stress the promiscuity of early watembezi women and the physical and social distance their various enterprises carried them in prewar Nairobi. Open solicitation by both men and women characterized this form as well. My evidence indicates that the watembezi form took place in the African villages as well.[59] Early watembezi prostitutes were both immigrants (among whom Maasai, Kalenjin, and Kikuyu dominated) and majengo-born, from the villages in Nairobi and those in Machakos, Kitui, Fort Smith, and Ngong. Almost all these prostitutes except the Maasai tended to become Muslim,[60] but this was part of an overall tendency for Africans in early Nairobi to convert to Islam and had little to do with prostitution in and of itself.

Prostitutes' earnings in this period seem to have been relatively high. Of the nearly three hundred prostitutes arrested in 1909 almost all were capable of paying a fifty-rupee fine, and the Nairobi Chief of Police moralized that "the Indian and native population of the town provided an easy source of gaining riches and finery."[61] Bujra and I both found that many young women already established in Nairobi prostitution returned home to bring younger sisters back to town with them, but it is impossible to tell whether this is evidence of the comfort of Nairobi life or the extreme dislocation of rural life, or both, in those years. Many of these older women were later able to receive a hefty bride-price for their younger sisters, and in some cases to pass on their urban property to them when they died.[62]

Prostitution during World War I

The Great War came as a surprise to Europeans in East Africa. The punitive expeditions against the Giriama and the Turkana had not adequately prepared the commanders of African troops for wartime labor mobilization. The ever-increasing operations against the Germans further and further into Tanganyika—and by 1916 back into Kenya in retreat—created a demand for labor in unprecedented numbers and unprecedented confusion. In all, over 179,000 men from the protectorate served in the Carrier Corps, units supplying military support systems and transport on a massive scale, and about 11,000 men from the protectorate served in the King's African Rifles (KAR). The absence of so many men from rural production alarmed administrators somewhat, but the military's demand for locally grown foodstuffs kept prices at least as high as they had been before the war. Official anxieties seemed justified when the rains failed in 1918, and an already weakened population—including sick returned Carriers—was hard hit by the influenza epidemic of that year.[63]

Most Carriers did not pass through Nairobi, but KAR troops did, primarily men from Nyasaland, Nigeria, and the Gold Coast, as well as men from the protectorate. Senior KAR officers, generally South African, Rhodesian, and British soldiers, were also stationed in Nairobi, which became a small-scale garrison town. KAR wages were more than double those paid the protectorate's few skilled laborers, and European officers earned considerably more. Carriers' wages for unskilled work remained at about prewar levels, but for skilled work—in offices or carrying machine guns—they were relatively high.[64]

During the First World War the professional identity, or role, of the prostitute—a woman who earned her entire livelihood through the sale of sexual relations—emerged on a large scale in Nairobi and was visible to both Africans and Europeans. Such an identity had been rightly or wrongly visible to European officials earlier, as in Nairobi and Nakuru in 1909: without the corroboration of oral data we cannot tell how accurate these accounts of professionalism were, or if there were other labors in which the identifiable prostitutes engaged. We do know, however, that those women's prostitution was firmly situated within their labor as daughters for their natal families. Prior to World War I, in Nairobi at least, prostitution was an activity many women willingly combined with cultivation and trade. It is clear from the informants quoted earlier in this chapter that Nairobi's Africans did not live in a world divided into prostitutes and respectable women, a world in which prostitution was a specific occupation, or even a concept that the woman herself would use to describe her work.[65]

This seems to have changed during World War I. The evidence I have indicates that many women already engaged in watembezi prostitution abandoned all other work in the early days of the war and took to full-time prostitution. Many were said to have rented beds or mats in the back rooms of stalls in the Indian Bazaar, where they took the soldiers they solicited outside the Bazaar; others were said to have rented rooms in the mud huts that passed for African lodging houses in central Nairobi, to which they brought the men during the day and night. Obviously, some of the women who prostituted themselves had lived in lodging houses and the Indian Bazaar before World War I, but there is no evidence that they derived their entire incomes from prostitution in those years. My informants were adamant that the World War I Bazaar prostitutes neither brewed liquor nor engaged in petty trade, and many were said to have maintained rooms in the African villages of wartime Nairobi and used the Indian Bazaar as business premises only.[66] Moreover, it appears that women had begun to see prostitution as a livelihood for themselves during the war. A Kikuyu-ized Maasai widow of a householder in one of Nairobi's African settlements told Bujra that after her husband's death, between 1913 and 1918 "I didn't get another husband. There was *another way* then."[67]

By 1915 an identifiable role of the prostitute, complete with dependent males, had emerged full-blown in the eyes of administrators. It is difficult to tell whether or not prostitutes were an autonomous social category or the one that most effectively demonstrated the laziness of African men, an idea useful to the administration whenever their attempts at Carrier Corps recruitment failed. For example, when only three volunteers came forward to join the Corps at double local wages in Malindi in 1915, martial law was declared in the town and two hundred men were "forcibly collected. This 200 was . . . mostly composed of loafers and 'scallywags' living on the earnings of women."[68] Here we see that "the prostitute" was not necessarily a role denounced by the state but one invoked to accompany the criminalization of men's reluctance to work. A year later, professional prostitutes not only dressed the part, but were seen to corrupt young girls. According to the District Commissioner in Kericho, "hundreds of these women pass backwards and forwards every year between the Reserve and Nairobi, Nakuru, and . . . unsettle the minds of the girls in the Reserve with their gaudy apparel and jewelry and their tales of delights of a life of ease in the various towns."[69] During World War I prostitutes were officially described as urban workers, but as women with close relationships in town and countryside.

Without first-hand accounts it is difficult to establish all the differences between the women who became full-time prostitutes during World War I and the women who had prostituted themselves in prewar Nairobi. According to a few women who had either observed prostitutes when they were children or later heard stories from older women, the women who practiced the watembezi form in and around the Indian Bazaar or in Nairobi's lodging houses were older than the women who had prostituted themselves in the fields and crossroads of the pre-1914 city. Many wartime prostitutes were said to have been widows, or women already established in Nairobi community life. I have no evidence of new immigrants in Nairobi practicing prostitution at this time, although it seems unlikely that none did; it is possible that those women, however, returned to their homes after the war. Many pre–World War I prostitutes gave substantial portions of their earnings to their families; it seems likely that some war- ⅄ time watembezi did the same. It was said that some women who had taken up full-time prostitution during the war built huts in one of the African settlements with their earnings; more, however, bought livestock which they kept on their families' farms. Those women who did neither, and who were regarded as "stupid" because they hid their money in their rented rooms, had enough cash on hand to build houses in the official African location when it was created in 1921–22.[70] There is not enough evidence to prove that the "professional" wartime Nairobi prostitutes were using their incomes to support their natal families, but the indications that they went home regularly or kept livestock there suggests that they did.

Housing, Policy, and Prostitution, 1900–1918

In general, colonial African cities were designed (sometimes years after their foundation) to contain and maintain pools of competitively cheap male laborers, who in theory would return to their rural families as soon as their contracts ended. They all supposedly had families whose farms would provide them with the foodstuffs their wages did not allow them to purchase. This emphasis on housing the single male laborer was in Nairobi a vast contradiction from its inception, given the condition of African ⅄ family life in the rural areas from the turn of the century to the years of rapacious Carrier Corps recruitment. However, Nairobi's labor requirements were until the mid-1920s seasonal, and until about 1914 the African settlements were able to house and feed and contain the city's work force.

Nairobi's early African settlements—Pangani, Mji wa Mombasa, Masikini, Kaburini, and Kileleshwa—were built without any formal land grants on land with good drainage, and all but Pangani were under the control of Muslim Swahili headmen. The settlements were hierarchical, with an early marriage age for women and a late one for men. Amina Hali said that in Kileleshwa "they didn't think a man your own age would know how to take care of you, the best kind of man to marry was your father's age"[71]—a fact that was probably responsible for the number of teenage widows who engaged in watembezi prostitution during World War I. From their foundation in the first years of the century, a male and female ⅄ property-owning petty bourgeoisie existed in each of these villages; most householders built four- to eight-room huts in which they lived, renting

out the remaining rooms. The monies from which they built urban property had been earned primarily from the sale of services—whether gun
bearing or prostitution—to the Europeans, Indians, and Africans who
hunted, traded, and worked in the protectorate,[72] and the sale of agricultural produce to settlers and African laborers alike. By 1915 each village was said to have between 150 and 200 huts.[73] Another settlement, for
Sudanese soldiers at Kibera, was established under military administration in 1912 and was not demolished.[74]

Why was it necessary to demolish three of these six settlements to popu-
late a native location? In the years before 1920 the rhetoric of urban segregation was the rhetoric of medicine and sanitation. Segregation was
equated with control over those diseases each race inherently had and
could, by residential proximity, transmit. Obviously, medical issues were
pressing in the early colonial city—by 1907 the Indian Bazaar had been
burnt down and rebuilt three times because of plague—but sanitary segregation did not reach ideological proportions until after 1912. Until
then, complaints about "native prostitutes" were expressed alongside
complaints about "disorderly or other objectionable persons," the same
vocabulary used to describe the casual poor in England.[75] In 1914 Dr.
Simpson's *Report on Sanitary Matters in the East African Protectorate, Uganda,
and Zanzibar* was published and provided a new gospel for the Municipality of Nairobi Council (MNC). The *Report* insisted on rigidly segregated quarters for Europeans, "all but the highest class" Indians, and "the
primitive African" as "absolutely essential" to "the healthiness of the lo-
cality."[76] In this way prostitutes and the "other objectionable persons" of
prewar rhetoric were declared diseased. By 1918 the MNC met "to consider the question of venereal disease," which could be solved, they urged,
by establishing "the Native Location as the first measure towards the controlling of native prostitution."[77] Unlike the Contagious Diseases Acts of
Victorian imperialism,[78] in Kenya there was no question of examining
and quarantining prostitutes or of separating them from their communities; instead, "controlling" meant removing non-Africans from the contamination of African prostitutes. It meant segregation.

In most colonial African cities with European populations disease was a
potent metaphor: medical evidence provided the legal means for the removal of African populations and sustained their separation.[79] But in
Nairobi as diseases and purveyors of diseases merged in the eyes of the
administrators, the control of urban space became more than the control
of infection: it became control over African social and sexual relations.

The rules for the native location, drawn up at various intervals between

1911 and 1914, exemplified this. The location was conceived to house all Africans legitimately residing in Nairobi; Africans were to be allowed to own property but not to buy and sell it; they could only transmit it to designated heirs. According to one unimplemented rule, residents could be removed from the location if they were not of good character. It was also ruled that no one other than residents could enter the location between 10 P.M. and 5 A.M.[80] Such rules were designed to keep the supply of employed labor fluid while limiting the mobility and non-African associations of watembezi prostitutes. Such rules revealed a shift in colonial thinking: Africans were to be contained not because they were diseased, but because they were Africans. Control over Africans' housing became control over urban Africans.

Whereas before 1912 urban policy formulations contained within them ruminations on African marriage policy,[81] there were no such niceties in the plans for the location. Nairobi's Africans were to be lodged in small rooms (about sixty-four square feet) and forced together in communal bathing and toilet areas, and their social life was imagined and then dictated: although the African villages were predominately Muslim, the location was built without a mosque, and a 1915 meeting of the Native Location Committee allocated 10 percent of the plots to Muslims and proposed that housing for one thousand African Protestants be set aside.[82] The location also cut Africans off from the arable land in Nairobi.

The sole criticism of these rules came from W. McGregor Ross, Director of Public Works from 1900 to 1922. He noted the criminalization of urban Africans and accused the Committee of believing

> that if they arrange to remove excrement and supply roads of access and potable water, they have done all that the most exacting of natives could possibly require. As a matter of fact we do more than this for draught oxen in the PWD stables. Anything in the way of ordinary human liberties and privileges, which non-criminal sections of the population ordinarily enjoy in civilized communities are to be restricted wholesale in the interests of "proper organization" (whatever that may be held to cover) and "thorough sanitary conditions."

He added that PWD laborers would be "much more subjected to the importunities of prostitutes" in the location than they were in the PWD plot.[83]

The proposed location was postponed by the war but also by administrative inertia: the Medical Department had been badly embarrassed by the failure of the proposed Somali removals in 1918.[84] The real spur for the demolition of Masikini, Kaburini, and Mombasa villages was pressure from the Indian community to survey those areas for their own residential use.[85] Kileleshwa was left standing until 1926, Pangani was not demolished until 1939, and Kibera was not demolished at all. Medical arguments may have provided the evidence, but property values and political pressure provided the motivation for successful African removals. By 1920 the value of residential land—especially land with good drainage, essential to the control of malaria—may have meant more to the Municipality than smallpox. In 1923 the Principal Medical Officer admitted, "the people from the destroyed villages had never been particularly badly housed. It was primarily the situation of their housing, not the class of housing, which was open to objection."[86] In 1924 Normal Leys wrote, "The gist of the whole matter is that an urban proletariat cannot exist decently and healthily on wages of £ 4 to £ 15 on land worth £ 200 to £ 500 an acre."[87]

Starting in early 1921, householders in the three villages scheduled for demolition were given one and two months to build new houses in the location, after which their old homes were to be destroyed. This meant that property owners could use their rents to subsidize their new buildings, and, perhaps more important, it enabled and indeed encouraged Africans who had recently acquired disposable property to build there as well; the MNC refunded them two months' ground rent if their house was finished by then. This enabled many women who had profited from wartime prostitution to turn their earnings into real estate. The location was not actually peopled until early 1922, however, when the MNC transported the willing householders of the old villages, along with their building materials, to the location and destroyed the houses of the unwilling ones.[88] The landlords seem to have named their new home after this harassment: they called it Pumwani, meaning "resting place."

Conclusions

Between 1890 and 1919 prostitution, both as occasional work and as a profession, emerged in what is today Kenya. Because of the paucity of firsthand accounts for this period, it is difficult to determine exactly who prostituted herself (or indeed, himself) for what end; nevertheless it is possible to see three distinct kinds of accumulation from prostitution: scrounging, women's work within her natal family, and independent capital accumulation. These three kinds of accumulation—why someone prostitutes herself—appear again and again in this study, but in the early period the amount of overlap between the three is surprisingly small.

Scrounging is frequently characterized as a survival strategy,[89] a term that masks the desperation and the day-to-day decisions involved in such prostitution.[90] Scrounging in this case is perhaps most analogous to begging: for many, it is perhaps the option most frequently available when begging fails, as it seems to have done along the railway lines between 1899 and 1900. Scrounging did not seem to continue in a way that gained the attention of the European observers who noticed well-dressed and well-organized prostitutes in the years before World War I, which testifies to the very real profits to be made from prostitution in the growing townships of the new colonial economy, and the relative speed with which East African rural economies were reconstructed. Indeed, it would seem from the incidence of once-pawned Maasai women as turn-of-the-century householders in Machakos and Naivasha that many women made a rapid and permanent transition from scrounging to prostitution for what seems to have been independent accumulation. This transition is the only overlap between the different kinds of accumulation that I can identify with the available data.

On the other hand, prostitution that was women's family labor seems to have been widespread throughout the years 1899–1918, and the women who prostituted themselves for this end do not seem to have moved into independent capital accumulation at all. Such prostitution—the sale of tasks normally available only through marriage—returned to the woman's family the exchange value of those tasks, often far in excess of the values that under normal or better circumstances her marriage would have transmitted to her father's household. These prostitutes seem to have come from families for whom the loss of livestock had been extreme and rapid, generally Maasai before about 1907 and Kalenjin in increasing numbers between 1905 and 1914, and from all accounts their prostitution provided cattle for their fathers' households as surely as their bridewealth would have done had there been any young man among their people capable of paying a respectable cattle bride-price. Indeed, in Central Province the daughters who stayed home were taken away from home by their fathers and married in the districts where the bride-price was higher.

It was primarily through their daughters that fathers were able to replenish their herds; sons' participation in wage labor simply took too long to acquire livestock in numbers sufficient for their fathers to maintain their position relative to the rapidly rising fortunes of cultivators. Moreover, sons' earnings tended to go to buy their own wives, and this probably weakened their fathers' control. In such situations the labor of daughters was historically more reliable: through daughters' marrying or becoming prostitutes, household heads could control the labor of a younger generation that was already mobile and ensure that some of what was earned in the new colonial economy could be returned to their own rural enterprises. It is altogether possible that women's labor migrations, such as those of Kalenjin women in 1909 that had so impressed Leys, served to reduce conflicts with their natal households as their brothers left home to work or become squatters on European estates.[91]

Independent capital accumulation—Amina Hali's "extra money"—began at the turn of the century, and by the start of World War I, full-time prostitution and women's use of their earnings from prostitution to establish themselves as household heads seems to have been widespread in Nairobi and coastal towns, and was easily identifiable by both African and European observers. In the years before 1914 the women who prostituted themselves for themselves had no characteristic ethnic affiliations; they tended to be Muslims, majengo-born or immigrants from areas where destocking had been less severe than the combination of smallpox and famine.

We will see more about independent accumulation in later chapters, but it is important to understand that it contains within it the nearly revolutionary notion that women can be household heads. In Nairobi they initiated and moved the cycle of family formation—complete, in some cases, with younger sisters' bridewealth—into the new urban centers, where the constraints on the reinvestment of their earnings were the absence of arable land and the residential requirements of sanitary segregation, established by law and enforced by fire and bulldozer. Women's independent accumulation was not able to manipulate the stunted capitalism of the protectorate in the ways that a generation of working daughters did in rural East Africa, and perhaps for this reason it was less noteworthy to the European observers who provide the bulk of data for this period.

3

Prostitution and Housing in Nairobi, 1919–29

It is generally held that though the native in his own reserve is an estimable person of many virtues his detribalised cousin that lives in the towns is the scum of the colony. Nairobi may disprove this. Existing conditions are dangerously bad and apt to breed bad citizens in the dark and evil abodes of vice and disease. The native however is indomitable and rises superior to the conditions which have been forced upon him.

E.B. Hosking, Memorandum on the native locations of Nairobi

At home, what could I do? Grow crops for my husband or my father. In Nairobi I can earn my own money, for myself.

Kayaya Thababu

At no time was the relationship between Nairobi's housing policies and prostitution clearer than during the 1920s. By 1923, when Pumwani was fully established, what seems to have been a new form of prostitution emerged and flourished there, following the MNC's bylaws to the letter. At the same time, African casual laborers in the commercial areas squatted on valuable real estate and engaged in more aggressive forms of prostitution. After 1924, however, the rigid enforcement of urban sanitary regulations and the legal limitations on where Africans could rent rooms brought about a decline affecting the watembezi form for three or four years. But by the end of the decade high African employment and prostitutes' ability to pay high rents brought women, with renewed camaraderie, back to the streets of central Nairobi.

Nineteen-nineteen and 1920 were years of intense contradictions: the African reserves were recovering from World War I, famine, and epidemic while the areas settled by Europeans required increasing amounts of cheap labor to take full advantage of the postwar boom.[1] To increase the supply of labor to settler farms and state enterprises, "legislation to prevent idleness" was called for by settlers and Governor Northey. After 1919 increases in the Hut and Poll Taxes obliged men to seek wage labor, which District Officers, private labor recruiters, and chiefs—whose cooperation would be noted—were to "advise and encourage" by "every possible lawful influence." Moreover, the system of labor registration (*kipande*) often made it difficult for men to leave a given employer. The resulting scandal, in which missionary leaders complained, with some restraint, that "compulsion could hardly take a stronger form," forced the administration to remove "encourage" from its circulars,[2] and left the colonial state in Kenya defensive and fighting for its own particular brand of autonomy against settlers and the Colonial Office.[3] The practice of coercion relaxed somewhat after 1925, but by that time many thousands of Kenyan men had become participants in the wage labor economy. In 1923 there were 129,000 men at work, 152,000 in 1925, and 169,000 in 1926.[4]

Wage Labor in Nairobi

The violence of 1920s labor recruitment made the option of employment in Nairobi attractive to many African men; wage labor in Nairobi seems to have been free of many of the disciplinary abuses that had so often characterized agricultural labor. Nairobi employment paid relatively well in the early 1920s, and while those wages were reduced somewhat by the high cost of living there, Nairobi offered a variety of jobs, and opportunities for the very small number of mission-educated Christians to use their English-language skills. Such skilled Christian Nairobi workers were often young men who owned rural land; non-Christian African supervisory workers in state and private enterprises tended to be Muslims who had served in the colonial police or the military during World War I.[5] There is some evidence that the men employed in semiskilled and unskilled Nairobi occupations were a little poorer than their counterparts were in 1913; in addition to those men working to pay bridewealth and accelerate the process of family formation, there were a number of men working to find the wherewithal to establish families, with or without land.[6]

Although the demand for unskilled labor was high in the early 1920s, it rose sharply after 1926 when Nairobi entered a construction boom. Between 1926 and 1930 public expenditure in Nairobi quadrupled, and the demand for low-paid public employees was great.[7] This meant that men in unskilled and semiskilled labor could extend their stays in Nairobi, despite the growing body of pass-law restrictions on the time allowed for job hunting. In 1927 the Native Affairs Department reported that out of twenty-five thousand Africans in Nairobi, twenty thousand were adult males in registered employment. This proportionately high employment remained constant until 1929, when the African population was estimated at 32,000.[8]

By the end of the boom, two housing estates were provided for the work force, although not for construction workers. In 1929 the MNC completed Quarry Road for its African employees, on the site of the old Carrier Corps camp; it continued to be known as Kariokor. It consisted of forty-seven brick buildings, each containing four ten-by-ten-foot rooms, each to house three or four men or one married couple. According to the proposal for its design, couples had "proved the best employees . . . healthier, steadier, and so more reliable." Each building had a communal cooking area and a toilet outside, with a tap for running water. Also in 1929 the Government built Starehe, between Quarry Road and Pumwani, for three hundred of its employees, in a similar style.[9] Outside of domestic service, private employers did not provide housing for their laborers in Nairobi, despite repeated complaints by the state.[10]

Rents in Quarry Road and Starehe were based on those in Pangani, 10/ per room.[11] When divided by the three or four men each room was supposed to house, these rents approached those in Pumwani—between 2/50 and 5/50, depending on the size of the room; Pangani rents tended to be high because of the wealth of the community[12]—but they were well out of the reach of married workers, had their wages been high enough to support a wife in town. Laboring men who lived in Pumwani and Pangani shared their rooms with several others in order to reduce their individual expenditure on rent; my data indicate that men from Pumwani had more spending money than did men in Pangani in the 1920s.

Because of currency fluctuations and changes in coinage between 1919 and 1922 and exaggerated written accounts,[13] it is difficult to establish wage rates before 1924. In general, however, Nairobi wages after 1924 were higher than those available in the countryside. In 1927, when one out of every seven of the 160,435 men at work in Kenya was employed in domestic service, a house servant working for Europeans in Nairobi could sometimes earn about three times as much as the 7/ paid a man for doing the same work in Kiambu.[14] Such discrepancies increased the flow of unskilled labor into Nairobi, and this in turn seems to have helped maintain the stability of low and decreasing wages in unskilled employment between 1928 and 1929 (see table 1).

The fluctuations in the value of the silver rupee, discontinued after

TABLE 1　Average Wages in Shillings per Month,
without Value
of Rations, Nairobi

	1924	1925	1926	1927	1928	1929
Domestic service						
House/garden staff		10	12	12	12	12
Cook	14	20[a]	30[a]	23	36[a]	30[a]
Gunbearer	15	15	15	15	15	15
Unskilled construction		16	20	20	20	14
Unskilled state	13	14	18	18	18	11
Semiskilled			38[a]	24	24	27
Supervisor/clerical	26	26	28	30	36	46

SOURCES:　Michael P. Cowen and J. R. Newman, "Real Wages in Central Kenya,
1924–1974," essay, Nairobi, 1975, notes; Farouk Mohammed, Calfonya, 13 March
1977; Ziro wa Bogosha, Pumwani, 18 March 1977; Salim Hamisi, Pumwani, 29 March
1977; Soko Kagawa, Pumwani, 10 December 1976; Ahmed Hussein, Pumwani, 1
April 1977; Odhiambo Okinyi, Shauri Moyo, 23 February 1977.

NOTES:　These figures are based on a very small number of individuals and are at
best preliminary. I have not attempted to average into these calculations the time spent
looking for work.

[a]Data from written source only.

1922, increased the prices of all commodities that were brought into Nairobi by rail.[15] This meant that Kikuyu farmers from Kiambu and Limuru could sell vegetables in Nairobi for better prices than they would fetch locally, but still for less than those vegetables transported to the capital by rail. On the whole, retail commodity prices in Nairobi rose until 1924; then they began to decline. The prices of only two basic foodstuffs increased substantially between 1924 and 1929: the price of a pint of milk increased by one-third to 0/40 in 1929, and the price of potatoes doubled, to 0/8 per pound in 1928. The price of maize flour, however, increased only a penny to 0/10 between 1926 and 1929, and rice decreased in price almost 10 percent per pound and cost 0/34 in 1929. The cost of a pound of sugar declined 35 percent to 0/33 in 1929, and a pound of tea decreased even more, from 3/75 in 1924 to 2/36 in 1929. The prices of beans and cabbage both decreased about 25 percent by 1928, to 0/13 and 0/11 per pound respectively. The price of bread also declined steadily: a one-pound loaf cost 0/48 in 1924 and 0/40 in 1929.[16] Between 1924 and 1929 African wages in most occupations remained fairly constant, so the decreases in commodity prices in that period increased Africans' real wages.

Malaya Prostitution in Pumwani, 1922–29

By late 1923 it appeared that many single women had adjusted to the lack of mobility that the creation of the location had forced upon them[17] and that they had done so in a way that both minimized the tensions of a community that had been hastily thrown together and maintained relationships between women who were often simultaneously friends and competitors. This was the malaya form, where the sale of domestic labor was arranged and consummated inside the woman's place of residence. In Pangani and in the villages that were demolished to create Pumwani, women who were prostitutes frequently had their own rooms, but my data suggest that these women met their customers outside of their homes, in the watembezi form.

Compared to the watembezi form, malaya prostitution offered a more-extensive set of domestic services for sale; the woman provided the short-term lease of whatever else was in her room: bedding, water, food, utensils. Starting in the 1920s malaya prostitutes insisted that they did not state the price until the man was about to leave:[18] this enabled the woman to charge for all the domestic labor she had performed and all the commodities that were used. Moreover, the woman did not immediately define herself as a prostitute, or her space—an important concept for women occupying sixty-four square feet—as belong to a prostitute.

Malaya prostitutes did not solicit men. A woman who went to Pumwani in the early 1920s said, "When I was young, we didn't go out to find men, we'd stay in our rooms and the men came to us. They would knock on the door and ask me if I was free to go with them."[19] However, many malaya women of the mid-1920s emphasized a relationship between their ability to provide a full range of domestic amenities and their being sought out by men. Kayaya Thababu, a Meru woman who went to Pumwani from Nyeri town in about 1925, explained how men knew to come to her room.

> They knew that the house belonged to a woman who never had a husband, so they knew it was a safe place to come because the owner had no husband to beat them. If a man saw me and liked me, then he would come to my door and knock and ask to come in. . . . The best way to find men was for them to come to your room and you talk, you make tea for him, and you keep your house clean, you keep your bed clean, you have sex with him, and then he gives you money. . . . I didn't go openly looking for men, and men came to my room with respect, no one could

tell that they were boyfriends and not my husband just from
looking.

Malaya prostitutes provided the amenities working men needed. To a
lesser extent this was true of watembezi prostitution, but in that form,
without any real link to the woman's place of residence, men had the option of providing some of the components of domestic labor—food or a
place where sexual relations could take place—or of doing without them.
⨍ The relationship of malaya prostitution to wage labor was more direct.
The gap between what a man required to return to his work daily, fit and
productive, and what he could afford influenced the conduct of the malaya form in the 1920s.

What kinds of men came to Pumwani's malaya women, and how long
did they stay in their rooms? A night-long visit to a prostitute, or "full-
time" as it was often called in Nairobi, could be very profitable for malaya
women; in the 1920s they usually received between 1/ and 3/75 for full-
time visits—some of the difference depended on how much food was provided. Interviews with men showed that it was primarily the self-employed
(householders, smiths, and merchants) or skilled service sector workers
(hotel staff, house servants, gun bearers) who could afford night-long
visits. Men with skilled or clerical jobs, particularly in state enterprises (the
MNC or the Railways, the largest single employer in Kenya) could also afford full-time visits to prostitutes, but not as frequently as could tinsmiths
or cooks.[20]

While these data are not conclusive, they nevertheless indicate that
wages in the private sector in colonial Kenya were too low to allow the men
who earned them access to all the amenities a night with a malaya woman
could offer. Perhaps for this reason, by the mid-1920s at the latest, malaya
prostitutes became available for daytime visits (called "short-time" in Nairobi), either for sexual relations and some small amounts of food or for
food and conversation. Just as the self-employed and skilled workers of
the 1920s paid prostitutes 20 or 25 percent more for preparing food, men
in unskilled and semiskilled jobs could purchase a less-extensive range of
food and sexual relations during these daytime visits.

The daytime visits meant that a malaya woman's room was available to
men during the day and evening. Daytime visits also gave sexual intercourse a value equal to that of other domestic acts. Amina Hali, who
moved to Pumwani when Kileleshwa was demolished in 1926, described
how the daytime visits could be made profitable.

> If you spoke to these men, and told them about yourself, and kept your house clean, and gave them bathwater after sex, he would give you a few more pennies, and if he liked you he would come again, and if he came again, even to greet you, you would give him tea, and if he came again for sex you would also give him tea, and then he would have to give you even 75 cents. . . . If a man knew you and came to you regularly, he could give you as much as a shilling, but if he was a stranger to you it would be 25 cents.

Malaya women managed to charge for conversation. A woman would be paid, Amina Hali claimed, according to how effectively she presented her needs. Men were not natural providers, but they could be convinced: "In those days it depended on the way you talked to a man. If you are hungry and you don't tell the man how hungry you are, he can't understand. That is why it depended on the women, on myself, on what I am going to say to this man until he understands me and pays me."

Both Amina Hali and Kayaya Thababu stressed a correlation of the more domestic services available, the more often men will come, and the more they will come back: prostitutes and customers from the 1920s said that the men who repeatedly visited the same prostitute paid slightly more than they had done initially.[21] In both the watembezi and the malaya forms customers occasionally became boyfriends or even husbands,[22] but only women who had been malaya prostitutes in the 1920s spoke of this happening as though it had been achieved methodically. In these descriptions malaya women said that, by making their domestic labor continuously available, they were creating relationships from which they themselves would profit.

The economics of the daytime visits are not difficult to understand. As public expenditure increased in Nairobi, the male migrant labor force grew from twenty thousand in 1926 to an estimated twenty-eight thousand in 1929. These figures are in fact probably low, since there was a steady flow of men looking for work entering Nairobi during the dry seasons.[23] Certainly African men outnumbered women in Nairobi, but without any kind of records for female immigration, the proportion of men to women is difficult to estimate, as it has been for the entire colonial era. In 1938 a survey of Nairobi's African laborers by their employers showed that there were just over eight adult males for every adult female in the city.[24] This figure was important for its application in the 1940s, as we shall see, and in the historiography of Nairobi,[25] not for its accuracy.

Given the historical invisibility of women whose occupations were both illegal and indoor, it is unlikely that these ratios represent the true number
of African women in Nairobi, In 1932, for example, when Nairobi had
five thousand fewer African residents than it had in 1929 (see chapter 4,
table 2), the ratio of African men to African women was reported to be just
under two to one in Pangani and three to one in Pumwani.[26] Bujra has
suggested a sex ratio of six men to every woman;[27] I think a slightly lower
sex ratio—four or five to one—would be more accurate, except for periods of exceptionally high male employment, 1926–29 and 1940–45,
when there were times when a sex ratio of six to one was plausible.

Sex ratios, in and of themselves, do not determine the conduct of prostitution, but they do affect and influence its rate of profit. The price of a
full-time visit in Pumwani in the late 1920s was between 1/ and 3/75; the
higher prices invariably included breakfast. A conservative estimate of
one full-time visit a week at 2/ and ten daytime visits totalling 2/50 would
have earned a malaya woman 18/ a month, an income well above unskilled
male wage levels. In Nairobi in the late 1920s the unskilled laborers who
could not afford to spend the night with a prostitute were willing, however, to spend some portion of a shilling for sexual relations during the
day and perhaps a bath and some tea. This enabled malaya women to take
advantage of decreasing commodity prices, especially after 1926, when
the prices of tea, sugar, and bread all dropped substantially. Malaya prostitutes from the late 1920s said that their deference and their cleanliness
encouraged men to return, and however brief a repeat visit was, men who
knew a woman fairly well paid slightly more than did strangers. The 0/25
a malaya woman received in most daytime visits was, when taken in the
aggregate over a three-year period in which a large proportion of men
were in paid employment, a substantial means of capital accumulation. In
this way, Amina Hali acquired the 600/ to pay for a house in Pangani in
1930/31. Other women bought livestock with their earnings.[28]

Malaya Prostitution, Islam, and the Pumwani Community

The malaya form did not come into being solely to satisfy the needs of
migrant laborers. It came into being in a community in which privacy was
at a premium, in which the communal bathrooms and latrines had no
doors.[29] Malaya prostitutes were tenants and neighbors and householders
and friends in such a community, in which their movements were largely
restricted to where they lived and in which they were, even as established

members of the community, competing for scarce housing with their laboring boyfriends and customers.

Malaya prostitutes of the 1920s said that their work was conducted "in secret" and that they were safe from official censure. They claimed—and this was articulated as frequently about the 1930s as it was about the 1920s—that "the police could not arrest a woman for being in her own room."[30] Malaya prostitution mimicked marriage and so conformed to the location by laws. Such prostitution had its constraints, however. Wambui Murithi, a successful watembezi who went to Nairobi in 1928, observed that in Pumwani "the women stayed like wives, they went with whoever came to them." The secrecy and the privatization of the malaya form helped reduce residential tensions, and their real or imagined potential for violence, in early Pumwani. The malaya form limited the risks for men seeking out women, and it did not involve those people who were not prostitutes in anything that might appear to be, either to neighbors or administrators, illegal or dangerous. If anyone was to be in danger, it was the malaya woman herself.

Malaya prostitutes of the 1920s said that they did nothing when a man refused to pay them—a risk inherent in naming the price last. Fauzia Abdullah, who went to Pumwani in the mid-1920s, said, "If a man didn't pay me, I wouldn't do anything because I wouldn't want anyone outside to know what was happening." Zaina binti Ali was more explicit. The malaya daughter of a wealthy Nandi prostitute, she was born in 1936 but had internalized the values of her mother's generation in a way that many women born in Pumwani did. If a man refused to pay,

> I couldn't do anything like start a quarrel because then your neighbors would know that you are really a prostitute and you were supposed to be doing your work in secret. I mean that my people, the Muslim people here in Nairobi, often knew that a woman was a prostitute but she will have their respect as long as she doesn't bring this to their attention. If she has boyfriends, she must do it in such a way that she does not cause her neighbors to be ashamed that they live near her. So if a man refused to pay a woman, she really can't do anything to him because she wouldn't want to shame herself in front of her neighbors, and she wouldn't want to be made to leave her house because of fighting. And what if a woman did fight, and was beaten up very badly? She would be hurt, and it would be her neighbors who had to pay for the taxi to the hospital. In Majengo women

were supposed to be prostitutes in secret, and no one liked it
when a woman was open about being a prostitute.

This quotation is especially important because binti Ali is herself a
property owner. She is part owner of a building in the Pumwani Renewal
Scheme of Calfonya, having been moved there from the stone house built
by her mother in Pumwani in the 1920s and inherited by her and her sister's three children: she had grown up knowing she would one day own
the house. Yet when she described her own prostitution, its conduct and
behavior was determined by the norms of the malaya form, not the fact
that she owned property. The vitality and viability of the malaya form
stemmed from its articulation of and with the concerns of urban tenants.

According to malaya women, their neighbors in Pumwani, landlord
and tenant alike, were tolerant of prostitutes so long as the prostitute took
it upon herself to insulate her neighbors from the potential for violence
and disruption that her labor involved. For prostitution in Pumwani to be
secure enough to be profitable, malaya women had to camouflage all the
actions that made prostitutes vulnerable to arrest and censure: solicitation, promiscuity, being known as a prostitute, and to a lesser extent,
rowdiness and drunkenness. "In the old days prostitutes were respectable
women . . . they lived quiet lives and their neighbors never complained."[31] Malaya women from the 1920s insisted that no one could tell
"who was a prostitute and who was not."[32] Indeed, malaya women did not
seem to think that their prostitution set them apart from their neighbors;
other social categories were at least as important. One malaya woman observed that she and her cohorts in Pumwani were said to be older than the
women who had been watembezi prostitutes during World War I, and this
too made their work safer because "arrests never happened to women
who were widows."[33]

All of this helped to secure for malaya women their position as tenants
in a highly competitive housing market. Tenants who paid their rent were
virtually impossible to evict (those who did not pay were locked out of
their rooms and their belongs taken against back rent), but sometimes
they could be harassed into moving, especially when the landlord wanted
the room for a relative or friend. A prostitute could be made to leave when
the landlord's pressure, usually in the form of increased rent, led to constant bickering. Kayaya Thababu moved to another house after such harassment in about 1929, because "men don't like to come to a house where
they know women are quarreling, so I looked for another place and
moved." While such indirect evictions of malaya women do not seem to

have been commonplace, they reveal how willing malaya prostitutes were to minimize tensions where they lived. Many of these malaya women occasionally engaged in watembezi prostitution on the streets near central Nairobi, but they never described such streetwalking as having values or norms or an ideology; when they spoke of their own prostitution, they described the malaya form. When other women in Pumwani described these women's streetwalking, however, they spoke of the "respect" they showed by meeting men in River Road or the Indian Bazaar.[34]

The secrecy of the malaya form allowed some women to maintain, if not create, friendly relationships with women who were otherwise their competitors. For women raised in Nairobi there was a true sense of community, of responsibilities and obligations and relationships that were said to be more important than the wealth derived from prostitution. Miryamu Wageithiga was taken to Nairobi as a small child by her father's brother's daughter in about 1900; in about 1920 she went to Mombasa but stayed only about three years "because I was a new person in Mombasa and although I was new to men, and they went with me and gave me money, I didn't have any friends who could help me and I didn't find a permanent boyfriend." Amina Hali described how her friendships with other women helped her to carry on malaya prostitution while she was married, in about 1928: "My husband would not know I had a boyfriend, I used to do a little trick. I would take the present from my boyfriend to one of my woman friends and then after a few days that woman would come to my house when my husband was at home . . . and my friend would say 'I have new earrings but I want you to wear them first, it is a present from me' and then I would thank her and take them back."

Other malaya women did not speak of reciprocal relations between women. The women who went to Nairobi in the 1920s described how the secrecy of the malaya form was maintained in practice. Mwana Harusi bint Oman, who came to Pumwani from Murang'a in 1922, said that, if she found out a woman was a prostitute, "I wouldn't have heard it from the woman herself, and when she and I talked, she wouldn't say that someone had given her money for sex, she would talk about other things, like her home, or how she was poor. . . . in those days women didn't brag about men giving them money." Kayaya Thababu, who came a few years later, was more cynical. She said that secrecy concealed distrust: "In those days women talked a lot about how poor they were. We would sit and talk and complain about our boyfriends, one woman would say her boyfriend only gave her sugar, another would say her boyfriend never even gave her sugar. . . . and all the time these women would have a new *kanga* to

wear. . . . Besides, if you talked about your money someone might think
to steal from you."

Why did malaya prostitutes from the 1920s have such different relations with women who were their peers? The answer may have had more
to do with the process by which they became Muslim than it did with their
common occupation and place of residence. The vast majority of malaya
prostitutes in Pumwani in the 1920s were converts to Islam, and most of
them converted after they came to Nairobi. From my interviews it appears
that Muslim converts had fewer reciprocal relations with women their
own age and occupation than did women who were born into the faith.
According to Koranic law, any Muslim man can convert any non-Muslim
so long as he does so in the presence of two Muslim witnesses. The convert
is given a Muslim name by which he or she is known afterwards. In the
practice of Islam in Nairobi, many Muslim women converted women.

For many women who went to Nairobi between 1918 and 1924—years
of famine, epidemic, and land losses—Islam provided new parents, often
replacing ones who had died. For women running away from their husbands, Islamic parents accepted divorce. Conversion was described as a
social, not an individual, phenomenon: "you know, those men who converted us, we had to treat them like our fathers and call them our fathers."[35] The majority of the women I interviewed from the 1920s were
converted by men. A sizeable minority, however, told of being "helped"
when they first came to Nairobi by older Muslim women who exchanged
free housing for domestic labor (it was usually women who had been
watembezi who could afford a month's rent when newly arrived in Pumwani) and gave them their Muslim names. Very often they taught the
younger woman Swahili.[36]

While these older women may not have performed formal conversions,
they seem to have taken their role as guardians very seriously. The pro-
moted behavior that was in some ways different from the rural rules and
values the younger women had left. Hadija Njeri, a Kikuyu in her late
teens when she went to Pangani in 1918, was very specific about her relationship with her Muslim mother.

> She was a Kikuyu, but she was a Muslim . . . called Mama
> Asha. . . . She's my first mother because she's the one who
> helped me when I came to Nairobi, she's the one who gave me
> my first place to live, she taught me to speak Swahili, and she's
> the one who gave me the new name of a Muslim woman. She
> made me become a Muslim, that's why I call her my mother
> and her own born sons my brothers. . . . You know, in those

days no man would love you if you already had a baby. Most of the girls, they waited until the baby was born and then they would kill the baby or abandon it to die. . . . In those days you couldn't tell your real mother that you were pregnant, your real mother could never allow you to have a baby when you weren't married, she must not know, she would never allow for me to let the child live. . . . Many prostitutes here in Nairobi had old woman mothers who cared for them and gave them names like Mama Asha did for me. . . . That's the kind of woman who can teach you the right way to act in town. They would say "now you are my daughter, don't kill the baby, you must take care of the baby." That's how I learned that the mother I met here in town was better than the mother who gave birth to me, because she is the mother who can hear that you are pregnant and tell you truly the right thing to do. She will not tell you to kill the baby. This woman you meet here in town, this Muslim woman, she's a good woman, she could never join in secret talk about how to kill your baby.

Infanticide seemed to have been a grim fact of rural life in the 1920s.[37] An urban mother, unfettered by any need for a respectable bride-price, forbade infanticide and sanctioned illegitimacy. She was also the confidante of the young woman she converted, especially about intimate matters that were presumably the subject of dire rumors, and this bonding between generations would have placed real limits on what a young malaya convert might confide in women of her own age. In this way the older Muslim women established some of the norms for urban East African culture. These were demonstrably different from those offered by Western religions. A Kipsigis woman told Bujra that she had been a practicing Catholic for many years when she had an illegitimate child in Nairobi. "She claimed that when the priest came to hear of this she was refused the sacrament. 'I was bitter and very angry,'" and she went to a prominent Pumwani Muslim and asked to be converted.[38]

There were of course many reasons why almost all malaya women became Muslims in the 1920s and early 1930s. Bujra has suggested that some malaya women may have converted in the hope of gaining "a patron amongst the more rich and successful in the community."[39] Perhaps more important, Islam, unlike most Bantu-speaking societies, allowed women absolute ownership of huts: they could own and dispose of houses. However much this right had been undermined in the past, Muslim women who acquired property were quick to use British laws and colonial situations to maintain and defend it.[40] By the early 1930s half of Pumwani's landlords were women, but those women comprised 80 percent of the location's Muslim landlords; in Pangani the proportions of Muslim landlords and female Muslim landlords were higher.[41] In Pumwani, childless property-owning malaya women frequently designated as their heirs the young women they had sheltered in town, or a woman they had brought from their homelands while she was young.[42] This was literal class formation: the creation of bonds of place and property between two women who were seemingly kinless. I know of no cases where a malaya prostitute transmitted property to a man she had befriended, and of no cases where a Muslim man left his house to a woman he had converted.

The male property owners in Pangani and Pumwani were mostly Muslims until the early 1930s; male Christian landlords did not seem to make the same mark on the community that Muslims did until about the same time. Most male Christian landlords came to householding through porterage or KAR wages, and in the 1920s had good jobs in town and did not reside in Pumwani day in and day out; their wives managed their houses.[43] Wealthy Muslim men from the coast, however, were noted for their generosity toward women in the 1920s.[44] Kayaya Thababu learned about Islam from her Swahili boyfriends: "I thought . . . it would help me with them if I became a Muslim," and she asked her Muslim father to show her "how to cook and eat like a Muslim person." Amina Hali, born and raised in Muslim Nairobi, claimed that being a Muslim not only made her a skilled provider of the correct domestic services, but also prepared her for her professional dealings with men: "There was a very special way Muslim women were supposed to behave . . . she must bring water and wash the man first, then herself, then she will cook food if it's morning, tea in the afternoon, but it is not right for Muslims to go right from sex to cooking, they must wash before they touch anything in the house."

Malaya prostitutes seem to have become Muslim at a slightly greater rate than did male newcomers to Nairobi in the 1920s.[45] The religion offered new converts entry into urban social life, and access to the generosity of the Muslim community; it provided a home. The pressures on immigrant women to become Muslim were strong, as a Kamba woman who came to Pumwani in about 1934 explained.

> When I first came to stay in Nairobi I noticed things, and I wanted to find people I could eat with and stay with peacefully. The Muslims told me I couldn't eat or stay with anybody because you know in those days everyone in Majengo was a Mus-

lim, and if you went to visit them, they would feed me separately from the family because I had no religion. Then I decided I wanted to become a Muslim so that I could join the people of Majengo. No one objected . . . they welcomed me very warmly, an Mkamba man converted me, he had been a Muslim for many years. Even today I am still a Muslim, I can go anywhere because I am a Muslim, I can always join Muslim people, talk to them in correct Swahili, and even stay with them for a while.[46]

"Joining the people of Majengo" meant living in the social milieu that secrecy and deference and respect and tolerance necessitated. Nairobi's African urban culture was not just the creation of Muslim property owners, but the specific result of the challenges to their hegemony brought about by young women and men who had problems specific to the post–World War I era and who came to live in the city.

The Administration of Prostitution outside Pumwani, 1920–29

Historical data, especially when obtained from written sources, are a function of visibility: when someone is doing something that an observer finds noteworthy, that person and her ascribed actions are more likely to enter the written record than are the actions of someone sitting at home. The women in Pumwani who "stayed like wives" have no documentary history. The women who lived elsewhere, however, appear in archival sources, as much because of where they lived as how they lived.

Under the Indian Penal Code, developed by Thomas Babington Macaulay for India in the 1830s and 1840s and grafted onto East Africa by the Foreign Office in the early years of the century, prostitution was not a crime but soliciting was. The IPC had been designed to regularize the punishment of felons in India and to criminalize the purchasers of illegal goods and services at least as much as the sellers.[47] Such well-intentioned laws were probably beneficial for colonized peoples, but they were cumbersome and impractical for settler societies. Officials in Kenya routinely tried to circumvent the IPC, which gave them little or no power to move self-employed men and women off the streets.[48]

Having criminalized solicitation, the IPC acknowledged that prostitution was not a vice but a relationship between men and women. For the colonial state, problems arose when local labor relations were sufficiently capitalist that the work of urban men differed fundamentally from the work of urban women and had to be policed accordingly. In Kenya the active enforcement of the IPC would have filled the jails with too many working men; the IPC did not distinguish between urban entrepreneurs and the wage laborers they served. Labor registration had left the unwaged unregistered and all but outside the law. Denied a legal apparatus with which to facilitate the wholesale removal of any group from the city's streets, the state had to become more subtle than its criminal law to deal with prostitutes.

Once Pumwani was established, it became illegal for all African women, regardless of how they earned their livings, to reside outside the location or Pangani. Moreover, it was illegal for Pumwani residents to be away from their homes after dark without the written consent of their employer, and it was illegal for non-Africans to come to Pumwani between 7 P.M. and 6 A.M. All of this meant that after 1922, Nairobi watembezi—and some of their customers—were not only noteworthy, they were vulnerable to arrest on grounds that had nothing to do with prostitution.

Nevertheless, few women in the 1920s were arrested for prostitution, and even fewer for living outside the location. Indeed, the women who lived outside the location claimed that their place of residence allowed them to avoid arrest: "in those days it was not legal for a woman to walk on the streets outside Majengo, but if you had a room there and the police stopped you, you could say you were coming from the shops, and go to your home."[49] The women who were arrested did not seem to consider it a legal issue at all: "those arrests were all because of jealousy between African peoples."[50] Women spoke of bribing policemen or having sex with them to protect themselves from arrest, but if a woman was arrested, she or her woman friends would pay the fine.[51]

If prostitution appeared uncontrolled to streetwalking prostitutes, how did it look to individual administrators and the colonial state? From a close reading of the Kenya National Archives, the progression of administrative control over prostitution is not at all clear. Neither the police nor the jails could accommodate massive arrests of anyone—the heyday of pass-law violations was yet to come—and those police who received extra monies from prostitutes had every reason to counsel against arresting them. By the start of World War I prostitution was viewed as a residential problem—one that would either expand or be contained—that spread disease and interfered with the racial segregation that had recently been declared Nairobi's destiny, and thus came under Medical Department authority.

In his work on bubonic plague in Cape Town, Maynard Swanson suggested that infectious disease was the "societal metaphor" that ordered racial segregation in the tropics. Illness applied to racial and ethnic categories ideas about contamination that had been applied to casual laborers in Victorian England.[52] This was true of Nairobi in a roundabout way, since sanitary segregation involved changing ideas about which nonwhite race carried the most diseases. Until the early 1920s the state maintained that Indians, because of their "incurable repugnance for sanitation and hygiene," were more diseased and dangerous than Africans, who were, for once, "more civilized . . . being naturally cleaner." Unfortunately, Africans tended to imitate those around them, so that "the Indian is . . . the despair of the sanitarian; he is a menace not only to himself, but to the native of this country."[53] Indeed, in 1916 there was a strong suggestion by B. W. Cherwitt, Nairobi's Health Officer, that African prostitutes living in the Indian Bazaar acted as a buffer between Indians' contagious diseases and Nairobi's European population. Cherwitt wrote that if the prostitutes were removed from the Bazaar their rooms would rapidly fill up with "400 or 500 lower class Asiatics" because "to overcrowd is an inherent tendency in the character of the Asiatic," and such overcrowding would cause "the spread of plague, smallpox, and the poor physique, debilitated condition and unwholesome appearance of so many Asiatics" throughout Nairobi.[54] The creation of Pumwani in 1922 released the land of the demolished villages for Indian residential development,[55] which was to reduce overcrowding in the Indian Bazaar. Prostitutes continued to rent rooms in the Indian areas, but tolerance for their presence waned as Africans themselves came to be seen as polluting as Indians had been.

The Medical Department was the only branch of the colonial state that could effect the removal of urban communities. Until the early 1920s it did so by establishing the diseased nature of those nonwhites inhabiting property in too close proximity to the city's European population. The Medical Department made places of residence illegal. The criminalization of space was the colonial state's response to a penal code in which most waged and all unwaged work could not be criminalized. In the 1920s the state sought to control prostitution through housing, not the courts, at the same time prostitutes were using housing to sell their labor.

From 1910 to 1921 the Medical Department in Nairobi was headed by several men, all of them sympathetic to settler interests. Cherwitt, in addition to strong opinions about Indians' health, tried to argue that property ownership by nonwhites increased the possibility of contagion, and as Medical Officer of Health in 1917 may have falsified a report of plague in a last-ditch attempt to remove Somalis from Eastleigh.[56] His successor as

Medical Officer of Health was in 1918 a lone voice opposing the creation of Pumwani, because "the vast majority of the inhabitants of the existing villages are undesirables who should not be permitted to reside in the township at all," and their concentration in one place would "foul the area."[57] In 1921 Dr. A. R. Paterson became Chief Sanitation Officer; he was then rotated through a variety of positions until be became head of the Department in 1932. He was a concerned and innovative administrator who believed that Africans could be taught health and hygiene, and he and his staff were extremely critical of the state's slow funding of sanitary matters.[58] By the time he took over the Medical Department in 1932 he had a reputation as "long winded, and the tendency displays itself in his written productions even more than in the spoken utterances, but . . . he is inclined to be a visionary."[59] Indeed, there is some evidence that he lost a few sanitary battles precisely because of sledgehammer methods.[60] Paterson's interest in prostitution and the diseases it spread was nil, and he had little interest in the rhetoric of inherent racial characteristics. Instead he saw town planning as the key to disease control, and by 1922 his mission in Nairobi was to provide better drainage with which to prevent malaria and create sanitary single-family dwellings for Europeans and Indians alike. With these goals, he was to structure and criminalize watembezi prostitution in the 1920s.

Watembezi Prostitution and Sanitary Segregation, 1919–24

The oral sources for the watembezi form in this era are slim: a few men's accounts, a few women's recollections of activities they had seen or heard about when they were young. The written sources are unlike any others in Nairobi's colonial history: three remarkable letters protesting prostitution in Nairobi, written by two young Christian Baganda working there, and the Medical Department's thoughtful replies and hastily compiled census of prostitutes.

African housing was scarce in postwar Nairobi, and homelessness was such a fact of African life in Nairobi that in 1920 the Vagrancy Law was amended to include anyone who, without the owner's consent, was found "lodging in any veranda, outhouse or shed, or unoccupied building, or in a cart, vehicle or other receptacle and not having any visible means of subsistence."[61] But between 1919 and 1923 women rented rooms or built huts on the streets and in the gullies that surrounded central Nairobi. River Road, the main street that linked white Nairobi to its eastern suburbs and a generic term referring to the adjacent streets of Racecourse Road, Canal

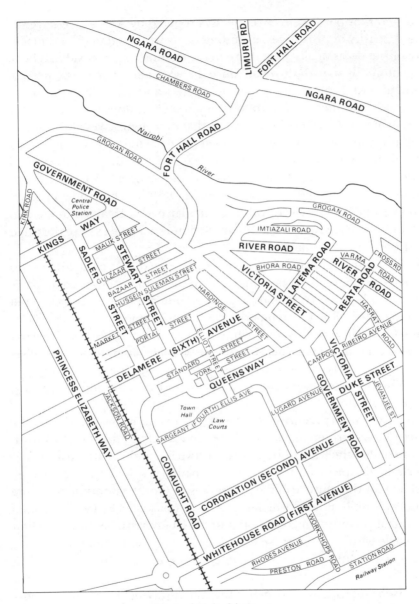

Central Nairobi streets

Road, and Campos Ribeiro Avenue, was reputed by Africans to have the highest density of prostitutes, including many who lived in Pumwani and Pangani but occasionally went there in the daytime. River Road had been in a continuous state of disrepair since the war. The women who lived in Pumwani and Pangani took men to bushes and alleyways; the other watembezi took them to the rooms they rented in houses owned by Indians, to huts and makeshift structures that they themselves built. Indian and European men either accompanied the woman to her room or took her to their homes, where, in theory at least, they could provide some of the domestic amenities.[62] Europeans and Indians paid women well and kept the prices charged African men high: 0/30 for short-time in about 1920 to about 1/50 in 1924. Although similar prices obtained in the outskirts of Nairobi, in River Road few or no domestic services were provided to African men in the daytime.[63]

By all accounts the watembezi form practiced in the River Road area was raucous—women called out to men and to each other: they tended to live near each other and frequently argued among themselves, but were not violent.[64] River Road watembezi were famous among Pumwani prostitutes for their relations with white men.[65] Nevertheless, in the early 1920s—years in which the state's considerable attentions were elsewhere—they attracted no official notice. They did, however, attract the attention of two young, educated, Christian African men, and they in turn notified the state.

Calling themselves representatives of "the people of the exterior dark," in three letters written to Paterson between July 1923 and May 1924 (with carbons sent to the King of Buganda) the two Baganda provided a vivid, if melodramatic, picture of watembezi activities. In their first letter they called not for the censure of the prostitutes, but for the punishment of the "owners of the building" who let it "for such business." The young men hinted that prostitution contributed to the labor crisis, because "some of the people who . . . visit these lewd females are contracted with various infections and suffer. . . . and become weaker and unfit to do any sort of work."[66]

Paterson met with the two men at the end of July, but he or his superiors waited until mid-October to commission a census of prostitutes; he admitted the timing was poor, since many buildings occupied by prostitutes in River Road and Canal Road had just been closed on sanitary grounds and the watembezi tenants were either "on the move" or divided between Pangani and Pumwani. The census itself revealed a total of 213 prostitutes (the Chief Sanitary Inspector, "with considerable experience in Nairobi," suggested this was too low). There was no mention of how the census was done, but a few items suggest that the women themselves were asked about where they lived. For example, a European property owner was identified only as Mrs. Rheims, and the names of many Sikh landlords were simply given by a nickname, Kalah Singh:[67] *kalah* is the Gujurati word for black, by which Gujuratis frequently refer to all male Sikhs, whose most common surname is Singh. It is unlikely that these were the names listed with the Land Office, and lessees would have known the names of their lessors, but tenants may well have called their landlord by the same name their Gujurati boyfriends used.

The rents charged African prostitutes are the most illuminating part of the census. Even though it is impossible to tell how long a woman lived in one place—the Baganda were later to estimate that the average watembezi working life was five months, after that "everything on their part no doubt goes ill; as they have now nothing . . . to feed themselves"[68]—they provide some concrete data on what women earned and how profitable different areas were. Rents were high, as they had been for several years. As early as 1914 it had been noted that Africans who rented accommodation from Indians outside the all-African areas paid more per room than did Europeans in the middle-class white suburb of Parklands.[69] Rooms on Campos Ribeiro Avenue shared by two women cost 20/ to 22/ per month; rooms on Racecourse Road shared by two or three women cost 16/; from Quarry Road to Swamp Road two or three women shared rooms that cost between 15/ and 18/; in the Swamp, in buildings or in huts, two women usually shared rooms that cost between 10/ and 12/, except in the sublet Grogan Estate, where three women shared rooms that cost between 20/ and 22/, and where one woman rented a room for 14/.[70] These women's individual expenditure on rent ranged from between 5/—what they might have paid for a room of their own in Pumwani or Pangani—and 11/, almost four times Pumwani rents. While there is no way to be certain if these rents devoured watembezi profits or indicated great ones, it seems likely that they imply high earnings, as 1/50 for short-time would suggest, since there were cheaper rooms—and malaya prostitution—available to these women in Pumwani in 1923.

Both the Baganda and the census takers were concerned with the prostitutes' ethnicity. Most of the prostitutes were identified by their place of origin; in 1923 tribes, particularly non-Kenyan tribes, were not an essential feature of colonial discourse. There were sixty-one Kikuyu women; fifty-eight from Uganda; thirty-nine Nandi; twenty-seven from Bukoba in northwest Tanganyika; fifteen from Lamu; twelve Somalis; and one lone

Swahili. There is little that can be generalized from these totals, however.
The number of Kikuyu women reflected the proximity of Kikuyu areas to
Nairobi and the land alienation that was taking place under the white settlement schemes of the early 1920s. The high number of Ugandan
women would have followed from the severe dislocation of World War I in
rural Uganda. Bukoba had been captured and all but sacked by two thousand India Army and KAR troops in 1915, and had been raided for able-
bodied men in the mass levy of 1917.[71] Nandi women had been a presence
in Nairobi prostitution for many years, and they were the women most
identifiable—and available—to Africans as River Road watembezi.[72]
These were all women who chose to live outside the Muslim preserves of
Pumwani and Pangani. Indeed, the presence of Muslim women from the
East African coast—from the same places that the generous Swahili men
of Pumwani came from—would indicate the profits and the interracial associations that were to be found in the River Road.

A few days after the census was completed, Paterson wrote to the Chief
Native Commissioner that structural improvements had rendered the
brothels of Canal Road "desirable residential areas" and that the Baganda
had reported that there was no more public solicitation there.[73] Indeed,
they wrote to thank Paterson, to inform him of the new whereabouts of
watembezi in central Nairobi, and to request Government aid in sending
home the women from Uganda and northwest Tanganyika, "who are always trying to obtain money for passages."[74] Paterson immediately wrote
to the Chief Native Affairs Commissioner, pointing out that if demolish-
ing unsanitary buildings had the effect of "scattering prostitutes throughout the city," even if they were openly soliciting men, their conduct was no
longer a concern of the Medical Department but was instead an administrative issue, "particularly as the possibility of repatriation has been
raised." He went on to say that the Medical Officer of Health would of
course supply the Native Affairs Officer with the evidence that would facilitate the administration of urban Africans.[75]

The watembezi the Medical Department had made homeless, whom Paterson thought "would probably stay on the move," became increasingly
vulnerable. At the same time, however, Paterson wrote that he wanted to
remove "the casual laborers in the commercial areas. . . . The natives with
whom we are really concerned do not at present command any housing of
their own worth the name and are never likely to be able to provide much
for themselves."[76] The removals that followed were a miniature history of
the city itself, the removal of unwanted people from valuable land. In Nairobi the unwanted people were invariably African entrepreneurs, evicted

with laws and building regulations, to make room for "desirable" residential and commercial locations. In the early 1920s an African female labor force, and from many accounts their dependents,[77] were removed from central Nairobi so that Indians and Europeans could live and work there. Starting late in 1923, African prostitutes—and presumably other self-employed Africans as well—were literally driven off the newly paved streets of the commercial areas and into the malaya form in Pumwani or Pangani or into marginalized watembezi prostitution in suburban Nairobi. Some women may have gone home; those who attempted to remain were faced with high rents and worsening circumstances in the central city.

Watembezi prostitution in central Nairobi began to decline after 1924 as there were fewer and fewer places for African women to live. After the demolitions on Racecourse Road and Canal Road in 1923, single-family dwellings and shops were built there for Indians.[78] As more improvements were made in the name of sewage, pest control, and progress at River Road, Campos Ribeiro Avenue, and Ngara Road, watembezi began to occupy shanties on the northern end of River Road, behind the Norfolk Hotel, and behind the mosque on Government Road.[79] In 1924 the Baganda reported that prostitutes lived in fewer, more deplorable houses that they built themselves or rented from Indians.[80] Later that year Nairobi's Medical Officer of Health claimed that there were at least three hundred Africans living "in premises unfit for human habitation" outside the locations. These dwellings were built of mud or, if a woman was particularly well-off, of wood and tin, and they were regularly knocked down or burned down.[81]

This destruction of African housing, even the carts and sheds of the 1920 Amendment to the Vagrancy Laws, in areas where it was safe and profitable to be watembezi virtually eclipsed the form in central Nairobi after 1924. In River Road prices for short-time in 1924 were higher than they were in 1926.[82] There are no written references to open prostitution taking place in that area between 1925 and 1928, and while this does not indicate the completeness with which the form was banished from the streets, it does show the extent to which watembezi numbers were reduced and their visibility diminished during those years.

Watembezi Prostitution, 1927–29

Starting in 1927/28 watembezi prostitution began to emerge in the River Road area once again. By then Nairobi was in the midst of a boom, the number of employed African men was high, and some of the improved buildings in River Road and Racecourse Road were being rented, in small numbers and at high rents, to African women. Wambui Murithi rented an upstairs room in River Road for 50/ in 1928, a vast increase over the early 1920s rents in the same area and more than ten times the 1928 rents in Pumwani.

That watembezi could afford such rents was part of Nairobi's overall prosperity. Another part of that prosperity that led to the renewed visibility of watembezi was the number of automobiles in Nairobi. In 1928 there were five thousand cars in Kenya, most of them in Nairobi and all of them owned by Europeans or Indians.[83] For men seeking women, the car enabled the driver to find a woman with comparative ease and safety and to take her to a place where sexual relations could take place. For watembezi women the car gave a concrete idea of what a man might be asked to pay. "River Road," said Wambui Murithi, "was a place for finding men with cars. . . . If they were Asians, you could even ask for 10/, they couldn't tell you they didn't have it."

Watembezi prostitutes of the late 1920s risked arrest and harassment, but their profits seem to have been high. In 1927 the price for short-time in the eastern end of Racecourse Road was as high as 5/.[84] Wambui Murithi was about twenty when she went to River Road in 1927/28, already divorced from the half-Kikuyu son of an Indian shopkeeper she had married in her home in Nyeri. She pointed out that living in River Road gave her access to Europeans and Indians, as well as skilled African laborers: "Women who stayed in River Road, we were very clever. . . . In River Road you could walk back and forth, back and forth, and you could find all kinds of men that way, white men, Asian men, Africans men with jobs . . . they all had to pass that way, and you could call out to them and take them to your room because your house was so near, women in Majengo didn't see Asians or white men just strolling by." Murithi explained the geography of Nairobi in terms of interracial access, profits, and safety for both customer and prostitute. "In River Road, sometimes you could go as far as Government Road to look for men," but Indians "never went past Quarry Road" to find women because they "feared to go to Majengo." Such fears had their advantages, however: Indians generally paid only slightly better than did Africans, but "they paid more in Majengo because they were frightened." But Indians lived and worked in River Road, so "if you had a regular boyfriend who was Asian or European, then he could visit you at any time."

The high rents in River Road meant that women shared their rooms: in her first few months in Nairobi, Murithi lived with the woman with whom she had come to Nairobi, a divorced Kikuyu like herself; later she lived with a woman who had been in Nairobi for a few years. Roommates cooperated in their work in ways that malaya women did not, as they joined together to establish work rhythms and allocate space: "It was very good to share, because if your regular boyfriend came and you weren't home, someone could go find you. And if I was on the street and saw that my friend was going with a man, I knew I couldn't bring a man to that room for half an hour. . . . But sometimes we went with men in cars, so we didn't need our rooms." Having roommates and friends also enabled Murithi to avoid arrest: "We never went out at night alone. We went, two of us, three of us, and if the police stopped us we would just say we were looking at cars, and go home together, and only go out again if the police had gone."

When malaya women occasionally walked the streets of River Road and Racecourse Road in the late 1920s, they were vulnerable to arrest precisely because they worked alone. The police "used to tell us we were too proud, and if we were alone, walking in the road, they would arrest us at the slightest excuse."[85] Some malaya women learned how to negotiate the streets: "You could be caught walking alone in the streets at night, then . . . turned in for vagrancy. Otherwise you could go anywhere if you had a companion."[86] Others did not and were arrested frequently: "women who came only in the night to look for men, women from Majengo or Pangani, sometimes they got arrested, but not for looking for men, for vagrancy."[87] In contrast, Murithi and her roommates "looked for men in the daytime." She herself was never arrested in the six or seven years she lived in River Road. Moreover, "we knew the police, sometimes we went with them, we gave them presents sometimes." Malaya women often had sex with policemen to avoid arrest, but "if you went with a policeman you didn't expect much money, I'll tell you that."[88] If a woman was arrested in the River Road area, her friends would pay the fine, usually 30/ or 40/, "if she had been in Nairobi for any time at all."[89] Nandi women were said to be the exception to this; when they were arrested in the 1920s and 1930s "an older woman, someone from their home" paid their fines.[90]

During Nairobi's boom a few women from the agricultural districts of Kiambu and Limuru began to supplement their incomes by occasional watembezi prostitution in Nairobi. They came to Nairobi in the daytime to sell vegetables and then went with African workers in Pumwani and Pangani or, after 1929, the Municipal Quarry Road estate, "and only those of us who saw them . . . knew what they really did."[91] Their absence was noted at home as well: late in 1928 Chief Kinyanjui of Kiambu asked the Local Native Council to take action against those married women who were going daily to Nairobi, ostensibly to sell vegetables but in fact to prostitute themselves there.[92] Married or single, these women seem to have been responding to the other side of the boom in Central Province: increased agricultural production on land already so overcrowded that women with limited access to land, married or alone, could not maintain their previous standard of living through cultivation, if they could cultivate at all.[93]

When the Quarry Road estate for Municipal employees opened in 1929, it was rapidly occupied by semiskilled and skilled men: at rents of 4/ per man in a three-bed room they were the only ones who could afford to live there, although there is ample evidence that these men reduced their rents by subletting their floors to men less well-off than themselves. Built to house 460, within a few months it held twice that number.[94] With such a population, Kariokor became a site of considerable watembezi activity almost at once. It was a place to find men with salaries and nearby rooms in an area where Africans could legally live and walk. In January 1930 fifty women were found living there, a few of them the single residents of the 12/-cubicles designed for married couples.[95] For watembezi, such rents in such a place would have been a bargain in the late 1920s.

The women in Kariokor captured the imagination of Africans in Pumwani in a way that more-visible watembezi had never done: Tabitha Waweru and Margaret Githeka, who had been ten and twelve in 1930, insisted that the Municipality had given prostitutes rooms in their Quarry Road estate rent free. Outside of the estate as more and possibly younger watembezi gathered at the roundabout that linked Racecourse Road and Quarry Road, Indians and, to a lesser extent, Europeans began to seek women there. Police surveillance increased, but profits remained high.[96]

Conclusions

The rumor known even to children in Pumwani in 1930, that prostitution was approved by the colonial regime, was astute: prostitution was essential to the smooth running of a migrant labor economy on the scale Nairobi required in the 1920s. Colonial administrators were to say as much less than a decade later. Prostitutes were not given housing, but outside of the areas being prepared for non-African occupancy, they were not evicted either.

Just as the forms of prostitution followed from women's access to housing, prostitutes' social relations were often determined by the situation of the housing in which they lived. The secrecy and isolation of the malaya form, the prostitution of women waiting in their own rooms in the firm belief that "no one could tell who was a prostitute and who was not," meant that women worked alone and risked arrest on the occasions they went to River Road. Watembezi women in River Road, however, shared rooms and work rhythms; they cooperated in order to allocate time and space fairly and to protect each other. But the form of a prostitute's labor, and her practice of it, were part of the community in which she lived, whether Pangani or Pumwani or River Road. For all the atomization of their work, malaya women were active participants in the communities of Pumwani and Pangani. Malaya women made themselves available for most of the day and night to attract the widest range of Nairobi's labor force and to maximize their profits. They inconvenienced themselves—by tolerating no payment, by moving house—to keep the peace where they lived. They converted to Islam so they might be better received and attract a more lucrative clientele.

The values malaya women articulated had to do with being good neighbors and responsible tenants and loyal friends (although not always loyal spouses). These women thought of themselves as friends and neighbors and tenants—even when they owned property—and converts and daughters; they did not describe their prostitution as separate and distinct from their other urban relationships. Indeed, when these malaya women described their work fifty years later, the relationship they described as crucial to the conduct of their chosen labor form were relationships with their women friends—the same relationships that Wambui Murithi called "good" for watembezi prostitution in River Road. With very few exceptions, female friendships—across or within generations—were seen by women like Miryamu Wageithiga as more important than any number of customers, and for women like Amina Hali, they were a way for accumulation to take place.

While prostitutes helped maintain African communities in Nairobi in the 1920s, the colonial state worked to segregate them. Pumwani constructed and policed itself, with considerable help from prostitutes, but the new Indian areas were shaped by Medical Department goals. Racial communities had to be segregated not only to contain their own characteristics, but to protect other races. This was by no means a new ideology, but it was one that the state in Kenya could not implement until the 1920s, when the boom allowed for the literal construction of segregated, sanitary neighborhoods. The ease with which "lower-class Asiatics" had lived with Africans was made illegal, for a few years at least. The realities of the Depression in Nairobi, at least until 1937, were to undermine the rigidity of official segregation and were to make malaya women in Pumwani and Pangani less isolated and more cooperative than they were in the 1920s.

4

Malaya Prostitution, 1930–39

By the 1930s the malaya form had become an accepted feature of life and housing in Nairobi's African location. Prostitution was how many women got by: "we were hungry, we had to go with men to get money or have no money."[1] It also served "the needs" of working men while saving the state the cost of providing family housing:[2] Pumwani became the site of the reproduction of male labor power in the city. The conduct of malaya prostitution changed, however, as women—particularly those who first practiced the form after 1930—responded to the decreasing numbers of men in wage labor in the early years of the decade, to the rapid increase in the number of employed men after 1937, and to the housing shortage caused by that increase and the state's ill-conceived urban policies.

These changing labor requirements were mirrored in the administration of Africans in Nairobi. From 1930 to 1936 the MNC's major concern was where Africans could live in town; they wanted to keep them in certain areas and out of others, some of which had long been occupied by Africans. The state made where Africans lived—rather than with whom, or for how much rent—a legal issue. Indeed, as the planned removal of Pangani seemed at last within their grasp, officials tried to control how long Africans could stay in the few areas where their presence was already legal: administrators' paranoia ran deep about how long African workers actually worked in town—at some highly inventive rates of pay—as the state sought to reduce the amount of time an unemployed African could be in Nairobi.[3] After 1937 the state focused its attention on the conditions in which Africans lived—or tried to live—in Nairobi. The decade of the 1930s was characterized by a numbers game of dawn raids and population estimates that generated strange, if conservative, figures of homeless Africans by the late 1930s.[4] Only after the artisans' strikes of the late 1930s did the state acknowledge that the housing market it had created encouraged profiteering by the large numbers of private African landlords who charged rents that caused "hardship" to the average African worker.[5] But it was because the administration was focused on issues of housing conditions that it related high rents to high employment and the subsequent overcrowding. In fact high rents had reduced African real wages in Nairobi throughout the 1930s. The overall impact of the Depression in Nairobi was to reduce the number of men in wage labor and reduce their spending money while their individual expenditure on rent increased despite the decline in population.

Labor, Housing, and Rents, 1930–36

In the early years of the Depression Nairobi's labor requirements dropped sharply: public construction was at a standstill, and in the rural areas jobs and wages were drastically reduced in estate agriculture, so laborers returned to their homelands and, wherever there was room, household production. The African population of Nairobi declined after 1930 and only achieved its 1929 level again between 1936 and 1937 (see table 2), by which time many unskilled Africans appeared to be willing to work for "reduced wages and increased tasks . . . without complaint."[6]

As the population decreased so did the demand for available African housing, which was substantially less crowded between 1931 and 1934 than it had been during the boom of the late 1920s. Many rooms were empty. The MNC lost almost £1,500 in rents from Quarry Road in 1931 because of vacancies.[7] The MNC reduced rents in the early 1930s, but African landlords did not, largely because doing so would not have brought

TABLE 2   African and Total Population of Nairobi, 1929–38

Year	Africans	Total	Year	Africans	Total
1929	32,000	47,457	1934	27,000	47,000
1930	28,000	49,000	1935	28,000	50,030
1931	27,350	47,943	1936	28,000	49,600
1932	26,765	47,465	1937	38,000	61,300
1933	23,174	41,685	1938	40,000	65,000

SOURCES: Nairobi Annual Medical Reports, 1929–32; Nairobi Medical Officer of Health Annual Reports, 1933–39.

them increased profits. Renting out two rooms at 7/50 per month would have amounted to almost the same income as renting out five rooms at 3/ per month: "my father was a good man and in order to live peacefully with him you had to pay the rent he wanted."[8] If several tenants had to share their rooms to pay the 7/50, this still gave the landlord spare rooms in which to house family members or friends. Some polygynous landlords housed their wives in the empty rooms—Tabitha Waweru's father had two wives in 1925 and eight when he died in the 1950s, Margaret Githeka's father had six—while other accommodated their adult children or allowed old friends to live for free.[9]

In Pangani, where the 1929 population had been roughly estimated at 4,000, a dawn raid in 1930 found 2,226 people living in 335 houses; in 1931 improved census methods revealed a population of 3,177 living in 312 houses. In Pumwani in that year there were 3,996 people in 317 houses.[10] By reckoning the number of occupants per room from these figures, I want to suggest that the gross overcrowding that characterized African housing in the late 1930s and after was not constant throughout the decade, as some historians have indicated.[11] Pangani houses had five or six rooms each.[12] Assuming an average of five rooms per house, in 1930 there would have been slightly less than seven people to a house or just over one per room, and in 1931 there would have been about ten tenants per house or two to a room. In Pumwani, where the older houses have six to eight rooms, at an average of six rooms per house in 1931 there would have been almost thirteen people per house or slightly more than two per room. Indeed, in 1932 the Municipal Native Affairs Officer (MNAO) reported that a very few houses in Pumwani had six lodgers each, while the rest had more.[13] While a single room in Pumwani or Pangani did not insure great comfort—a very large room was ten feet by eight feet, with poor ventilation, poor waterproofing, and nonexistent insect-proofing—they were conditions of some privacy and, above all, some expense.

The evidence that has been taken to indicate overcrowding, such as the 1930 dawn raid in Pangani that found people "sleeping on floors and in passages as well as several in one bed,"[14] was more likely proof that many laborers could not afford to rent single rooms, and so either had to share them or settle for part of the veranda. The housing market in Pumwani and Pangani was such that landlords would willingly rent space in passageways to men who could not afford to share a room, which suited the needs of casual laborers and men who only came to Nairobi to work for short periods. But the expense of Pumwani and Pangani drove working Africans into illegal occupancy elsewhere: between 1934 and 1936 Africans were found squatting in the commercial areas, and in Upper Parklands and the exclusive white suburb of Muthiaga.[15]

Depending on the size of the room, rents in Pangani increased from between 5/ and 6/ in 1929 to between 6/ and 9/ by 1937, when the average rent was said to be 7/50, with bachelors (a favorite Medical Department term meaning men in paid employment) paying 4/ or 5/ each when sharing a room. In 1932 rents alone supported 80 percent of Pangani's landlords. In Pumwani rents were between 5/ and 8/ in the early 1930s, and between 8/ and 11/ from about 1934 to 1937, after which in most cases they more than doubled.[16] Nevertheless, the relationship between landlord and tenant was personal. Rents in Pumwani and Pangani and the squatters' settlements could be negotiated or could be late, or both: "it all depended on the landlord, some would help you with a special rent, if they knew you or were from your home, and some charged everyone the same rent, because they wanted the money."[17] Municipal housing was unpopular and uncrowded enough for the MNC to reduce rents in 1933 in an attempt to attract occupants: the cost of a single cubicle was lowered to 5/ and a three-bed cubicle to 9/. Despite the low rents Quarry Road did not fill up until the high employment years after 1936.[18]

Between 1930 and 1937, rents increased, while wages decreased (although at a slower rate), so that many laborers could not afford to rent or even to share rooms. In 1932 the MNAO asked Indian contractors to provide housing for their African employees, many of whom were found sleeping outside Pumwani, where rooms cost 8/, for which "their wage of say 14/ a month is insufficient."[19] In Pumwani and Pangani "a few people shared their rooms to save money or because they worked at different hours."[20] But without sharing accommodation with more than the average number of room occupants—that is, one other person in Pumwani and Pangani in 1931, not to mention sleeping on building sites or in passageways—wage laborers would have been paying extremely high rents, even in the Municipal estates (see table 3).

As rents increased and the number of wage laborers decreased, landlords gave empty rooms to a relative or a friend. Other tenants tried to share their rooms. The shared rent, however, represented an increasingly large proportion of a month's wage. For example, a gardener who in 1929 was earning 12/ per month and sharing a 4/ room in Pangani with three others would have paid 1/ rent. In 1935 a gardener's wage was 16/; if he was sharing a 6/ room in Pangani with one other, his rent would have been 3/, more than half of the increase in his wages. Cowen and Newman have

TABLE 3 Average Wages in Shillings per Month,
without Value of Rations, Nairobi

	1929	1932	1934/35	1939
Domestic service				
House/garden	12		16	17
Cook	30		18	20
Unskilled agriculture	13	14	12	13
Unskilled state	11	12	10	11

SOURCES: Michael P. Cowen and J. R. Newman, "Real Wages in Central Kenya,
1924–1974," essay, Nairobi, 1975, p. 4; Soko Kagawa, Pumwani, 10 December 1976;
Thomas Mukama, Eastleigh, 10 March 1977; Omolo Okumu, Pumwani, 2 March 1977.

argued that until 1938 the value of wages remained high, even in situations of their actual reduction, because of the overall decline in retail commodity prices. But in Nairobi it seems likely that real wages were reduced
between 1930 and 1937 by increased individual expenditures on rent.

After 1932 non-Muslim wage laborers, faced with insecure housing and
the prospect of more dawn raids, began to move out of Pangani and into
Pumwani and Quarry Road, especially after rents were reduced there in
1933. The revenues available to Pangani prostitutes declined. Some malaya women left Pangani to engage in watembezi prostitution in River
Road, but returned when they could no longer afford the rent; others
were arrested.[21] Younger Muslim women went directly from Pangani to
Pumwani; Miryamu binti Omari had gone to Pangani with her parents in
about 1920; she left in 1932/33 because "I was starting to move with men,
so I decided to find a place in Pumwani. . . . I knew it would be a better
place to find men with jobs."

Changes in Malaya Prostitution, 1930–36

The changes in the malaya form that can be identified from oral sources
took place in Pumwani, where in the early 1930s rooms were readily available to those women who could afford to rent them. A few daughters of
Pumwani householders were given their own rooms, from which they
could practice the malaya form. However, there were a limited number of
men in paid employment to visit them, and those who did had relatively
little money to pay them.

The women who came to Nairobi in the early years of the Depression
did not come specifically to follow the labor supply, but once in town their

livelihoods were very much affected by its reduction. The women from
Central and Eastern Provinces who became prostitutes in Nairobi after
1930 did so because of the increasing congestion and lack of opportunities
in their rural homelands, where they claimed to have been mistreated, as
widows or divorced women or even as young brides, because their people
were poor. "Trouble is what showed me Pumwani, problems make you
find anywhere to stay," said a Kamba woman who came to Nairobi in about
1934.[22] Peculiar to the 1930s were women who said that they left home to
escape forced marriages,[23] as families tried, largely unsuccessfully, to secure land rights through marriage.[24] The immigrant women who went to
Nairobi between 1930 and 1935 were able to find rooms without relying
on older Muslim patrons, but they converted to Islam nonetheless and
practiced the malaya form with secrecy and discretion; in this they were
like the malaya women from the 1920s who continued their work well into
the Depression.

There were, however, other ways in which their prostitution was different. Malaya prostitution in the 1920s was profitable because men with jobs
had at least 0/25 to 1/50 to spare each month; women trusted men to pay
when asked and to sometimes return and, when they did, to pay more. In
the 1930s increased individual expenditure on rent consumed working
men's extra shillings, and by 1933 at the latest, many young malaya
women began to ask for payment in advance, both for short daytime encounters and night-long visits, even when breakfast and bathwater were
included in the latter. Women said they did this because "I had no reason
to trust the man."[25] Young malaya women who asked the price last did not
do so to maintain proper Muslim decorum, but to guarantee their own
safety: "If a man refused to pay me . . . I would have to let him leave. . . .
If I was inside with him what could I do? . . . I could not force him."[26]
Malaya women in the 1930s were able to increase their profits by increasing the number of visits by men, not the number of services provided during each visit. Men were encouraged to come and go fairly quickly, albeit at
relatively high prices: short-time in Pumwani and Pangani cost between 1/
and 2/50. Men paid these amounts, but no more: none of the semiskilled
laborers I interviewed had spent the night with a prostitute in either Pumwani or Pangani between 1930 and 1935.[27] The young malaya women of
the early 1930s emphasized sexual relations as prostitutes did at no other
time. Mwanisha Waligo, born in Mji wa Mombasa in about 1913, took over
an empty room in her father's house in Pumwani late in 1930 and became
one of many women to inaugurate the practice of a slightly altered malaya
form. She stressed that sexual intercourse was the most important thing

women could sell to men: "If you were a woman you had to go with men to get money, it was impossible not to get money from men. . . . In these days it was not dangerous to be a prostitute, any woman could be a prostitute. That was our job, to go with men to get money. . . . The problem women had in those days was how to work hard in bed to get money, and to talk to a man so he gave you a lot of money."

Sexuality—not cleanliness, not respect, not secrecy—was central to prostitutes' descriptions of prostitution in the 1930s, as it was at no other time. The malaya women who began their prostitution after 1930 rarely talked about the importance of domestic tasks; indeed, many would only cook food if men brought it as a gift,[28] as men took advantage of the low commodity prices during the Depression. The women who did not cook food used food as a metaphor for sexual intercourse. When I asked Miriam Musale, who came to Nairobi in about 1936, what kind of men paid best, she said, "I can't explain about what kind of men, it's like when someone is hungry and eats. The men came, they asked me the price, we went together and he left." Hadija Njeri, a watembezi woman throughout the 1930s, said of one of her customers, "He was hungry for sex and I was hungry for money." She described what appealed to Muslim men in erotic terms: "walk slowly . . . like you had no bones, then you could get Muslim men to marry you."

Malaya women's minimalist reproduction of labor power was a consequence of the decrease in men's real wages. Monica Nyazura, who came to Pumwani in 1936/37 and combined wazi-wazi and malaya prostitution, said she demanded payment in advance because "that way I was sure to get a man, I was sure to eat that day." She had observed the more formal malaya practices to be unprofitable.

> I thought it was a bad idea. There was one woman . . . she lived near me in Digo . . . she was born here, she was a pure Swahili, and she would wait until one of her boyfriends came for the whole night, she would go with him and feed him in the morning, she would even make bathwater for him, and you know water is not free in Pumwani, and then her boyfriend would tell her that this week he had no money, and when he came to see her again he would bring money, and she would never see that man again. Or she would get 2/ for the whole night, she would take whatever the man gave her, and in those days the water and tea and food cost 75 cents at least. So I ask you, which is better, to get 1/ for sure . . . or to wait with food and milk for a man who might only promise me money?

Malaya Women and the Emergence of Danguroni, 1934–38

After about 1934 one neighborhood of Pumwani came to be associated
with the new, more commercial, and highly competitive practice of the
malaya form. This area was called Danguroni, a corruption of the Por-
tuguese word for dancer and used in its locative form to mean a part of a
town where prostitutes live.[29] Residents divided Pumwani into four parts;
these divisions were bounded by the streets that quartered the location.
Majengo was the area with the deepest ties to coastal Muslims and was considered the center of Islamic respectability; in the 1920s, along with Mashimoni ("many in the pits") to the east, Majengo was the site of formal
malaya prostitution. From Majengo, the Pumwani divisions were based on
accumulation, decorum, and, according to Muslims, degree of Islamicization. South of Digo Road were Digo and Danguroni, where the new version of the malaya form flourished after 1933. The area of Danguroni
existed in the 1920s but had no specific name or identity until the
mid-1930s. Digo had no separate identity at all; it was generally subsumed
into Danguroni, except by a few women who were at pains to point out
that things were slightly different there. Women who lived in Danguroni
in the 1930s did not distinguish between Danguroni and Digo,[30] possibly
because they themselves had come to live in the area because of the reputation of Danguroni, not Digo.

Young prostitutes probably went to Danguroni because housing was
available there for women new to Pumwani. By 1934 the rent for a room
for a single woman in Danguroni was 10/ a month, "because it was a place
for business," while rooms in Majengo cost 8/.[31] This increased rent,
which was to be dwarfed by the rents charged throughout Pumwani in the
late 1930s, marked the first time that Pangani landlords capitalized on
prostitution.

After 1934 Danguroni was known as a center for the malaya prostitution of immigrant women. Its reputation was such that Miriam Musale, a
malaya woman who never earned much money herself, attributed her
own circumstances to the fact that she abided by the norms of Majengo,
where she had a room. She never questioned Danguroni's reputation.

> I've never lived in Danguroni, but I had a friend who used to
> stay there, and I used to go to greet her, we used to talk. Every-
> one knew that the women who stayed in Danguroni were rich
> prostitutes, I didn't have to ask my friend if she was rich, I knew
> she was. The poor people like me, we mixed with people here
> in Majengo and it was hard for us to get a lot of money because

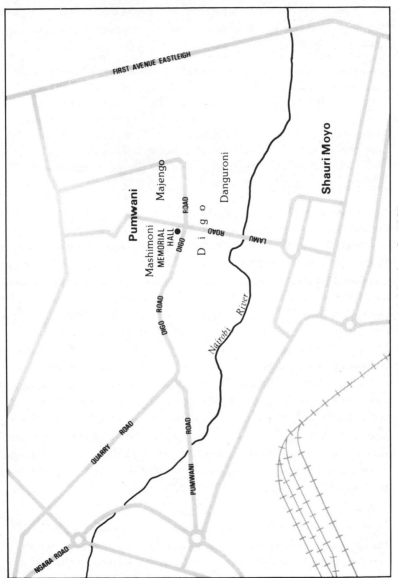

Pumwani neighborhoods, 1935

we had to wait for the men to come to us, but Danguroni was a special place for prostitutes so most of the men went there.

This seems to have been true. When I asked Salima binti Athmani, a Kamba woman who came to Danguroni in 1934/35, about Danguroni's nicknames—*mji wa malaya, kambia wa malaya* (prostitutes' town, prostitutes' camp)—she angrily responded that

> Danguroni was not a place to make jokes about, it was really a place for finding money. . . . I can't explain to you how good Danguroni was, because it was really the best place I could have lived at that time. . . . I used to go with different men and make a lot of money, and then I became a strong woman, I ate well, I had lots of money, then I would remember my sons. . . . first I built a house on my husband's farm for them, and then I paid the bridewealth for their wives.

What made prostitution in Danguroni so special, and so profitable? Most of the accounts of its reputation come from women who lived in Majengo, where they claimed that prostitution was markedly different from that in Danguroni. According to Zaina Kachui, who came to Pumwani in 1935/36, men in Majengo "had to come to the door and ask 'can I come in?' and if you are a prostitute you can say come in, if you are the wife of somebody you can tell him no, you are a wife, and those men, they could not feel hurt, they would just go to another door and look for a prostitute . . . but in our side of Majengo it was hard to know if somebody was a prostitute or not, but Danguroni was known for prostitutes, everyone knew about it." Men in the 1930s went door to door with aplomb and respect and, in Majengo at least, what appeared to be less trepidation than malaya women had attributed to them a decade before. Salima binti Athmani's account of her own malaya prostitution in Danguroni, however, revealed a more commercialized form, one that was neither secret nor hidden from neighbors, and one in which there was a volume of business that could be profitably manipulated.

> We used to stay inside our rooms and if a man came it was up to you to ask how much money you wanted . . . if you asked him he had to give it to you. . . . In those days you never saw ten or twenty men moving around to find a woman like you do today, the men used to be more frightened, they used to come politely, one at a time, and one would knock on your door. . . . The men used to fear that you would be the wife of somebody and they would be beaten up if they entered your room, so if a

man talked to you through the door, and trusted you, and you told him you were alone, then you can let him come in and you'll have sex. After that the man will call a friend and tell him "now I can show you where you can find a woman." And . . . if the first man who came to my house had to pay me, let's say 5/ for short-time, then all the friends of his I had sex with that same night would have to pay me 5/.

Five shillings is too high a price for the early and mid-1930s: 2/ to 3/ seems to have been the short-time rate in Danguroni then, or about fifty cents more than the prices that obtained in Majengo or Pangani.[32] What accounted for the high profits in Danguroni was not the amount individ- 𐤀 ual men paid but the frequency and the volume of their visits. Salima binti Athmani described a kind of prostitution that protected men: the negotiations that established trust as well as the amount of services to be performed took place on opposite sides of a closed door, safeguarding men from irate husbands and the risks inherent in continually going door to door. This was certainly audible to a woman's neighbors. Either the neighbors and landlords did not object, "also they were doing their business at the same time you were,"[33] or a new norm of community behavior had been formatted in the more commercial malaya prostitution. Women in Danguroni did not need to fear eviction before 1935, when there were still empty rooms available to them in Pumwani, but after 1936 the housing market was as competitive as it had been in the 1920s, and malaya women had every reason to stay in Danguroni, where a night's earnings could be three or four times what they would be in Majengo.

No food was provided in these visits; women only cooked for the men who brought food, or for special friends.[34] Nevertheless, men received more than sex from their visits to women in Danguroni. They received, for pennies more than short-time would have cost them elsewhere in Pumwani or Pangani or River Road, some security in searching out a prostitute. This was a luxury—for which they paid perhaps fifty cents extra— in a city where men were out on the streets—in the case of some casual laborers, all the time—vulnerable to increasingly strict pass and vagrancy laws, soliciting the women who remained inside their rooms. For laboring men, harassed out of overcrowded rooms in otherwise empty Pangani houses and chased off the building sites and verandas on which they slept, Danguroni offered a respite not only from official surveillance and intrusion, but from the Muslim community that, elsewhere in Pumwani, demanded their decorum and circumspection even as they sought out prostitutes.

Men's fears of male violence had long affected the conduct of Nairobi prostitution. Malaya women of the 1920s and 1930s spoke of customers' anxieties about offended husbands, and how men preferred to repeat visits to women they already knew to live alone or to visit married women at prearranged times during the day, a precaution for which they sometimes paid extra. A few men reported paying a woman in advance only to have her announce that her husband was due back momentarily.[35] Danguroni's reputedly high proportion of malaya women, and the freedom to negotiate fairly openly with them, offered laboring men a convenience and a safety for almost the same amount that a man would spend going door to door in Majengo.

In Danguroni the first man to approach a prostitute may well have received some small favors from his friends in exchange for his having led them safely to an available woman. While this process may have occurred in Majengo as well, it did not happen in a way that the woman was aware of, and this is significant, both in terms of women's consciousness and women's earnings. For a malaya woman to have known that a man was recommending her to his friends would have severely compromised her sense of secrecy and respect; if a woman acquiesced to this new sensibility, it is possible that she gave the man a discount.

Danguroni also served a function for the state as well. It was a place where male labor power was reproduced and contained, at least occasionally. Men could take their recreation outside the areas where they were constantly liable to arrest and harassment, but they then did so in a place known to the authorities. In part because of Danguroni, the colonial state did not have to search sheds and goat pens—practices that waned in the high-employment years after 1936—to find men in violation of vagrancy laws. The site of reproduction became a gathering point, and thus a place of containment and tacit surveillance. Such a place was crucially important because the state's attempts at housing designed precisely for these purposes failed to accomplish them.

Perhaps the best example of the vitality of the malaya form in Danguroni was in that area of sexuality about which the colonial, settler state was most ambivalent—sexual relations between white men and African prostitutes. Brief sexual encounters between wealthy men and prostitutes have generally been seen a paradigmatic of the exploitation of poor women, but an exploitation that could lead to social acceptability.[36] Victorian men, for example, defended "sexual access to working class girls as a time-honored prerogative of gentlemen."[37] Recent imperial history has

portrayed the sexual relations between local women and the first European colonizers in Victorian rhetoric—women's consent is taken for
granted—but also as a laudable exception to the "stiff and aloof social relations of the twentieth-century empire."[38] The situation in Danguroni,
however, was more complex than the language of privilege and empire
would allow. Danguroni suggests that the extent, intensity, and duration
of these sexual relations were under the control of the women themselves,
not the men. Danguroni raises the question, what if brief sexual encounters between classes and races were the prerogatives of the poor women, ⸸
proof of prostitutes' ability to shape these relationships to their needs and
their work?

Nairobi prostitutes, particularly in the 1930s, had no illusions about
their relations with white men: "white men didn't touch your breasts if
they wanted you, those white people weren't looking for women to be
wives to marry them, they wanted someone for a short-time."[39] Europeans, however, paid so much more than Africans and most Indians did
that women made jokes about men's generosity in racial terms. Mwanisha
Waligo said that if an African man "gave you 6/ you were happy and you
were lucky. Probably he was a half-caste."

In Danguroni the conditions of sexual relations remained the same
whether the customer was white or black: male networks brought men to
malaya women for exceptionally profitable short-time visits. While Indian
men rarely ventured into Pumwani, European men "used to come with
their houseboys, he was the one that brought the white man to us."[40]
Sometimes men came with taxi or rickshaw drivers—"the rickshaw came
very quickly when wazungu called"—who would deliver them to a woman
and pick them up later "because when some white men went with African
women they didn't want anyone to see them in the morning."[41] The servant or the driver would make an appointment with a woman he had selected in a way that did not seem of any great concern to the prostitute:
"maybe he had come to me once, maybe he was of my tribe, maybe he
came just by chance, but he would come, talk about the white man and we
would set a time . . . a white boyfriend . . . wants to come for sex and it
would not be safe to go to a total stranger."[42] This was the conventional
wisdom repeated even by women who admitted, "I myself never had a
white man from a taxi driver," since servants and drivers had passes that
allowed them in and out of the locations at night.[43] In this malaya form,
servants and drivers, not the white man, made the appointments and
brought the woman foodstuffs she did not have to cook for them.

He used to send his houseboy with presents . . . sugar and oil,
everything I needed. Sure, and the mzungu himself would not
come, he would send the boy, and that was not money for sex, it
was a gift, to help me. . . . if someone came to my house he
would think he was in a store, but he wasn't in a store, he was in
the house of a prostitute. That was when I lived in Danguroni.
When the white man needed to come and see me, he had to
send the boy to tell me to be prepared for him, to tell me the
day he was going to come. Be prepared, he'll come today, that's
what the boy would tell me.

Under no circumstances would the woman pay the servant: "he came with
the white man, and the white man had to pay him," but "if he came in the
daytime I might feed him . . . and if he worked for a white man I saw a lot
I might help the houseboy with 5/ if he asked."[44] Malaya women did not
retain men to serve as go-betweens with white men: "How could I know
when a European would want to go with me?" said Asha Mohammed, who
began malaya prostitution in the Pumwani Extension of Shauri Moyo in
1939. She explained that there was a racial division of labor in appointment making: "if a white man wanted me, if he saw me and did not know
any Swahili, he would send his servant to ask where I lived and then they
would both come at night to talk to me."

   The European man himself "used to come at night, have sex, pay you,
and then go away"[45]—relations identical to those sold casual laborers. In
Danguroni race and wealth did not determine the nature of sexual relations; the prostitutes did that. Race and wealth instead determined the nature of relations between masters and servants. In Danguroni the specific
form and the specific location of sexual relations remained constant whatever the man's race or income; only the remuneration changed.[46]

Labor, Overcrowding, and Malaya Prostitution, 1937–39

The number of men employed in Nairobi rose dramatically at the same
time commodity prices began to increase: between 1938 and 1952 the cost
of living rose at an annual rate of between 6 and 8 percent.[47] This and the
even more rapid increase in rents in the late 1930s diminished real wages.
Nairobi workers' ability to circumvent high rents by sleeping wherever
they could had maintained real wages and undermined the city's racial
segregation in the past. By 1937, however, even the sheds and the verandas of the vagrancy laws were crowded, and the state worried about the

sheer number of casual laborers on the city's streets, attracted by "the glitter of the city, the almost unbelievable temptation of the shop windows."[48] While the state feared the consequences of underemployed Africans looking in shop windows, they failed to provide the housing that could provide a contained social life. By 1938 the state had built forty-eight units of married workers' housing, while squatters had built hundreds. Private employers saved money by putting their employees in Quarry Road, which was overcrowded again by 1937. Elsewhere African workers saved money by sharing rooms with as many laborers as possible, or by moving into the squatter settlement of Mathare, where rents were somewhat lower than those in Pumwani but premises almost as crowded, or into Eastleigh, where rents were higher but conditions substantially improved.[49]

Between 1937 and 1945 rents rose in Pumwani and what was left of Pangani: in 1938 rooms in Pangani cost about 18/ per month, unless the tenants had been there a long time, in which case it was much less. In 1939 in Pumwani rooms rented from 15/ to 26/, and the MNC set rents in the 176-house Pumwani Extension at between 19/ and 27/ per room.[50] But these rents were frequently offset by tenants' sharing their rooms with several others. For example, Clayton and Savage report that in 1938/39 laborers sometimes slept seven or eight to a room.[51] Six employed men sharing a 18/ room would have been paying 3/ each—a hefty piece of an average wage of 23/ per month, but the same cash amount they might have paid for less-crowded premises in 1935, when their real wages were higher. For those Africans who lived in the locations, the proportion of income spent on rent remained between 15 and 19 percent in the 1930s, but by the end of the decade the conditions of overcrowding were more oppressive than were rents.

In 1935/36 Wambui Murithi moved from River Road to Pumwani, where she had requested and received a plot from the MNC providing she could build a house on it in one month. She managed to build her house in stone and rented out the rooms to young women. Not all former prostitutes did that, however; a building owned by a single woman no longer guaranteed safety to men in Pumwani, and a few older women tried to suppress competition in their houses.

> In those days there were many landlords who were prostitutes and if she was a good woman she was not jealous of younger women coming to town. You were looking for men and she was looking for men, you cannot feel jealous. Some of these women helped younger women, they gave them advise or helped them

learn Swahili. There were some big prostitutes who were
jealous and they rented to men only . . . they just refused to
rent to any woman alone.[52]

A number of landlords, first in Danguroni but later in Majengo and
Mashimoni, built outside rooms. These were additional rooms of mud
and poles, usually measuring four feet by eight feet, built along an outside
wall of a Pumwani house; the entrance to the room was from outside the
house, not along the common passageway that went through the house.
Obviously, the increase of two or, where there was room, four rooms increased landlords' incomes. The rooms were relatively expensive and extremely cramped, but they were rarely shared by laboring men; instead
they were excellent residences for women practicing the 1930s version of
the malaya form, and the wazi-wazi form.

High employment, higher rents, and dense overcrowding—and the
state's ambivalent relationship to migrants' social reproduction—meant
that in Pumwani the reproduction of male labor power was structurally
minimalist. By 1938 the colonial state was as cynical about the needs and
wants of their labor force as it was about the disruption—and opportunities—their labor requirements brought to rural Kenya. In his massive report on "the conditions of housing and employment of natives in
Nairobi," Eric Davies, the MNAO, addressed the facts of the migrant labor
economy in blunt economic terms. Malaya prostitutes, he wrote, were a
necessary part of African life in Nairobi: they could reproduce male labor
power cheaply and effectively enough for the state—without even taking
up very much space—and save the Municipality the cost of family housing
and family wages.

> 25,886 males employed and living in Nairobi have only 3,356
> female dependents in the town. This is a proportion of just
> over one to eight. A demand arises at once for a large number
> of native prostitutes in Nairobi. . . . The immigration into Nai-
> robi of young Kikuyu girls is continually mentioned by the
> Kikuyu Local Native Councils urging that steps be taken to
> stop it. The position here is aggravated by the lack of proper
> native housing; whereas the needs of eight men may be served
> by the provision of two rooms for the men and one for the
> prostitute, were housing provided for these natives and their
> families six rooms would probably be needed.[53]

What is perhaps most important here is that Davies conceived of prostitutes as part of the migrant labor economy in Nairobi, the part to which

the state had allocated the tasks of social reproduction; it welcomed the benefits of prostitutes with close and stable ties to the working class. But in these years the state's allocation of new housing, and the arrangements of younger malaya women, were redefining and reconstructing those ties: in this way, social life in Pumwani and Eastleigh and Mathare was transformed, but not through the efforts of the state.

Some of the men whose rents were reduced by sharing their rooms had a little extra cash to spend on prostitutes, and those women who emphasized short-time sexual relations began to increase their earnings. The shortage of housing in the late 1930s led some malaya women to share rooms. These women developed strong friendships—Zaina Kachui and Miriam Musale shared a room for almost a year—with even more cooperative behavior than was typical of malaya women in the 1920s: "And the good thing about those times was, two women would go with the same man and not be jealous; my friend and I, we could go with one man. If we were sharing a bed and a man comes and decided he wanted both of us, I would not feel jealous. That way she'll get her money and I'll get my money: no jealousy."[54] This is a far cry from work performed in secret, yet it was deferential, compliant, polite, and indoors. Elsewhere prostitutes divided tasks so as to guarantee their safety and increase their earnings. Muslim women and women from societies that practiced male and female circumcision were said to avoid peoples who did not, primarily the Luo of Nyanza. Amina Hali said that in the 1920s many Muslim prostitutes had Luo customers "in secret"; the men were at risk only when the lovers knew each other well enough to quarrel and the woman accused the man of forcing his attentions on her. As circumcision became a symbol of Kikuyu cultural unity in the wake of missionaries' chauvinism of the late 1920s (although the Kamba, Meru, and Embu practiced circumcision as well), the division between circumcised and uncircumcised became an issue around which other tensions were organized. Luo men told of being sent away by women they had already paid, but prostitutes privately assured me that this rarely happened, and many Muslim women said they had had Luo boyfriends at one time or another.[55] By the late 1930s the pressures on women who went with Luo men were said to be severe, especially in Christian Pumwani: "if a Kikuyu woman went with a Luo man and it got to be known to people . . . she would even be told to leave the room she was living in."[56] When Zaina Kachui, a Kamba, went with Luo men first in the Kikuyu and settler coffee-growing area of Thika and later in Majengo, she would ask a woman friend "to stay in the doorway, to take care of Kikuyu and Wakamba men because if they would meet that Luo man inside my room they'd beat him up badly." Luo men paid her extra "because they weren't circumcised . . . when you went with a Luo man you must keep it a secret, and keeping the secret costs 7/," an amount that men confirmed and other prostitutes denied for the late 1930s.[57] The woman who watched the door, however, did so for friendship, not the money: "she was my friend, if she needed money, I would help her, if she was hungry, I would feed her, if she was going with a Luo man, I would watch the door for her and if I had money, I would not ask her to pay me for watching the door." In the 1930s such friendships existed even with the women had close ties to older Muslim women.

Some malaya women shared rooms with men and women who were not prostitutes, and they engaged in an even more modified malaya prostitution. Men came to them and made appointments, and then they either accompanied the man to where he lived or went there later. Sometimes these women were married or in relationships of long standing, sometimes they lived with siblings, and sometimes they lived with their Muslim "fathers" or, less frequently in the 1930s, "mothers," who had converted them to Islam and who sporadically supported them in exchange for cooking and cleaning.[58] The women who lived with their Muslim "mothers" or "fathers" generally "slept out" with men in rooms that were "not terribly crowded,"[59] although these women's frame of reference for overcrowding may have been somewhat askew, as neither of them had been in Nairobi in the early 1930s. Such women seem to have received small payments; they often went to the man's room and asked the price last and took "anything he felt like giving me"[60]—in marked contrast to Danguroni, a few hundred yards away—but a wise strategy when alone in a man's room with his friends nearby.

The price for short-time decreased throughout Pumwani after 1936/ 37, from as low as 0/50—the amount the Davies Report allowed for "amusements" for both married and single men—to 1/ or 1/50,[61] in part because of the competition from wazi-wazi women. The late 1930s were a time when women knew how many men earned very little (see table 4), and prostitutes' awareness of male poverty changed their conduct. Mwanisha Ahmed came to live in the Pumwani Extension of Shauri Moyo in 1939 and combined the wazi-wazi and malaya forms; she asked for 1/ for short-time "because I was poor and those men were poor."

Despite the increasing numbers of working men, the cost of living was increasing at a rate that prohibited many women from returning to full-scale malaya prostitution; the men who came to Pumwani did not earn

TABLE 4   African Wages in Nairobi, November 1938

Monthly Wages in Shillings	Number of Adult Employees
Up to 10	280
11 to 20	15,661
21 to 40	9,069
41 to 80	1,727

SOURCE: Eric R. St. A. Davies, MNAO, "Some Problems Arising from the Conditions of Housing and Employment of Natives in Nairobi," Nairobi, August 1939, typescript, Housing of Africans in Nairobi, MD 40/1131, p. 7.

enough for malaya women to feed them and still make a profit. But as the number of men living in Eastleigh and Mathare, bordering Eastleigh, increased, a few young women began to practice the malaya form in all its domesticity there starting in about 1938. Among these women were malaya and watembezi women who had lived in Pangani and who had come to Eastleigh when Pangani was finally demolished in 1939; other malaya women said they first came to live in Eastleigh when they were domestic servants for Goans, Indians, or Seychelloise, and were given housing there.[62] By 1938 the prices for short-time and for night-long visits—including breakfast—were higher in Eastleigh than in Pumwani.[63]

While there was some malaya prostitution practiced in Mathare in the early 1930s,[64] the form came to be practiced with renewed finesse there and in Eastleigh in the late 1930s. Mathare was a squatter settlement with no legitimacy at all; Eastleigh accommodated Indians, Goans, Seychelloise, and Somalis. Police did not enter houses in Eastleigh searching for illegal residents, but they did patrol the area, so that African prostitutes were fairly restricted—or at least vulnerable to arrest—in their nighttime movements. The watembezi women who had come to Eastleigh either had to take up malaya prostitution or go to town to look for men. Eastleigh itself seemed to offer very little for watembezi: "Sometimes you go to find men and you don't find them," complained Hadija Njeri about living there after 1938. Watembezi prostitutes in Eastleigh were often arrested, but because of the benign neglect with which prostitution was policed in the late 1930s by a state overwhelmed with unheeded, unenforceable pass laws, these arrests were often regarded as private matters between the arresting officer, presumed to have been rebuked, and the woman. The police could not begin to repatriate women who had been in Nairobi since the early 1920s—"I told the mzungu, if I went back to my room in town it won't cost the government anything"—and most of the adult women who were arrested for prostitution between 1935 and 1939 were given minimum fines.[65]

Women in Wage Labor and Prostitution, 1937–39

Historians of western Europe and North America have argues that prostitution becomes widespread after an initial demand for female labor encourages women to leave the protection of their families and go to work; as work becomes more industrial and the demand for women's labor drops, women are forced into the streets to make ends meet.[66] Christine Stansell has argued that in New York City it was the increasing number of working-class women who occasionally prostituted themselves that shocked reformers, not the number of prostitutes themselves.[67] Families' ability to "protect" their daughters was often an abstraction, however, and the demand for women's labor cannot be studied in isolation from the prevailing wage structure and the reasons women worked. In this section I argue that women's participation in wage labor does not necessarily reflect changing notions of respectability or women's decreased participation in casual labor: in Nairobi wage labor was after 1937 an option available to a few women, and many of those women used wage labor—sometimes their own, sometimes someone else's—to reorganize the way they prostituted themselves. Prostitution may have supplemented the low wages paid working women, as many scholars suggest,[68] but those women simultaneously used their wage labor as a way to increase their earnings as prostitutes. For women who wanted to acquire property, or return home wealthy, or refinance their families—regardless of how successful they might have been— prostitution was not a substitute for wage labor, it represented a way to avoid wage labor, for themselves and for their dependents.

In Nairobi the increased employment for women after 1937 influenced which labor form or forms a woman chose for her prostitution. In 1938 there were 237 women legally employed in Nairobi. All of their occupations involved the sale of some specialized task of domestic labor: there were 164 child-care servants (ayahs), 58 hospital ward attendants, and 15 licensed brewers who supplied the MNC's African beer hall in Pumwani. There were also a number of male and female part-time sweepers of Government and Municipal premises, who were not officially counted. The licensed brewers earned 42/ per month; the ward attendants averaged 37/; ayahs averaged 30/, a decrease from their average wage of 34/ in 1934; ayahs employed in Indian household earned somewhat less; and the sweepers earned below 12/. In the same year, 2,227 "house-boys and personal servants" working for Europeans earned an average wage of 28/50 per month; the average wage for all domestic servants in European employment was 22/50. The Government's 215 "office boys and messengers" earned a monthly average wage of 28/40, and the 63 railway clerks and telephonists earned 74/ on average.[69] Thus in the late 1930s the small number of women who had jobs earned wages not unequal to those offered men, particularly in domestic service.

The large population and high rents of the late 1930s meant that the domestic servants housed on their employer's premises shared their rooms[70] either with co-workers or friends (who may or may not have been charged for rent). Many working women had to share their rooms to save money or to earn extra money. The working women and women sharing rooms who prostituted themselves did so as employees—women with rooms had a need to appear respectable in and around those rooms.

Wanjira Ng'ang'a, a Kikuyu woman who went to Nairobi in 1937/38, described how she and a woman friend left agricultural wage labor in Murang'a to seek their fortunes in the city: "We decided to go to Nairobi because my friend said that she had gone with European men and they paid a lot of money, and the best place for us to find money would be Nairobi. But when we came here, she got a job as an ayah for Asian people and they gave her a room in Westlands, so we both lived there and every morning she would wake up early and go to work, while I would go out and look for men." Since she was sharing a room with a woman whose continued employment—and housing, on which Ng'ang'a relied—depended to some extent on a respectable appearance, Ng'ang'a practiced the watembezi form, not because it was more profitable, but because it was more convenient for her friend's work.

> I would walk up and down the streets, or I would stand at a corner, and if a man asked me to go with him I would tell him that I had no place to go, and could we go to his house. Sometimes, they were African men, and they were somebody's servants we could go to their rooms, but sometimes we couldn't and then we would go to the bushes, just for short-time. But it if was an Asian man or white man who wanted to go with me, then there was no problem, we could go directly to his house.

Ng'ang'a sometimes arranged for men to come to her shared room, with carefully planned appointments "on Saturday . . . because I didn't want those Asians to be suspicious of me, so if I had an African man, I'd tell him to come on a Saturday, and then my friend would tell the Asians that my cousin was coming to visit me."

This is more than another example of the cooperation between women who shared rooms. This is an example of time and work discipline in self-employed casual labor, the development of diligent work habits and work rhythms in prostitution, not waged employment. As Frederick Cooper has pointed out, European officials and employers throughout Kenya complained that waged workers could not be made efficient and obedient until they feared dismissal. The painful lessons of unemployment, "the sanction of the sack," was "the ultimate basis of production in a free labor economy." Casual laborers and the self-employed were immune from this sanction, "for all that was at stake when they contemplated an hour's loafing on the job or joining a strike was a day's pay, not a job."[71] But prostitutes in suburban Nairobi organized their form of labor and its labor process, space, and time around the sanction of dismissal, and made appointments with men for Saturdays, the day on which "cousins" were likely to be off work.

In 1939 Ng'ang'a's friend got another job as an ayah, and she herself went to work for a Sikh family in Nairobi at 30/ a month including her own room, "but that was less money than I found for myself in Westlands, so I quit the job and went back to looking for men." The regularity of wage labor, in and of itself, was less profitable and less desirable than prostitution for Ng'ang'a.

Other employed women lived in Pumwani between 1937 and 1939, and those who supplemented their wages with prostitution tended to use the legality of "having business" in European and Indian areas to solicit men there. Elizabeth Kamya, a Ganda who worked as an ayah in Nairobi in 1937–39, lived in Pumwani first with her brother, then alone, and then with her sister who came to join her in 1939. She claimed that most of her income during those years came from watembezi prostitution in central Nairobi, where "some wazungu would just motion with their hands to get into their cars, and you would just go with them somewhere near the forest, just outside of Nairobi, and they would give you as much as 40/, and then they would take you back to River Road or Government Road or wherever they found you." Kamya lost her job at the start of the war and stopped going to town to find men. In an atypical opinion of the efficiency of the local police, she was frightened of arrest and deportation because "I was not a Kenyan, I could have been sent back to my country, and what was I to eat there? . . . When I went to Government Road . . . I had a letter saying I was the employee of somebody, but when the war started I had no job, I had no letter, and then the police would have reason to arrest me."

Another Ugandan woman, Hadija binti Nasolo, came to live in Pumwani in 1938, while she was working as an ayah for a European family. She then worked as a part-time sweeper in a Nairobi police station. While she practiced a fairly cautious malaya prostitution from her room in Pumwani, she used her job as a sweeper to meet well-paid European men, one of whom took her to hotels outside of Nairobi, because "he had a wife and we couldn't meet at his house." Such contacts made her part-time job lucrative: "he'd give me 50/ and it was like a thousand to me in those days." Indeed, the fact and the fantasy of a woman having a legal job that would give her access to wealthy and generous European men, who might also act as mediators in the face of government sanction, appears again, particularly during World War II.

Conclusions

In the 1930s the spatial divisions within Pumwani, and within Nairobi, became pronounced in ways that influenced the conduct of prostitution. The malaya form itself changed dramatically within a few hundred yards as Danguroni emerged as a center for prostitution. The watembezi prostitution in late-1930s Eastleigh was as different from that practiced by Wanjira Ng'ang'a in Westlands as Ng'ang'a's was from Elizabeth Kamya's in Government Road. The racial segregation and town planning orchestrated in the 1920s led some women to practice the watembezi form with great care and specificity.

Perhaps because of the availability of rooms in the African settlements in the early 1930s, space and housing meant more to prostitutes in that decade than community values did, as the communities in Pumwani and Pangani expanded and contracted. Prostitutes in their own rooms exerted immense control over their customers, black and white; prostitutes who went to men's rooms took what they were given. By the end of the decade, many watembezi women saw European men as potential protectors. These various relationships—to housing, to place, to customers—may well have been condensed in the emphasis 1930s prostitutes placed on sexuality when describing their work. They recalled their sexuality with pride, the way a decade before malaya women had boasted about the cleanliness of their rooms. Sexuality may have been how women articulated the control and self-reliance that easy access to housing must have meant to them: they could talk, however much in jest, about themselves, not about their rooms.

But such an emphasis on sexuality, and such minimal social reproduction, may also have reflected prostitutes' turning necessity into a virtue: rents eroded men's wages to the point that malaya women's rate of profit could best be secured by their discarding the sale of various domestic tasks. But malaya women did not abandon social reproduction; in part of Pumwani, they refined it. The prostitution that flourished and was to continue to flourish in Danguroni made men—even the most occasional and casual of laborers—safe. It protected them from the norms of Muslim Pumwani, and it availed them respite from the harassment and surveillance of life lived in verandas and passageways, where they were the tenants of Pumwani Muslim landlords. Danguroni was successful because it met men's needs: it maintained and reproduced a social life that was impossible a few hundred years away, and illegal where they worked.

5

Prostitution, Production, and Accumulation: The Origins and Development of the Wazi-Wazi Form in Pumwani, 1936–45

While there had been a few historical tensions between watembezi and malaya women in Nairobi, these had been based more on colonial zoning than on African attitudes. Malaya and watembezi women almost never worked in the same area. Many malaya women had occasionally practiced watembezi prostitution; if anything, they had a tolerance and respect for the form itself, but doubts about its safety and rate of profit. These tensions did not affect the conduct of prostitution as much as it affected patterns of African occupation outside legal and illegal African settlements. But starting in the mid-1930s, a new form of prostitution emerged in Pumwani, one that was not generally practiced by malaya women, and especially not by Muslim malaya women. The wazi-wazi form transformed prostitution in Pumwani. Whereas watembezi and malaya women had occasionally spoken with disdain for one another, malaya women almost invariably condemned the wazi-wazi form and its practitioners. This animosity represented more than competition over urban incomes; it represented urban women's responses to different patterns of accumulation and, more important, reinvestment.

The Origins of the Wazi-Wazi Form, 1936–40

In wazi-wazi prostitution a woman found men—and men found a woman—while she was sitting outside the door of the house she lived in. Pumwani residents say that the form was called wazi-wazi because it was associated with Haya women from the Bukoba District of Tanganyika: the Ganda, who preceded the Haya into Nairobi by decades, called the Haya "Waziba" after Kiziba, the Haya chiefdom nearest Uganda.[1] In Swahili,

103

however, *wazi* means "open" or "bare" in the sense of free access or the availability of space; doubling the noun intensified its meaning and provided Muslim Swahili speakers with a pun that condemned wazi-wazi behavior and its Haya practitioners.

The wazi-wazi form seems to have been originated by women from Tanganyika and Uganda who sought quick profits but feared the possibility of arrest and deportation that watembezi prostitution courted. The prostitutes from Bukoba who were in Nairobi in the early 1920s did not practice the form, since it is unlikely that women sitting outside their rooms in the shambles of River Road and Campos Ribeiro Avenue would have escaped the attention of the Baganda observers. Indeed, no one seems to have heard of wazi-wazi prostitution before 1936, especially in Danguroni, which was to become even more notorious for its practice there during World War II. Salima binti Athmani, who lived there between 1934 and 1943, said, "When I came to Danguroni I never saw . . . this thing of women putting their chairs outside, waiting for men." Haya women did not seem to move into Danguroni until the start of World War II: "when the KAR came, then there were Waziba in Danguroni."[2] In the rest of Pumwani, however, after 1936 the wazi-wazi form seems to have emerged as a daytime option for Haya women and some women who were otherwise malaya prostitutes. As the number of laborers in Nairobi increased so did the need of newly arrived women to become more visible, particularly those who lived outside Danguroni and had no neighborhood reputation to lead men to their doors. After 1937 many newly arrived Christian wazi-wazi women rented outside rooms in Pumwani.[3]

The earliest first-person accounts of the wazi-wazi form I have are from two women, Monica Nyazura, an Nzinza from Mwanza in Tanganyika, and Rehema binti Hasan, a Muslim Sebei from the Kenya-Uganda border, both of whom lived in Mashimoni in 1936. Nyazura said that she waited for men to come to her room at night, but "in the daytime I might sit outside my house and start talking with a man who seemed interested in going with me." Rehema binti Hasan had lived with a succession of men as they worked in Bungoma, Murang'a, and Thika before she came to Pumwani in the mid-1930s. She indicated that the increased male population of Pumwani accounted for the success and popularity of the wazi-wazi form, which she was as a social phenomenon: "we used to sit by our doors and wait for men to come to us, and they did."

Women who combined wazi-wazi prostitution with their malaya practices gained visibility without risking police harassment. While sitting outside their rooms, women could do many things without inviting suspicion—watch children, prepare food, or sew. Sewing became increasingly common as more and more women from Christian families, many of them veterans of mission homecraft classes, went to Nairobi and the prostitute population of Pumwani ceased to be mainly Muslim. Although their visibility scandalized many Muslim malaya women, in late-1930s Pumwani the wazi-wazi form allowed some malaya women to establish relations with male laborers new to the town. Moreover, the wazi-wazi form served to free men from their dependence on other men and male networks to lead them to willing women; it is possible that the wage laborers who wanted to be rid of any financial obligations to other men might have more cash to spend on prostitutes, and might do so regularly. As the price for wazi-wazi women was negotiated in advance, with the man and the woman both outside the woman's house, men did not have to fear that they would be assaulted by an enraged husband on whose door they had inadvertently knocked. In Danguroni the wazi-wazi form freed women from the risks inherent in negotiating a price and a visit with a man they could not see. As more and more men in Pumwani worked, married women and women in long-standing relationships could practice wazi-wazi prostitution and thus not have men coming to their doors. The form was especially convenient for women with small children living with them and no nearby kin—and this applied to foreign women perhaps most of all—as they did not have to ⨍ arrange for child care, which they would be called upon to reciprocate, if they were only going inside their rooms for fifteen minutes or so.[4] Wazi-wazi prostitution was also very advantageous to women who shared rooms, for it allowed them to pay reduced rents without sharing the men who approached them as they sat outside their door. The structure of the wazi-wazi prostitution and its daytime practice—and the needs of its practitioners—dictated that the form stress brief sexual relations.

All of these qualities crystallized into the identity of wazi-wazi women, visible prostitutes available for short-time all day long, by 1938 at the latest. By that time the form was fully identified with foreign women. Indeed, by the start of World War II in 1939 the visibility and the security of the wazi-wazi form had a strong appeal for women who were not Kenyans. When Elizabeth Kamya, a Ganda, lost her job in 1939, she immediately ceased watembezi prostitution in Government Road because she feared arrest and, more important, deportation. She began to practice the wazi-wazi form in Pumwani, where she shared a room with her sister. "At the beginning of the war I sat outside my door and when a man came to greet me, we could go together." Kamya insisted that wazi-wazi prostitution was restricted to daylight hours, and thus more visible to the Pumwani community than any watembezi activities might have been, because "at night the soldiers were drunk, and it was dangerous for a woman to sit along outside her house at night. It was the women who went out to look for men at night who got arrested, and I didn't do that." Kamya explained why so many foreign women chose the wazi-wazi form: "they were very poor, and they feared arrest and deportation, but also they were new to Nairobi, so they didn't know where to find men." Margaret Githeka, the daughter of a Christian householder brought up in Pumwani, suggested that such caution gave them strength: "when they came to Nairobi for the first time, they were not frightened of anything because they didn't roam about in the streets."

The wazi-wazi form was particularly advantageous to men; they risked nothing in seeking a woman. The form was to benefit African soldiers as well, many of whom were from West and Central Africa. They knew little or no Swahili and were probably reluctant to enter a house and begin knocking on doors to find a prostitute. They would have been the group most likely to walk the streets in Pumwani, where the wazi-wazi form covertly allowed women to solicit men.

Wazi-wazi prostitution was invariably the sale of short-time sexual relations. A man would be served food only if he himself brought it, which rarely happened in the daytime.[5] Elizabeth Kamya drew a firm distinction between the men who visited her for sexual relations during the day and the men who spent the night with her: her wazi-wazi customers were mainly soldiers. "I had boyfriends, but they were men from here, from Majengo, and they stayed the night, but they didn't pay me more than the soldiers."

Like the malaya form, wazi-wazi prostitution was predicated on the fact that the woman had a room to which the men might purchase access, but most similarities ended there. Almost all wazi-wazi women demanded payment in advance "so no one could cheat me."[6] Wazi-wazi prostitutes, particularly the Haya and the Ganda, were said to be extremely aggressive, at least by the petty-bourgeois standards of Pumwani. They were said to beat up the men who refused to pay them, or to call upon their neighbors for help, or simply to take an item of the man's clothing, which some women claimed they sold immediately for cash but others said they held until the man brought them their payment.[7] Thus, wazi-wazi women were thought to value their earnings far more than they valued their security as tenants or the respect or privacy of their neighbors, even at a time when housing in Pumwani was scarce and overcrowded: they reversed the older values of the malaya form. Indeed, wazi-wazi women were reputed to have called out their prices from where they sat—prices that ranged from 0/25 to 1/8—to the men who passed by, and this seems to have helped to lower the price for short-time in Pumwani after 1937.

Ethnicity and Profits

From all accounts, Haya women were the most aggressive practitioners of the wazi-wazi form, which was named after them. They "just sat in the doorway and if they saw a man passing, no matter what tribe the man was, they would wave to him."[9] Even though malaya women of the 1930s did not select their customers on ethnic criteria, and no woman could discern ethnicity through the closed doors of Danguroni, it was Haya women who earned the reputation of going with any man at all. No other group of prostitutes was described in this way. The issue was not just prostitutes' promiscuity, but their interethnic promiscuity.

Throughout the colonial era, intertribal prostitution seems to have been more profitable than that between members of the same ethnic group. Prostitutes could describe this, but they could not explain it. Salima binti Athmani, herself a Kamba, said, "My tribe is my tribe. If an Mkamba man paid me 50 cents I would take it. I believe you have to choose what to do to get money, so I tried not to go with many Wakamba men. It was no use, no money, to go with them." A few African men complained that prostitutes of their own tribe were dull.[10] Intertribal prostitution also seems to have led to fewer arguments and complaints than paid sexual arrangements between men and women of the same ethnic group. Esther Akinyi, a Luo prostitute who came to Nairobi in 1937, said she tried to speak Kikuyu all the time so as to avoid the censure of Luo men. A less-pragmatic woman claimed that if a Kikuyu wazi-wazi prostitute "called out to a Kikuyu man by mistake, they would start quarreling with each other . . . and definitely the woman would be beaten up by the man."[11]

Haya women were different beyond the fact that they went with men of other tribes. An old Kikuyu man interviewed in Pumwani in the mid-1960s explained what was so specifically exceptional about the Haya: "There were some Waziba after the German War, but most came later, during the Italian War. That's when people started knowing about a tribe called the Waziba. Most people here hated those girls because they were not circumcised. In those days men were really proud. We wouldn't even speak to uncircumcised girls. . . . If one of your age group saw you with such a girl, he wouldn't eat meat at your house.[12]

The question of who would and who would not have sex with uncircumcised men had by the late 1930s taken on a significance greater than the extra shillings a woman might receive for the act itself. It had reached ideological proportions in a way that was absent from earlier periods. In the 1930s circumcision had become, especially among Kikuyus, a very different issue than it had been in the 1920s in the wake of missionaries' attempts to ban clitoridectomy among Christians in Central Province.[13] Women raised in Pumwani and Pangani in the 1920s insisted that it was their cohorts and not their parents who warned them "that it was shameful to go with such men while our own were circumcised,"[14] and if they did, "your friends would avoid you,[15] while women born in Pumwani in the 1930s were taught by their parents to avoid uncircumcised men.[16] By the late 1930s women and men, particularly Kamba and Kikuyu, had thought about what sexual intercourse with an uncircumcised person meant and expressed that meaning in emotional and erotic terms. Asha Mohammed, a Kamba Muslim, explained, "In my tribe our men are circumcised and that is a sign that a man is an adult, that he is ready for sex and marriage, and men who are not circumcised are not grown up, and they behave like children, that's what we call them, and having sex with an uncircumcised man is the same thing as trying to become a child again." A Meru woman who went to Pumwani from Central Province in 1939 complained that she did not "like the smell of uncircumcised men."[17] Margaret Githeka, a Kikuyu, said she rarely had Kikuyu customers because "Kikuyu men never like to have sex with women who had had sex with Luo men, they would say that they couldn't go with a woman who had sex with Luo men, I know that." Haya women brought no such cultural impediments to their work: "these women weren't circumcised, so it was no great shame for them to go with uncircumcised men and no one would hurt them if they did, so all the Luo men working in town went to Danguroni almost once a week."[18] Haya women were said to welcome uncircumcised Luo men and, perhaps for that reason too, were exotic to the men of Pumwani.

But laboring Luo men—7,273 in Nairobi in 1938 according to the Davies Report—were migrants with strong ties and large remittances to their homes in Nyanza. Mombasa had a reputation as a Luo town and had higher wages; more than half the work force in Nairobi was Kikuyu.[19] In Nairobi most Luos were unskilled or semiskilled, and many worked for the Railway; they comprised about a quarter of the city's labor force and were by no means well-off. Nevertheless, Luos were one of the two groups that prostitutes cultivated—either in profitable secrecy or, as in the case of the Haya, in great numbers. Luos, along with wealthy Muslim property owners, were the Africans who paid "the most money" with "the least trouble."[20] What made these men generous? In the case of Nairobi in the late 1930s and early 1940s, generosity seemed to be a function of wealth and fear. Both groups visited prostitutes, both paid well, eagerly, but they did not receive the same services or treatment: the rich men were treated to a full imitation of domestic life, and the working Luos received a rushed short-time. Asha Mohammed described how she waited on her wealthy Muslim customers; how much money they paid "was up to them. After I went with them, in the morning I would bathe and make them tea, and talk nicely to them and tell them I was alone with a child to bring up, and they would give me what they wanted." She did not provide bread, and with poorer men she demanded payment in advance: in this way, Mohammed was able to accumulate 166 goats and 12 cows by the early 1970s. Zaina Kachui, however, described another kind of malaya prostitution: "when I had sex with Luo men and my friend was watching the door, after sex the man would have to leave right away, he would not take tea, he wouldn't even spend much time getting dressed. Once his trousers were up, he would leave."

As more and more Haya women moved into Pumwani in the late 1930s, Luo men became a less specific segment of the population of customers. They became less willing to pay extra for women to have sex with them. By 1940, once Haya women were firmly entrenched in Danguroni and in Nairobi consciousness, Luo men became regular visitors there, if they had not been already; prostitutes newly arrived in Pumwani and Shauri Moyo did not regard Luos as a special kind of customer, good or bad. Naomi Kayengi arrived in Pumwani from Uganda in 1944 and found Luo men "nice" and her first customers, but there was nothing remarkable about them. Even Kikuyu and Kamba wazi-wazi women in Danguroni went with Luo men.[21] Zaina binti Ali, taught by her parents to stay away from Luo men during World War II, informed me in the 1970s that "I changed my opinions. . . . people are less strict today than when I was growing up, and there is no need to believe everything we were taught."

As Haya wazi-wazi women enabled Luo men to reconstruct the demand for prostitutes in Nairobi, they changed the mores and cultural practices of many Kenyan women; they also restructured how profits were available to many prostitutes. While this reconstruction certainly earned Haya prostitutes the scorn of Pumwani's malaya women, it was not the feature of wazi-wazi prostitution that was most resoundingly criticized in Pumwani.

The Role of Haya Migrants

The Haya prostitutes who captured the imagination of other women in Pumwani first went there in the mid-1930s, and by the start of World War II they went in great numbers. At that time, many had the funds to move into Danguroni at inflated rents; this reinforced its notoriety and gave it a new name, Mji wa Bukoba (Bukoba town), by 1942.[22] The association of the Haya with the wazi-wazi form dates from 1939, and in East Africa the form is specific to Pumwani. McVicar identified it as the *only* form of prostitution practiced in 1960s Pumwani,[23] a testimony to the secrecy maintained by malaya women.

In their 1957 study of Kampala and its suburb, Kisenyi, Southall and Gutkind observed that "highly commercialized prostitution is definitely characteristic of the Haya," which they illustrated with examples of Haya women being paid less than they were promised. They found no satisfactory explanation for such widespread Haya prostitution, but they did not identify anything resembling the wazi-wazi form in Kampala and Kisenyi. Haya women in both places combined watembezi and malaya prostitution but seem to have preferred the latter. The authors noted that the Baziba—Ganda for Waziba—Quarter in Kisenyi was "unusual for its concentration of prostitutes who sit in their rooms and wait for customers to come and hire them. These women are almost entirely Haya."[24] Elizabeth Kamya confirmed this for Kampala in the 1930s: "There was no open prostitution as the Waziba did here. In Kampala it was done more in secret and with respect."

Several authors have commented on the high proportion of Haya women engaged in prostitution in East African towns in the 1950s and 1960s; Kenneth McVicar found fourteen of twenty-five "full-time" prostitutes in one area of Majengo to be Haya.[25] Haya prostitution was so visible that in Nairobi a form of prostitution was named for them and in Kisenyi a district was. These scholars have called the prostitution practiced by Haya women "commercial"—a term so mystifying that it suggests that these authors perceived some of the same qualities that captured the popular imagination of Pumwani, where the Haya "were cruel women, they used to sit outside their rooms and sell their bodies without caring who saw them."[26] What these qualities were and what they meant in Nairobi, and what caused Haya migration to East African cities when, must be inferred from written sources. In the time I was interviewing in Pumwani, I could not find one Haya woman who had been a prostitute there between 1936 and 1946: all had gone home. This alone gives a compelling sense of Haya women's attachment to and involvement in social life in Bukoba. Written sources do not provide a very nuanced picture of why Haya women became prostitutes, but they do shed some light on Africanist academic thinking about prostitution.

The secondary sources from which a chronology for Haya prostitution outside the Bukoba District might be established are not very satisfactory. Southall and Gutkind provide the best summary for what must be considered the mid-1950s conventional wisdom on why Haya prostitution was so widespread. These causes range from the personal to the cultural. It was said that the light skin color of the Haya made them especially attractive to East African men, an idea very much favored by McVicar, but one that Southall and Gutkind flatly rejected: if East African prostitution was the result of spectrographic supply and demand, there were other women better suited for the task.[27] My own data suggest that while a few men paid extra to spend the night with women who were "so beautiful," this was not unique to East Africa, and that skin color in and of itself was not a factor men held dear.[28] Southall and Gutkind also suggested that prostitution was first practiced by the royal Haya daughters who were denied "normal marriage," and in true courtly fashion "their example spread." In fact, royal women resisted this practice well before the British banned it in 1919: they converted to Christianity and went to live in convents and missions.[29] It was also thought that Haya prostitution originated when German administrators had demanded beautiful Haya women as their concubines, but a German traveller in Bukoba in 1910 commented on the absence of Haya prostitutes there and the number of Ganda women "wandering through the country."[30] The view common in Bukoba was that Christian missionaries had required permanent and monogamous marriages, which encouraged fathers to increase the bridewealth. The young men who were unable to wed therefore "required other outlets" while those men who married behaved "as headmen rather than as lovers" and demanded that their wives work exceptionally hard to make up for the expense of matrimony, so much so that "prostitution became a welcome escape for women."[31] Such a theory does not explain why women escaped into a profession in which other men demanded their money's worth, and ignores the frequency of divorce among the Haya. Missionaries, however, tended to see the problem as cultural: the ease of customary divorce, and the *bisisi* institution by which illegitimate Haya children were the legal offspring of a woman's ex-husband, had by the Depression left many households with what were disposable daughters, women who had been disenfranchised since birth.[32]

The problem with these theories is not just that they are wrong. It is that in all of them African women are seen as more autonomous than anyone would view an African man. These women are not linked to anyone in their households in any way other than to run away; they have fathers but, according to these ideas, no mothers; they respond and imitate but do not decide or negotiate or plan; they escape but apparently never return home. These ideas did not explain Haya prostitution; instead they assume that the causes of prostitution dangle outside of Haya and East African families and economies. None of these theories even mention money. They do not explain why Haya women needed money and why they needed it so desperately in the 1930s, for that is why Haya women became prostitutes.

Bengt Sundkler, then Lutheran Bishop of Bukoba , gave the most reasonable chronology for Haya prostitution in the 1945 article in a missionary journal. He explained how coffee, a local, royal crop, was introduced by the Germans to Haya commoners' smallholdings in 1904. Christian Haya men became wealthy cash crop producers; most of their manual labor was done by migrants from Ruanda-Urundi. By the boom of the late 1920s, the cash bridewealth had risen to as much as 600/ or 700/. In 1929, when the world market price of coffee fell from 30/ to 3/ for a thirty-five-pound bag, men needed cash to pay their debts and their laborers. They seem to have sought cash in a uniquely Haya way: divorce. Unlike most East African peoples, Haya fathers returned bridewealth to the husband when a marriage was dissolved.

> Men had to find money, and the obvious means was to divorce a wife and get the bride price back in full. The fathers suddenly had to find 600/ or 700/ to return to sons-in-law. That meant ruin. Then the women found a solution. They had been taught during the "fat" years that they had a cash value. The lake steamer brought them in their hundreds to Nairobi and Kampala, and returning home years later, with bicycle and syphilis and umbrella, they were hailed as the economic saviours of their families. Prostitution became rampant.[33]

This is not necessarily the most dynamic view of Haya families, and it reveals little about the complex and subtle pressures that induced Haya women to volunteer to leave home, become prostitutes, and pay their fathers' debts. But it does tell us about the nature of accumulation in rural Buhaya: marriage was a source of fathers' accumulation, and divorce was a source of husbands' accumulation: whether a woman was leaving natal home or husband determined which way cash circulated through the Haya petty bourgeoisie. In this way, patrilineages redistributed cash. In marriage and divorce and after, Haya women of the Great Depression behaved as daughters, and this, perhaps more than anything else, set them apart from the women in Pumwani who accumulated capital as independent heads of households, for themselves. The malaya women of Pumwani knew full well that Haya prostitutes had values fundamentally different from their own, and they mystified those values as behavior that was shameful, aggressive, and above all, public.[34]

It would seem that while some Haya came to Nairobi in the mid-1930s, they only began to arrive in large numbers between 1936 and 1939.[35] Many of these women may have come from prostitution in Kampala and Kisumu and Moshi. According to life histories collected in Buhaya by Birgitta Larsson, Haya prostitutes often worked in several cities, staying in each for eight or nine months. During World War II, for example, one Haya woman worked in Kisumu, Nakuru, Moshi, Nairobi, and Mombasa.[36] But the Haya women who began prostitution in the mid-to-late 1930s did so in a more specific context; they seem to have been adjunct to intense coffee speculation and peasant resistance in their homes. Even as the price of coffee remained low, Haya farmers expanded production during the Depression, paid for in part in the face of declining bridewealth by fathers' rights to use their daughters as collateral for loans. Such subsidies for coffee production enabled Haya peasants to combat British attempts to legislate farming techniques.[37] Moreover, Haya mothers probably saw prostitution as a way to obtain their daughters' financial support, and it is altogether likely that young women were influenced by kinswomen who had been prostitutes in the early 1920s and 1930s.[38] Haya prostitutes of the late 1930s were intimately involved in the fortunes of Bukoba, and the fortunes of Bukoba were intimately involved with their work as prostitutes.

Even before the start of World War II there were enough Haya in Pumwani to fuel stereotypes about them and their community. These invectives were specific to Pumwani and the Haya: women who were prostitutes elsewhere in Nairobi in the late 1930s did not mention the Haya,[39] and the young Kikuyu watembezi who captured colonial attention during World War II never offended Pumwani's malaya population.[40] Indeed, Haya prostitutes were described, forty years after these women had first gone to Pumwani, with an awe and passion and with abundant details that I had never heard used to describe other prostitutes. When Margaret Githeka described the aggression of Haya women, for example, she observed that they found ways to make their work more profitable by making it more public. She said that when a man refused to pay a Haya woman,

> they would fight, and then the woman would start screaming for help, saying this man doesn't want to give her any money. The Waziba were the ones who started this screaming, saying that the man had to give them cash. And also they would start doing shameful things when a man tried to cheat them, they would start to abuse that man, and they would ask their neighbors to come, they would have a fight in front of everyone.

Haya women, apparently, took sympathetic neighbors for granted. The process by which Haya prostitutes came to live near each other was gradual, as women reported soon-to-be-vacant rooms to each other and alerted landlords to a tenant who would always be able to pay the rent—often 20/ or 25/ in Pumwani in 1940—at a time of a high turnover of paying tenants.[41] A few women pointed out that once Haya prostitutes came to live in the same house, they were able to offer each other physical protection and physical support when they fought with men.[42] Only when housing was exceptionally crowded did malaya women have the kind of cooperation that wazi-wazi women took for granted, and even then they did not fight with men. But Githeka understood that their aggression was not the result of neighborliness, let alone culture or temperament; it was about the importance of cash to Haya prostitutes "because it was this money that she depended on . . . and a woman would risk her blood to get her money."

Muslim women from the 1930s and 1940s regarded Haya as at best interlopers, outsiders who made no attempt to follow the conventions of life in Muslim Pumwani. Indeed, I have no evidence of any conversion to Islam by a Haya woman. Haya prostitutes made no efforts to settle in Pumwani. According to Zaina Kachui, "they needed money, that's why they were prostitutes. And every Mziba woman who was here made a lot of money but they never spent it here, they took it straight back to Tanganyika . . . they didn't want to be rich here, they wanted to be rich in Tanganyika. Those Waziba women didn't mean to come here and build here, they used to come and work and take their money home." Both Kachui and Miriam Musale were concerned that I understand that the Haya women they were talking about did not build in Pumwani: "Those women have gone home now and those stone houses you see were built by women younger than them," who came in the 1960s. They, and other prostitutes in mid-1930s Majengo, understood full well that Haya prostitutes were accumulating wealth, but also that they were accumulating it for their families in rural Tanganyika. While they were earning money as daughters, however, they were acting like sisters in Pumwani. Mwanisha Waligo said,

> In those days it was the Waganda and the Waziba women who were rich and they didn't buy any plots here in Majengo. If one of those women died by mistake in Nairobi her neighbors and friends who had come with her to Nairobi would take her clothes and money and body and go straight to her home. Those Waziba women wouldn't have graves here in Nairobi, they would go straight back to their own country. These women . . . were sending money back to their own country every week, and when they died they would be buried at home too, no matter where they died. When an Mziba woman died a neighbor would take the body and all the property to her father's house.

These observations were important to a generation of women in Pumwani who claimed that one of the main attractions of urban Islam was that the religion would arrange their burials.[43] But they also reinforced the knowledge that Haya prostitutes were outsiders, earning money only to send it home. Once at home, former Haya prostitutes were as scathing about the mores of Muslim Kenya as malaya women had been about them. One Haya woman told Larsson that another became a Muslim "because she wanted to eat. Her Islam was food only."[44]

Haya women's cooperation and sisterhood seem to have been based on common assumptions about their long-term economic goals and about their occupations. Nevertheless, as prostitutes, they were competitive with each other. Haya women seem to have reconciled their competitive roles and their solidarity in the one feature of wazi-wazi prostitution that was so resoundingly condemned by malaya women of the same era: they called out a price—one that was low—sometimes to men passing by, sometimes to each other in accusation: "you sell your vagina for one shilling."[45] This may have been an insult but it was also just below the average short-time price for 1939–40. While it has been observed that "verbal abuse and fights permeated the relationships prostitutes had with each other,"[46] the function of each abuse has not been explored. In calling out prices, whether in rage or in announcement, Haya women were manufacturing consensus: they were refining the marketplace in very basic terms. They were setting a minimum price, below which women might find it difficult to go and impossible to call out to men. This was to insure that no single woman could or would undersell the others, and that most wazi-wazi women could at least earn their subsistence without undermining the profits available to her neighbors or restructuring prices. It would seem that neighborliness, work, and patterns of accumulation, not ethnicity, were the basis on which wazi-wazi women maintained and defended price boundaries.

The Haya, Danguroni, and Prostitutes' Accumulation, 1936–1946

Once Haya women came to live in Danguroni, starting in the late 1930s, popular stereotypes and myths conflated, and it is difficult to establish a chronology for their origins, as the beliefs about Danguroni and Haya prostitutes came to coincide. This is not because my data are hard to date or because of my informants' sloppy thinking; rather it reveals how strongly that coincidence articulated the true nature of prostitution in Danguroni, and how malaya women identified that prostitution and condemned it only when its practice differed from their own.

Danguroni had been known as "a market for prostitutes"[47] that was "known to everyone in Kenya, so most of the men went there"[48] since the mid-1930s. The women who lived there between 1934 and 1938/39 were mainly from central and eastern Kenya; most had been married before going to Nairobi and seem to have been in their early or mid-twenties; prostitutes elsewhere in Pumwani were often younger. After 1939 the Haya and the less numerous Ugandan women who went to Danguroni were also said to be in their twenties.[49] By the time Danguroni became known as Mji wa Bukoba, the notoriety of the Haya and that of Danguroni conflated and were mystified more than either had been before. Danguroni was said to be frequented by African soldiers, some of whom introduced European troops to Danguroni, and within a short while, "it was home to them."[50] The financial success of women in Danguroni was greatly exaggerated—"those were the ones who got rich in the war"[51]— and attributed to their place of residence. Wazi-wazi women were considered "shameful" because they requested payment in advance, despite the fact that many of their accusers had done the same when they were malaya prostitutes in Pumwani in the 1930s.[52] Tabitha Waweru, a Christian born in Pumwani in the early 1920s, was more specific—and realistic—about Haya women in Danguroni.

> Ziba and Nandi women used to call to men walking by, that was in Danguroni . . . they used to call "come here, come here," and some of them became very rich, but most of them got

beaten up very badly, and they let their babies die. The Nandi
and the Ziba women were the first to throw their babies
away. . . . They used to kill the babies as soon as they were born,
and leave them in the toilets. Sometimes the police would come
and ask if we knew who the mothers were, but we could never
say for sure.

This is a balanced account of Haya prostitution in Danguroni: some
Haya (and their colleagues in Waweru's eyes, the Nandi; other women said
Ganda) became wealthy but many more were brutalized. What is important here is not that Haya women were "shameful" or "disrespectful" but
that their visibility and the beatings and the infanticide were objectionable, they invited the police to the doors of more respectable women in
Pumwani. While the actual number of police in Nairobi suggests that they
could not investigate infanticide very often, if at all[53]—indeed, during
World War II malaya women tried to get the numbers of police in Pumwani increased—it was not a rare occurrence in Pumwani in the 1930s and
1940s. Residents talked about it matter-of-factly—with less passion than
they spoke of the Haya—as yet another example of municipal untidiness,
more inevitable than shocking. Zaina Kachui complained that the young
women in Pumwani in the 1970s did not show the proper respect and hide
the rags they used to absorb their menstrual blood: "these days you see
bloody rags everywhere, in the street and in the toilets, they just throw
them out, it's the way I used to see dead babies in the toilets all the time."
    Muslim women were counseled against infanticide; part of living a
woman's life in Muslim Nairobi was keeping unwanted children: Hadija
Njeri, a woman so counseled, was at pains to distinguish Danguroni from
"Muslim Pumwani." There is, however, no concrete evidence that suggests that the Haya committed infanticide any more than anyone else. Although the bisisi institution meant that divorced women had no legal
responsibilities for their children, the Haya rate of secondary sterility due
to venereal diseases must have been fairly high. But infanticide is not a
crime people commit when they want to put down roots somewhere, and
this, perhaps more than anything else, may explain the association of infanticide with the Haya. Condemnations of infanticide embodied the
values of community and inheritance and family life, and were about the
place in which those values were applicable: these were the issues around
which women organized their animosity toward Haya prostitutes. The
wazi-wazi form contained an urgency and a fervor for accumulating capital that was alien to the malaya women of the 1930s and 1940s.

Danguroni in the mid-1930s had a reputation for prostitution, but not for "shame" and "disrespect." Even the rarified malaya form practiced there between 1934 and 1938/39 never antagonized or alienated malaya women in Majengo. Indeed, as Salima binti Athmani pointed out, some of the women who worked in Danguroni also lived in Majengo, and others moved there at the start of the war.[54] The communities were not then as separate as they were to become. Nevertheless, the malaya women who worked in Danguroni before 1938/39 seem to have practiced the form to earn money for their families, not for independent accumulation. Indeed, in Danguroni the ideology of patrilineal control was so strong that women who worked there saw themselves as transmitters of property between males. Salima binti Athmani gave virtually all of her earnings to her sons, by way of her estranged husband. She could not see the point of building a house for herself "because I already had my husband's farm. . . . If I had a plot, my sons would inherit it, if my husband had a farm, my sons would inherit it, so what's the difference?" The difference, of course, would have been years of tenants' rents. For binti Athmani property was something that passed through her, something that belonged to men. She was not accumulating money for herself, but for her sons, as a strategy for herself: in the late 1930s "I built a stone house on my husband's farm for them. . . . I decided that this was better than putting money in a bank." Danguroni in the early 1930s had been the site of familial accumulation, but it had been conducted within the confines of the malaya form, quietly, with secrecy and respect.

It was the Haya women in Danguroni, with their aggressive wazi-wazi form, their screams, and their fights, who scandalized women in the rest of Pumwani. The scandal was not the screams and the fights in and of themselves, but that the screams and fights literally announced and articulated family accumulation, prostitution that was urgent and desperate because fathers and husbands needed money urgently and desperately. The wazi-wazi form in Danguroni was the prostitution of rural petty-bourgeois cash crop producers, a different group altogether from malaya women. The most identifiable wazi-wazi practitioners in Danguroni, the Haya and the Ganda, were from societies in which cash crop production had been introduced into peasants' smallholdings at the turn of the century. The initial boom in cotton and coffee prices financed and then reinforced fathers' control to a degree that may never have previously existed. The vicissitudes of international markets and colonial marketing practices left that control as dependent on production and international prices as it ever was on the obedience and loyalty of kin. It may be significant that the wazi-wazi prostitutes I know about who lived outside of Danguroni during the late 1930s and early years of World War II, most of whom were not Haya, accumulated as malaya women, for themselves.

Outside of Danguroni, in the rest of Pumwani, malaya women did believe in acquiring property for themselves, even when no one else did. In Pumwani and the African settlements throughout the colony, women from societies in which they could not own property built houses and rented out the rooms at extremely profitable rates. For the most part, malaya women came from households engaged in subsistence production, although most of the food crops produced in central Kenya after the 1920s were selected for the marketable value of their surplus.[55] They were the daughters of families that eluded impoverishment barely and regularly. Almost all malaya women—*all* malaya women of Majengo—retained control over their earnings; they might have purchased livestock for a brother's bridewealth or given lavish gifts to their families at one time or another, but they prostituted themselves to support themselves, to head their own households, to purchase and transmit real property. This control was Amina Hali's "extra money" and Kayaya Thababu's distinction between Pumwani and her rural homeland: in Pumwani "I could earn my own money, for myself." Miriam binti Omari was more concrete: prostitution allowed her to buy for herself the things men had given her.[56]

Malaya women who were born in Pumwani also retained control over their earnings, in ways that informed the geography of African property ownership in Nairobi. Tabitha Waweru was born in Pumwani in 1925, the daughter of a polygamous Christian householder. She left her father's house to practice the malaya form—combined with some wartime watembezi prostitution—because "I decided that even if my father had property it was not mine, it belonged to my father; so I came to Mathare and built this house and rent the rooms." Margaret Githeka's father was a Roman Catholic householder with six wives; she began to practice the malaya form in the mid-1930s, and in 1962 she built a house in Mathare because "I wanted my money to do me good." These women represented a different kind of accumulation from that of Salima binti Athmani, working "for my sons" in Danguroni a few hundred yards away, the same year Githeka left her father's house. Other less successful Pumwani- and Pangani-born malaya women controlled their incomes as well. Mwanisha Waligo, the daughter of a well-to-do Majengo householder, frittered away her meager earnings; she claimed she spent whatever windfalls she received helping her woman friends. She remained somewhat dependent on her father until he died when she was fifty, but at not time did she give money to her parents. Ibrahima binti Musa, the daughter of a Kileleshwa householder who went to Pangani and the to Pumwani in 1935 as a wealthy tenant, supported her mother with her earnings from prostitution, but only after her father's death when she took over as the head of the family. Women who were the daughters of the urban petty bourgeoisie—men and women whose accumulation already represented a break with lineage loyalties— did not return their incomes to their respective patrilineages; they kept them for themselves.

Malaya women effectively established themselves as household heads: they created new lineages that they themselves founded. They purchased or built urban property, which they struggled to maintain as independent, or at least to keep outside the control of preexisting patrilineages. Childless malaya property owners in Pumwani frequently designated heirs for their houses, most often young women they had sheltered in town or those they brought from their rural homes.[57] Malaya women with children passed their property to their offspring, sometimes by primogeniture, sometimes by sharing: illegitimate children for whom no compensation was paid to the mother's father were legally the descendants of the mother and not the father.[58] If a woman did not formally designate an heir "on the paper that allowed her to own the building," then the MNC would "take over the building" when she died.[59] Yet many childless malaya women did just that,[60] in a clear rejection of family ties: it was by careful deliberation that malaya women guaranteed that their property would not be returned to the lineages into which they were born. According to Tabitha Waweru,

> some women were really rich and when they got old, because they didn't have any family living around Nairobi, an old woman would choose another woman and tell everyone "this is my heir." She would have to love you, really, to do that, but it happened a lot. To become an old woman's heir you would have to cook for her, clean for her, wash her clothes for her, everything. Then one day this old woman will take the young woman to the DC's office and say "this is my daughter, I want her to get my property when I die." She would do this the first time she felt sick, and the DC would write it down . . . . A lot of women in Majengo did this, they befriended old women, and they got property in this way.

I know of no cases where childless malaya women designated males as their heirs, a process that would have transmitted the property to the young man's lineage. Such rejection of their families of origin seems specific to the malaya form: women who had acquired urban property through their watembezi earnings designated a brother's or sister's son as their heir, thus transferring their property back into a patrilineage, but not necessarily the one into which they were born. Wambui Murithi built her parents a house on their farm but sent most of her earnings to support her dead sister's children who lived with their father; in the 1950s she designated her sister's oldest son as heir to her house, which meant that the house would eventually belong to the lineage of her late sister's husband, not her own. The state did not attempt to routinize African urban property transmission until the late 1940s.[61]

Malaya women's property often had to be protected from their patrilineages. When a Kikuyu malaya woman died in 1942, leaving a stone house valued at £ 600 to her only child, a daughter, rural kin arrived in Pumwani and claimed that the house was rightfully theirs under customary law. Colchester, the MNAO, decided under a rather Pumwani-ized version of English law that the house belonged to the daughter.[62] In the 1930s, however, malaya women had to struggle against the state almost as often as they did against their patrilineages. "It has always been difficult for women to inherit property, even in Majengo the DC had to be called in when a woman left everything to her daughter, even if she had no sons."[63] In designating heirs and rejecting their patrilineages, malaya women were founding lineages that, taken in the aggregate, comprised a class. They were transmitting to women and men the property around which a whole range of relationships and opportunities and situations was organized. It would seem that the state was offended by this stabilizing influence on the relationships of African workers to men and women who lived slightly outside the law but with a firm commitment to community life in Nairobi, not by prostitution.

In 1938 (the same year the Davies Report explained how prostitution "served" Nairobi's needs), when the state began to create a respectable working class in words and memoranda, it did so at the expense of Pangani and Pumwani landlords, who were suddenly declared diseased, detribalized, and degenerate—all the adjectives that had been applied to casual labor a few years earlier—in the same memos and reports. The removal of Pangani raised the question, What was the state to do with landlords whose property had been demolished?

That removal, originally planned for 1921, was postponed because of the very usefulness of Pangani's landlords; they capably housed part of Nairobi's work force in years when labor was in short supply. When plans for its demolition finally got underway during the reduced labor require-

ments of the Depression, it took six years of debate, testimony, and deliberation for the state to decide against full or even reasonable
compensation for Pangani landlords. But if reasonable compensation was
out of the question, so was their retreat into tenancy: these landlords had
been able to house a work force with more control and better organization
than anyone else had done; their services were needed, their newly
formed lineages were not. After a prolonged debate, the MNC offered
175 Pangani householders, over 100 of them women, the right to come to
the newly constructed Pumwani Extension, where they were allowed to
hold lifetime leases on rooms for 4/ and 5/per month, to collect and keep
the rents that they set in all but one-third of the houses (where the MNC
set rents), but not to sell or pass on the property when they died. The Extension was called Shauri Moyo before it was opened; the name "just
emerged"[64] and literally means "heart business" in Swahili, a reference to
the painful decision to take up the state's offer, which enabled women to
continue their work as landlords but not to create the ties of place and
property that bound wealthy prostitutes and poor immigrants to a vision
of Nairobi in which Africans worked and prospered and belonged.

The state had attacked not working prostitutes but successful retired
ones. It was not that the state objected to private landlords, even when
they were prostitutes: indeed, the conduct of the malaya form was well
suited to the housing of Nairobi's work force. It was what the landlords
did with their property that was cause for alarm. Officials did not act
against prostitution; they moved against urban class formation. For malaya women the unrestrained patrilineal accumulation that was taking
place in Danguroni at the same time that all the houses in Shauri Moyo
were being taken over by displaced Pangani landlords must have revealed
how precarious their position in Nairobi was. It would seem that when, in
the mid-1970s, these same malaya women condemned wazi-wazi prostitutes in Danguroni as "shameful" and "disrespectful" and for bringing
the police into Pumwani, they were not just condemning the conduct that
had eroded their late-1930s profits: they were alluding the state intervention in African accumulation and social life.

Nevertheless, the ties of place and property and work were created in
other, more subtle (and more impoverished) ways between generations
and, somewhat less often, between genders. The idea that young women
could and should acquire property was in Pumwani in the 1930s advocated by older women, many of whom had not acquired property themselves. These were the older Muslim women who sometimes aided younger
immigrant women, teaching them and housing them, although it did not

require much patronage to find a vacant room in Pumwani in the early 1930s. Zaina Kachui explained how a woman who neither housed her nor converted her (she had become a Muslim in the early 1930s, in Thika) taught her that prostitution was accumulation, not an act of degradation or exploitation.

> These days I do not have to beg anyone to give me a place to sleep. . . . I got help from a woman who was staying hear me, this was just when I was learning to speak Swahili, she was the one who told me to take money from men. In those days I feared to take money from going with men, because I was frightened that if I asked for money they would call me a prostitute. But that woman, she used to tell me, "if you don't get some money from men, I'll beat you." And because I feared that she would beat me, I took money from men. You know, if that woman hadn't helped me, I wouldn't even have a cup to drink from today. . . . that money I earned, I used it to buy the things I needed.

It was the old woman, not Kachui, who did not trust men's capacity to provide for their lovers. She believed that the real risks for urban women came from marriage, or worse, a promise of marriage:[65] permanent boyfriends earning Nairobi wages meant dependence. Kachui described how her own attitude toward long-term relationships changed, and how broad her definition of property became.

> In those days in my heart I wanted one boyfriend to stay with, and that woman told me "you are stupid, you want to stay with a man and he can't help you to get your property, you must find men to pay you cash." . . . and she would tell me how angry she would be to find me with a boyfriend who was helping me little by little. She said she wanted me to stay alone and be a prostitute so I could have my own things. She was the first woman to help me in Nairobi, without her I wouldn't have a cup to drink out of, or a bed, of that I am sure.

Monica Nyazura, who combined the wazi-wazi and malaya forms in Majengo starting in the late 1930s, lived with several men. She incorporated them into her household and supported them with her earnings. She often went with men while in these relationships: "It depended on how much money my husband and I needed, because he was going to be able to eat the money I made this way. So if a man came, and we needed money, and my husband was inside, he would go out and visit someone while the

man and I went together for short-time." In Nyazura's combined wazi-
wazi and malaya prostitution, adult males were adopted into her household as dependents; malaya women, however, never supported men other
than their own sons.

Salima binti Athmani, who began working in Danguroni a year or two
before Kachui and Nyazura came to Pumwani, had a substantially different ideology of gender relations. In her opinion boyfriends were natural
providers, men who looked after all of a woman's immediate needs, except whatever need she might have to support her children and to accumulate and reinvest capital.

> In those days you had to have a boyfriend. Without a boyfriend
> you will eat what? So I always had a steady boyfriend but I was
> also doing my business and I had to find two places to live, be-
> cause when I was with my boyfriend I had to pretend I wasn't a
> prostitute, so my boyfriend paid the rent and helped me with
> clothes and food and everything here in Majengo, but I also
> kept my permanent room in Danguroni for my business. I paid
> the rent there myself. And you know my boyfriends would
> never find out that I went to Danguroni to sell my body there.
> That was a good way of life.

But in such a way of life, the bonds of place and property were easily
disconnected, or at least severely bent: they were made to take place in
separate locations. Boyfriends were neither included nor excluded from
accumulation in Danguroni; they were, as some women said infants were,
removed from it: relationships were made separately from the processes
of accumulation, particularly the accumulation of capital destined for
rural East Africa. In this way Haya wazi-wazi women were aggressive to
the men who visited them in Danguroni and loyal to their fathers in
Bukoba: no lasting ties were forged in Danguroni. It was this separation,
the aggressive conduct arising out of the strength of women's family ties—
on which family members living elsewhere depended—that accounted
for the professionalism attributed to wazi-wazi prostitutes. It was perhaps
a logical contradiction that this professionalism reinforced the belief that
Danguroni was a place notorious for prostitutes while everywhere else—
rural Africa and Majengo—was where respectable women lived.

Conclusions

On the whole, the form of prostitution a woman practiced determined
what she did with her earnings. My data show that the circumstances un-

der which prostitutes acquired property in and out of Nairobi throughout the colonial era were directly related to the vitality of agricultural production of the woman's family of origin. Women from households engaged in subsistence farming, however inexact the term might be when applied to central Kenya, practiced the malaya form for a good part of their careers and were the women who retained control over their urban incomes. These were the women who waited quietly for men to come to them: their respect and deference accompanied independent accumulation. The more aggressive forms of prostitution, in which women sought men without secrecy and often with a lot of noise, accompanied the most conventional female behavior. The women who chose the wazi-wazi form, or the mid-1930s Danguroni version of the malaya form, were generally women from families engaged in cash crop production. These women, whose families constituted a rural petty bourgeoisie, did not acquire wealth for themselves, and almost all of them returned home—sometimes after their earnings had—where their monies came under patrilineal control, or they acquired property in their homes that would eventually belong to their patrilineages. Like a generation of watembezi prostitutes in the years before World War I, these women and their families used prostitution to refinance their failing agricultural ventures.

In the early colonial era the daughters of pastoralists practiced the watembezi form almost exclusively. In the 1930s, however, the watembezi form seems to have been practiced less specifically, at the same time that profitable African pastoralism declined: women engaged in it periodically or because it was necessitated by where and with whom they lived. It was not a form of prostitution that women practiced exclusively, but one that women either practiced occasionally or avoided altogether. Squatters in the settled areas of the Rift Valley went from pastoralism to subsistence and wage labor in the 1930s, when they were forced to sell livestock,[66] and their few daughters who became prostitutes in Nairobi in those years practiced the malaya form. Wangui Fatuma, from Molo in the Rift Valley, did not practice the watembezi form because she "feared the police," although she said she had realized that prostitutes were only rarely arrested, but she had no reasons to take such risks.

6

Constructing Classes: Gender, Housing, and the State in Kenya

Pumwani and Pangani thrive on the lodging system. You get a perfectly decent boy who has been a houseboy for some time and who has lost the art of living in the reserve, and he will probably buy a little house and let out the lodgings at the rate of 10/ a room. It is really a little gold mine.

E. B. Hosking

Q. What did men do to get money in the old days?
A. The old men had houses which they could let and get money, and the others used to work, except for the young boys who could not find work.

Chepkitai Mbwana

Housing was not essential to colonial enterprises in Nairobi—unskilled African laborers had been doing without it, on and off, for years—but the issue of African housing, and its meaning to the state and landlords alike, provided the rhetoric with which colonial officials and urban Africans contested the urban landscape. The facts of housing and homelessness had perhaps less to do with sheltering workers from the cold highland nights than with competing groups' abilities to contain those men in units ready-made for a supervised social life. Colonial officials were less concerned with housing urban Africans than they were with controlling them; African landlords were less concerned with civic notions of order than they were with accumulation and establishing urban networks. At the same time African women articulated and combated their own structural weakness through the acquisition and defense of urban property. The relationship between private landlords and the state was in practice dialectical: the rigidity of colonial attempts to control urban Africans all too often made their presence in Nairobi illegal, as well as their property ownership and the methods of its acquisition.

The state's attempt to manage urban Africans by housing them was social engineering in its basest and most structural form. Dividing a city into areas designated legal and illegal for African occupancy forced Africans into decisions about law and legitimacy, and authorizing the size, shape, and, by 1940, materials for African housing had everything to do with official expectations about what African life should or could be. The grim dormitories of Kariokor and the even grimmer rooms in Gorofani and Marurani in the 1940s belied the official pronouncements about the benefits and stability of family life. African landlords controlled the labor force concretely: their rents often created the condition of homelessness that so frequently distressed the state, and their rules of conduct determined the behaviors of many of Nairobi's African population. African tenants had their own ideas about housing, space, and families, and the proper relationship between them, and they were often active critics of the social engineering to which they were subject.

Until the 1930s housing policy was primarily concerned with where urban Africans might live. In Nairobi the state allowed both legal and illegal settlements, often gratefully. The real pressure for the destruction of the independent villages in order to create Pumwani came from the Indian community, not the administration. Policies of the mid-1930s demonstrated that officials approved of former prostitutes renting rooms to wage laborers; they objected to these women—and any number of men— owning property and passing it on, with the sense of place, community, and continuity that implied. After World War II officials' revulsion at African Nairobi and their broader notions about how to control and order social change led them to see housing as a way to construct genders and the obedience and responsibility that such sexual and marital roles implied. The number of housing schemes of the late 1940s, with their copious documentation and publicity campaigns, suggests that the state was trying to structure African class relations through gender relations: skilled literate workers were to be allowed to live with their families. But individual Africans landlords were never, in my experience, so grandiose as to see themselves constructing anything but buildings; they saw the acquisition of real property as a personal goal. Africans claimed that unemployment and property ownership were the poles in an urban life cycle, in which householding was the result of a well-spent, frugal urban life. Property was the way earnings could be turned over to chosen heirs; they saw it as class formation at the turn of the century, and they continued to see it that way in the late 1940s. Colonial officials expressed this somewhat differently: well into the 1930s they saw African landlords as profiteers, scoundrels who had found a foolproof way of not working.

Locating Landlords

Well before World War I, colonial officials had made a distinction between urban, detribalized Africans and the mobile, rural migrant laborers. Between June and November 1911 John Ainsworth, easily the most experienced administrator in Kenya and then Provincial Commissioner at Kisumu, wrote three memos on African urbanization. They were on the whole concerned with where Africans should live, not with the quality of their life or the nature of their relationships. The first and third were concerned with permitting Sudanese and Swahilis to remain in the townships in which they already lived,[1] and were in part a response to 1910 attempts to remove Swahilis from agricultural smallholdings in Kikuyu and Limuru.[2] The second was about the problem of those Africans who "appear to wander away from their reserves in an irresponsible manner" and then settle in townships "to avoid tribal control";[3] apparently, the distinction between migrants and townsfolk was not as clear as Ainsworth presumed. Nevertheless, he proposed a location policy for all urban Africans, with rigorous policing of the younger population: they were not allowed into townships unless they had work there, and they were to be ordered home once their employment was over.

Ainsworth identified the Sudanese and Swahilis as ex-Government servants, porters, askaris, and ex-slaves: "toil and age in some cases, and the advent of the Railway in others" had rendered them unemployable, especially since the government wage levels they had been paid at the turn of the century were not available in provincial stations. All of this, Ainsworth wrote, "left them homeless and disorganized. They have become detribalized, demoralized, and decentralized, and so they congregate round what centres there are . . . and carry out a semi-indolent existence by petty-trading."[4] The permanent urbanization of these men and women was to be an administrative convenience: "If they are cleared out of one Province they will go to another; they must go somewhere. So the matter is in no way assisted by moving them about. Indeed, if they could be settled down definitely it would be an all-round advantage." To this end Ainsworth proposed that an urban African location be established in each township, to accommodate "the increasing movement" of young men seeking work. Location building plots could be leased at four rupees a year, and residents would be liable for a Poll Tax of 6 rupees annually; defaulters would be put to work for the Government one month for every four rupees due. The location would enable Sudanese and Swahilis to continue in petty trade while controlling some of the "vagabonds" who were to become such a regular feature of colonial rhetoric. Ainsworth envisioned the location to be an urban village, with each migrant building his own bachelor hut; lodging houses were expressly forbidden.[5] Since the annual ground rent was to be the equivalent to at least a month's wage,[6] illegal lodging houses were the instantaneous result.

Younger, able-bodied Africans posed a different problem; those who did not work did not belong in towns. Ainsworth allowed that many such youths had come with the hope of employment, but the relations they formed with those Africans already residing in townships "generally . . . knock any idea of this description out of their heads, and they resort to a vagabond life." Ainsworth's plans to rid townships of offending Africans—especially women living there without parental consent—called on the state to institutionalize the authority of African families, the betterment of which could best be attained by Government intervention. Many elders "did not know how to proceed" to "get their sons and daughters from the Townships" and had appealed to the state for help.[7]

It is important to understand that such policies were not the response of administrators thin on the ground, nor were they naive assumptions about African social life. Ainsworth had been in Kenya since 1895; he had been in Ukambani at the height of the famine; he had probably seen African families at their weakest. It was unlikely that he had any illusions about the power of elders to control their sons and daughters in the postconquest labor, marriage, and cattle markets.[8] The ideals and policies that followed from Ainsworth's 1911 directives on urbanization were deliberate constructions of African social life, rural and urban. The only unemployed Africans who were allowed to remain in townships were the old and detribalized; those who were to be sent away at considerable expense were young men and still-marriageable women.[9]

These categories of young and old, of runaway daughters and loyal ex-servants, of migrants and long-term townsmen, were ways of distinguishing tenant from landlord. These were conventions of colonial rhetoric, and they helped to deny the ambiguous aspects of urban life. These categories were frequently gendered and always aged, and at different times one group was supported at the other's expense. But it was landlords who occupied a unique position in colonial thinking and colonial reality. They were at once a group constructed by the state—with its own ascribed history and characteristics that made it dependent on state power—and an autonomous social group with an existence independent from European political authority. As a result they often confused and flustered the colonial state. Official descriptions of landlords often contradicted each other precisely because the meaning of landlords was so contradictory to colonialists. In the poorly timed and unsuccessful attempt to move Somali householders out of the area just east of Nairobi township in 1915–17, the Medical Officer informed his superiors "that the Somali . . . is not employed by the public or Government to any extent." Three weeks later Chief Secretary Bowring demanded that the Colonial Office stop the evictions because the Somalis "work as Askaris or Interpreters for Government." Within a few months, however, Somali headmen had bought the freehold plots on which they resided, which were not subject to township rules.[10] Typically, landlords had gone about their business of acquisition and accumulation without regard for the State's definition of themselves.

Landlords were at work well before World War I; they only came under official censure in the 1930s, when they were lumped with the unemployed and criminal elements, the classes most dangerous to a state that was not firmly in control of city life.[11] Unlike the state, private African landlords were able to control many aspects of their tenants' behavior—which unsupervised public housing, such as it was, could not do—and they took responsibility for repairs and the cleanliness of communal areas.[12] They treated their houses as investments, the way a class would. They built up ties of rights and obligations. Abdullah Gitau, a Pangani landlord, judiciously manipulated his resources to build a stone house in Pumwani in about 1939. Two of his tenants, Asha binti Juma and her husband, Mohammed Macaria, returned home to Murang'a while they waited for him to finish the house, which took about a year. Gitau sent a message to them when the house was completed. Thirty years later, when Macaria died, Gitau evicted a woman and installed binti Juma in a smaller room, so that she "would save some money but not have to leave the house."[13] Sometimes a landlord's rights and obligations were more instrumental and more gender-specific, particularly when the housing was illegal. Wanjira Ng'ang'a built a house in Buruburu in which she and other prostitutes lived from 1942 to 1952; she supported her tenants through lean times, menstruation, and pregnancy because "that is how I made sure they would help me. We were women, we stayed in the same place and we were all made in the same way." Indeed, when "the Mau Mau fighting began and all the houses in Buruburu were demolished and I was homeless,

I had to start all over again finding money, so I went to Bahati and stayed with a woman who used to be one of my tenants in Buruburu."

Landlords represented the religious and propertied communities to which they belonged. Muslim landlords, with their greater access to social institutions and networks in Kenyan urban centers before 1939, took an active role in socializing their tenants to the prevailing norms of city life.[14] Landlords who were also prostitutes had a vested interest in minimizing any sort of aggressive behavior; Kayaya Thababu pointed out that men stayed away from houses where women quarreled. Peacekeeping efforts were not confined to Muslim landlords, however; householders of all religions settled minor disputes and discouraged activities that might attract the police. Landlords who were or had been prostitutes taught their tenants the harsher realities of town life. Many forbade their tenants to brew illegal liquors, while others advised younger prostitutes to take only cash gifts so they could not be accused of receiving stolen goods, and to do nothing when a man refused to pay them.[15]

African landlord's accumulation served the state in ideological and practical ways; the high rents they charged, "beyond the capacity of the average native to pay without hardship,"[16] sent more men to their rural homes or into urban homelessness than the pass laws did, and gave the state its self-righteous tone in condemning landlords. In 1939 Governor Brooke-Popham claimed that landlords' "profiteering" had caused the artisans' strikes of that year, even though the first such strike had been by Railway apprentices housed by their employer.[17] The description of African landlords exploiting African laborers was part of a larger development in 1930s official thinking, a growing awareness of class differences between urban Africans; this was to become commonplace as colonialists portrayed landlords and tenants as completely antagonistic. In this vein official reasoning attributed the not-so-apparent failure of Mau Mau in Nairobi to the fact that Kikuyu tenants would not join forces with their Kikuyu landlords.[18] In the attempts to demolish Pangani, mid-1930s administrators identified in annual reports a group of casual laborers and "criminal characters" who along with the Africans who housed them preyed upon the wage labor force, "the average native." These predatory criminals, rich and poor alike, were a restatement of the unrespectable poor, or residuum, of Victorian social reform—the men and women whose livelihoods did not depend on the order and discipline of capitalist production, but on their wits instead. Not only were such classes a threat to the state's definition of order, but they were held to be a threat to those classes already participating in the state's conception of social life, with the state's rules and methods. The unrespectable poor were characteristically described in biological metaphors that revealed their infectious power: they were polluted, they had degenerated, they could contaminate: "we have got to protect the bona fide worker from the parasite class of native."[19] The equally orderly metaphors of decolonization replaced medical terminology for many years, but the unrespectable poor reemerged in the development rhetoric of the 1970s: they became the urban informal sector. In the antiseptic language of the day, age, gender, and biological metaphors were rarely used, but the old colonial categories remained. The urban informal sector was a restatement of older ideas about Africans in towns, that African capitalists were engaged in the intense exploitation of a young labor force, even though that exploitation kept them off the streets.[20] Given the persistence of these ideas about African landlords in Kenya, the colonial state's deliberate attempt to get rid of loyal, legal ones in the 1930s becomes all the more significant.

The Demolition of Pangani Village, 1930–39

Pangani was the oldest "uncontrolled" African settlement in Nairobi, built around the turn of the century on land granted by John Ainsworth or, according to some bold landlords, Queen Victoria. By 1930 it was the richest African settlement in Nairobi, with two mosques and more stone buildings than Pumwani; it housed laborers at least as well as anywhere else, at rents competitive with those charged in Pumwani.[21] Pangani had first been scheduled for demolition in 1919, but the labor shortage of that year thwarted plans to disrupt African housing in Nairobi. Its demolition was further delayed as the Municipality vacillated over Pangani householders' demands for compensation. Although a few houses were torn down in the early 1930s, in November 1933 the MNC postponed further evictions until the publication of the Kenya Land Commission's *Report*, the result of land litigation in Central Province, which would suggest an average assessed compensation above which the Municipality need not pay. The Report was published in May 1934. Despite the MNAO's recommendation of £ 10 compensation, the amount was fixed at £ 50. Armed with more documentation and census figures, in June 1936 the Town Clerk ordered the demolition of the thirty-six houses owned by landlords who had lived in Nairobi less than six years, the rhetoric of age in action. Despite the KLC recommendations, no houses had been built to accommodate the evicted residents; within two months the Colonial Office received a complaint that this policy was sending a daily average of twenty men, women, and children into the streets "sleeping in the open bitterly cold." By October this policy was reversed at the insistence of the Colonial Office which, after the Northey Circulars of the 1920s, had become extremely wary of supporting policies that might cause Kenya adverse publicity. The MNC agreed not to evict people who had nowhere to go to in town or rural areas, and with a loan from the Kenya Government began constructing the 175-house Pumwani Extension, designed to accommodate 155 fewer Africans than had lived in Pangani in 1931.[22] In 1937, when Pangani was again overcrowded, the MNAO recommended that no more houses be torn down until the Extension was completed, and it was not until June 1938 that the fifty final eviction notices were served on Pangani householders. The settlement was officially demolished in 1939, although squatters moved in a few months later.[23] During this entire period, the squatter settlements of Mathare and Buruburu were untouched.

This sequence of events reveals two distinct trends. First, that the exclusively medical arguments that had been used to facilitate the removal of African entrepreneurs and householders in the 1920s had been replaced, by the mid-1930s, by a cumbersome array of committees, experts, and the Colonial Office itself—which still could not fully remove an urban population. The demolition of Pangani took place, or failed to take place, in a wider context of disputed land rights in central Kenya, and the increased documentation represented not only a movement away from specifically sanitary arguments for urban social control, but also the power and viability of African landlords. Second, it reveals that the group under attack in the demolition of Pangani was the landlords, not the labor force. Indeed, the early 1930s plans to relocate potential workers did not include Pangani at all, but focused on the Sudanese soldiers' settlement at Kibera.[24]

The attack on landlords took the appropriate form of attacking their heirs, not their tenants. As early as 1931 E. B. Hosking, then District Commissioner of Nairobi, wrote, "The old Nubian is a man to whom the colony owes much, but the second generation and the hybrids arising from mixed unions are degenerate." He complained that there was now "all over Nairobi a race of detribalised natives, born to prostitutes," mainly Muslims who lived by letting out lodgings, "who cannot be sent home because they do not know to what reserve they belong, or . . . the reserve to which their fathers belonged." Nairobi "had no place for these parasites."[25] Two years later the state's expert on Pangani landlords testified that if they could be sent "back to the reserves the chances are that their children could grow up to be decent people. If they continue living in town there is little hope of that."[26] Some of these younger landlords were the same women that malaya women had struggled to install as their heirs.

The demolition of Pangani has nevertheless been described as a masterstroke of urban labor policy, "consciously designed to use segregation in the town as a means to obtain cheap labor."[27] But cheap labor was by the mid-1930s readily available from rural Kenya, and, as we have seen, the cheapest labor power had its own relationship to segregation in Nairobi: men slept in the streets. The 1930s location policy, much of which was worked out in the memos and meetings about the evacuation of Pangani, was the means by which African labor would be segregated in part from other races but, much more important, from other, unwaged Africans within the town. In this way the rhetoric of urban African indolence shifted to include not only elderly landlords but the sort of tenants they had attracted by 1936, as Deputy Governor Wade defended the evictions in Pangani:

> The nucleus of the inhabitants are old men and widows, strict Muslims according to their lights, detribalized, deruralized, and obviously incapable of being accommodated anywhere but near a town.
>
> Such veterans are mainly ex-soldiers, porters, and personal servants . . . who played a useful and honourable part in the pioneering days. . . . Round this respectable nucleus have gathered . . . natives, generally from local reserves, who live by their wits and on their fellows. Retired prostitutes have set up lodging houses, which are also brothels and refuges for the criminal classes. . . . nearly all are undesirable in Nairobi. Most have assumed a veneer of Islam but the tenuity of this can be judged by their addiction to illicit brewing and drunkenness. They are neither detribalized or completely deruralized: they prefer the amenities of town life which gives them a greater scope for their criminal proclivities. . . . I see no reason why they should be encouraged or permitted to live in Nairobi to prey on the working population.[28]

This account shows the centrality that African social relations had come too have in 1930s housing policy: what worried Wade was the community in Pangani, not anyone's degree of Islamicization. The image of a respectable body attracting unemployed Africans around them was a potent one, and one that continued well into the 1950s.

Who were the Pangani landlords? According to the state's own figures, they were a fairly unremarkable group, no more the victims of "toil and age" than wage laborers were. Of 293 householders owning 312 houses, 247 were Muslim, 12 were Christian, and 34 claimed to be pagan; 121 were women, all of them Muslim, and 172 were men. Although Kamba and Kikuyu Muslims had their own mosques there, 146 landlords were Kikuyu, 25 Nandi, and the rest "various tribes" only a few of which appeared to be Kamba. Only 29 landlords were born in Nairobi—people who would be called "pure Swahili" by their tenants—the rest came from rural East Africa. There were 146 who had been in Nairobi for more than ten years, and of those, 90 had been there over twenty years, but 72 had been there between five and ten years, and 74 had been there less than five years. Two hundred thirty-three landlords made their livings exclusively from their properties; of the men landlords, 25 were also skilled laborers and another 13 were domestic servants.[29]

The state had its own history of Pangani landlords, best represented by the officially sanctioned testimonies before the KLC.

> We, after embracing Islam, become detribalized and consequently lose claim to cultivating land of our ancestors and are compelled to go to townships and seek our living by employment or trade, we have been driven to this unenviable position by (1) reason of our religion, (2) lack of any organization, and (3) the omission of the Government to set aside tracts of land where we could . . . follow the occupation of our forefathers . . . in agriculture.[30]

This was pure John Ainsworth, although he saw labor, not Islam, as the source of detribalization. What was perhaps more remarkable than a spokesman for Pangani's Kikuyu Muslims describing his complete detribalization and disorganization was his ubiquitous complaint. Similar kinds of helplessness and compulsions applied equally well to non-Muslim migrant laborers, who came to towns because of land alienation, or taxation, or crop failures. There was nothing special in this account except the ways in which it was privileged by and for the state; it argued, after all, that propertied Muslims were without organization, without authority, without community—without the very things that made landlords a specialized group in a specialized community. Such a construction made property owners seem hapless and adrift in complex political processes, it reduced urban living to a fact of religious life, and it showed landlords to be separate and distinct from their tenants. At the Kenya Land Commission, the MNAO translated for the landlords who concurred: "It is a very bad thing for a Mohammedan native to be returned to his reserve," as it would be "as though we were thrown away. . . . We do not drink *tembo* the same as pagans do, neither do we kill goats by strangulation."[31] Such a construction enabled colonialists to try to make a city without landlords and to make landlords be landlords without property.

The Allocation of Housing in Shauri Moyo, 1936–38

Between 1936 and 1938 the MNC abandoned its more fanciful plans for what to do with dispossessed Pangani householders—including placing some in an urban almshouse and sending another 145 to a "detribalized native village in the reserve"—and offered 175 lifetime leases on the houses in the Pumwani Extension at a reduced plot-holding fee. They were to be allowed to collect and keep the rents, but they could not dispose of their leases or pass them on to biological or designated heirs. It took over a year for the requisite number of Pangani landlords to accept this offer, and well over one hundred of those who did so were women, representing at least 90 percent of Pangani's women landlords. The remaining landlords took their 1,000/ compensation and built illegally elsewhere, a clear indication of their disdain for the state's policies and its notions of legality, or retreated to well-connected tendencies in Pumwani. For Pangani householders the new estate seemed designed to be the opposite of an African settlement; one said that the houses were built in a straight line, "as an example."[32] By 1938 the Extension became universally known as Shauri Moyo. Administrators took the name, and its immediate adoption, to mean that the landlords felt they had no real choices, a striking example of the official denial of squatters' settlements but also an example of Africans' ability to control the names of public places. But one former landlord said that the name meant that the landlords who went there were not forced to do so, although they were forced to leave Pangani.[33] "In those days it was better because the government informed people before you had to move, they gave you a date of when you had to move. . . you could even find out where you were being moved to."[34]

Forty years after the demolition of Pangani, former tenants recalled its community and organization. Landlords were, of course, neither detribalized nor deruralized: they were what every colonialist wished for every wage laborer, people who travelled between town and countryside regularly. Landlords maintained ties to both places. Salim Ibraham was a Pangani householder, born in Uganda; his mother "had a house in Pangani before he did." When Pangani was demolished he took his compen-

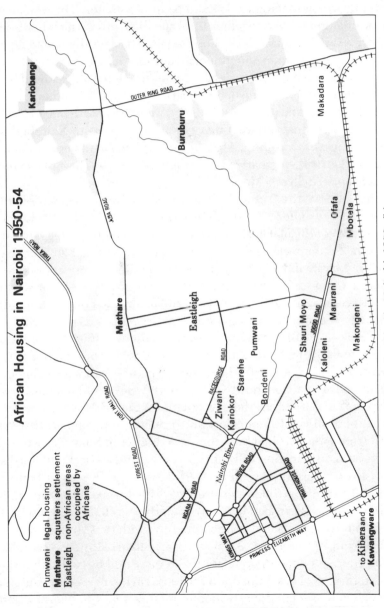

African Housing in Nairobi 1950-54

Pumwani — legal housing
Mathare — squatters settlement
Eastleigh — non-African areas occupied by Africans

Kariobangi

Buruburu

Makadara

OUTER RING ROAD

JUJA ROAD

THIKA ROAD

Mathare

Eastleigh

Ofafa

Mbotela

FORT HALL ROAD

FOREST ROAD

RACECOURSE ROAD

Ziwani

Kariokor

Starehe

Pumwani

Bondeni

Shauri Moyo

DOONO ROAD

Maruani

Makongeni

Kaloleni

NGARA ROAD

Nairobi River

RIVER ROAD

KINGS WAY

PRINCESS ELIZABETH WAY

MACHAKOS ROAD

to Kibera and Kawangware

African housing in Nairobi, 1950–54

sation and returned to Uganda; his mother, however, went to be a landlord in Shauri Moyo. On one of her many visits to her son she brought his recently widowed daughter back to Nairobi with her. The woman and her granddaughter lived together until she died, after which her granddaughter moved to Pumwani.[35] Long-term urban residents had equally far-flung networks and commitments. Fatuma Ali was the daughter of a Yao man from Malawi and a Kamba woman; she actually was raised by another Kamba couple. She divorced her first husband when her children were in their teens and married a man and went to live with him in Eldama Ravine. Her first husband went there to bring her back to Nairobi to witness her daughter's wedding. After her second husband's death she went to share a room with her married daughter and her daughter's husband in the newly opened Shauri Moyo.

In Shauri Moyo the "respectable nucleus" was put to work while their children were disinherited. In this way the social controls of Nairobi Islam, and even of the malaya form, would be carried over to the new estate without the clutter of class formation and community that had been so difficult to penetrate in Pangani. The former landlords were allowed to select their tenants, set the rents (in all but one-third of the houses, where the MNC set the rents), collect and keep them, for 4/ a month plot-holding fee. Money was not the object here: Shauri Moyo's 175 cement-block houses, built by a European contractor at a cost of 2,400/ to 3,300/ each, had been built by the MNC with a loan of £ 46,000 from the Kenya Government. The 175 landlords who came to Shauri Moyo were being paid, and paid well, to manage the MNC's property; they could not pass it on.[36] Many years later, however, the new tenants in Shauri Moyo conveniently ignored the history of demolition and removal and claimed that "rich women from Pangani" had built the stone houses in Shauri Moyo themselves,[37] in an affirmation of women's agency and African landlordism.

Who was supposed to live in that property? The fifty-eight houses in which rents were controlled were reserved for former Pangani tenants; they were supposed to pay between 7/ and 9/ each. In the rest of the houses rents were supposed to be competitive with those in Pumwani, between 19/ and 27/ a room.[38] But by the time Shauri Moyo was completed in 1938, Nairobi's African population had increased by twelve thousand, to forty thousand. The competition for rooms in the new estate must have been fairly intense, particularly among migrants new to Nairobi, and it seemed to many that "most of the people from Pangani went to Pumwani."[39] Those who went to Shauri Moyo had very specific reasons for doing so, however. "In those days there was a great deal of discrimination by the Swahilis against African Muslims. . . . in Pumwani there was only one mosque and it was dominated by Gunya and Digo men, so my mother decided to go to Shauri Moyo rather than be looked down upon as a Kikuyu Muslim in Pumwani."[40]

Structural Solutions

The MNC had not initially wanted to build Shauri Moyo in stone. They had only done so under pressure from Paterson of the Medical Department. He had originally been a sanitation officer and had long championed improved building materials as a way to order and govern African social life. While his staff frequently blamed insanitary conditions on the lack of supervision, Paterson had for several years hinted at an African potential stifled in unhealthy surroundings. As early as 1925 he claimed that "enlightened" farmers realized that the expenditure on good housing would be recouped in productivity,[41] and in 1930 wrote of Nairobi,

> times have changed since 1924 and even the casual laborer of today is not the red blanket savage of 1923. The boys in these dormitories, even the poorest of them, have now some ambition to be clean. Many are endeavoring to read and write and in many corners I saw laborers sitting with slates, and whatever may be thought of the value of the 3Rs at least it may be said that they might have been more dangerously occupied, and . . . given some facilities for study and recreation these boys would use it. As it is however they must sit among bugs and stale posho in filth and squalor. . . . sooner or later the beer shop must present greater attractions.[42]

But in the early 1930s Paterson had to battle official tendencies that wanted all Africans, no matter how industrious, clean, or ambitious, returned home rapidly. According to the MNAO, H. A. Carr, there was no reason "that one cannot expect more advanced natives, such as clerks, ex-non-commissioned officers, etc., to go back and live in the reserves." It would in fact be an advantage for "the uneducated" if "the more highly educated natives" could be made to "reside in the reserve when their work outside is done."[43] But Paterson wanted cities stabilized, not made more fluid than they already were. By 1938—the year before strikes paralyzed Mombasa and cement houses were finished in Shauri Moyo—Paterson argued that unhealthy buildings posed greater threats than beer halls, or even literate Africans. "To allow continued wattle and daub building in Nairobi," he announced, would result "not in economy of any kind either for the employer or the town, but in inefficiency, ill health, large expenditure on medical and public services, no small amount of social unrest, and no small danger of industrial and civil disturbance."[44] The ban Paterson introduced on temporary building materials brought together the divergent official goals of removal and sanitation: stone meant stability, not just of structures but of political and social institutions; it was also too expensive for most Africans to build in. Thus stone meant a degree of state control that could not be exerted over wattle and daub, corrugated iron, or wood. The same materials that could pacify a working class could ruin a group of landlords.

In the late 1930s this was a contradiction only to some members of the administration; it was a deliberate policy of the Medical Department. In 1938 a group of Kikuyu and Kamba Muslim "old Pangani landlords," represented by Shams-ud Deen, the Legislative Council member who had opposed the 1936 Pangani evictions, requested permission to build wattle-and-daub lodging houses in Pumwani. Among their supporters were E. B. Hosking, who as Nairobi's DC had advocated the hasty removal of these same landlords from Pangani in 1933 and now hoped that the MNC would relax its ban on wattle-and-daub housing so that these men could help alleviate the housing shortage, and the Financial Secretary of the MNC, who wrote that, while stone buildings were a "laudable ambition," they were "hopelessly out of relationship to the general standard of native income and . . . we must be satisfied with the good instead of the best."[45] Paterson's reply demanded once again that private employers subsidize better housing for their labor force, but did not speak at all to the health hazards of wattle and daub or even the new stone order. He responded instead with the official rhetoric of the early 1930s, in which helpless landlords required the protection of the state. The "best interests of these old Muslims" were not served by allowing them to spend £ 28 more than they had received in compensation on wattle-and-daub lodging houses, because "sooner or later they would again be required to move, and just as in the past they would once again find themselves in difficulties, and at a time when they would still be older than they were two years ago."[46] The purpose of stone structures in the late 1930s was to keep a labor force circumscribed—in places where they could read but not drink—and a landlord class excluded.

The State as Landlord

Sanitation, crime, and literacy all had a meaning to colonialists. Sickness and crime were both characteristics of African housing that could spread over to European areas—where Africans worked daily—and infect the population. Literacy was something quite different, even more menacing, a quality that could spread from Europeans to Africans without control. After 1936, when housing policy ceased to be a sanitation issue and became one of controlling African class formation and its related tensions, the state sometimes allowed itself to build in "very temporary materials." In 1946, when the rapid pace of public construction had been outstripped by squatters building in Kariobangi and Mathare, the state hastily built Marurani, between Shauri Moyo and the Railway estates, in wattle and daub, in order to provide 1,120 bedspaces at a subsidized 5/ per space. Within a year, Marurani developed a vibrant social life of brewers and antipolice riots, and was demolished in 1950–51, two years ahead of schedule.[47]

The colonial state of the wartime and postwar era was a very different landlord than it had been in the 1920s and 1930s, when it had been so ineffectual that decaying animals and bucket latrines were left unattended despite the continual complaints of the Medical Department.[48] The colonial state was, however, never fully in control of its older estates. In 1939 the African Advisory Council was established to involve respectable Africans in the government of the locations, but also to allow the state a toehold—largely through Africans from the coast—in Pumwani and Shauri Moyo.[49] The postwar public landlord invaded African private life in ways that private African landlords had never done. Crime—the meaning of which was to take on a special significance after 1946—is a telling example. By the early years of World War II, well-intentioned administrators blamed crime on slum conditions and the high rents private landlords charged: "when ten natives are crowded together in a room, the opportunities for petty thieving which may be the beginnings of a criminal career are as numerous as the frequency of such petty thieving shows."[50] But private landlords took care to socialize migrants: Wambui Murithi cautioned her young wartime watembezi tenants not to accept gifts from soldiers, lest they be liable to arrest for receiving stolen goods. In the 1930s and 1940s neighbors and landlords reported women suspected of infanticide to the police.[51] Public landlords took more drastic measures and restructured African living spaces. In 1947 Nairobi's Medical Officer of Health claimed that "Africans' hospitable nature" caused tenants to take in job-seeking relatives and friends and that many of these people were "too urban minded" to return home and so they "turn to a life of crime." Gorofani, the Municipality's newest housing estate, would halt this process—and save the MNC £ 15,000 in construction costs—by reducing the floor space of each room from the proposed fifty to forty square feet. This was only a "retrograde step" if one ignored the facts of Nairobi life for "mere theoretical ideas." Thus each of the expected five tenants per room in Gorofani, with "as much and probably more floor area than he 'enjoys' in the present grossly overcrowded quarters" (which, in Pumwani, had fourteen square feet more floor space), would be loath to accommodate friends there. If they did, "efficient supervision and enforced discipline would eliminate cases of illegal occupation."[52] Crime was to be contained by limiting the amount of space in which a male migrant would live.

Starting in the late 1930s housing was a way to construct or prohibit family life: the state built accommodation for over 8,700 Africans in eight estates (not counting the houses added to Pumwani and Shauri Moyo), rigidly divided between bachelor quarters (in the overwhelming majority) and family housing. The presence or absence of a kitchen referred not only to what the state expected working men to spend their money on, but to visions of male and female behavior. Men in dormitories were to have occasional relations with women who would cook for them, somewhere; the men who earned enough for family housing were to have wives—and specific rooms—for cooking their meals. Starting in 1939 administrators began to suggest that families alone were not a sufficient alternative to beer halls, but that the quality of communication within African families might be. In 1939 the Governor wrote to his successor that African women

> must receive education not only in cooking food and looking after babies, both of which I admit are very important, but also sufficient to be able to read native books and papers so they shall be able to talk on an equal footing with their menfolk. I believe the African who takes quite an intelligent interest in European affairs, gets fed up when he goes back to his hut and finds his wife can think and talk of nothing but maize, manure, and goats. Thereupon he goes off to his counterpart of the club. . . which may become a sort of talking shop, and possibly a centre of disaffection.[53]

Making wives companionable—disregarding the agreeable, saleable con-
versations of the malaya form—meant constructing urban housing appropriate for such families. The estranged, educated African man, falling
into dissent and violence because there was no one to talk to at home, became a powerful colonial fantasy, equalled only by the remarkable
qualities attributed to housing for married workers. The opening of the
houses for ninety-six Railway employees and their wives in 1938 was
hailed as a medical breakthrough: those houses alone were said to have
reduced the Landhies' number of venereal disease cases by one-third, or
677.[54] Such figures described not only the nature of colonial ideas about
African sexuality, but colonial fantasies about the power of stone houses to
shape African sexual behavior.

The new married residents of wartime and postwar housing estates
were to be totally unlike those families who were called "degenerate . . . hybrids" when the state sought to remove them from Kibera and
Pangani a decade before.[55] The new ideal was proposed by Colchester in
1941: men from Nyanza could bring their wives to town without risking
the loss of land rights, so that the Luo artisan, mainly in Railway employment, was "the healthiest figure in Nairobi in body and mind. . . . He is
usually accompanied by his wife and some children. He earns as good a
salary as the average clerk, he returns home for a longish leave every three
years or so, and looks forward to retiring on a gratuity after twenty years
or more of service."[56] Such families were to be "an urban working class"
given "the fundamental unit of association and community, the
home . . . created in bricks and mortar."[57] Perhaps equally important,
they were not supposed to be landlords themselves or stay in town once
they retired. These new families were to reside in houses designed with
specific spaces for sleeping and cooking and to have specific relationships
in which these tasks were to be performed. The new urban African families were to be literate, relatively well paid, and respectable. Indeed, the
locations' supervisory staff was Africanized to indicate the new respectability of literate, urban Africans. When dances at Memorial Hall in Pumwani were said to attract drunks, Dedan Githengi, the Welfare Officer for
the Locations, organized a dance to which only couples would be admitted, "an evening which the best type of African would not be ashamed to
attend and to bring his wife."[58] The new urban African families were to
have men who worked and women who cooked, families in which the services and obligations of the malaya form were concretized into ideas about
wage labor and its total reproduction, a regime so arduous that starting in

1947 many women left this kind of Nairobi monogamy and established themselves in malaya prostitution in Pumwani and Shauri Moyo.[59] In practice, however, nucleation was subverted as couples in Kaloleni brought wives' mothers or husbands' brothers' sons to live with them.[60]

But the amount of family accommodation built by the state was quite small, a mere 13 percent of the total housing constructed between 1940 and 1950. The rest was bachelors' quarters, "bedspaces" as they were known, with subsidized rents and catering to workers who earned between 50/ and 150/ per month; in contrast there was one housing estate for married workers who earned between 150/ and 350/, and two, Ziwani and Kaloleni, for workers earning 350/ to 500/.[61] What kind of social and civic life was envisioned in a city composed of estates of single, unskilled men and many fewer estates for married, well-off families? Communities were planned with "a measure of social control and to prevent the spread of unsatisfactory conditions"[62] without regard to ethnicity, despite half-hearted pleas in the administration to govern the city through tribal associations,[63] to be salary specific: people would live near those who earned what they earned. The state's desire for control, and its attempt to construct genders sparingly, in a benevolent image of English workers' families, had not effaced class differences among urban Africans; it made them concrete. The bonds of community, the sense of place and property that the state had been so eager to dismantle in the mid-1930s were apparently absent in the new estates, where men were linked only by their wages and their proximity to each other. The MNAO, Tom Askwith, observed that "responsible Africans" were concerned about crime in Nairobi and "the breakdown of morals and the disintegration of customary law."[64] The Superintendent of the African Locations, Tom Mbotela, complained about the number of armed gangs that made "the law-abiding resident afraid to go abroad at night." According to Askwith, in the past it had been easier to control the African locations not just because the population was smaller, but because the population was "by nature" more law-abiding: "Africans have now adopted an attitude of opposition."[65]

Such opposition and the pressures of the postwar housing shortage led some liberal voices in the administration to urge a return to private landlords. Askwith suggested that Africans be allowed to build small wattle-and-daub houses "sufficient for a family" and one or two lodgers,[66] thus limiting African accumulation as well; two years later Vasey also suggested that "a more healthy moral situation is likely to develop with a system of one or two lodgers in a family house."[67] Such housing, exactly like that available in the squatters' settlements of Kariobangi and Mathare, was never adopted by the state, but its rhetoric was clear: married couples were not only supposed to control each other but the labor force around them.

The final insult to the state's attempts to house male migrants came four months after Mau Mau was officially declared a State of Emergency. The settlers' *Sunday Post* blamed the revolt of the state's conceptualization of urban space: "there is no better breeding ground for crime, no better forum on which real and imaginary grievances can be ventilated and enlarged, than an overcrowded hovel of 'bedspaces' dimly lit by a flickering oil tin light, with nothing to do in the early hours of the evening after work but grumble."[68] Those communities of working men, those estates without landlords or brewers or prostitutes, bred dissent.

One of the state's solutions to a crisis engendered by "the concrete forest"[69] of their own construction—social and material—was to reinvent African private landlords. By 1953 there were calls to allow Africans the civic pride and responsibilities that came from property ownership:[70] Pumwani was to be reproduced in a much more expensive version. In 1953 Makadara was opened as an estate in which loyalist or rehabilitated Africans could build houses and hold them in usufruct. To make sure that Makadara would not become like Pumwani, the state allowed plot-holders five years in which to build their houses, in materials and for a price set by the City Council. Most of the plot-holders and tenants were Kikuyu.[71] As for its own housing, the colonial state added what was possibly an unintended degree of menace to the estates it built for African civil servants in 1954. They were named Ofafa and Mbotela, for two African high-ranking civil servants assassinated by Mau Mau.

Conclusions

In the invention of the colonial state, landlords were tired, old, dependent on official goodwill and tolerance; in reality, African landlords were dynamic, committed, with close ties to their tenants and communities. Until the 1930s the imaginary landlords of official rhetoric and the real landlords of African settlement rarely met: policy was constructed for the former and routinely subverted by the latter. Private landlords built, owned, and supervised African housing in Nairobi; Pumwani was based on a preexisting system in which landlords were autonomous. They set the rents they charged, for example, and were not criticized for this until 1939. They evicted the poor and reduced money wages at monthly intervals, something pass laws could not do at any point in their enforcement.

The state appreciated all these benefits, even when it did not acknowledge them. This contradiction was deployed in housing policy again and
again: African property was held in usufruct (no small contradiction in an
economy where all migrants are supposed to return home), and in the
1930s at least, legal settlements were demolished more often than were
illegal ones. In 1939, after three years of criminalizing and denigrating
landlords, the state attempted in Shauri Moyo to make landlords do their
work without the promise of inheritance and community. But for all the
rhetoric about pride and place and taking care of the helpless, private
landlords were seen as the most-reliable sources of social control. During
Mau Mau, when the state itself was under attack from Kikuyus, it returned to private landlords, and allowed Kikuyus to build in usufruct in
Makadara.

The state's own forays into housing Africans revealed colonial assumptions about African gender relations and their place in making a stable
labor force efficient and productive. Officials tried to control African
male migrants' behavior without landlords or communities. By the late
1940s changes in space requirements in migrant laborers' housing were
introduced as a way to restructure the "hospitable" nature of Africans.
The postwar segmenting of Nairobi into housing for unskilled single men
and housing for skilled workers' families showed how far the state would
go—and how much it would spend—to construct African social life in an
attempt to create more polite labor relations than had been seen in Mombasa and Nairobi in the late 1930s. The state hoped that skilled workers
would become dependent on place and property, not because they owned
it but because it came with the job. African landlords, however, had no
illusions about the reliability of wage labor; they did not see housing as a
way to structure gender and family relationships. Their social relations,
the complicated interactions of coastal Muslim elites and new immigrants,
constructed gender. Indeed, if they were prostitutes, they had their own
ideas about the meaning of gender and the role of men and women in
their lives, and these ideas depended on their form of prostitution, not
their property ownership. But these women, and male landlords, built
housing as a way to join the ranks of the urban petty bourgeoisie, to construct classes.

7

Prostitution in Nairobi during
World War II, 1939–45

When the Italians were here . . . those were the wealthy days for women. I would work cutting spices in the daytime, come home, wash, and go out looking for men at night. You know, work comes when there is a problem, and the war was a problem and it gave work, and it is funny, really, because when there was a war, and the Italians were here, I had no problems.

Zaina Kachui

Historians have observed how a large military presence expands the demand for prostitution and a wide range of temporary relationships: prostitutes provide companionship for men otherwise denied women friends, relieve the grim boredom of barracks life, and provide a social life that does not remove men from their working units.[1] The nature and content of this expansion, however, and its changing relationship to the kind of prostitution offered nonmilitary men has not been fully explored. It is necessary to find out which aspects of prostitution expand and which contract to meet the special conditions and burdens of wartime. In this chapter I show what it meant for prostitutes to have their services, sometimes in a truncated form, so greatly in demand.[2] For these reasons, wartime brought renewed vigor to official concerns about who prostitutes were, what diseases they carried, and what social ills they represented.

The War and Wage Labor

The war increased Nairobi's labor requirements rapidly: in 1939 there were said to be 41,000 Africans in the city; in 1941 their civilian numbers were estimated at 70,000 and in 1944 at 66,500. The numbers of non-

Africans in Nairobi also increased during the war, thus increasing the number of households employing African domestic servants. The Indian population of Nairobi was 17,700 in 1939; by 1941 it had risen to 22,000. In March 1942 the government blocked Indians returning to India and began what was in effect the conscription of skilled Indian workers and artisans, most of whom became permanent employees of the Railway, residing in Nairobi. In this way the Indian population of Nairobi reached almost 32,000 in 1944. The war effort also increased the number of Europeans in Nairobi: there were 6,800 living there in 1939, 8,000 by 1941, and 10,431 by 1944.[3]

There was also a large military presence in Kenya during the war: three Royal Air Force bases (one in Eastleigh); Royal Engineers at Thika, Eldoret, and Nairobi; twenty thousand Italian POWs; four camps in and around Nairobi housing King's African Rifles (East and Central African soldiers) in training programs and in transit to and from combat in Southeast Asia; and a total of nine thousand troops of the Gold Coast Regiment (GCR) of the Royal West African Frontier Force (RWAFF) involved in the defense of East Africa from June 1940 to October 1941. GCR troops, called Golgos in Nairobi, were rumored to be violent and dangerous off the battlefield. Actual numbers are difficult to ascertain, as the War Office did not maintain centralized records of how many African recruits served in each regiment, but by the end of December 1940 there were seventy thousand African and European troops in British East Africa, the plurality of which were in Kenya.[4]

All of these men were housed in camps that employed African labor as cooks and cleaning staff, at wages well above those paid by Kenya's Europeans and Indians. This "introduced an element of competition out of all proportion to the needs and commonsense of the situation," editorialized *The Mombasa Times* in 1942. Mombasa had the largest military population of any city in Kenya, and letters to the editor "complained that servants were demanding 40/ from settlers since they could get 30/ from the army with much less work."[5] Not only did the military presence in Kenya lead to rapid, if irregular, increases in the wages of privately employed domestic staff (see table 5), but the increased European and Indian populations of Nairobi increased the number of men earning those wages. The number of servants employed in wartime European households was such that a 1944 ordinance restricted the number of servants Europeans could hire to three per European.[6]

In 1941 there were 22,054 domestic workers in Kenya, rising to nearly 30,000 by the end of the war, nearly twice the 1939 number. Ninety thou-

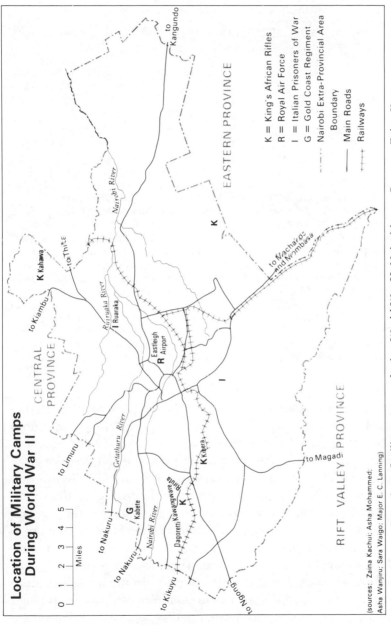

Location of Military Camps During World War II

CENTRAL PROVINCE

EASTERN PROVINCE

RIFT VALLEY PROVINCE

K = King's African Rifles
R = Royal Air Force
I = Italian Prisoners of War
G = Gold Coast Regiment
Nairobi Extra-Provincial Area
Boundary
Main Roads
Railways

Miles
0 1 2 3 4 5

(sources: Zaina Kachui; Asha Mohammed;
Asha Wanjiru; Sara Waigo: Major E. C. Lanning)

to Kangundo
to Thika
to Machakos and Mombasa
to Magadi
to Ngong
to Kikuyu
to Nakuru
to Nakuru
to Limuru
to Kiambu

Nairobi River
Riaruaka River
Getathuru River
Nairobi River

K Kahawa
I Ruaraka
R Eastleigh Airport
I
K Kibera
K Kibera
K
G Kabete
Dagoreti Kawangware
Riruta

Location of military camps during World War II, Nairobi area. Sources: Zaina Kachui, Asha Mohammed, Asha Wanjiru, Sara Waigo E. C. Lanning.

TABLE 5　Average Wages in Shillings per Month,
without Value of Rations, Nairobi

	1939	1940	1941	1942	1943	1944	1945
Domestic service[a]							
Kitchen/garden staff	17	21	22	23	26	29	32
House servant	18	26	34	36	40	41	38
Cook/barman	23	37	40	64	47	60	54
Unskilled KUR	25	30	36	45	45		
Semiskilled	27		24	40	24	45	45
Artisan	70		60[b]	73[b]	105[b]	78	75
Driver			70	80	80	80	90
Clerical		60	60	48	48	101	102

SOURCES:　Farouk Mohammed, Calfonya, 13 March 1977: Thomas Mukama,
Eastleigh, 10 March 1977: John Mwakalili, Shauri Moyo, 6 March 1977; Joseph
Njoroge, Pumwani, 26 March 1977; Ahmed Hussein, Pumwani, 1 April 1977; Salim
Hamisi, Pumwani, 29 March 1977; Ziro wa Bogosha, Pumwani, 18 March 1977;
Odhiambo Okinyi, Shauri Moyo, 23 February 1977; Omolo Okumu, Pumwani, 2 March
1977; Richard Mulembe, Pumwani, 18 February 1977; Mutiso Katumbe, Pumwani, 16
March 1977; Opiyo Oyugi, Pumwani, 28 March 1977; Habib Hasan, Pumwani, 2 April
1977; Michael P. Cowen and J. R. Newman, "Real Wages in Central Kenya, 1924–
1974," essay, Nairobi, 1975, pp. 27–29.
NOTE:　The number of informants is very small, and these figures are at best
guidelines to African earnings.
[a]Wages at time of engagement, primarily in European households or hotels.
[b]Includes self-employed Africans, whose earnings varied greatly.

sand Africans were employed in agricultural wage labor in 1945. In that
year 39 percent of Nairobi workers were employed in private, nonagricultural enterprises. Clayton and Savage have asserted that these figures represented a new sophistication in unskilled workers seeking the
best-paying jobs,[7] but in fact wartime wages for unskilled Kenya and
Uganda Railway (KUR) employees were consistently higher than were
wages in unskilled domestic service. Nevertheless, during the war unskilled domestic service offered greater opportunities for advancement—
with greater rewards—than any other form of wage labor. With the increase in the number of households requiring servants at relatively high
wages, occupation switching and promotion within the household were
common occurrences, and it is possible to envision a competitive situation
previously unknown—or previously unidentifiable—among Nairobi domestic workers. A charitable cook or employer could teach an unskilled
African kitchen attendant the skills and recipes he could take to a cook's
job elsewhere; in 1942 this would have enabled a man to double his wage.[8]

Similarly, gardeners could sometimes learn to become syces. Expertise could be delayed or withheld as well. House servants and garden servants in less-affluent households did not have many opportunities to become skilled, and my data suggest that they changed jobs less frequently than did cooks or kitchen servants. But domestics' earnings were high enough in the war years for many men to purchase sewing machines or scrap tin and go into business for themselves.[9] Although certain wartime malaya practices were organized to reduce tensions between the soldiers and POWs they befriended, it is possible that such conduct was not extended to the domestic servants who visited malaya women: the competitive elements of servants' wartime employment were minimized by patronage and dependency within the workplace.

As table 5 shows, clerical wages—earned by 5 percent of the African work force in 1942—were competitive with those of skilled domestic servants only between 1942 and 1944. A war bonus, for example, was extended to African civil servants only in January 1943.[10] In comparison, soldiers were paid very well: KAR and RWAFF troops destined for combat received 45/ a month, and the East African Pioneers (garrisoned in camps primarily in North Africa and the Middle East) received, before deductions, 32/ a month, most of which seems to have been sent back to the soldiers' households. In 1943 the District Commissioner in Machakos estimated that soldiers had sent over two million shillings home.[11]

The first of Kenya's eventual twenty thousand Italian POWs surrendered to troops of the Third GCR and Fifth KAR just over the border in Ethiopia in 1940. They were frightened of Ethiopian reprisals and were by all accounts fairly relieved to be captured by a British army and willingly walked into internment camps in Kenya, a few of which they helped build. According to Thomas Colchester, then MNAO, the colony simply "had no resources to be nasty to them," and they were let out in groups to work on projects, primarily road work and construction. The POWs were treated above and beyond the letter of the Geneva Convention: when pasta proved impossible to import, an Indian family began to produce it with the labor of five POWs released into their employ to improve its quality; when musicians among the POWs volunteered to form an orchestra, instruments were loaned to them by administrators and settlers. After 1942 over fifteen thousand POWs were outside of Nairobi. Many were used as drivers and machinists and received small amounts of spending money for their journeys. With such treatment, only two Italians escaped: they climbed Mount Kenya, raised an Italian flag, climbed down, and surrendered.[12]

The war only marginally increased the demand for female wage labor. In 1944, when by the most conservative estimates there were over five thousand households employing servants in Nairobi, the total number of women employed in nonagricultural wage labor in all of Kenya was 2,218—and this figure includes casual and monthly employees.[13] This figure can only represent a large number of English and Goan women employed as ayahs. In Nairobi a few women could work preparing spices for resale to the army, as Zaina Kachui did. Women were hired daily and were paid by the weight of the chilies and ginger they gut; it was said that the most a woman could earn this way was 1/25 a day. Few women would have chosen to work thirty days each month, but working fifteen days would have meant earning 18/75. This was extra money to be sure, more than half an unskilled worker's wage and a sum that would have allowed prostitutes to increase their wartime profits or to choose their customers more selectively than they might otherwise have done.

Not only were African money wages high during the war, but rents began to decline slightly after 1939. In Pumwani a single room cost between 13/ and 15/ between 1940 and 1945, for people who had been in Pumwani a while, with slightly higher rents for newcomers.[14] This reduction was in part due to the increased revenues some landlords received from their outside rooms, and in part to the illegal African-owned wattle-and-daub houses being built daily in the squatter settlements and Mathare, Kawangware, and Buruburu during the war, offering tenants rents low enough to force some Pumwani landlords to reduce their rents.[15] The promise of wartime employment seems to have increased the number of tenants per room in Pumwani, so that lower rents were shared by fewer occupants than there had been in the late 1930s. Nevertheless, three semiskilled laborers in a 15/ room would have paid between 11 and 25 percent of their monthly wages in rent, or about the same proportion as late-1930s tenants in Pumwani paid. Rents in Shauri Moyo ranged from 12/ to 25/ per room between 1940 and 1943, but sharing rooms could reduce the cost per tenant there as well. By contrast, the rooms rented specifically to prostitutes in Buruburu cost 15/ during the war. African rents in Eastleigh rose from 22/ in 1940 to 35/ in 1943/44,[16] but it is unlikely that these rooms were occupied by laboring men.

Commodity prices rose steadily during the war, at an annual average rate of 13 percent. One pound of maize meal that cost 0/4 in 1938 was 0/10 in 1945; a pound of rice cost 0/19 in 1940 and 0/31 in 1943; potatoes were 0/6 per pound in 1940 and 0/13 in 1943. Bread cost an average 0/35 per pound during the war and thus was hardly an alternative to locally grown starches. Cooking fat doubled in price between 1938 and 1945, when it cost 1/75 a pound. The price of sugar rose slightly and gradually to 0/25 in 1945. The prices of beans and cabbage were highest in 1942, but by the end of the war both cost just slightly more per pound than they had in 1940, 0/17 and 0/13 respectively.[17] Milk, starting in 1940 legally sold only from inspected premises, after twenty years of complaints that African hawkers diluted the milk they sold in Nairobi, cost 0/25 per pint carton in 1940 and 0/29 in 1945.[18] These consistently higher prices meant that there were no foodstuffs that Nairobi residents could switch to in order to save money. A Government report of 1942 claimed that "lower paid servants of both Government and Railway must be in a state of malnutrition. He feeds well for a short period after wages have been paid but inadequately for a variable period before payment day."[19] This could only have meant a diet that was proportionately more expensive and sporadic for Nairobi's privately employed domestic servants and most of the city's semiskilled wage laborers, who earned less than unskilled Railway employees. Moreover, the price on nonfood essentials rose faster than food prices did: a blanket cost between 2/ and 5/ in 1938 and 8/85 in 1945; a cake of soap cost 0/22 in 1940 and 0/55 in 1945.[20]

A series of droughts in central Kenya between 1942 and 1945, aggravated by African producers' reluctance to plant maize, given the low prices of marketing boards guaranteed for it, led the government to begin rationing wheat, bread, rice, and maize starting in March 1943. In Nairobi, wage laborers' registration for the scheme was put on their kipandes; those not formally employed could obtain food through traders' shops, Pumwani and Shauri Moyo landlords, churches, and, for Luo, Luo Union, which had been recognized by the MNAO in 1941. Black markets thrived: women from Kiambu and Machakos carried vegetables and charcoal to Pumwani and Shauri Moyo daily, where they resold their produce to shopkeepers who prospered during the war.[21] Men and women not legally employed and living in Mathare and Eastleigh frequently purchased black market foodstuffs in Ruaraka from hawkers who came from Kiambu and Thika. Africans who lived in Kawangware and Buruburu either had small gardens of their own or purchased food from neighbors who did.[22]

The Essential Commodities Regulations reduced the rate of food price increases but also served to increase food prices for those who were not formally employed. After 1943 malaya prostitutes living in Pumwani and Shauri Moyo were often unable to acquire enough food daily to make a profit on the meals they provided for the men who visited them. Malaya

women living in Eastleigh, particularly Kikuyu women, could provide
meals and appeared to have more success increasing the price of a night-
long visit by about 2/ over what was often charged in Pumwani.[23] Christian prostitutes, wherever they lived, could obtain food through churches.
Haya women, however, who were said—by their Muslim neighbors at
least—to be fairly regular churchgoers, did not substantially increase
their prices during the war, but they did not provide food for their customers either.[24]

During World War II, occupation switching—in and out of Nairobi,
and in and out or upwards in domestic service—was the primary mechanism with which Africans could raise their average monthly wages to keep
ahead of the increase in prices, especially when the increases in food
prices were maintained after 1943. This produced a large and mobile
male work force, of which soldiers were a substantial part. Prostitution in
Nairobi changed to accommodate the size and special needs and characteristics of that work force.

Juvenile Prostitution

Teenage watembezi prostitutes were first observed in 1937/38, when the
roundabout linking River Road and Quarry Road was said to be frequented by fourteen- and fifteen-year-olds, most of whom were Kikuyu.[25] Before the outbreak of the war, however, administrators did not
seem overly concerned with this phenomenon. Indeed, the Davies Report
did not call it a problem, but suggested that such immigration was the inevitable consequence of African housing in Nairobi. But Davies's successor as MNAO, Thomas Colchester, was appalled by the presence of
juvenile streetwalkers; mainly because of their youth, but also because the
form of their labor connected them to Kikuyu taxi drivers, who he saw as
involved in "every kind of illegality" and "up to every trick"—robbery and
fencing stolen goods—during the war. European soldiers reputedly
asked drivers to take them to Eastleigh, where the juveniles walked the
streets adjacent to the RAF base. Under Colchester's direction, the young
watembezi were frequently arrested for pass-law violations; those judged
to be under fifteen were not formally charged but were sent home as soon
as possible. Many such teenagers were arrested several times over; some,
Colchester claimed, as they returned to Nairobi: they were especially vulnerable because of their youth and their presence on the streets. Colchester described the control and repatriation of juvenile watembezi in the
language of urban sanitation: "it was like streetsweeping."

How serious a problem was juvenile prostitution, what kind of issue was it, and what did a sudden administrative interest in its control signify? While nineteenth-century reformers and twentieth-century historians have been shocked by the prostitution of teenage girls in the streets and brothels of burgeoning cities,[26] even when the actual number of young girls was small and nonexistent, Mark Thomas Connelly has argued that political concerns over juvenile or child prostitution conveniently "reduced the complexities of urban prostitution to the problem of victimized children."[27] Juvenile and child prostitution was, in many periods of reformist zeal, a phony target, one that allowed states in which sexuality and social reproduction were diffidently conflated to initiate repressive measures against sexuality. Officials' well-motivated concerns about juvenile prostitutes translated into actions that weakened young women's ability to reproduce their families and lineages.[28]

Juvenile prostitution was not new in wartime Nairobi, although the scale of juvenile prostitution probably increased at that time. How young were these women? Many were Kikuyu and thus would have been between ten and fifteen at the time of their circumcisions, the most-reliable means for establishing their ages. But by the 1930s women's circumcision years' names were localized almost to the homestead,[29] so there is no firm way to establish which name occurred when. Sometimes women knew the more widespread name of the boys' circumcision year in which they were born, and thus a date could be established. Moreover, given the number of immigrant women engaged in wartime prostitution, women's perceptions of their own and others' ages are also important. Wangui Fatuma was born in 1922 and ran away from her squatter family when she was between fourteen and sixteen. She feared arrest so much that she became somewhat of an expert on its preconditions, and observed that the women who were arrested during the war were younger than she was, which would indicate that some of these juveniles may have been in their late teens. Gathiro wa Chege went to Nairobi from Murang'a early in 1939, when she was nineteen or twenty. She said, "We were young so men came to us" when she stood on the street in Eastleigh. Either she realized this later and passed the insight on to a researcher, or her youth had been remarked on at the time: in either case she thought herself young during the two years she practiced the watembezi form in Eastleigh.

Neither Colchester nor I have statistics about the ages of Kikuyu prostitutes, but my data suggest that many of the women from central Kenya were in their mid- to late twenties when they went to Nairobi during the war.[30] Some of the women were of course younger, but it is possible that they did not represent the majority of wartime Kikuyu prostitutes, or what many teenage prostitutes returned home after the war. Faith Wangoi went to Nairobi in 1939/40 from Nyeri shortly after her circumcision, when she would have been between thirteen and sixteen. Edwina Kamau was born in 1925 in Kiambu and was on the streets of Eastleigh by 1940. Beatrice Nyambura went to Nairobi at fourteen and worked as a laundress for an Indian midwife; the year before she had earned 6/ per month picking coffee in Kiambu. On the whole, women in their mid- to late twenties went to Nairobi because they were alienated from their families; teenage prostitutes went because they were not. Sara Waigo, a twenty-seven- or twenty-eight-year-old widow who went to Nairobi form Murang'a in 1939, said, "Don't think if someone was helping me in my home I could have left it," but Nyambura went home to Kiambu several times a month, and members of her family visited her regularly.

Although methods for establishing women's ages are not exact, it does not seem that these juvenile watembezi were any younger than were women who were beginning to practice the malaya form in the same years. Christian women born in Pumwani tended to know the year of their births, so it is possible to know their ages at various points in their careers. Tabitha Waweru, for example, was fourteen at the start of the war; by the time she was seventeen she was engaging in very sophisticated streetwalking in central Nairobi. Margaret Githeka began prostitution at fifteen or sixteen; she had two children by the time she married at nineteen. Both of these women were the daughters of householders; neither was driven to prostitution by parental neglect or parental poverty. Both said that the decision to become a prostitute had been based on other decisions about accumulation, property, and inheritance, and the likelihood of spousal support in colonial Nairobi. "A woman could become rich if she believes in working hard and saves her money and at long last she would be able to buy a house."[31] The issue here is not the maturity with which teenagers made such decisions, but that these decisions were made at fifteen, unmade at seventeen or nineteen with respective husbands, and made and unmade again as relationships and financial planning dictated—especially as children added a new dimension to questions of inheritance, obligations, and property. This was equally true of watembezi women, regardless of their age: Faith Wangoi returned to Nyeri with a child and savings before the end of the war and stayed there until 1963; Edwina Kamau went from prostitution to hawking to prostitution to hawking to shopkeeping after the war. Gathiro wa Chege left all but the most occasional prostitution with Indians in 1941 to become a licensed hawker

when she went to live with a man, with whom she stayed until 1956. Beatrice Nyambura supported her own child and her sister's children with her
earnings as a laundress, ayah, and prostitute. She eventually decided to
become a prostitute because it paid the most money: "it wasn't likely that a
woman would get a job that paid as much as twenty-five boyfriends." The
young Kikuyu girls who shocked administrators at the Kariokor roundabout in the late 1930s or in Eastleigh in the early 1940s were about the
same age or older as the deferential practitioners of a revitalized malaya
form in Pumwani. This did not represent any decline in African morals or
age at marriage—which seems to have been at its 1978 mean of just under
eighteen[32]—but rather the early age at which women assumed adult responsibilities, both for themselves and their families.

Who were these teenagers? The rhetoric about young runaways, cast
adrift in heartless cities, alone and unprotected, never to return home,
conjured up an idyllic image of rural life that could be easily contrasted to
the city where young girls met their ruin. Anxieties about runaway daughters enabled African men—more vocally after the war than before—to
sentimentalize agrarian life and rural families. The specifically Kenyan
objections to juvenile prostitution contained an appeal for more bucolic
and authoritarian solutions to the relationships of migrants and women
and slums. It is perhaps significant that the official who was most concerned about juvenile prostitutes was also concerned with maintaining African "units of social cohesion." Colchester claimed he had recognized the
first African ethnic association because a "tribe" was a family, a "unit of
association" and loyalty. Davies, his predecessor, the man who did not object to "the immigration . . . of young Kikuyu girls," had opposed ethnic
associations and had refused to recognize Luo Union.[33] The official in-
stitutionalization of "tribes" during World War II reflected a growing official belief in the ability of rural society to solve the complex problems of
poverty, landlessness, and forced marriage.[34]

What happened to these young women when they went to Nairobi may
not have been as desperate as the rhetoric of runaways often implies. Even
in a Nairobi of seventy thousand Africans young women did not drop out
of sight; instead they sought people who spoke their language, and they
tended to find people who either came from the same area as they did, or
people who could easily point out such men and women. The home a
woman had left behind had a different meaning when deployed in Nairobi. When Gathiro wa Chege went to Pumwani, she found another
woman from Murang'a who also "had nowhere to live and was sleeping on
a veranda but together we went to a house owned by another woman from

Murang'a, and she gave us a small room at 18/," a bargain for 1939. Edwina Kamau stayed with a woman her brother had known. Margaret Githeka said that the women who came from Kiambu to Pumwani were invariably seen by someone they knew from home. Some women had a healthy fear of such urban networks. Wangui Fatuma did not want to return to her family and the marriage they planned for her; in about 1939 she went to Mombasa because she heard that a relative of her father was working in Nairobi: she was sure he would find her and take her home.

All of these women were Kikuyu, and the relative ease with which they settled in the capital revealed the growing presence of a large Kikuyu community in Nairobi at the start of World War II. By 1947 55 percent of the legal work force in Nairobi was Kikuyu,[35] and it is likely that an even higher proportion of the illegal one was comprised of men who spent part of the week in Kiambu or Murang'a and part of the week in Nairobi. The extent of Kikuyu social life in Nairobi was such that Sara Waigo, going to Shauri Moyo in 1940, got by speaking Kikuyu and did not begin to learn Swahili until the mid-1950s. Many women used ethnic communities to join new communities: Naomi Kayengi, a Gisu from Uganda, did not stay with other Ugandans in Pumwani, but lived rent free with an old Nandi woman for whom she cooked and cleaned, as arranged by a friend of her late husband's sister. Many other women, but by no means a large proportion of immigrant women, became Muslims.[36]

Watembezi Prostitution

Supply and demand are only part of what makes prostitution profitable, but it is in wartime watembezi prostitution that their interaction can perhaps best be seen, and not be overestimated. Put simply, the war increased the number of women engaged in watembezi prostitution and decreased the age at which women first practiced the watembezi form. For the most part, Nairobi's streets had been the terrain of the experienced because of police surveillance;[37] the young women who went alone to River Road in the late 1920s were arrested for vagrancy until they learned their way around the police. But as the numbers of men on the streets increased, and as police priorities shifted away from solicitation, women seem to have taken to the streets in unprecedented numbers. The risk of arrest, earnings, physical safety, and work relationships of wartime watembezi women varied not according to supply and demand, but by which streets they walked. Arrests of juvenile watembezi took place in Eastleigh and on the main roads linking Eastleigh to Kiambu and Thika. Older watembezi women were sometimes arrested, but wartime judges generally considered the arresting officers to be rejected suitors, so these women's fines remained relatively small.[38] None of this, however, should be taken to mean that juvenile and older watembezi prostitutes in other parts of Nairobi did not fear being arrested and act on those fears, regardless of the policy or efficiency of the Nairobi police.

The women who were considered the wealthiest wartime prostitutes began their careers with watembezi prostitution in Eastleigh and, to a lesser extent, Government Road. These were virtually all Christian Kikuyu women, and some of them—Ruth Nyokabi, Mary Nduta, and Margaret Wainana are the best-known examples—went on to even greater financial successes after the war's end. According to women who claimed to have walked the streets with them—perhaps a fact, perhaps a common exaggeration—these women were born around 1925 and were on the streets by about 1942 at the latest, or when they were about seventeen.[39] These women and perhaps a dozen others, mainly Kikuyu, but some Kamba and Kalenjin, said to be older, owned individual houses in Eastleigh by 1947.[40]

It is easy enough to dismiss these successes by pointing out how small a proportion of wartime watembezi ever bought houses or cars with their earnings; nevertheless, they represent financial gains far greater than any previously realized from prostitution. The success of women like Ruth Nyokabi and Mary Nduta demonstrated how much money even a small proportion of women might earn, and how much of that money could be earned by walking in Eastleigh and Government Road. Malaya and waziwazi women who remained in Pumwani during the war reported receiving between 0/25 and 2/ from African civilians for short-time, 3/ from African soldiers, 5/ from British soldiers, and from 2/ to 5/ from POWs. These amounts seem consistent with the going rates charged at army camps after 1942. Watembezi women and their African customers reported short-time prices between 1/ and the more frequent 2/, which was the wartime short-time price in Quarry Road. Short-time prices in Eastleigh, however, were 5/ for African civilians and POWs (who do not seem to have gone there in large numbers), while soldiers of all races paid nearly twice as much.[41] Even without an increase in their volume of business, the women who lived in Eastleigh and those who went there for watembezi prostitution could earn substantially more than other wartime prostitutes.

Prostitutes in Nairobi had always known that hard work and diligent savings could make them wealthy—providing the state did not demolish their houses without compensation—but wartime watembezi prostitution moved prostitutes' accumulation well beyond the realm of mud houses in squatters' settlements. Part of this had to do with women actively seeking European men, and their awareness that white men had more money than did African men. Prior to World War II prostitutes had treated each white customer as a windfall, as someone who came when his servant remembered where a woman lived. Some women continued to do this during World War II. Mwana Himani bint Ramadhani knew that European men paid more because "they had the most money," but never ventured out of Pumwani to find them. Neither did Miriam Musale, but taxi drivers and African soldiers brought white customers to her. When they did not know any Swahili, the Africans "talked for them" and negotiated a price double the one they themselves were charged for short-time. Ibrahima binti Musa also stayed in Pumwani during the last years of the war, and taxi drivers sometimes brought white men to her: "these men knew many women; if they found you on the day an mzungu wanted a woman and on that day you needed money, then you went with him." Europeans were not seen as special or wealthy or generous; they were men like any others, more cautious in approach, perhaps, useful on a "day you needed money" but not worth going out and looking for. Similarly, Asha Mohammed lived in Shauri Moyo during the war; she had a number of white customers but no real sense of the profits available from them. Indeed, she worried that the clothing and furniture white men gave her would make African men think she was too expensive for them to approach. These women did not deliberately seek out European men, and of the four, only Asha Mohammed acquired property.

But the younger, more-aggressive watembezi women saw things differently. They saw European men as rich, generous, and possessing access to the state that could, by a simple piece of paper, legitimate, or at least enhance, prostitution. These were the women who went regularly to Eastleigh and Government Road to find white men. Although there was no consensus on the prices Europeans paid during the war, it was generally held that they paid substantially more than did Indians—who paid between 5/ and 7/ short-time—and reports of 30/ from European civilians were not uncommon. Europeans also gave food in addition to cash. Moreover, before 1945 Europeans were said to be more tolerant of small children than Africans were.[42] The women who could systematically meet white men could do very well for themselves.

Many of the women who deliberately set out to find white men were in their late teens during the war. Tabitha Waweru was typical, if ingenuous, in her description of how she and her friends—two of whom she insisted were Ruth Nyokabi and Mary Nduta—would go and look for Europeans, and the advantages that such men could bring to her practice of the watembezi form.

> Because the police didn't bother us in the daytime, we used to go to Government Road. We would meet white men while they were shopping. If you knew a bit of English it helped . . . he would say "show me your house" and then you'd tell him how to get to your house, or even take him there, that's better . . . in those days no mzungu felt shame to go with a dirty woman from Majengo. . . . When he met other wazungu, or the police, he would say "she is my ayah." Wazungu were clever people; he'd write a letter to show you were working in his house; you could go to Eastleigh, anywhere, during the night when you looked for men and not have any trouble with the police, even though you were not working for him at all, he was just one of your boyfriends. And when you parted with that white man he would not ask for the letter back. . . . They were the ones who showed us how to eat biscuits, they were the first people who brought roast meat for us women, and eggs. They'd give us food in addition to money, but they never insisted we feed them; they'd just buy food for us. Wazungu men said they didn't care if we were poor and our houses were dirty, when they liked you, you could become rich.

This is a description of very serious, very deliberate prostitution: a young women whose watembezi prostitution in one place at one time of day enabled her to make walking the streets safer in another part of Nairobi at another time of day. Sometimes Waweru took her toddler, his hair combed "like the Afro style you see today," with her to Government Road in the daytime because "wazungu like to see babies" and the police would be less suspicious of her. She also took the initiative in speaking her desired customers' language. Elsewhere in Nairobi, the absence of a common language kept short-time prices low. The war brought many Europeans to Kenya for the first time, and watembezi of that era referred to white man's skill in African languages as a gauge of what he might be expected to pay: "if a white man speaks good Swahili, you can be sure he learned it from an African man who taught him African prices."[43]

Watembezi believed that their associations with Europeans could offer protection as well as money and food. Wartime watembezi agreed that a letter "proving" employment in a European household was the best protection a prostitute could have. After 1942 Gathiro wa Chege used her hawker's license "to go to River Road and look for Asian men with cars . . . with that license you know the police could not arrest me . . . that way I got my own money." The women who did not go to River Road or Government Road, usually women in their twenties, tried other methods to avoid the risk of arrest. Some women did not go out at all at night.[44] Others went out at night only with military men—because "the police . . . feared the KAR; if they saw you with a KAR man they would not stop you"—or left secure accommodation in Pumwani to live nearer KAR camps.[45]

After the completion of the RAF base in Eastleigh in 1940, military men and watembezi began to congregate there, and soon European men specifically interested in finding prostitutes went there as well. Some went to the steps of the Pumwani Maternity Hospital, built in the early 1930s, where off-work taxi and rickshaw drivers would find women for them, almost at random.[46] Rickshaws were made illegal in 1942, amid groundless but grandiose accusations of pimping—one rickshaw man was known as "kingi ya malaya" in 1941–42, although it would seem that this title was bestowed on him by men, or by himself, and not by prostitutes—after a year of African complaints to the MNAO that rickshaws were demeaning.[47] This gave Nairobi's European- and Indian-owned, African-driven taxis a monopoly on ferrying men in and out of Eastleigh ad Pumwani. Taxi drivers were not without radical politics, but they were probably not as criminally inclined as the MNAO believed. They occupied a position in the world of individuated labor that has sometimes been ascribed to domestic servants: they were for the most part skilled illiterates who worked closely enough to Indians and Europeans to become acutely aware of the political issues and disparities in standards of living.[48] Taxi drivers, perhaps not unlike servants, were in sexual matters consultants to their European fares and may have established bonds of trust, familiarity, and reward with such men that brought men temporarily together in collegial relations. At the same time, these male interracial relations allied taxi drivers with the least-aggressive wartime prostitutes, the women who were available to the white men cab drivers brought to their doors—if the woman needed money that day. These relationships also maintained the short-time price in Pumwani, as African drivers and soldiers taught white men the current rates, thus circumventing supply and demand. Colchester's objections to juvenile watembezi and criminal taxi drivers conflated two different aspects of African social life. The women who actively searched for white men had no need of taxi drivers, especially those who told European men African prices, and looked for ways to avoid go-betweens by having documents to prove they were someone's ayah. In practice, taxi drivers were associated with the women who quietly stayed home in Pumwani, in secrecy and respect, unaware of or unconcerned about the benefits of white customers. The juvenile watembezi and the Kikuyu taxi drivers were both the most visible of laborers and those whose work linked them most intimately to European men, but they did not work together or rely on each other very often.

In 1942 Pumwani was declared off-limits to African troops after repeated brawls, and while it is difficult to say how this affected women whose primary source of income came from watembezi prostitution, it did increase the number of African soldiers going to Eastleigh to find women. After 1942 many young watembezi began to move from Pumwani to Eastleigh, where they could rent a room for between 22/ and 30/ per month, or double what they then paid in Pumwani.[49] Most of these women had shared rooms in Pumwani, but they tended to live alone in new accommodations in Eastleigh or Shauri Moyo, and they used their premises for occasional malaya prostitution. Some of the cooperation engendered in their earlier years of streetwalking carried over into these women's practice of the malaya form and informed the wartime and postwar conduct of prostitution in Eastleigh. For its younger, largely Christian prostitute population, Eastleigh was known as a place where "prostitutes never fought," never expressed a jealous word about another's success, and where childless prostitutes were often asked to look after another prostitute's child for a night in exchange for 20 to 33 percent of what the woman earned in that time.[50] It would seem that the collegiality of youthful streetwalking led some women to pay other women for domestic tasks, rather than entering into reciprocal child-care relationships—which might erode a woman's rate of profit—or depending on their kin, practices that were commonplace in wartime Pumwani or Shauri Moyo.[51] Older Muslim prostitutes who had lived in Eastleigh since before the war and had combined the watembezi and malaya forms for years had no close ties with other prostitutes of the same generation.[52]

In late-1930s Pumwani, the interaction of the wazi-wazi and the malaya form increased the price for short-time slightly and decreased the price for night-long visits. The special conditions of wartime created virtually separate markets for prostitutes: military men including POWs who came for short-time and by their networks stabilized prices at just above their late-1930s levels; white men whose custom was secured without networks and whose short-time price was over ten times more than African soldiers paid; and the African men who spent the night, some of them rich and some of them poor, who were charged according to their abilities and the goals of malaya women. But young women living in Pumwani, particularly those with small children in crowded rooms, could prostitute themselves most profitably outside of Pumwani, whether in Eastleigh or in Government Road. Women such as Tabitha Waweru practiced the watembezi form but thought of themselves—and their accumulation—as malaya prostitutes; juvenile watembezi were like any other women who identified primarily with the watembezi form: they sent most of their money home.[53] The profitability of watembezi prostitution in Government Road and in Eastleigh during the war represented a renewed vigor of interracial prostitution and represented the decline of those areas previously associated with profitable watembezi prostitution, River Road and the Quarry Road roundabout, where the most successful watembezi women lived on the streets on which they walked. Eastleigh continue to feature the highest prices for prostitution between Africans well into the 1960s.

Malaya Prostitution

Perhaps the most important change that took place in the malaya form practiced in wartime Eastleigh, Pumwani, and Shauri Moyo was that it was so readily combined with the watembezi form. Women combined the two forms in what seemed a new way in Nairobi, or at least in a way that the practitioners had not previously described so openly. Most of the malaya women who came to Nairobi before 1939 practiced both forms in their working lives, but few practiced both simultaneously over a period of several years, and even fewer described having adjusted their behavior to accommodate both forms.

Throughout the war the malaya form remained the safest form of prostitution. As African residential areas expanded to the west of Pumwani and into the new quarters of Starehe and Ziwani and into Shauri Moyo and, quasi-legally, Eastleigh, the malaya form moved as well: "There were a lot of women who had Asian boyfriends and they got them places in Eastleigh so they wouldn't have to go to Majengo to be with their girlfriends. That's how Eastleigh came to have so many prostitutes by the end of World War II."[54] The most notable incursion of the malaya form into central Nairobi was the Silver Building on Campos Ribeiro Avenue, between River Road and Government Road at the southern end of the area designated for Indian commercial and residential use, a feature of Nairobi zoning that had historically accounted for the rooms illegally rented to African prostitutes in River Road. According to a detailed, anonymous letter to the Chief Secretary in 1942, the building's owner, Mangal Dass, had sublet it to an African man for 250/ a month, and it brought in a total monthly income of 840/.[55] The tenants included many malaya women who practiced the form with all the circumspection, secrecy, and decorum of its 1920s version, and some watembezi, who were said to bring men back to their rooms. The building was not a brothel in anything but common European parlance; it was instead a place where prostitutes lived and worked: the administration knew about the Silver Building—and called it a brothel—but no arrests were ever made there.[56] Some of the tenants were said to have become householders in Mathare or Kariobangi, but no one could provide me with actual details or names. Similarly, no one I spoke to could identify the African subtenant; Colchester said there was no subtenant, while others said that the African was merely the agent of another wealthy Indian: whoever he was, if indeed he existed and was actually a he, he was extraneous to the concerns of wartime prostitutes, an other landlord of temporary accommodation.[57] Their concern was with their own safety, and "the government didn't give a woman any problems if she was a prostitute in secret."[58]

In Pumwani and Shauri Moyo the malaya form was greatly influenced by the wazi-wazi prostitution practiced in Pumwani. In wartime Pumwani the full-time price charged by malaya women seems to have been kept low by the short-time price charged by wazi-wazi women and the increasing number of men who came there seeking short-time relations. Possibly because of the number of foreign men visiting Pumwani, many malaya women asked for cash in advance as they had done in the 1930s.[59] In Shauri Moyo, where the wazi-wazi form was not practiced at all, malaya women who had recently come to Nairobi adopted some of the more assertive wazi-wazi practices. Asha Mohammed, a Kamba Muslim woman who first went to Shauri Moyo in 1939/40, said that if a man refused to pay after spending the night with her, "I'd call my neighbors, and if it meant fighting for me to get that money, that's what would happen." Malaya prostitutes in wartime Pumwani did not speak of enlisting their neighbors' aid. But in the newer community of Shauri Moyo, neighbors were called upon to help prostitutes obtain their payment, by both Muslim and Christian malaya women.[60] By the end of the war, public and often violent denunciations of nonpaying customers were an accepted feature of the malaya form, although less in Pumwani than anywhere else, and one that many observers eventually ceased to frown upon. As Hidaya Saidi, born near Nairobi before the turn of the century, noted, "When I was young, men used to beat up women; today women beat up men. That's the biggest change I have seen in my life here." Mwana Himani bint Ramadhani went to Pumwani from Mathare in 1930; in 1976 she claimed, "Most of the women here used to beat the men who didn't pay them."

The young women who combined the watembezi and malaya forms often practiced a more circumspect and respectful malaya prostitution than many women in the 1930s had done. In Pumwani, Eastleigh, and to a lesser extent Shauri Moyo, the war marked a return to the full-service malaya prostitution of the late 1920s, complete with secrecy and deference but, generally, payment in advance. "If I had a man for the night, I would wake up early in the morning, wash myself, and prepare his bath. After he bathed tea would be ready and after drinking he would go away."[61] The deferential, price-last malaya form that flourished in the 1920s was as influenced by low commodity prices as it was by the scarcity of rooms in Pumwani. Women asked the price last not only to include in it all the tasks they had performed during the man's visit, but to maintain an appearance of respectability in an overcrowded location in which Muslims virtually controlled housing, and where an affront to Muslim mores was thought to invite eviction. During World War II, however, with high commodity prices, restricted access to many foodstuffs, and rooms readily available in Eastleigh to women who could afford them, deferential, full-service prostitution seems to have emerged, as the tasks sold were thought to be more valuable than the commodities they involved. Part of what men purchased from malaya women was a validation of their ideas of proper gender relations—that women cooked for men, and served them, in polite obedience. In Eastleigh between 1939 and 1945 the price for night-long visits varied from 5/ to 13/, and the proportion of that amount (between 20 and 30 percent) that women said was for breakfast was almost identical to the proportion of the cost of a night's visit that men spent on food when they themselves brought it, and slightly more than the entire short-time price during the early years of the war.[62] Based on this data, it would seem that malaya women in Eastleigh provided breakfast at cost; profits lay in the work of cooking and preparing breakfast and building a relationship.

Young malaya women cooked and made tea for men and cooperated with each other. When Sara Waigo had a child in the early 1940s, the woman with whom she shared a room in Shauri Moyo supported her, through prostitution, for almost a year. In Pumwani, when Margaret Githeka met men while she was married, from 1937 to 1947, she would "ask the man for cash, and then I'd hide it until I really needed that money. If he wanted to give me a present I'd explain to him that my husband would be very jealous, but that he could ask another woman to bring me that present and say she had brought that thing for me." In Buruburu, Wanjira Ng'ang'a supported her tenants through hard times. Such cooperation of young prostitutes, whether immigrant or majengo-born, whether Kikuyu or Swahili, whether Muslim or Christian, was to be a unique feature of the wartime malaya form and a commonplace feature of life in Nairobi's African villages, legal and illegal.

The Maintenance and Reproduction of Labor Power in Wartime Prostitution

The war created a dilemma for malaya prostitutes. In the past they had been able to increase their earnings by supplementing sexual relations with food, domesticity, bedding, and bathwater. But during the war the majority of men who would normally comprise the most regular customers of Nairobi prostitutes—men without women nearby—were soldiers and POWs, men who had their daily food and shelter provided by organizations that did not, as a rule, allow them to eat and sleep anywhere else. Most of the men who came to malaya women had only a short time to spend with them, and probably could not be induced to pay extra for a few slices of bread. Given the increase in food prices, some malaya women probably welcomed the opportunity to stop providing food, but those women who had profited by serving food had to find other ways to increase their earnings. Some malaya women began to reorganize their sale of domestic labor, so that one aspect of it—whether sexuality or sewing or cooking—could gain them either preferential access to the camps or the repeated patronage of military or POW personnel in their own homes. Some women used one domestic task to practice the watembezi form, and others used another in the malaya form.

Such specialization became even more important after 1942, when the army pressured Colchester into declaring Pumwani off-limits to military personnel. Pumwani had been the site of numerous brawls among Italian POWs and GCR and KAR troops between 1940 and 1942; even after the GCR returned to West Africa in October 1941 their reputation for violence remained. The administration could not have increased the number of police patrols in Pumwani without reducing police manpower in the European and Indian areas of Nairobi at a time when the crime rate was rising, but they could declare Pumwani off-limits to African troops. This saved the MNC money and the political complications that might arise from police arresting soldiers or military police entering Pumwani. Declaring Pumwani off-limits was not an indication of the severity of its violence but a way to maintain the separate administration of African civilians and African soldiers.[63]

Although many African soldiers continued to come to Pumwani—there were still no serious police patrols—the number of white men delivered by taxis to malaya women decreased. The white man who visited Elizabeth Kamya once a week since the start of the war stopped coming, as did many other soldiers, but she "still made a living." Monica Nyazura and a British soldier worked out what she said was a common ruse to enable him to come to her and, perhaps more important, for her to go to him at his camp.

> These white men were usually soldiers and they used to come here to find women . . . but after a few years the Golgos started beating up the white men and other people, so the whole army was banned from coming to Majengo. After that, the only way an mzungu soldier could visit you was to bring you some of his clothes and then on a day like Saturday you would tie his clothes together and take them back to the camp, and you could go with him there, because the gatekeeper would let you in, because you would say the you brought the soldier his uniform that you had repaired. Some did this every week with their European boyfriends . . . any woman who did not have some reason for going to the camp, like returning a uniform or a letter saying she was an ayah taking a message, was arrested.

Such access to camps was especially useful to women like Nyazura, who had combined the wazi-wazi and malaya forms since the late 1930s, and who had lost earnings when Pumwani was declared off-limits. Although she herself claimed that this access hardly made her rich, Zaina Kachui claimed that the women who went inside the caps could "make almost 100/ in a week that way"[64]

While letters and respectable, if unlikely, cover stories were important features of successful wartime prostitution, malaya women tended to organize their work around appointments and the performance of a specific nonsexual domestic task. This was designed, possibly through a painful process of trial and error, to attract many men, each of whom was to believe that these tasks were performed for him alone. Between 1939 and 1941 two battalions of the GCR were garrisoned at Kabete. Tabitha Waweru described how her organization of appointments and of cooking was necessary in her relations with several GCR men at once.

> I used to cook for them; they told me what they ate in their country and I made it for them . . . most of the food they ate

was beef, and they brought a lot of food for me in those days. . . . Most of the women who went with Golgos never went hungry, their houses were filled with food. . . . Golgos were the first men to open our brains to how to get a lot of money from men . . . because they paid so much money, women like my-self, we found a way to get six or seven of them in one week, in secret. People used to say Golgos ate each other, but this was not true. They fought each other a lot. . . . If two ever met in my room they would fight, and after that, the one who was there first, he would cut off my ear, this is what they said they would do if they saw me with one of their friends. So when a woman went with a Golgos man the most important thing she could do was remember the day of her appointment and not make an appointment with any other man for that day.

Golgos had a fabulous reputation for violence against women—they were said to cut off women's ears, or cut the distended earlobes of Kikuyu women, in jest and in anger[65]—but it was not the appointments in and of themselves that mattered: it was the illusion of sexual loyalty. Women who went with GCR men took appointments seriously, just as they took learn-ing to cook West African dishes seriously: they learned how profitable prostitution could be. When GCR had regular leaves, it would have been fairly simple to arrange to see different GCR men on different days.

Wanjira Ng'ang'a rented a plot of land in Buruburu after the birth of her first child in 1940. She built a house there and rented out the four rooms to prostitutes, mainly Kikuyu and Kamba women, for 15/ each. At first Ng'ang'a brewed beer, but by 1942 she stopped, thinking it was too big a risk for the money she earned. Buruburu was on the road connect-ing Thika (and the KAR camp near it) to Nairobi and Machakos, and POW and military drivers formed a large part of Ng'ang'a's clientele. She described how she and her tenants managed household appearances to minimize the potential for conflict between POWs while maintaining reg-ular customers.

I myself was afraid of fights, so I only had one Italian boyfriend at a time, but some women used to have more than one . . . and such women would give each man a certain day of the week, and on that day and that day only he would come. That's be-cause the bedsheets those Italians stole for us had numbers on them, and the women with more than one Italian boyfriend would remove the sheets that did not belong to the man and put them on the ones that did on the day he was to come. This

way there could be no jealousy, no fighting, because when an
Italian came he found the sheets with his number on the bed.

The effort required for illiterates to memorize serial numbers should
indicate how seriously and effectively women took the business of keeping
appointments. Indeed, it is altogether possible that the POWs did not
rigorously check the numbers but only made sure that there were numbers on them. Whereas Nyazura used a domestic task as a means of gaining access to a man, Waweru and Ng'ang'a organized their labor time to
give the appearance of single-minded devotion to one man, by matching a
man to "his" day of the week.

In these quotations it is clear that the feeding and bathing of military
labor power was not essential to these transactions; the state took care of
that for soldiers and POWs. What was in fact being maintained in these
examples was an illusion, the importance of which can best be gauged by
men's willingness to pay for its continuation. Sexual intercourse was only a
part, and I suggest a small part, of what these women spoke of having offered. They presented an illusion of sexual loyalty and appeared to wait
for one man only at a prearranged time: they did not act like prostitutes,
available to whoever came by. How flimsy this appearance was depended
on how closely the participants cared to look at it: no wartime prostitute I
spoke to reported soldiers or POWs inquiring how they spent the other
nights of the week. Such illusions were part of the reproduction of labor
power: the appearance of such loyalty—to so many men—minimized the
tensions between men who were in otherwise competitive situations. For
those women who confused appointments the danger to themselves was
real enough, but it was recognized as a by-product of the violence between
men that would take place.

While soldiers' relationships with each other on the battlefield have
been described as intimate and politically instructive,[66] soldiers' relations
with each other before and after combat could be very tense. Soldiers
awaiting demobilization were often justifiably on edge, as this was their
last chance to receive full compensation and redress grievances.[67] The
lives of Italian POWs must have been frustrating in the extreme. But what
did soldiers and POWs get out of the elaborately maintained fictions of
sexual loyalty, and what did appointments give them that they could not
obtain in the camps in which they lived? Military life combined hierarchy
with labor discipline in vivid ways: a Kamba song praised the ability of the
British Army to make dogs follow orders.[68] Appointments enabled military men to enjoy their leisure time without compromising their sense of

status and rank.[69] Prostitutes clearly did not know the ranks of the men who came to them, but soldiers were all too keenly aware of their own rank and that of the man they saw leaving a woman's room. Appointments enabled many soldiers to maintain the proper distance from each other even in the dense housing of Shauri Moyo and Pumwani. This was especially true for the GCR, whose long-standing regimental arrangements of order and status were disrupted each month as four hundred replacements arrived from British and French West Africa, most of them raw recruits who confounded the intimacy of the pre-1939 Regiment.[70]

Labor power is reproduced and maintained by much more than the number of calories prepared by one person for consumption by another. Indeed, nutritional insufficiencies were commonly remarked on by Kenya's Medical and Labour Departments.[71] What constitutes the reproduction and maintenance of labor power is the social context in which the calories—and what the calories are often metaphors for—are prepared and consumed. How does a context reproduce labor power? In prostitution, it does so by fulfilling the needs of the paying participants. The needs that are met by sexual relations—their frequency, duration, and nature—and the allocation of food and shelter within sexual relationships are determined by wider ideologies, not biological absolutes. In Nairobi wartime prostitution, men sought the kinds of relationships that they believed they needed, the relationships that most closely approximated the contexts in which they wanted to receive intimate relationships, including food and shelter. Their labor power was reproduced and maintained by the degree to which they were satisfied with the arrangements they had thus authorized.

The use of appointments during World War II represented a growing awareness on the part of Nairobi prostitutes of men's lives and social relations. Prior to the war, with the possible exception of Danguroni in the mid-1930s, most prostitutes did not seem to have a clear idea of what men did to get money, how they behaved with their friends and co-workers, and how they and their friends and co-workers organized their social lives. Malaya women from the 1920s and 1930s said that if one boyfriend came while they were with another, they might complain, but that was all they would do; "I would tell them that they had not paid my bridewealth, I was not married to them, they could not feel jealous."[72] It would thus seem that soldiers and POWs made their preference for exclusively maintained visiting days clear to malaya women. This in turn suggests that the relationships soldiers and POWs entered into during the war were those that maintained the social life from which they were otherwise removed.

The Watembezi Prostitution of Malaya Women, 1942–45

The actual number of troops in Kenya is impossible to obtain, but estimates suggest between thirty and fifty thousand in the years 1942–45, not
counting the POWs. There were seventy-five thousand Kenyans in military service, including voluntary labor, in 1944.[73] These figures represent
a fluid population—many were out of the country, and many were in an
around Mombasa—but there were probably between five and eight thousand soldiers garrisoned in and around Nairobi at any given time, and
many of these men went to Pumwani and Shauri Moyo whenever they
could.

Central African KAR and RWAFF soldiers were new to Kenya, knew
little or no Swahili, and were thus probably reluctant to knock on doors in
Pumwani or Shauri Moyo and ask if there was a woman available to them
inside. They seem to have flocked to Danguroni in the early years of the
war, where they went with wazi-wazi women for prices negotiated with a
show of fingers.[74] The men of the Gold Coast Regiment of the RWAFF
had a reputation for violence, rape, drunkenness, and cannibalism made
worse, according to some evidence, by long-standing antagonism between
them and Central African troops in the KAR.[75] They were also frequent
visitors to Pumwani.

The repeated fistfights GCR or KAR initiated with everyone, but especially with POWs, became a regular feature of life in Pumwani before
1942, to the distress of many older, established malaya prostitutes. Early
in 1942, before the off-limits posting, an informally organized group of
Muslim malaya women, most or all of them householders and said to be
Swahili, Bajuni, and Kalenjin, went to Colchester to request increased police protection in Pumwani. They offered to provide information to the
military police. To make their point, they gave a donation of 2,000/ for
British war charities, which he accepted,[76] but Pumwani was declared off-
limits nonetheless.

Although some African soldiers did go to Pumwani seeking women after 1943, when there were fewer police than there had been in 1942, those
who did so usually went with wazi-wazi women.[77] Many malaya women,
however, took advantage of the fact that there were hundreds of men just
a few miles' walk from Pumwani (see map). Many women who had previously practiced the malaya form began to join together to go to the KAR
and POW camps at night. Early in the war a few women had gone alone to
places near the camps at night, but only when there was a civilian employee who could tell soldiers that there would be a woman available that

evening.[78] The watembezi prostitution of malaya women that developed after 1942 was substantially different and seems not to have involved any of the same women.

These women were both Christian and Muslim, residents of Shauri Moyo and Pumwani, and had been in Nairobi for between two and seven years. They left Pumwani and Shauri Moyo in groups of five and ten and walked to the camps, keeping off the main roads.[79] Some of these women identified so strongly with the malaya form that they refused to acknowledge that this might be called watembezi prostitution. Farida Monteo, a malaya woman who went to Pumwani from Pangani in about 1939, was adamant that her trips to the camps were conducted "in secret" and not by streetwalking: "That was wartime, that was different, but we never took the road, we travelled through the bush, and there were four or five of us walking together, we weren't doing anything wrong. . . . We were not looking for men while we were walking, we were walking to one place to find them, we weren't like those women who walk up and down the street and call to every man and car they see."[80]

Once outside the camps, however, women did call out to men. The women themselves did not know precisely how the men knew they were there and got outside, but "they would know somehow. As you know one hyena and another hyena can't miss each other."[81] At the POW camps the Italians were always said to have condoms ready,[82] which suggests a great deal of official sanction or at least tolerant guards. Guards in both military and POW camps had access to these women as well, and presumably to gifts and payments from the men they let out.

Because many of these soldiers and POWs did not know any Swahili, and because it was probably also important to keep noises to a minimum, most of the negotiating outside the camps was conducted in sign language. A man would point to a woman and say, "Mimi taka" (I want you) to her; she would hold up a few fingers to show her price in reply. In this way, women tended to underprice themselves. The prices charged for sexual intercourse on these excursions were very close to the short-time prices these women had charged in Shauri Moyo or Pumwani, between 2/ and 5/ for KAR and GCR men—whose salaries were about 45/ a month—and almost invariably 2/ for POWs.[83] Time was a factor depressing these prices: standing in the bushes outside a military installation was not the place to hold out for 10/. But the combination of speed and a high volume of business—a few women claimed to have gone with five and six men a night—gave these streetwalking malaya women fairly high earnings.[84]

These walks to the camps changed the social relations of the women who went on them. Women who had previously prostituted themselves within the isolation of the malaya form—which Farida Monteo and Asha Wanjiru had done for six or seven years—were beginning to work together, deciding when to work and where to work and how to get there. They were also sharing the space they used for sexual relations, thus briefly abandoning the notion that no one could tell who was a prostitute and who was not.

Soon after the collective trips began, *wakora*, a word usually translated as "thugs" or "rogues" but meaning in fact the most-organized sector of the criminal elements so frequently mentioned in 1930s and 1940s urban policies, began to attack women as they returned from the camps, beating them and taking their money. The women responded by asking their regular boyfriends to wait for them at a prearranged place not far from the camps to escort them back to Pumwani and Shauri Moyo.[85] Sara Waigo, a Christian Kikuyu woman who had come to Shauri Moyo in 1940, described this process.

> Wakora would follow women when they went to the Italian camp, and then they would wait for these women in the road, because they knew the women would be returning with a lot of money. But in those days every woman had a regular boyfriend, an African boyfriend, so we used to go in a group, many women, and every woman had told her boyfriend to come and escort her on the road after she finished her work at the camp. So we used to go to the camp and our boyfriends would come and wait outside the camp for us to finish, and then they used to walk us home so we would be safe. Also this way the police would never guess we were prostitutes, we looked like wives. But before we made this arrangement with our boyfriends we used to be beaten very badly by wakora, and we had our money stolen, so we decided to ask our boyfriends to come and collect us outside the camp.

This was considerably different from wazi-wazi prostitution and the wartime watembezi form; in this malaya form women linked their work and relationships in new and intimate ways. It would seem that, starting in about 1940, having a boyfriend was becoming less of a liability for a prostitute, or was a liability with which a prostitute might comfortably live. Gathiro wa Chege lived with a man for about fifteen years starting in 1941, and kept her occasional watembezi earnings a secret from him; she sent most of the money to her mother. But malaya women like Waigo and

Monteo and Wanjiru were actively soliciting their boyfriends' help in their prostitution and were extending ideas about men as protectors to African men. Indeed, some of the more useful fictions of the malaya form—that no one could tell who was a prostitute and who was a wife—were mobilized and updated and given credibility precisely by the inclusion of boyfriends. Like the kindly letters and gifts given prostitutes by white men, these men escorted their girlfriends for love, not money. According to Asha Wanjiru, women did not share their earnings with the men who walked them safely home: "if you wanted to you could give him some, but if you didn't you would only have to buy him food, cook it, and eat with him."

The 1942 donation and request for police protection by established and well-to-do malaya women and the watembezi prostitution of somewhat younger malaya women after 1942 show the degree to which cooperation increased among malaya prostitutes in Pumwani and Shauri Moyo during World War II. Compared to malaya women of earlier years—women who might help a friend or pay her fine—these women acknowledged that they should act together because they shared a form of prostitution: it was work, not friendship or religion, that made wartime prostitutes form groups. In the late 1970s researchers studying Nairobi expressed dismay that the city's informal sector—prostitutes, brewers, hawkers, pickpockets—did not think of themselves as proletarians.[86] But why should they? Prostitutes were not proletarians. Malaya prostitutes were pettybourgeois women who actively controlled profit-generating enterprises— the sale of sexuality, the sale of domestic skills, the rental of rooms, or all three—for which they provided the labor. Malaya prostitutes demonstrated a petty-bourgeois consciousness during World War II when they petitioned the state for increased police protection of their property and when they transformed their relations with their boyfriends in a way that safeguarded their property. These were not impoverished women desperately trying to make ends meet; these were women engaged in complex collective groups the purpose of which was to protect their earnings.[87]

Venereal Disease, the State, and Prostitution

Whenever large numbers of prostitutes interact with military populations, venereal diseases tend to become major preoccupations of military and state officials. Most of the peacetime efforts to control prostitution in the nineteenth and twentieth centuries were cloaked in the language of disease control. In much of the English-speaking world, the legal efforts to control venereal diseases involved limiting prostitutes' movements; similarly, colonial African attempts to control diseases had to do with controlling Africans' movements as well. In much of the Western world, prostitutes were often defined by their promiscuity, not whether or not they took money for sex.

In Kenya, unrestrained female sexuality was not seen to have the same causal relationship to venereal disease that it was seen to have elsewhere. This was probably due to ideas about African sexuality in general, and those ideas had the overall effect of making officials believe that English legislation was inappropriate for Africa. The British Contagious Diseases Acts of 1864, 1866, and 1869, which spread rapidly through English-speaking parts of the empire, created an apparatus in which women identified by police as "common prostitutes" were registered and subjected to periodic vaginal examinations; if they were found to be infected with a venereal disease, they were to be incarcerated for up to nine months in a hospital containing a locked venereal ward. These laws were immediately opposed by feminists demanding their repeal because they blamed prostitution and venereal diseases entirely on prostitutes, and not on the middle-class men whose sexual appetites made prostitution an attractive option for poor women.[88] Such laws would have been prohibitively expensive to implement in Africa, but it is possible that Contagious Diseases laws, or the regulation of prostitutes, raised questions about gender, race, class, and their relationship to conceptualizations of male and female lust[89] that would have complicated the business of colonial rule, which consistently saw African sexual behavior as something beyond legislation. There was, for example, no attempt to control female age at marriage through age-of-consent laws in colonial Africa, nor was there any specific colonial construction of "normal" sexuality.[90]

In Kenya the rhetoric of disease control was winding down by 1936 in the debates over urban policies; thus the wartime administration of prostitution was social, not medical. The goals of colonial officials were to protect soldiers from thefts by prostitutes and their associates and to banish young girls from the dangers of Nairobi's streets. To these ends, arrests were made. Protecting any group from venereal infection was not the administration's goal, and the military presence in Kenya during the war did not lead to medically administered crackdowns on local prostitutes. Indeed, Kenya's medical officers seem to have been baffled by military views that prostitution was a vice that the state ought to suppress. In 1943 the Port Health Officer at Mombasa wrote that the main concern in the meet-

ings held routinely to discuss prostitution and the high incidence of venereal diseases in H. M. Navy appeared to be "the abolition of sexual
intercourse between Europeans and non-Europeans." He went on to report that the increase in free medical services to sailors a year earlier had
made "the regulation of prostitution very much less of an issue" for the
Medical Department on the coast.[91]

This separation of medical issues from the administration of prostitution characterized Kenya's Medical Department and military even before
World War II, and accounts for many of the differences between colonial ✝
and metropolitan medical thinking about prostitution. The introduction
of prophylactics in the late 1930s may well have encouraged an official
policy of treating venereal diseases when they occurred. But on the whole
the administration of prostitution in Kenya was an extension of forty years
of urban policies. In 1938 the Medical Officer in Meru urged the KAR not
to deport prostitutes living near military camps because "their place would
be taken by others" and diseased soldiers "would infect the fresh women
so there would be no solution to the problem." Instead he suggested "distribution of stout rubber goods" recently imported into the colony, free
medical treatment for prostitutes and soldiers alike, as well as his own services as a lecturer on "the evil aftereffects of gonorrhea."[92] Technology
and expertise, not criminalization, were to be enough to protect African
soldiers. There was no legislation that empowered District Officers or the
KAR to remove women simply because they were prostitutes near military
camps. Civil administrators repeatedly proposed increasing prostitutes'
access to medical treatment during the war. In 1942 Paterson, fearing a
postwar epidemic of venereal disease, unsuccessfully proposed free treatment for prostitutes in Nairobi's Infectious Diseases Hospital.[93] Prostitutes were clearly seen as diseased, but their treatment was not considered an issue important enough to merit the use of state funds.

Such ideas about who was diseased and who should be treated meant
that the rural, nonprostitute populations of Kenya became the arena in
which the administration of venereal disease treatment took place. This
was not a neutral policy; given the infertility caused by untreated gonorrhea and syphilis in women, the Medical Department sought to construct
a demand for paid venereal disease treatment based on infertility. In
1939 the drug M&B 693 was first introduced in Kenya. Originally designed to combat pneumonia, it also proved effective in treating gonorrhea. This was a major breakthrough; the earlier treatments required
repeated draining of the urethra, a painful process many patients did not
complete. Paterson made the drug available to different groups at differ-

ent times and at different rates. It was issued free to the KAR in 1939.
Later that same year, Paterson proposed that it be sold to the Maasai to
cure their high rate of female infertility and to induce them to sell cattle, at
competitive prices, to meet Nairobi's growing requirements for beef. He
wrote that the Kajiado Maasai

> could at long last be persuaded to sell their cattle for the pur-
> chase of the drug . . . the Masai now appreciate that the ster-
> ility of their women is due to the high incidence of
> gonorrhea. . . . They realize that unless they do something
> about it they will die out as a tribe. As a result, babies are now
> more important to them than cattle . . . the discovery of the
> drug 693 has provided an unrivaled opportunity for encour-
> aging the Masai not only to sell large numbers of cattle for the
> provision of Medical Services, but to get into the habit of selling
> cattle.[94]

Beef was the main issue here, not babies. Areas with birthrates as low or
lower than the Maasai were neither given nor sold M&B 693 until the end
of the war.[95] But this emphasis on the sale of the drug, which was given to
pneumonia patients free, made the wartime treatment of venereal disease
a men's issue. Men, and not women, were made conscious of its evils and
consequences. It was male Maasai who heard the grim warnings about
their tribe dying out and male Maasai who were to sell their cattle to buy
drugs. In military rhetoric, male responsibility became male instrumen-
tality as armed forces lecturers announced "You have often blamed
women for failing to bring forth children and you sent them back to their
fathers. What should be done to you, though, if you cause the woman to
become sterile?"[96]

Ethnicity, Sexuality, and Illness in Wartime Nairobi

During the war Haya prostitutes continued to be regarded as "shameful"
interlopers whose manners and morals were "disrespectful" by Pumwani
Muslim standards, even when Muslim women adjusted those standards to
incorporate some aspects of the wazi-wazi form. The war, however, was a
time of interlopers. How these outsiders were perceived, and how these
perceptions were organized and transmitted, were essentially narratives—about violence, about sexuality, about ethnicity, and about
disease—that became part of African discourse in Nairobi. Such narratives were often no more than rumor and gossip; only occasionally were

they written down by European participants. But taken together, they provide information about social life that might otherwise be invisible to historians.

Rumors and gossip are often difficult to put into a precise chronology. While the dates for the GCR presence in Kenya are known (mid-1940—they had been en route to East Africa when war was declared—to late 1941), accusations against GCR men continued for at least a few months after they had gone; these stories obviously had a meaning beyond the amount of time these soldiers spent in Kenya. Stories about women's sexuality, particularly the emergence of a specific notion of Ganda female sexuality and a propensity for gonorrhea, and specified groups of men who most appreciated that sexuality, are harder to put into any analytical sequence, but both began during World War II.

Although there were diffuse stories of GCR cannibalism from World War I,[97] the stories from World War II were specific, violent, and sexual. Their reputation for frequenting prostitutes was impressive. Zaina binti Ali was nine when the war ended—six when the GCR left Nairobi—but she knew who the Golgos were: "they were black soldiers in the KAR and whenever they had money and were given permission to go out of their camps they always came to Majengo to find women." Their commanders agreed: however often it was said that "the West African lacks initiative. . . he is an adept mover when sex is involved."[98] Many of the women I interviewed had heard that the Golgos were cannibals; a large number of women said they raped women and regularly started fights. A few women heard that they had eaten a woman in Nyeri, while others heard that they had cut off a woman's breast and eaten it, or, as we have seen, cut off women's ears.[99] The GCR's European superiors told stories that were anatomically similar: Ghanaian or Nigerian troops were said to have taken some of the first Japanese prisoners in India or Burma, in 1943. "They cut off their ears, fried them, and had a good meal."[100] Such descriptions—in which Nairobi prostitutes' only contribution were stories about GCR cutting off women's breasts—revealed a common vocabulary between European officers and Nairobi prostitutes in which all that was violent and sexual about African men was crystallized and confirmed. That this vocabulary was about West African troops may have been because of their unique characteristics or because of what they represented in wartime Kenya: it meant that GCR violence could be recounted without specific references to the tensions and conflicts of class and ethnicity within Kenya. Indeed, the fact that this vocabulary was shared between European men and Nairobi prostitutes indicated the respectability and authority each of these groups believed they possessed.

More than wakora, Golgos brought a specificity to the fact of violence against women, especially prostitutes: they personified it. Golgos epitomized what was good and bad about prostitution: generous and dangerous men, not as a contradiction, but as a daily possibility. The risks of being involved with them went beyond the physical: "The Golgos loved babies really, and if you became pregnant from a Golgos man, or even if you thought the father of your baby was Golgos, you should not tell him. . . . Otherwise, that Golgos man will take away the baby."[101] In outraged respectability women told stories about the GCR that emphasized their violence against women and much more vulnerable creatures. "They used to eat young boys and sometimes puppies. They used to come into town with sacks and look around for newborn puppies and when they found them they'd buy them for as much as 50/. And on their way home to the camp, they'd eat the puppies, without even cooking them . . once a man told me that he'd seen some Golgos in a peas-field eating the puppy that the man had just sold them."[102]

Violence and extravagance characterized GCR conduct. The women who knew them well, such as Tabitha Waweru, could speak about Golgos violence and identify the kinds of urban and sexual terrain they were defending with fists and knives. But even Waweru could not explain away their generosity. "When the Golgos came to Pumwani they used to come with 300/, and they gave it to us. At first we were surprised, we thought maybe they had stolen it from somewhere." Nor could she explain the comportment, with women at least, that gave rise to straightforward comparisons with Europeans.

> If I had a permanent boyfriend, a white man, he would buy me a yard of material, a bedsheet, and also a blanket, and he would write a letter for me saying he's the one who gave it to me. Otherwise the police will come and see I have a new blanket and suspect me of stealing it. Golgos men used to give us these kinds of presents, and we would ask for letters like the wazungu wrote, and they would give us those too.

Golgos revealed something fascinating about African men: they could cause bodily harm, but they could perform all the functions of white men as well. As the only soldiers in Kenya who did not come from colonies dominated by white settlers, GCR, particularly literate GCR, may have expressed this in many subtle ways. Indeed, by the time the last "odds and ends" of the GCR had left Kenya in June 1942, one of the regiment's lieutenants had become the first African to become a commissioned officer.[103]

It was also during World War II that a belief emerged among men about the sexuality of Ganda women. Prior to the war men found the women of one ethnic or religious group more attractive than another—because of how they walked, or the length of their hair[104]—but they did not express that interest in terms of sexual pleasure or expertise. Indeed, the earliest account I have of a man describing the extent to which he was satisfied by an individual prostitute was in 1939.[105] Since the man had been in Nairobi since 1929, it seems unlikely this observation was due to his youth or a generational change in open expressions about sexuality. Starting during the last years of the war, Ganda women received and maintained a reputation for sexuality that continued at least until the mid-1970s. We have already seen that Ganda women had been in Nairobi well before the 1940s. In those earlier years not only did they have no discernible reputation for sexual expertise, but they were often lumped together with the Haya for their public behavior: in the 1930s there was nothing to make them stand out as a separate ethnic group in African Nairobi. Ganda women who went to Nairobi in the 1930s did not see themselves as special in any way other than that they were foreign,[106] and Ganda women who went to Nairobi between 1940 and 1941 do not seem to have been aware of any erotic reputation.[107] But for the most part, men who went to Nairobi after about 1939, even Ganda men, spoke of the pleasures of Ganda women.[108] By the end of the war Ganda women knew their reputation and were willing to capitalize on it: women who stayed in their rooms in the early years of the war walked to the Railway Quarters starting in 1945 "because I heard that men from Tanganyika paid very well for women from Uganda."[109]

Wartime prostitutes, particularly those born in Nairobi, had stories of their own about the Ganda, involving venereal diseases. "There was one Ganda woman who brought this disease to Kenya, she was called Grunet," said Tabitha Waweru, who went on to describe the woman in personable detail. Describing the orchitis of syphilis, she explained that "grunet happened to men only, it was when their testicles became really big, that's why we called them grunet." She and other women linked the disease to aggressive prostitution. "That sickness used to be with Waziba and Nandi women because they went with Ganda men."[110]

Here we have men's ideas about Ganda female sexuality, and a prostitute's critique, a counterdiscourse of venereal infection. The dialogue of pleasure and danger was not contained in one narrative, as it was with the

Golgos, nor did they contradict each other; the counterdiscourse was a caveat, but a powerful one. Venereal diseases were to take on a special importance in postwar Nairobi, so that the remembered association of Ganda women with syphilitic infection thirty years after the war is important. Accusing Ganda women of bringing syphilis was also a way for contemporary Nairobi prostitutes to deny their own fragility and vulnerability, to place themselves in healthy opposition.[111] In these stories the notion of the Other was constructed, not by colonialists eager to justify the brutalities of their enterprises,[112] but by the colonized themselves.

In recent years popular stereotypes about Africans in general and African prostitutes in particular have come into being in an attempt to identify aquired immune deficiency syndrome (AIDS) as an African disease. Although much of the initial research that spurred such claims has been reexamined and found flawed, it left us with the impression that Africans were licentious and diseased. The nature of transmission was said to be different in Africa than in North America and Europe, due to African patterns of culture rather than those of labor migration, the general level of health care, and epidemiology. Assumptions about African sexuality influenced medical diagnoses and efforts at disease control.[113] As a way to construct an explanation for a horrifying disease, this was not all that different from what Nairobi's malaya women said about Ganda prostitutes during World War II: that *they*, not themselves, slept with many men, and *they* were the ones who got sick.

Conclusions

In wartime Nairobi the three forms of prostitution interacted with each other to produce a discernible regional price differentiation. The low short-time price charged by wazi-wazi women in Pumwani increased the short-time price for malaya women there, but led to an overall decrease in the full-time price for the practitioners of both forms. These low prices may well have encouraged young teenage prostitutes—immigrant and Nairobi-born—to practice the watembezi form outside Pumwani, as they went to Eastleigh and Government Road. Short-time prices in Eastleigh were high at the beginning of the war, and when many of these watembezi moved there after 1942 and began to practice malaya prostitution, they continued to receive high fees: these women faced no competition from wazi-wazi neighbors. Indeed, many of their neighbors were watembezi prostitutes during the day and helped keep Eastleigh prices buoyant. The movement of watembezi into Eastleigh, and a general eastward movement of the profits in Nairobi prostitution, seems to have reduced the earnings of watembezi in River Road, where women earned the same cash amounts they had earned in the 1920s.

Even with these geographical disparities in earnings, women often moved from one form to another in the course of a day, as Tabitha Waweru's wartime career shows. This may not have been a unique feature of wartime prostitution, but it was a phenomenon that wartime Nairobi prostitutes reported more explicitly than their predecessors had. Some women brought the norms of one form into the practice of another, so that the Pumwani malaya women who went to find men in KAR and POW camps charged the same prices they asked in their own rooms—thus reinforcing the price differences between themselves and malaya women in Eastleigh—while insisting that such trips were not streetwalking. These changes were part of a larger change within the malaya populations of Pumwani and Eastleigh, where younger women—sometimes veterans of the streets—cooperated with each other in ways that the isolation of the form had previously made difficult. When Pumwani malaya women took up their collective version of the watembezi form, they engaged their boyfriends in their work in ways that were new to the malaya form. The war seems to have brought about, or coincided with, prostitutes' growing awareness of men's needs—sometimes enforced by men's violence—so that appointments with African men took on the seriousness that appointments with European men had a decade before.

The influence of one form of prostitution on another was more evident during the war, not because the forms had been more rigid and discrete before 1939, but because the wartime situation—the influx of soldiers, the GCR, rationing, Pumwani being declared off-limits—required more rapid and conscious adaptations than we have seen in any other time in Nairobi's history. Thus, young malaya women from Pumwani and Shauri Moyo had no difficulty practicing the watembezi form and in some cases rationalizing it as malaya prostitution. Other malaya women used the provision of specific domestic services to gain access to barracks where they practiced the watembezi form. Watembezi women who had frequented Government Road and Eastleigh switched to full-fledged, and full-service, malaya prostitution once they acquired their own rooms in Eastleigh, where they showed complete deference to the men who visited them, and where they continued the cooperation of their watembezi days into the malaya form. But malaya women in Shauri Moyo, even when they

were the tenants of former Pangani prostitutes, had by 1941 copied some
of the behavior of wazi-wazi women and began demanding payment in
advance.

The women who recounted their wartime experiences to me were astute and articulate. But another reason that the interactions of the forms
are so clear during World War II was that colonial attempts to control
prostitution were so minimal. The constraints on women's behavior were
the fear of arrest, the fear of wakora, the fear of GCR, and the fear of
venereal diseases. These fears were potent, but they did not determine the
conduct of the forms; they determined where and when and with whom a
woman chose to conduct a specific form of prostitution.

8

Prostitution, Crime, and Politics
in Nairobi, 1946–63

The study of postwar labor and housing in Nairobi has recently been over-shadowed by the study of postwar violence in Nairobi. David Throup and John Iliffe,[1] in very different books, depict a Nairobi that was violent and dangerous, where criminal gangs merged imperceptibly into the militancy of Mau Mau. Throup provides the most impressive melodrama: "the 30,000 Kikuyu and members of the related Embu and Meru people subjected the 12,000 Nyanza Africans to an unending reign of terror."[2] Throup was echoing the postwar MNAO, Tom Askwith, who had proposed a reign of terror of his own: "the gangs must be hunted out in an almost military fashion by highly mobile and numerous bodies of trained police."[3] In their writings, even liberal officials saw violence—and its specifically African characteristics—everywhere, so that by late 1948 members of the African Advisory Council worried that football "had become the successor to tribal warfare."[4]

How extensive was this crime wave and who did it affect? The kind of streetwalking—and the kind of street social life—that took place in the African locations after World War II stood in stark contrast to the complaints reported monthly in the African Advisory Council meetings. Pumwani was apparently safe enough to attract single women and men, some of them inebriated, to the dances at Memorial Hall, without their being robbed,[5] and was safe enough for poor women to walk together in the late afternoon, "just out . . . if we saw a man who seemed to like one of us, we told him where he could find us."[6] Individual women in fact felt safe enough to walk to other locations specifically to look for men, particularly men of other nationalities.[7] But African Nairobi was also dangerous enough for liberals like Askwith to speak of violent repression, for shopkeepers to worry about when their husbands were late returning from work,[8] and for members of the African Advisory Council to be stoned as they drove away from meetings.[9]

Either one set of facts is wrong—which seems unlikely—or both are true. If they are both true, then they describe two different gendered and salaried universes of risk and danger. The crime of postwar Nairobi was against property, specifically the kind of property that skilled men could afford. Shortly after Tom Mboya, then a sanitary inspector in the Medical Officer of Health's office, moved to Kaloleni in 1950 his guitar, his suit, and his blanket were stolen.[10] But crimes against women, and particularly crimes against prostitutes, decreased markedly after World War II.[11] Indeed, former malaya women in Pumwani looked back on the late 1940s as a period when the rule of law was authoritative and responsive.

> Before Mau Mau, in the days of the English, when a girl was pregnant and she wanted to throw her baby away . . . her neighbors in the same house would report her to the police if she tried to kill the baby, and the police would try very hard to find out if the women killed the child, and women came to fear killing newborn babies because they were afraid of what the police would do to them, they were frightened of going to jail.[12]

If prostitutes feared jail and officials feared lawlessness, what was the nature of authority in postwar Nairobi? As violence ceased to be against women and began to be against the respectable male urbanites whom the state was then attempting to legitimate, officials identified with the fears and complaints of these men and began to moralize and legislate the need for state control over male violence.[13]

Postwar Wage Labor

Who had gone to live in Nairobi after the war to create such diverse accounts of social reality? Throup's assertion that "the returning *askari*, who spurned the retraining courses at Kabete and quickly dissipated their gratuities, the angry squatters expelled from the European farms in the White Highlands, and the dispossessed *ahoi* of Kikuyuland, sought refuge in Pumwani"[14] reflected earlier notions about the dangers of the laboring (or recently unemployed) classes and implied that the skilled, the literate, and the regularly employed would not stoop to dissent or dishonesty. But the postwar employed and unemployed were not so disparate as to be mutually exclusive categories.

The economic growth of the postwar era was unparalleled; in addition to the number of small, Indian-owned manufacturing firms that had begun during the war, between 1946 and 1951 five foreign-owned industries set up factories in and around Nairobi. But the high employment in industry, estate agriculture, and construction failed to absorb the reserve army of semiskilled labor recently demobilized from the military. Skilled workers only fared as well as the labor market allowed: John Mwakalili was a 50/-a-month house servant when he joined the KAR in 1940; after the war he worked as a mechanic earning 250/ a month. But Joseph Njoroge earned 50/ a month as a gardener in Nairobi in 1940, when he enlisted in the KAR. Upon his demobilization he worked as a truck driver's assistant for 150/ a month for three years and then was let go; after a year he got a job as a house servant for an Indian family in Eastleigh for 60/ a month.

Construction work, which was perhaps the biggest growth industry in Nairobi until 1950, was seasonal and largely unskilled. Indeed, as private and public construction boomed after 1948, the number of unskilled and semiskilled manual laborers looking for work in Nairobi kept wages artificially low and falling. Postwar European immigration to Kenya expanded the demand for skilled domestic servants but seems to have reduced the number of domestic servants per household. Until the early 1950s wage laborers moved out of agriculture and into domestic service and unskilled urban labor, but this did not drive money wages up as it had done twenty and thirty years before. Ex-servicemen and men forced out of military domestic service experienced a dramatic drop in their money wages.[15] The wages of any number of men, whatever their career changes, increased only 10/ or 20/ per month between 1940 and 1950.[16] (See table 6.)

At the same time, the growing skilled, well-paid work force encouraged an informal sector of their own: hawkers, practitioners of traditional medicine, bottle sellers, barbers—all became occupations men practiced while they waited for openings at their skill level. The structure of the locations changed as older men went into the informal sector to wait out the lean times of the labor market. Some demobilized servicemen became shoemakers, barbers, or tailors immediately after the war; many returned to formal sector employment after a few years.[17] In this way they were indistinguishable from the unskilled men who alternated stints of wage labor with self-employment as smiths, traditional doctors, or bottle sellers in the

TABLE 6   Average Wages in Shillings per Month,
without Value of Rations, Nairobi

	1945	1946	1947	1948	1949	1950	1951	1952
Domestic Service								
Garden Staff	32	31	37	34	38	43	40	40
House servant	38	39	43	44	40	55	60	65
Cook	54	46	47	52	60	55		
Unskilled manual	25	26	26	27	33	27	27	36
Semiskilled	45	46	40	42	46	50	58	60
Artisan	75	58	63	77	90	105	110	115
Driver	90	90	80	79	80	80	115	105
Askari/guard	46	30	30	30	30	30	30	30
Supervisor			40	80	68	70		

SOURCES: Notes generously loaned me by Michael P. Cowen and J. R. Newman; Ziro wa Bogosha, Pumwani, 18 March 1977; Ahmed Hussein, Pumwani, 1 April 1977; Odhiambo Okinyi, Shauri Moyo, 23 February 1977; Thomas Mukama, Eastleigh, 10 March 1977.

postwar years.[18] Both groups together straddled conventional notions of a skilled urban work force and the unemployed, and merged into the "out of works and undesirables" that the colonial state tried to have removed from Nairobi annually.[19]

This is not to suggest that postwar Nairobi was without its poor, its unemployed, its perpetually disgruntled: such people were of course there. But on the whole "the rogues and the vagabonds" that various branches of the urban administration had been talking about for years were of a different order in the years immediately following World War II. This was not so much because they were more in opposition to the colonial state than previous residents had been, as Askwith suggested, but because they were more skilled, possibly more educated, and certainly more savvy as to how to evade the controls of an overburdened urban administration.

Crime in postwar Nairobi was not only sophisticated, it was interracial. While the police were generally thought to be too poorly educated to be of much use, criminal gangs were thought to be well organized, and there were a "vast number" of receivers of stolen goods. Some receivers were police informers; they were Africans, Indians, and Europeans: each tended to take the goods "their race could most innocently dispose of." Clothing theft and resale was the only crime that was said to be all African; other stolen items were transported in trucks driven by Indians or, less frequently, Europeans.[20] Crime in postwar Nairobi was, if anything, more professional than the construction industry. Moreover, such communities of lawbreakers, with their interracial connections, their networks, their social identity, were as much a part of postwar Nairobi as was the African Advisory Council. The nature of such groups has not always been readily identifiable, but their importance—in matters pertaining to politics, property, race, and gender—has been unmistakable. The historiography of the Anake wa 40 has, for example, described it as a nationalist group whose armed robberies won the support of Nairobi's populace, a group of ex-soldiers that disbanded in 1949 because "of a lack of public support," and "a criminal gang" that supplied prostitutes to Nairobi's Indian community, respectively, using shreds of evidence to prove each position. For example, it was said that the group supplied prostitutes because its alleged leader was found with women's clothes in his Ziwani home. In fact, he was a tailor.[21]

For those on either side of the law, however, rising commodity prices reduced real earnings. Maize flour, beans, and rice more than doubled in price between 1946 and 1952. During that time the cost of sugar doubled, that of milk increased by one-half, and that of bread by two-thirds. Only the cost of potatoes and cabbage remained relatively low in the postwar years, although the price of cabbage increased by 60 percent by 1949 but dropped to its 1945 price in 1950. Between 1945 and 1952 the price of kerosene rose nearly 70 percent and charcoal increased by 50 percent.[22]

Rents also rose, but not as steeply as they had in the late 1930s, as the MNC subsidized rents in its estates. Single rooms in Pumwani rented from between 13/ to 26/ in 1946, depending on the size of the room, its location within Pumwani (the lowest rents tended to be in Digo and Mashimoni, and then only among Muslims), and how well a tenant knew a particular landlord. By 1950 the lowest Pumwani rents were 16/ and 32/. Rents in Shauri Moyo were competitive during this period, about 25/ per room, and ranged from 10/ to 35/ in Bondeni and Kaloleni. Single rooms were considerably less in Bahati and considerably more in Ziwani. After 1946, rents in the squatter settlements of Mathare, Buruburu, and Kawangware increased to between 20/ and 30/ per room. This seems to have been because the cost of building materials had so increased that the initial expenditure for building a shanty in wood or even wattle and daub was such that householders had to charge high rents to recover their losses, and this may have served to put low-paid wage laborers into densely crowded rooms in Pumwani. In African-owned houses in Eastleigh, rents doubled and trebled to between 70/ and 80/ after 1947 because, as one tenant said matter-of-factly, the owner "had to repay a loan."[23] Such rooms in Eastleigh, however, were out of the reach of laboring men.

Married workers' housing had been taken up seriously by the MNC after the war. This increased the number of families living in Nairobi as the
purchasing power of even artisans' wages plummeted. A 1950 survey of
Nairobi workers—which did not count heavy drinkers, regulars at football matches, and men who missed work because of illness—showed that
their average monthly cash expenditure was about 18 percent more than
their wages, usually managed by loans from friends, kin, or credit from
retailers.[24] For workers with resident families the proportion of debt must
have been much higher, as it must have been for the sickly or the heavy
drinkers. A few skilled workers' wives obtained hawkers' licenses to sell
cooked food or permission to open tea kiosks;[25] others shared their quarters with single male laborers to reduce rent, or took in homeless relatives.[26] Not only was the new nuclear ideal undermined by unskilled
workers, cousins, and grandmothers, but as skilled and unskilled workers
were strapped by the rising cost of living after 1948, the colonial references to friends and kin who crowded the best-designed African housing
became fact.

The attrition rate from Nairobi's married workers' housing estates
seems to have been fairly high. A number of postwar prostitutes said they
first went to Nairobi to live with their husbands, whom they abandoned to
go to Pumwani and Shauri Moyo. The friends and relatives of the Luo
artisans Colchester had celebrated spoke of how disruptive urban life was
for marriage.[27] I think it would be wrong, however, to attribute such postwar marital breakups to the pressures of Nairobi life: these women
claimed to have left their husbands because of the drunkenness and repeated beatings, two of the main reasons why rural wives, particularly
those from western Kenya, said they left their spouses in the same years. A
few rural women claimed to have left their husband because he took a second wife, however, which husbands in married workers' housing in Nairobi did not do. Such monogamy may have been evidence of a change in
urban Kenyan men or of the decline in urban skilled workers' wages, or of
both.[28] When these women left their husbands, they generally took their
children with them, went to live in Pumwani and Shauri Moyo, and supported themselves through prostitution.

Welfare Associations and Prostitution, 1946–52

Runaway wives were harassed in a new and more intense way after World
War II. Starting in the late 1930s—the same time that the MNAO called
the immigration of young Kikuyu prostitutes into Nairobi inevitable—

ethnic unions from Kavirondo and Nyanza requested recognition in Nairobi and help in locating "runaway daughters."[29] Most of these groups were recognized during the war, starting with Luo Union in 1940, as "units of social cohesion."[30] Frequently these groups were amalgams of Christians and Muslims, skilled workers and householders, and stated as their goals the use of Memorial Hall in Pumwani—built in 1925 and hardly used at all in the 1930s—for dances or meetings, to be represented at official functions, such as sporting events and talks; and "to vouch for the affairs of members of their community . . . enquiry as to whether or not a woman is really someone's wife."[31] By 1946 the enquiries into African women's private lives took place in earnest: there was an unconfirmed report that the Kikuyu General Union (KGU) "was holding their own court to punish wayward girls and return them to their homes."[32]

It would be inaccurate to assume that welfare associations represented a recently constituted African patriarchy joining forces with colonial sexism to control and contain female behavior. Even a notion of African patriarchy, with undifferentiated attempts to control female behavior, does not hold up to the evidence. In 1946 the Bukoba Association in Nairobi split between the prostitutes, who provided most of the funds, and its male membership. The separatist Bahaya Union in Nairobi repeatedly voted against joining other, Tanganyika-based Haya associations, as Haya prostitutes protected their contributions and their organization.[33] The activities of most welfare associations were in fact opposed by the colonial state, which repeatedly remonstrated with them that they were usurping judicial powers and making civil matters out of problems that belonged in Native Tribunals. Indeed, Kikuyu welfare associations had repeatedly asked for criminal prosecutions for the men—lovers, customers, or the truck drivers who brought women to Nairobi—who led women astray.[34] Welfare associations were not only demanding rigid controls on women, they wanted the right to police male behavior as well. The colonial state and the ethnic welfare associations represented substantially different versions of access to and control over African private life, each with different rights, responsibilities, and obligations.

What did the welfare associations want? Between 1946 and 1952 they wanted extraordinary powers and extraordinary tolerance. In 1946 the KGU attempted a roundup of uncircumcised Kikuyu men in Nairobi, which failed. In 1948 the Women's Section of the African Workers Federation, Mombasa, requested an end to hawkers' licenses and demanded "to know why a European can go about with an African woman, but whenever an African goes about with a European woman he must be taken before

Court."[35] In that year interracial prostitution was not an abstraction on the coast. It was supposedly "common knowledge" that women from the Polish refugee camp at Nyali "were prostituting themselves with Africans" without arrests or censure.[36] In 1950—two years after the Kikuyu Central Association extended its oath of unity into Nairobi to carefully selected trade unionists, criminals, taxi drivers, and prostitutes[37]—the KGU identified four groups of women who should be allowed to remain in towns: those legally married and living with their husbands, householders, registered domestic servants, and "old prostitutes who have lived this way for a long time and cannot find alternative means of employment." The rest were to be sent home. They asked that the dignity of women be protected from abusive men, "no matter if he is a European, Indian, or an African." Indeed, they asked for the creation of a civil code "governing fornication or prostitution" applied to "Europeans, Asiatics, and Africans without discrimination." They asked that the men arrested with prostitutes be jailed as well and made to pay the woman's transport home. They asked that the laws relating to native custom be strengthened by the colonial state. They demanded more clinics to treat venereal diseases. They asked that any taxi driver carrying young women without parental or spousal consent "be severely punished, have his driver's licence suspended or cancelled and stopped from buying any more petrol for that particular car." Both the KGU and the Kalenjin Union asked that Kikuyu and Kalenjin women who worked as ayahs "who were found to be incapable of doing a satisfactory job" be reported to them.[38]

While postwar colonial social engineering was an attempt to control African men's private lives by controlling their time and controlling their space,[39] the welfare associations sought to control men's private lives by controlling their relationships and their mobility. Occasionally the associations ventured into the uncharted waters of controlling women's work, but on the whole the vocabulary and the categories that accompanied the creation of respectable, nucleated urbanites in the 1940s were internalized—with substantially more dissent and debate—by those very Africans who earned enough to be deemed respectable. The KGU were not the passive victims of the social engineering of the late 1940s; they took the invasion of private life to heart. They envisioned an authoritarian world in which reliable men entered into responsible relationships that were backed up by laws that could control the movements of wives and children. So strongly did the KGU believe in matrimony, for example, that they wanted a law to forbid members of different tribes to live together, but "legal intermarriage between tribes is right."[40] But the ideology that made

men as responsible for prostitution as runaway women were was not simply the result of the emerging self-consciousness on the part of Nairobi's
menfolk; it came in part from the membership of the KGU. According to
the colonial state's stooge and then Assistant African Affairs Officer, Dedan Githengi, the reason the KGU was ineffectual in sending women
home was "because Kikuyu women are allowed to hawk foodstuffs in the
town" and because "the Union's work is prejudiced and will continue to be
prejudiced as long as it allows young women who have run away from
their husbands to be members."[41]

Nevertheless, it was prostitutes and not truck drivers who were most
easily identified and harassed. According to Colchester, the KGU did fine
prostitutes immediately after World War II,[42] but KGU stalwarts insisted
that prostitutes were not fined. The organization was founded to maintain "the dignity of women." Sending women home was welfare, and
proof that the KGU had strong urban-rural ties. Between 1946 and 1952,
when complaints were received from aggrieved fathers and husbands, the
appropriate runaways were identified by informers, mainly women but
sometimes ex-soldiers in the years immediately following the war, whose
information was said to be "*very* exact." These informers were salaried
monthly by the KGU, and their identity was known to the African Affairs
Officer. The young women so identified were then interrogated by older
Kikuyu women, generally the informers: if they claimed to be married,
they had to show proof, and if they were prostitutes they had to explain
exactly why they had left their husbands. Young single women were sent
home to their parents (as were "poor young boys," in far fewer numbers
than women), who paid for their transport home: parents were overjoyed
at getting their daughters back.[43] Despite all this, the KGU was fearsome
enough for at least one gang to make a living masquerading as the KGU,
detaining and fining Nairobi prostitutes.[44]

Luo Union, with presumably fewer Nairobi prostitutes, was less discrete
in matters of repatriation. Women in the Nyanza countryside in the late
1940s and 1950s passed on what may well have been a conventional wisdom, that Luo Union made women dress "in clothing cut out of an old sack
with a gaping hole in the front and the back, without panties, and these
women were made to walk down the street in public and later they were
taken to the bus that would take them home."[45] In the wake of Operation
Anvil in April 1954—when thirty thousand Kikuyu, Embu, and Meru
were arrested in one day in Nairobi—Luo Union's attempts to control
female behavior, and female apparel, became almost punitive: "If a Luo
woman was caught by Luo men they'd make her strip and make her wear a

dress made out of sacks and then they'd make her walk around where everybody could see her and they'd denounce her as a prostitute." To Luo women, it looked as if Luo Union had the support of the state: "Luo Union would persuade the police or judge to send her back home to Nyanza with a police guard."[46] Bylaw 8 of Luo Union made it an offense "for a Luo girl or woman to take money from her underwear pocket." Although colonial officials took a year to ask Luo Union to remove such unenforceable bylaws,[47] in May 1954 Luo Union Women's Branch was formed, to police Luo women *and* men: "we wanted to organize and mobilize women and girls when we found that men were harassing women, dressing them in sacks and sending them home without looking at each case properly."[48]

The first President of the Women's Branch, Salome Ogai, was less concerned about underwear than she was about making sure that women accused of prostitution were actually prostitutes. She did this in ways that made Luo intraethnic prostitution as dangerous as interethnic prostitution was. While Ogai insisted that "decent Luo women were not gesturing to Kikuyus with their hands," knowing that a woman had no husband was not enough; Luo men were recruited by Luo Union to ask their friends about certain women; sometimes they went with Luo women and informed on them afterwards. Once a woman was identified as a prostitute, Luo men went to physically remove her from her house; she was taken to another woman's house and then escorted to the bus station. Luo Union paid the woman's bus fare and paid for the escort. Both single and married women were sent back to their parents. Once at home, Luo Union would alert someone to watch the woman there.[49]

Prostitution in Pumwani and Shauri Moyo, 1946–52

The hard-and-fast distinctions among watembezi, malaya, and wazi-wazi forms were already becoming frayed during World War II as women combined the forms to meet the special opportunities and constraints of wartime. In the postwar era even the most dutiful of young Muslim malaya women allowed themselves the luxury—and profits—of frequent streetwalking; new immigrants combined watembezi and malaya forms daily. Malaya women in the 1920s and 1930s had sometimes gone to River Road to look for men but did not always admit, let alone announce, that they combined both forms. Nevertheless, women of the late 1940s considered themselves malaya prostitutes and supported themselves as independent household heads with their earnings. Women occasionally practiced the malaya form without rooms of their own, but with characteristic malaya accumulation and community. For example, after an illness Farida Monteo was evicted from the room she had lived in Pumwani for twenty years, but the owner allowed her to sleep on the veranda for free. After almost a year she had saved enough to build a shanty in Mathare and used her monthly income of 80/ to rent a room in Pumwani.

The watembezi form, with its distinctive patterns of accumulation and reinvestment, lost some of its specificity in the postwar era. On the whole, women used the watembezi form to supplement the earnings available from malaya prostitution, not to support rural households. This was not because rural households were so well off in the postwar era, but that the problems of soil erosion, land shortage, too many or too few cattle could not be solved by a few years of daughters' streetwalking, just as they were not solved by remittances from sons' and husbands' migrant labor.[50] Wazi-wazi identity in the postwar era remained more fixed; these women combined wazi-wazi prostitution with nighttime malaya prostitution but almost no streetwalking. The ability of wazi-wazi women to maintain their social identity was reinforced by new arrivals from Bukoba. After 1946 the reputation of Danguroni began to fade rapidly, but the area retained its ethnic specificity and was known sometimes as Wazi-Wazi or as Mji wa Bukoba despite the fact that many Haya immigrants went to live elsewhere in Pumwani. By 1948 or 1949 it was becoming known as Digo, of which it was a part.[51] All of this means that after 1946 it is really not useful to examine the forms of prostitution individually; instead, postwar Nairobi had a fluidity—of streetwalkers, customers, and absentee landlords—that gave the regional variations of prostitution within the city's African locations a meaning they had not had since the 1920s.

The prices paid prostitutes seemed to be regional in this era. In general, the short-time price of between 1/ and 2/ obtained in Pumwani until at least 1952. Women in Shauri Moyo said that "it differed from man to man" and that women "felt jealous" and "kept our earnings a secret," but it was about 2/ for short-time. There was no wazi-wazi prostitution in Shauri Moyo, because it was "small" and known only for malaya prostitution.[52] Such reliably low prices seem to have increased the volume of business in Pumwani, especially for wazi-wazi and some malaya women, after 1948. Their customers were not the unemployed or even poorly paid construction workers; they were skilled laborers, domestic servants, or self-employed African men, living in the more expensive, if occasionally illegal, housing in Ziwani, Eastleigh, Mathare, and Kawangware.[53] These men went to Pumwani as an earlier generation of European men had

done, to find women. It seems unlikely that this exacerbated tensions between the African locations, as the Pumwani unemployed and underemployed would not have been keenly aware of prostitutes' clientele, and
most Pumwani Muslim elites also frequented wazi-wazi and malaya
women in Pumwani.[54]

Many of the men who went to Pumwani and Shauri Moyo were KAR
veterans. As such, they already knew the area, they were also veterans of
countless lectures on the evils and consequences of venereal diseases, and
they had a healthy respect for the relationship between gonorrhea and
female infertility, and their own role in transmission and infection. Many
probably subscribed to the responsibilities articulated by ethnic welfare
associations. In any case, prior to World War II it was generally said that
men preferred to visit prostitutes who had no children. These women
would request less money, and as one woman pointed out, "children make
noise and want attention the first thing in the morning, and that is not
what a man goes to a prostitute for."[55] After the war, however, prostitutes
noted for the first time that "some men feared that a woman without children had gonorrhea and that they would get it, and those men would only
go with a woman who had a child already."[56] Prostitutes with children, including women recently arrived from the Railway Landhies, were sought
out by men. Many women who had small children during World War II,
and who had taken up the wazi-wazi form because of its safety or convenience for child care, did as well from wazi-wazi prostitution after the war
as they had done during it.[57]

Not all prostitutes with small children practiced the wazi-wazi form between 1946 and 1952, however. Declining real wages meant that the
methods earlier generations of watembezi women had used to find well-
paid men no longer worked; the short-time price in River Road was no
better than the short-time price in Pumwani and was substantially more
risky. Many women from Pumwani took to daytime watembezi prostitution in the new locations built especially for single men. By 1950 some of
these men were welcoming women with children as much as KAR veterans had done a few years before. Mary Masaba, a Christian Gisu woman
from Uganda who had come to Nairobi late in 1945, described how she
went to Bahati in the early 1950s—where a bedspace cost 6/ per month
and a room 21/—and was received in a way she contrasted vividly with her
treatment by the white men she met on the road. "I had a child I always
carried around, I couldn't afford to have a ayah, and a white man couldn't
stomach the idea of you coming with a child to his house, but the Africans
were all right about it." She even moved to Bahati for a while "because it

was cheaper for me to stay with men there, because I wasn't paying any rent and that way I could save a bit of money. . . . but finally the contract of the man I was living with ended and he went home, and by that time I had saved some money, so I decided to come back to Majengo."

Between 1946 and 1950 Masaba had combined the malaya form with some daytime watembezi prostitution in Pumwani; the latter allowed her to visit men in their rooms without disturbing her children. Her practice of both forms was straightforward: "the prices were 1/ for short-time and 5/ for the whole night." She knew that other women asked for more money,

> but others like me did not. It was like this, I didn't have money and I needed to get some: if a man knew he could go with me for 1/, he would, and I wouldn't have to worry about bargaining or fighting or abuse, and if he knew that it was 5/ for the whole night, he would pay me that in advance, and I wouldn't have to spend money on tea or anything in the hopes that he would give me a few cents in the morning. Don't you see, I had five children, I had lived with several men, and it was simpler for me to go with a man who knew in advance what he was going to pay me.

Here was a prostitution well-articulated as a way to keep the peace, to minimize tensions and conflicts and, by the late 1940s, expectations, as was price-last malaya prostitution of twenty years before. Many women in Shauri Moyo did the same, but tried to ask for 2/ for short-time: "I didn't have any money when I did that, also these men were poor, they didn't have 5/, so there was no point in fighting them for money."[58] Such low prices were partly maintained because men exchanged information about it ("everyone knew the price") and because it was "simpler" for the women themselves. Masaba's prostitution must have earned her between 45/ and 60/ per month at least, much more than unskilled laborers earned between 1945 and 1950. But during those years she paid 23/ per month rent (37/ after 1952), raised five children, and supported at least as many men through periods of unemployment and low-paying jobs. By her own account she lived comfortably and was able to send all five children to primary school. In 1977 she was living on money she had saved and contributions from the two sons who shared her room. She had fared well but was fairly typical of women who began their prostitution after 1945, in that she had never been able to earn enough to invest in urban or rural property. Masaba understood this and did not describe her prostitution in

terms of the acquisition of property or possessions, as malaya women did
earlier, but as an alternative to reliable spousal support: "Everybody needs
money, don't they? Women need money too, so what else can she do besides prostitution if she can't find employment and she has got children to
support? And maybe a woman never had a capable husband, so probably
she will turn to prostitution so as to make a living for herself and her children." It is perhaps significant that Masaba volunteered that what she valued about her life in Nairobi was her control over her time, not her
earnings, as malaya women twenty years ago had done. "At home, every
minute would have to be accounted for, I would either have to be working
in the farm, or looking after children, or cooking, and there was always
someone to tell me what to do. Here my time is my own."

Price-first malaya and daytime watembezi prostitution seems to have
lowered the price for short-time sexual relations throughout Pumwani
and, to a lesser extent, Shauri Moyo. Between 1946 and 1952 the short-
time prices of wazi-wazi women ranged from 1/50 (the price of a pound of
maize flour in 1951) to 3/ (the price of packaged milk in 1949).[59] These
were barely better than their wartime prices, and some wazi-wazi women
responded to their declining incomes by attempting, with limited success,
to fix their prices. We have already seen the implicit ways that prostitutes'
prices were maintained at existing levels—by men exchanging information or Haya women calling out their prices—but this was the first deliberate attempt by prostitutes to establish and maintain a fixed short-time
price. This seems to have begun around 1948; it was initiated by Haya
women, but the actual organization was by wazi-wazi women living in adjacent houses, not by ethnicity. Juliana Rugumisa, a Haya woman who began wazi-wazi prostitution soon after she went to Pumwani in 1948,
described how Haya women living in one house in Mashimoni decided to
raise their short-time prices. "We all agreed never to go for less than 2/.
Most of the women who decided were Haya, but we asked our neighbors
to help us. Some of our neighbors were Luo women; some were Nandi."
These women were also Christians. My data suggest that in 1948 price-
fixing was confined to a number of adjacent houses in Mashimoni and
possibly Digo; it is difficult to say if it had spread to other houses in Pumwani, in the absence of direct evidence. It seems unlikely that it did, however, because women like Mary Masaba had already deflated the short-
time malaya price. In 1954, even with the special risks and opportunities
of Mau Mau, a new Muslim arrival in Pumwani was informed by the men
who came to her door that the short-time price was 2/, not nearly as "generous" as the short-time price she had been used to in Mombasa a few

weeks before.[60] There was no short-time price-fixing in Shauri Moyo, although many malaya women charged prices equivalent to those in Pumwani.[61]

But the presence of price-first malaya women and daytime watembezi walking openly through Pumwani and Shauri Moyo scandalized older Muslims and even young Muslim prostitutes who combined both forms: "it was one thing to go in the street to look for men . . . it was another to let your elders know you were doing this."[62] The values of the older Muslim malaya form remained, but they were simply not practiced as often, or as profitably, as they were preached. For Nairobi-born Muslim women, once they decided to take up prostitution, the malaya form was, by virtue of their upbringing, religion, and sense of community, all that was available to them. Fatuma Ali, for example, was already widowed by her second husband when she moved to Pumwani in 1952 to practice full-service malaya prostitution, with so little success that she eventually took a job as a street sweeper. Ibrahima binti Musa, the daughter of a Kileleshwa householder who had moved to Pangani and then Pumwani, repeatedly criticized the moral decay evidenced by the daytime watembezi prostitution of the late 1940s. Yet she herself engaged in watembezi prostitution at night, "but I did it with respect and secrecy . . . never in the daytime when everyone would notice." She went to town to meet European men, using back alleys to go to the bus stop, and solicited African men at the dances ethnic welfare associations held at Memorial Hall, about a hundred yards from her house, after 1946. At those dances, she would inform African men that she was married, not because she was, but because she believed that this would insure their discretion and secrecy when they went home with her, so they would be careful not to disturb her mother in the next room.

Watembezi prostitution at the dances at Memorial Hall was a dependable, safe way for prostitutes to find men and to reduce the appearance of promiscuity that they believed would provoke male violence. The stabilization of Nairobi's labor force had created a new idiom in which men and women approached each other at those dances.

> If I was dancing with a man I'll touch him very hard on the arm three times and then he'll ask me in a whisper "are you married?" and then I would be happy, I would think today I have my partner. Now, because I had an appointment with this man I wouldn't go with any other man that night. In those days if you went with more than one man in a night they would fight each other and someone might be killed.[63]

In just such ways violence against women, and violence between men, was for many prostitutes negotiable. Tabitha Waweru identified Kikuyu men as potentially belligerent but malleable.

> You can't tell a man you want 50/ for short-time because if he's a Kikuyu man he can beat you. I'll tell you how things were with Kikuyu men, the way things were at that time: if a Kikuyu man really loves you, and if he came to your house and spent the night there, I couldn't ask him for anything. But I'd wake up very early in the morning, make hot water so that he could have his bath, and have the tea and everything ready for him at the table when he's finished his bath, and after he ate and dressed, then he'll put the money in your kanga and leave it lying on the bed, because he was happy with you for what you did.

This is virtually identical to 1920s descriptions of how Muslim malaya women were supposed to behave with Muslim men. In the 1920s women spoke of how being Muslim enabled them to provide the domestic services that would be most appreciated; there was no risk of being beaten. Here we see the same malaya conduct twenty years later without any Muslims involved in it. Is this evidence of the Kikuyu "reign of terror" or does it represent something else? It is unlikely that Waweru's ideas about how to treat Kikuyu men came from her Pumwani childhood: she was the daughter of a polygynous Kikuyu father and a Giriama mother. She never thought of herself as Kikuyu, nor did she ever learn to speak the language. Her conceptualization of Kikuyu manhood was linked to her ideas about women's work and the nature of domestic services therein: in this instance, ethnicity was not a cultural absolute, but negotiable terrain. Indeed, this quotation reveals much more about Waweru's sense of her own social skills than it does about behavior unique to Kikuyu men.

Ethnicity was not, in the late 1940s, an emotional bond but a means by which some women assessed and guaranteed their safety. Lydia Nthenga, a Christian Kamba woman who had taken her children from her husband's room in the Railway Landhies in 1947, said she tried only to go with Kamba men because "he'll tell me where his home was and he was probably not going to harm me or cheat me or beat me if he thought I would eventually tell someone from his home what he'd done." Not every woman could afford the luxury of ethnic particularism, however. Louise Kaseem, a Toro woman who went to Pumwani in 1946 "because I was poor in Uganda," engaged in daytime watembezi prostitution and "welcomed every man. At that time I had no money and I had to go with whoever had money, I couldn't afford to choose one tribe over another." But other Ugandan women, particularly those who had lived in Nairobi for a few years, sought out those groups of men who would pay them the most.[64]

In both Shauri Moyo and Pumwani, the declining value of wages meant that better-off men could easily give prostitutes gifts instead of cash. If ethnic welfare associations were concerned with underwear, postwar malaya women were concerned with the outer garments they received as gifts—and the contexts in which the gifts were given—and how these might make them seem in their communities. Asha Mohammed worried that the clothes her generous European boyfriends gave her would alienate her neighbors in Shauri Moyo: "if an African man saw you in a beautiful dress like a European woman, they would think you were very expensive and not even try to make an appointment with you." Tabitha Waweru had no such compassion. While she waxed lyrical about the gifts Europeans and West Africans gave her, she complained that after World War II "these men from Kenya, my country, they'd buy a kanga for you and a kitamba and also a long dress. And that African man who buys you a long dress, he'll brag to his friends about how much money he spent on his girlfriend, but really he's hopeless. We never wore long dresses out." Clothing apparently was not just about conspicuous consumption or status or appearances: it had a different meaning to men and to women.[65]

Prostitution outside Pumwani and Shauri Moyo, 1946–52

The wartime experiences of many Eastleigh prostitutes—watembezi prostitution with generous European men and substantially less generous Indian men, and full-scale malaya prostitution with African men—continued well into peacetime, with the benefit of the relaxation of military patrols. A few women, like Tabitha Waweru, remained in Majengo, but many others continued to live in Eastleigh once the war was over. As the racial composition of Eastleigh changed, Muslim malaya women began to move there from Pumwani and Shauri Moyo, starting in 1946. Although watembezi women without the proper documents were sometimes arrested,[66] malaya women believed that Eastleigh would be safe for their work because of the circumspection of the form. Moreover, in Eastleigh Muslim malaya women extended the full services of the form to Indian men in a community that was still predominately Indian. Indeed, these women stressed that the religion they shared with Indian men made them especially able to serve them. Alisati binti Salim, born in Pangani and brought up in Uganda, moved to Eastleigh in 1946 from Pumwani, and rented a room there for 80/ per month. She volunteered that this was profitable for her, because "there were many Asian men living there, they owned the houses . . . and it helped me in my business that I had been brought up a Muslim, and I knew how to talk politely to these men, and wash myself and leave them bathwater after sex, and so it was good for me to live there."

Here we see once again the conflation of ethnicity and the malaya form: that men of certain tribes or religions behave in certain ways that the clever prostitute can negotiate her way around. Such ethnic constructions seem fairly specific to the malaya form; watembezi and wazi-wazi women did not talk about how different groups of men behaved. But do these quotations illuminate male ethnic traits and desires, or do they describe the characteristics of the full-service malaya form? Here were women smug in the knowledge that they knew how to please specific groups of men. These were women not overly concerned with ethnicity in and of itself. They were instead proud of their ability to manipulate the service and the deference of the malaya form to their financial advantage.

Such deference enabled binti Salim to build a house with her earnings; she was one of the few women who began prostitution after World War II who was able to do so. In 1951 she built a house in Kariobangi for 1,500/, although she returned to Pumwani to live as a tenant among Muslims. Malaya women in Eastleigh provided deferential, price-last, full-service prostitution. The full-time price was dear: men reported paying between 10/ and 20/—21/50 if breakfast was included—to spend the night. The African men who could afford these amounts were artisans, drivers, and senior domestic servants.[67] These men also visited women for short-time at a price of 5/, occasionally 3/, in postwar Eastleigh; 3/ to 5/ was about the intra-African short-time watembezi price there as well.[68]

Other women did less spectacularly, but nevertheless they did well: Edwina Kamau obtained a hawker's license shortly after the war; after a few years she went back to prostitution and then back to hawking again. She was able to lease a small shop in the late 1950s. Beatrice Nyambura worked as a prostitute, a laundress, a domestic servant, and a prostitute and was able to build a house in Mathare in about 1960.

Africans began to acquire property in Eastleigh shortly after the war. Between 1946 and 1948 all the new African landlords in Eastleigh were women, former or still-working prostitutes. By 1947 or 1948 the most successful wartime watembezi were known to other women as successful, aggressive young women already making money in other enterprises. By then, Ruth Nyokabi owned three houses in Eastleigh's Somali and Indian

area, Section 3, and Mary Nduta, who passed into legend when she purchased a secondhand Mercedes-Benz in 1960, may have owned a house in
Eastleigh by 1947. Margaret Wainana, who had earned enough through
prostitution to begin selling scrap metal at the end of the war, bought a
secondhand car in 1947 or 1948, which she was able to parlay into a fleet
of three or four taxis before the Emergency.[69] Less well known women
were said to have acquired property in Eastleigh only after they had made
threats on the lives of their Indian lovers, although others insisted that
they borrowed money from these men to pay for their properties, effecting illegal property transfers that were not registered with the Land Office until many years later.[70] The new owners certainly behaved like
women in debt: within two years the rents they charged doubled and
trebled to between 70/ and 80/ a room.

By 1948 and 1949 African property ownership in Eastleigh was becoming commonplace. Beatrice Nyambura lived there from 1938 to 1947,
when she got a job as an ayah and lived on her employer's premises in suburban Nairobi. In 1949 she returned to Eastleigh, and former neighbors
helped her find a room for 40/; within six months the rent had increased
to 70/ "because the house had been bought by an African woman and it
was her only source of income and she needed a lot of money." She tried to
return to the house where she lived in 1938, "but that house had been
bought by an African also and they wanted a lot of money for a room
there." Many women were willing to pay such rents, but the owners themselves, trying to maximize their profits, lived elsewhere, generally in
Asian-owned and, by their standards, cheaper housing in Eastleigh.[71]
Some women "made lots of money" in Eastleigh but did not stay there:
"not all of them wanted to stay in town, they wanted to farm."[72]

At the same time, a few Muslim malaya women in Pumwani had,
through slow and steady accumulation, been able to build wattle-and-
daub housing in Kariobangi, Buruburu, and Mathare. The restrictions on
expanding Pumwani and Shauri Moyo and the ban on building in wattle
and daub meant that they could only build in squatters' settlements. Most
of these women never moved into their new houses, however. They said
they did not want to live among Christians and be away from the Muslim
community in which they had lived for many years, so they stayed in Pumwani.[73] Thus absentee landlordism on a large scale became a feature of
African life in Nairobi. To the salary segregation of the municipal estates
was added the growing religious segregation of the squatters' settlements.
Nevertheless, the very illegality of the squatters' settlements and African-
owned houses in Eastleigh seems to have kept social life fairly quiet in

those areas. Women paying 70/ per month and entertaining Indian customers had a vested interest in keeping their surroundings peaceful, and
in places like Buruburu most of the resident landlords had been there
since the early 1940s and remained until the settlement was demolished in
1953.[74] Indeed, although Buruburu was said to be the home of Anake wa
40, it was tranquil in comparison to the municipal estates: there were antipolice riots in both Marurani and Shauri Moyo in 1947 and 1948 respectively, and the 1950 general strike, which was not nearly as violent as
officials anticipated, was orchestrated from Shauri Moyo and Pumwani.[75]
Prostitution in the squatters' settlements seems to have been fairly sedate
and expensive: as short-time prices between Africans in the River Road
area dropped sharply to 1/, the short-time prices in Mathare, Buruburu,
and Kariobangi were slightly higher than those in Pumwani and Shauri
Moyo—between 2/ and 3/—while the full-time price was as much as 2/
more.[76]

Mau Mau and Prostitution

The Mau Mau revolt, officially a State of Emergency from 1952 to 1960,
has been the subject of considerable scholarly attention.[77] Scholars dis-
agree as to the nature of the movement, sometimes to the extent of drown-
ing out the disagreements within Mau Mau. Much of this literature places
the origins of Mau Mau in generalities, either over increasingly insecure
Kikuyu land rights or over increasingly rapacious demands of Kikuyu
chiefs. But the search for origins has sometimes denied the specifics: the
massive oathings of 1948–52, the well-organized support from Nairobi
well into 1954, and the social rearrangements and factions of the forest.
From a colonial standpoint, the movement—for which Mau Mau is as
good a term as any to describe the fluidity of organization and
membership—was always a Kikuyu civil war: the State of Emergency was
declared after the assassination of Chief Waruhiu, not the murder of a few
settlers. Mau Mau was, at the beginning, very popular. In all, it was estimated that fifteen thousand Kikuyu went into the forest, where the movement split along the same lines that divided the labor market—literacy,
skill level, and degree of identification with Western values. Nevertheless,
for all the forest fighters' dissent and ill-advised strategies, it took ten
thousand British troops and massive detentions lasting until 1959 for the
colonial state to regard Mau Mau as defeated. Indeed, the counterin-
surgency efforts constructed an idealized movement of their own: even
though by participants' accounts Mau Mau had lost most of its popular

support by 1955, British troops were not withdrawn until after the capture and execution of Dedan Kimathi, leader of the best armed forest faction, in 1956. Emergency regulations stayed in effect until 1960.

Perhaps the aspect of the revolt that has been studied least has been the role of women and the gender rearrangements that forest life entailed. The participants' descriptions of these rearrangements are crystal clear: General China, Karari Njama, Joram Wamweya all have described the redefinitions of women's work that took place in the forest and the detention camps designed to cure the evils of Mau Mau oaths. The same men, in many cases, who wanted to criminalize men's behavior with prostitutes and runaway daughters in 1950 were to allow women to carry guns and insist on monogamous marriages in the forest three years later: the forest did not represent a break in Kikuyu social life but a continuation of the changing ideas about the place of men and women in African marriages and relationships. Debates within the forest were about gender, domestic services, and who should perform them: in 1954 the joint committee of Mount Kenya and Nyandarua forces discussed the bloody and unpopular Lari massacre by debating the nature of women, not the nature of loyalists; in 1954 Kimathi issued a circular to all forest fighters, demanding that women and not men do women's chores when they were in the guerilla bases; in 1955 Stanley Mathenge's forces administered a forest oath demanding that Mau Mau abandon any leader who refused to perform women's work and gather firewood and fetch water himself.[78]

Nevertheless, prostitutes have figured more prominently in Mau Mau historiography than did women householders or married women, armed or unarmed. As the British propaganda campaign commissioned increasingly bizarre oaths with which to condemn Mau Mau, prostitutes, menstrual blood, and genitalia became regular features of the confessions extracted under torture.[79] In the official reports on Kikuyu militant politics, prostitutes gained a dubious legitimacy they had not had before. African male politicians all but threatened the colonial state with prostitutes. Letters to the Kikuyu press claimed that the intensification of women's work in the terracing campaigns of the late 1940s would drive women into urban prostitution.[80] And the colonial state was threatened: according to the District Commissioner in Nyeri, a mass meeting held in July 1952 was "insinuated" with "over 40 bus loads of thugs and prostitutes, who were clearly under instructions to excite the crowd."[81] While the relations between Nairobi prostitutes and British soldiers during World War II were treated lightly, relations between Nairobi prostitutes and the police during the Emergency were given a new and predatory meaning: "prostitutes . . . lay 'tender traps' for African askaris . . . abducting them and later suffocating them to death" in order to steal their guns.[82] Cora Presley has suggested that such descriptions enabled colonial officials to trivialize women's political activism,[83] which seems likely, but they probably also indicated the extent to which prostitutes were visible as loyal members of, and contributors to, the militant political organizations.

Whether or not colonialists associated uncontrolled sexuality with uncontrolled politics, they defined a political landscape in Nairobi that was determined more by their own housing categories than it was by the actual realities of African life. When G. R. B. Brown, fresh from the unrest of Mombasa and newly installed as Nairobi's District Officer, wrote about the 1950 general strike, he complained that "the centres of trouble were the three overcrowded, poorly constructed slums" of Shauri Moyo, Kariokor, and Pumwani. Starehe, Ziwani, Kaloleni, Bahati and Makongeni "were not so seriously affected."[84] He was wrong, for by 1950 Bahati was a center for Mau Mau oathing, men from Ziwani attacked policemen in Kariokor, and the Mau Mau courts in the largely Kikuyu squatter settlement of Mathare added a certain wariness to social life there.[85] Pumwani and Shauri Moyo were fairly calm in the early 1950s; oathing took place secretly in both places but seems to have been, for men at least, a social event—some said it was given in the homes and on the business premises of non-Kikuyus—and continued in Pumwani at least until late 1953.[86] Mau Mau oaths did not add any particular danger to daily life in Pumwani and Shauri Moyo, but they did make daily life more tense; the element of secrecy strained the already edgy relations between Luos and Kikuyus, and the very possibility of oathing seems to have driven many Luo women out of political organizations.[87] Mau Mau clearly exacerbated whatever tensions existed between ethnic groups in Pumwani and Shauri Moyo; years later Muslims were to say that the greatest bitterness was between Kikuyus and Muslims, while Luos said that the greatest suspicion was between Luos and Kikuyus.[88] Kikuyus referred to the tensions Mau Mau caused between Kikuyus: oathed Kikuyus, for example, became wary of consorting with unoathed Kikuyus.[89] Nevertheless, support for Mau Mau in Pumwani was not a wholly ethnic or religious issue. The woman said to be the most active and adventurous supporter of the forest fighters—the one who brought them European beer—was a Muslim Boran Oromo prostitute.[90] Four hundred prostitutes—including a number of Kikuyu Muslims—were said to have been oathed in Pumwani and Eastleigh in the first months of 1950s; according to the oath administrators they were told to collect information; according to others, they were asked to contribute money frequently.[91] Some women said that there was an organization of oathed Kikuyu prostitutes, Sauti ya Malaya, "Voice of the Prostitutes," but others claimed that there was no such group, that the name had only been invented by informers who wanted to condemn individual women.[92] No one could say who led this organization, or if it was centered in Pumwani or Eastleigh. This kind of data—and the fact that it was discussed, not without some prodding, twenty and thirty years after Mau Mau— indicates how uneasy life in Pumwani and Shauri Moyo had been.

It would be a mistake to consider the activism of Kikuyu prostitutes the result of men's admitting them to their secret society. There had been women's political organizations with their own oaths in the Kikuyu areas for twenty years. Indeed, in 1947 there was a women's strike on coffee es- tates in Kiambu; in 1948 there were massive antiterracing campaigns by women in Murang'a; in 1950 women in Kiambu were giving the oath of loyalty to men.[93] Kikuyu prostitutes' political activism in the early 1950s was part of a larger pattern of women's political activism—for many women, second-generation protest—that swept Central Province in the postwar era: in women's eyes, occupation may have had little to do with it. While some officials had dismissed women's rural protests as the work of "outside agitators," administrators like Askwith, who was put in charge of rehabilitating male Mau Mau, believed that Kikuyu women's militancy was more violent and "far more rabid and fanatical than the males."[94]

Regardless of how prostitutes influenced or failed to influence Mau Mau, Mau Mau transformed prostitution and legal sexual relations in Nairobi. Mau Mau encouraged marriage in direct and indirect ways. In 1952 it was against "Mau Mau regulations" for an activist to live with a prostitute; one man was fined 80/ for just such an offense.[95] From the start of the Emergency, Kikuyu women were arrested for not having passes and jailed for between six months and a year.[96] When Beatrice Nyambura got out of jail in 1953, she bribed a Kamba cook 150/ to marry her in a civil ceremony so that she could obtain a pass. Years of casual liai- sons paid off: "I had known him for several years, not a permanent boy- friend but a friend, and I decided to ask him to do this because I knew he needed money." Marriage was the only legal means by which interethnic couples could stay together in Nairobi. As if the KGU had finally gotten its way, "during the Mau Mau fighting, Luo men who were in love with women here, particularly Kikuyu women, would become Muslims and let themselves be circumcised so that they could marry and live safely in town."[97] In 1953 Herbert Owiti, a Luo Catholic who mainly worked as a driver in and around Nairobi, was living with a Protestant Kikuyu woman;

they decided to become Muslims so that the woman would not be detained
as her brothers had been, so Owiti went to King George V Hospital to be
circumcised and a few days later formally converted to Islam. He changed
his name to Habib Hasan and paid his wife 100/ as bridewealth.

Stable or even occasional unmarried relations between Africans were
virtually prohibited, however. Malaya women were particularly defense-
less to the incursions of the police and the hastily recruited Home Guard.

> Mau Mau . . . was really a bad war, because . . . whenever you
> relaxed at home people would come knocking on your door
> and ordering you out, even if you were sleeping they would
> come and order you outside. In those days of Mau Mau if you
> had a boyfriend you couldn't allow him to spend the whole
> night at your house, because if the police came and knocked on
> your door early in the morning and found someone also living
> in your house they would arrest you and then you would go
> straight to jail. There were no trials or fines in the Mau Mau
> days.[98]

Most people in Pumwani claimed to fear the police more than Mau Mau.
Mau Mau could be "anybody. If you behaved with respect you were
safe."[99] "But the police were jealous people, if they asked for something
you had to give it to them. They had guns."[100] The Mau Mau gangs that
terrorized the African locations were, according to prostitutes, unarmed,
on foot, and substantially less competent than they were in their own accounts years later.[101] The police were much more in evidence: African
locations were surrounded by barbed wire, and Pumwani was raided
three times in one month in 1953, Bahati somewhat more often, without
netting much more than pass-law violators.[102] Nevertheless, prostitutes
maintained "you couldn't have a man spend the night with you. If you did
they could arrest you for keeping a criminal."[103] Nights were distinctly
uncomfortable in Pumwani: "sometimes we slept on the floor, because at
night they shot guns into your house and they couldn't hit you if you were
on the floor."[104] But even police raids in Nairobi reproduced the values of
the colonial state's belief in literacy, urban families, and respectability despite the violence they claimed to face daily. In 1953 Home Guards circled
the City Council's skilled workers' estates of Bondeni, Ziwani, Starehe,
and Kaloleni, entered each house, and gave each occupant a form to fill
out, requesting them to name suspected terrorists.[105]

The Home Guard in Pumwani were largely shopkeepers and property
owners, stalwarts of the Village Committee representatives on the Ad-

visory Council, and their dependents. The African Affairs Officer exerted considerable pressures on them to join the Home Guard, and Mau Mau exerted even more pressure for them not to do so. Between 1952 and 1953 a Zanzibari landlord, a Kikuyu Muslim householder and member of the Village Committee, a Hadhrami shopkeeper, and the daughter of a Meru Muslim householder and her Kikuyu Muslim husband, a Bahati shopkeeper, were all shot and injured. Muslims claimed this was proof of the bitter hostility of Mau Mau to Kikuyu Muslims in Pumwani and Shauri Moyo.[106] Muslims were generally free from the kinds of harassment ordinary Kikuyu faced, and were exempt from the Special Kikuyu Tax, used to defray the costs of making war, which rose from 20/ to 25/ between 1952 and 1956, when it was reduced to 15/ until it was abolished in 1959.[107]

But for many Kikuyus, becoming a Kikuyu Muslim was a rational choice. For a few women, informing for the Home Guard became a way to make up for some of the revenues lost when Pumwani was ringed with barbed wire; it was also a way to settle old scores. Freda Wambui, a Kikuyu prostitute, was said to have taken the name Fatuma at the start of the Emergency so that people would think she was a Muslim. According to a Ugandan Christian man who came to Pumwani in 1954, she was an informer and was "very strong and without pity for anyone—I have even seen her hit a man. She was the cause of many Kikuyu, Embu, and Meru being sent into detention."[108] A few people said she had sold the names of informers to Mau Mau,[109] and in the late 1950s she reverted to her Christian name and continued to live undisturbed in Pumwani.

What was Kikuyu—or Muslim, or Luo—ethnicity about that it could be taken up and then removed as political necessities dictated? If Luo-ness was not an indissoluble bond, how could being Mau Mau be one? The question here is not, I think, what is ethnicity about, but what do people call themselves, and why. The loyalties of Herbert Owiti or Freda Wambui were intensely personal, and the fact that they acted out those loyalties as Muslims reflected, not the nature of Nairobi Islam, but the nature of a colonial state that feared a fantastic vengeance from Kikuyu Christians and thus equated Islam with loyalty. Becoming a Muslim was a way to survive Emergency regulations; being a Kikuyu was not.

Housing in Nairobi was transformed by the Emergency. The fluid movement between African locations was halted by barbed wire; in 1953 Mathare, Buruburu, and Kariobangi were demolished and many residents went to live in the already overcrowded Bahati; others were detained.[110] By 1953 the colonial state broke down and allowed for a return

to Pumwani-style usufruct and private landlords. Makadara was opened
as an almost urban protective custody, a place where Kikuyus who had
been screened and declared "white," or loyal, could build houses on
Government-owned plots in Government-approved materials. The population was almost entirely Christian Kikuyus, including brewers, prostitutes, and former prostitutes who sold cooked food.[111]

Despite the absence of so many men—roughly eighty thousand were
detained between 1952 and 1959, mainly Kikuyu—there were only a few
legal jobs for women, and some were expensive to obtain. Some women
worked as street sweepers when Embu men were jailed, while permits to
hawk vegetables and sell tea and thus live legally in Nairobi were readily
obtained by bribing Dedan Githengi, Assistant African Affairs Officer,
until he was removed for his conduct in 1956.[112] The barbed wire around
every African location, the curfews, and the dangers of night-long visits
reduced malaya prostitutes' earnings and made the watembezi form pro-
hibitive for women without passes and dangerous for women with them.
Nevertheless, men paid prostitutes more than they had in the late 1940s:
during Mau Mau the short-time price in Pumwani, Shauri Moyo, and
Eastleigh was often 5/ and the full-time price 20/, although only a few
men spent the night with women; a Kikuyu man claimed that short-time
relations between Kikuyus were free during the Emergency.[113] But it is
possible that the ideology of Mau Mau, with its armed women boasting
that "the work of killing people like Waruhiu was the work of women and
girls,"[114] was antithetical to the deference of the malaya form. The sym-
pathizers of the men who gathered firewood and went on armed patrols
with their wives in the forest may not have wanted to be waited on by
women in town. Certainly between 1950 and 1958—the year before the
last detention camp closed—the number of men who reported bringing
foodstuffs to prostitutes was high, especially among men who had not
done so before,[115] although this may have had as much to do with curfews
as it did with new relations of domesticity. Nevertheless, in a time of food
shortages, such gifts may reflect changing notions of responsibility and
intimacy.

But even for the women who earned money from prostitution during
Mau Mau, there were few ways to hold onto it. Opportunities to bribe
were frequent, as were opportunities to make donations to Mau Mau, and
the advantages of doing both were compelling. Many people said that the
way most people weathered the Emergency was to give money and support to both sides. Officials certainly maintained that the city was controlled by Mau Mau, until five British Army battalions accompanied by

Police General Service Units "cleaned up" the city in Operation Anvil throughout April 1954.[116] Moreover, every night for the two years following Operation Anvil military control of the city was reasserted with a vengenace, and the residents of Pumwani were held in Memorial Hall while their rooms were searched. Street by street, people were rousted from their rooms at gunpoint, and marched to Memorial Hall—the site of so much accumulation just a few years before—where they were made to lie face down, one hand holding their passes or, in the case of established Muslims, residence permits in the air, while their rooms were searched. "We were told to leave our rooms open and cupboards and boxes unlocked; they said they were looking for guns but they took our money."[117] Similar raids took place as often in Shauri Moyo and Bahati.[118] Many women made arrangements to hide each others' money as one street was being searched and another was not, but the risks of sending children running through Pumwani as the army was moving in were too great, and almost no one did this after mid-1954. Instead, some women hid their money in the undergarments they acquired just for this purpose and hoped that they would not be searched, but none of these women were able to save very much money for very long.[119]

This was not an end to women's independent accumulation, but it did mean that the poor, the newcomers—those without links to the propertied classes—were without the means to save much money. Women who arrived in Nairobi in the midst of the Emergency did not manage to acquire property, although they managed to support themselves.[120] On the whole, the Kenyan women who had property before Mau Mau—whether or not it had been bulldozed—fared better than women who did not. Despite special taxes, arrests, and loss of loved ones, these women had the established ties of community and tenants that allowed them some respite from the burdens of the Emergency. When Wanjira Ng'ang'a's house in Buruburu was demolished in 1953, she went to stay with a former tenant in Bahati, "to start all over again finding money," with which she was able to build a house in Mathare in 1960. The absentee landlords from Kariobangi and Buruburu fared even better, since they were already well-situated in Pumwani and Shauri Moyo. The prostitutes who were said to survive the Emergency with their earnings intact were foreign-born women who had already invested some of their earnings outside Kenya. Hadija binti Nasolo sent small sums of money to her farm in Jinga, Uganda, as often as she could, "sometimes twice a week," with relatives, friends, and friends' children. Haya women were said to have done the same.[121]

Commissions and Communities, 1954–63

The Nairobi that had been violently reconstructed during the Emergency—whole communities of squatters demolished, large numbers of people removed, and social life rearranged for those who remained—was restructured, in plan and in action, by the women and men, prostitutes, workers, and colonialists, who regarded Nairobi as their terrain. The vision of colonialists is perhaps best represented by the *Report* of the East African Royal Commission, a bland fantasy document prepared between 1953 and 1955, in which all the ills of an unspecified present situation could be righted if Africans were allowed to own property in town. Africans' vision of the city was perhaps best represented by the old and new property owners—women dispossessed from Mathare and Buruburu forced into a striking reversal of class ties during the Emergency and building once again in Mathare once Emergency regulations were withdrawn. The fate of the women who had lived and worked in the city's new estate of Makadara, and the women who had swept the city clean while the ethnic group preferred for the job was considered too great a risk, represents perhaps a vision of community in Nairobi that colonialists and developers never imagined. The old Muslim networks, the informal sector, the residuum, could support the people the legal sector deemed redundant. Indeed, the squatters settlements and "overcrowded slums" already had the "responsible African middle class" which, having abandoned "the security of their holdings in the countryside," was "the first step in the formation of a healthy urban society . . . whose loyalties are directed towards the town rather than to their areas of origin." The settlements and the slums had what the East African Royal Commission conceived—thinking it was its own, original idea—as Kenya's future.[122]

During the Emergency, repression and reports of commissions of enquiry alternated, a rapid-fire discourse and counterdiscourse within the colonial state. One month after Operation Anvil the Carpenter Commission submitted its report on African wages, which recommended that a new minimum wage be established that would allow even unskilled workers to maintain a family in town, so that the African would thus be removed "from the enervating and retarding influence of his economic and cultural background." Such high wages would make labor more efficient, they calculated, and workers more afraid of losing their jobs.[123] This was designed to eliminate the dreaded "target" worker, who came to town only long enough to obtain cash for specific purposes, a concept that was not only erroneous in the mid-1950s—when many Kenyan women lived in fortified villages, and many men were jailed—but one that obscured the kinds of social life that subsidized and were subsidized by men who waited out lulls in the labor market. Migrancy and stabilization were to a large extent colonial constructions; they did not accurately describe the skilled men who became tinsmiths or herbalists while they waited for well-paid work. Similarly the men who lived with Mary Masaba or Monica Nyazura were not without a family presence; on the contrary, they were involved in complex relationships of cohabitation, obligations, and parenthood: they simply did not have their wives with them in town.

The minority report of the Carpenter Commission—written by Kenya's largest manufacturer of maize meal—argued that a stabilized labor force would remove women from farms and "ruin African agriculture."[124] The fate of African agriculture—the relationship of legally married African men to African women—formed the background for the official pronouncements on Kenya's future in the midst of Mau Mau. The East African Royal Commission proclaimed a strong interest in the "education of African girls," which they believed aroused the hostility of African men who thought "it would make them less willing to undergo the heavy labour in the fields combined with domestic drudgery that is their normal lot."[125] In this way, the commissions reflected some of the concerns of African welfare associations a few years earlier, that women's behavior be changed by changing men.

Such abstractions, and such roundabout ways of effecting social change proposed by the same people who currently held eighty thousand Kenyans in detention camps, were of course difficult to implement in a city that had been ungovernable as long as Nairobi had. New housing and new wages did not necessarily reproduce old relationships, or even bring about the desired new ones. The new landlords in the model estate of Makadara could not do for their tenants what the old ones in Pumwani or the new ones in Mathare could: as late as 1960, the sanction of the state did not provide community or loyalty. Thus, when Wanjira Ng'ang'a's house was demolished in Buruburu in 1953, she went to stay with a former tenant who rented in Bahati. In 1960 they each went to build in Mathare. Amina Hall had been disfigured in a argument with an Indian lover in the late 1940s, when she was in her fifties. When the money she had saved ran out, she gave up her room in Pumwani and slept in friends' rooms, or on their verandas in the dry seasons, until her death in 1976. Such generosity seems to have been fairly commonplace. In the early 1960s an old Pumwani householder, a Kikuyu Muslim who had built her first house in Mji wa Mombasa, asked a researcher,

> Do you think I'm a fool for helping all these old people? These
> women are very poor—they never had as much money as I
> had, so I let them stay here without pay. I never have any quar-
> rels with anybody because my hands have really touched a lot
> of money. . . . I help people so that God will be good to me.
> Your former tenants, if you were good to them and they meet
> you one day, they will help you. . . . The person who spends his
> money alone dies alone.[126]

But in Makadara the state's ideas about labor, its productivity, labor
market segmentation, and community could not be made to cohere. The
screened Kikuyu labor force housed there did not satisfy the needs of Nairobi's private employers, who were by 1956 "pressing for the return of
their Kikuyu employees who were removed during Operation 'Anvil,' as
they have found that the employees from other tribes who have replaced
them are unsatisfactory. . . . There is a general complaint about the low
output of work and lack of a proper sense of responsibility." Luo and Kamba were said to have missed the opportunity to show their initiative,[127] and
employers championed the seasoned Kikuyu migrants with their strong
urban-rural ties. This was probably more of a perception than anything
else: in the decade after 1955, there was a major increase in productivity.[128] But in Nairobi the condition of urban wage labor remained largely
the same. The reproduction of the labor force was still done by women:
those who did not provide sexual services sold workers cooked food. Beatrice Nyambura combined the malaya and watembezi forms in Eastleigh
during the Emergency. In 1954 Sara Waigo was one of many Christian
Kikuyu women sent to live in Makadara, at twice her Pumwani rent. Then
in her early-to-mid-forties, she decided not to prostitute herself, as
Makadara already had a large number of prostitutes, but "to stay with one
man the whole time"—a man she had known since the early 1940s and
who had been released from detention in 1955. Waigo did "another business there," selling cooked food. In the early 1960s Waigo and Nyambura
built their own houses in Mathare.

Less successful were the women in Makadara who entered the labor
force themselves. Nairobi's street sweepers had for years been an eth-
nically segmented occupation. Recruitment was almost exclusively limited
to the Embu of Central Province. It was also one of the worst-paid jobs in
Nairobi, and its duties included removing night soil. After Anvil, almost
all sweepers were detained; when no replacements were found, new recruits brought from Embu were also discovered to have taken a Mau Mau
oath.[129] Eventually, without raising sweepers' wages, the City Council re-

cruited women in Makadara. Gathiro wa Chege worked as a sweeper for several years, "until they said they were firing all the women," in about 1962. After a few months she was evicted from her room in Makadara because she was unable to pay her rent; she went to Mathare to live—still unable to pay rent—with a brewer, a woman who had been her neighbor in Kariokor. "She built a house and let me stay until it was torn down. Then she built another one." Although the basis of property relations—usufruct—was identical in Pumwani and Makadara, the social relations were not: landlords in Makadara simply could not, or would not, support their tenants the way landlords in Pumwani or Mathare did.

Why was this? The answer may not lie in the innate generosity of Pumwani or Mathare landlords or in the nature of property ownership and inheritance, but in the labor relations in both places and in the larger city. In Makadara most tenants worked outside the housing estate. In Pumwani and Mathare, many also worked elsewhere, but at least as many were self-employed, or independent artisans, or ran small businesses there and had, in Michael Chege's words, "a profound stake in the survival of Mathare."[130] They had the same ideals that landlords had: a belief in self-discipline, thrift, and individuality.[131] The bonds of place and community that landlords struggled to protect in the late 1930s were replicated in the cooperation of brewers, shopkeepers, prostitutes, and neighbors in Mathare and Pumwani.[132] It may have been not property ownership but urban self-employment that gave Africans the pride and civic responsibility the East African Royal Commission so desperately craved. Janet Bujra has argued that "the thin dividing line between self-employment and wage employment blurs the outlines of the working class" in Pumwani,[133] but it strengthened the bonds of place and neighborhood: men and women could not slip from wage labor to self-employment without accommodation, customers, and a social world to link them together.

Nevertheless, Africans built houses in Mathare. The East African Royal Commission recommended to the colonial state "that wherever possible Africans should be encouraged to own their own houses,"[134] and indeed, Africans built their own houses, wherever they could, but not in the spaces authorized by the state. The increases in wages of the late 1950s and the overcrowded conditions of Nairobi's legal African housing resulted in a vigorous expansion of squatter settlements starting slowly in 1958–59 and all but exploding by the early 1960s. Kawangware grew steadily. Mathare was once again inhabited in 1958, bulldozed, and a thriving village again by 1962.[135] Kaburini, an occasional squatter settlement between Quarry Road and the Hindu Crematorium, mushroomed late in

1962.[136] The political geography of Nairobi changed as well: Luo and Luhya migrants of the late 1950s were often unable to find accommodation in the municipal estates and moved instead to Kibera, where a dozen years later they outnumbered their Nubian landlords two to one.[137] Dagoretti, long the most densely populated area in Kiambu, was incorporated into Nairobi in 1963, and almost at once landowners built mud and then timber huts as rental properties.[138]

Who were these new squatters and tenants? They were not all gainfully employed. Between 1957 and 1962 the African population of Nairobi rose by an estimated fifty thousand; but between 1957 and 1962 the number of African men in registered wage employment dropped by eighteen thousand.[139] These figures reveal how many men were unemployed, but also how many men could live in Nairobi without formal jobs. The emphasis on male "unemployment" concealed male and female self-employment and the neighborhoods and networks in which these people operated. It provided a planners' label for the kinds of irregularity that had long been a feature of African labor in the city. Calling the informal sector "unemployed" denied the very communities developers were trying to build. For example, as Pumwani housed more and more "unemployed" men in the 1960s, it became more stabilized: half the male population had their wives with them.[140] In Mathare, and to a lesser extent in Kawangware, brewing became a source of revenue, cooperation, and community on a scale unknown before. New Kikuyu immigrants sent their children home to be fostered by their mothers, strengthening urban-rural ties, and brewers supported their boyfriends and husbands and uncles.[141] Providing housing for the new squatters was perhaps one of the best investments in the newly independent capital:[142] a few women from Pumwani became absentee landlords for a second time in the booming settlement of Kariobangi,[143] while Margaret Githeka and Tabitha Waweru, both acting on the advice of friends of their fathers, built houses in Mathare in the early 1960s. They and Sara Waigo and Wanjira Ng'ang'a and thousands like them were part of the responsible, urban African middle class that emerged, loyal to the town and not the countryside, but not in the places the colonial or independent state anticipated.

A new specificity of forms of prostitution—or a combination of forms—appeared in the new neighborhoods of the post–Mau Mau city. The wazi-wazi form remained specific to Pumwani for reasons that had to do with neighborliness, population density, and the accumulation strategies of the form. One Haya woman said that she did not move to Westlands in the early 1960s because "the rents are too high for me. Besides, I never stayed anywhere like that. In Mwanza I lived in a place just like Pumwani. You see, here there are a lot of girls from my home, and also many other people, all living close by. If I have any trouble, like a man tries to beat me, I can call for help. . . . It might be dangerous for me to live alone some other places."[144] Indeed, the wazi-wazi form did not spread to the less densely populated Shauri Moyo. As restrictions on African movements were relaxed toward the end of the 1950s, the European suburb of Westlands became the new Eastleigh, where African malaya women rented expensive rooms so as to be available to European men there. The watembezi form flourished in the early 1960s, as women in Eastleigh went often to central Nairobi and later to Westlands to find men. There is some evidence, all of it from colonial sources, that the watembezi prostitution of teenage girls was how poor urban households reproduced themselves.[145] By the mid-1960s some watembezi women moved to Westlands, as rents there began to decrease slightly when the area became more Indian and African.

Between 1960 and 1970 new slang terms emerged to describe prostitutes' work. These terms were used in addition to the labor forms and were substantially less specific; they described the context of the work in pragmatic terms. Women in Mathare referred to brief encounters as "quick service," after a local bus company.[146] Kikuyu women in Mathare said they were "selling their kiosks,"[147] a straightforward description of entrepreneurship and a conviction that their bodies were money-making enterprises. In Pumwani and Shauri Moyo and the Pumwani Redevelopment Scheme of Calfonya "short-time" was replaced by "a quick job" (full-time remained full-time), a man's term that described what men did, not the services and amenities that women provided. In Eastleigh in the mid-1970s watembezi prostitutes parodied women's participation in wage labor and their own work when they announced they were "going on duty." Women's use of these terms was a rueful comment on the vitality of urban prostitution, for "selling her kiosk" or "going on duty" described the extent to which prostitution had become, or resisted becoming, proletarianized.

Conclusions

No new forms of prostitution emerged in Kenya after 1939, and for the bulk of this period the watembezi form lost much of its specificity and became appendaged to the malaya form for some time. Even though in the municipal estates streetwalking had been more commonplace, if less lu-

crative, than ever before, land pressures and overstocking and out and out
warfare in rural Kenya and a rising cost of living in urban Kenya were such
that it was no longer a viable solution for farmers' daughters to prostitute
themselves for brief periods to restore a family's fortunes. For many
women, as streetwalkers in mid-1970s Eastleigh made clear, the watembezi form was not a good business or a money-making enterprise, but was
a reliable source of income. Late-colonial prostitution was not structured
by the specific characteristics of postwar Nairobi—a savvy and frequently
self-sustaining work force, a rising cost of living, and a politicized and
even militarized climate in the town—but by the specific requirements of
rural reproduction. As families were weakened by the progressive impoverishment of the countryside, prostitution became a less-viable family
strategy. Indeed, at least one characteristic of late-colonial Nairobi—the
self-sustaining work force—was in part a result of the conduct of prostitution in the city; the reliable incomes available to women like Mary Masaba
enabled them to support men through periods of unemployment.

But the very things that diminished watembezi accumulation in this
period made the malaya form more industrious. The eclipsed opportunities for urban property ownership during the Emergency allowed
long-term residents of Nairobi with strong neighborhood ties, usually
malaya women, to regroup and save money, and in the late 1950s and
early 1960s many of them built in Mathare. Indeed, the tendency of malaya women to become absentee landlords in Buruburu and Kawangware
and Mathare before the Emergency, and resident landlords in those
places after 1960, shaped social and political life within the city. Before
1953 Mathare and Kawangware and Kariobangi tended to be Christian
settlements of semiskilled workers; many of their Muslim landlords continued to live in Pumwani and Eastleigh. The violence about which colonialists complained was in fact very different in Shauri Moyo, Mathare, and
Pumwani, not because the nature of African activism and dissent was different in those areas, but because relations of place, property, and labor
were different in those areas. After 1960, Mathare and Kawangware became close-knit communities of Muslims and Christians, rich enough to
support large populations of brewers, in which resident landlords and
tenants shared a common goal of community wealth. For women like
Wanjira Ng'ang'a, bulldozed out of her home in Buruburu, property ownership in Mathare was as much the result of colonial repression as anything else, but the rapid increase in squatters' housing in the years
preceeding independence provided urban Kenya with the thriving

middle classes and urban communities that colonial commissions believed essential for orderly modernization.

But we have already seen how landlords and self-employed women had kept Nairobi orderly for many years. The association of these groups with crime and lawlessness was far less significant than colonialists imagined. On the contrary, in the postwar era prostitutes exercised considerable self-control and control over other prostitutes. Mary Masaba kept her short-time price low, so she "wouldn't have to worry about . . . fighting or abuse," while wazi-wazi women began to fix short-time prices and older malaya women informed the police about women they suspected of infanticide. Indeed, prostitutes stressed their ability to negotiate around male violence. African welfare associations sought to control African behavior, male and female, and asked the state to police private life. But the most fearsome, and according to some the most unexpected, crime was terrorism, which emerged full-blown late in 1952.

Mau Mau was a shock to the colonial state, which then subjected central Kenya to the most massive military repression British Africa had yet seen. But Mau Mau also contained its own rules, regulations concerning private behavior, courts, and factions. In the midst of the repression—in Nairobi until 1954, in the forest perhaps somewhat later—Mau Mau implemented its own vision of order, of regulated private life, of the proper relationship of men to women and the allocation of domestic tasks. In part because of how violently those visions were implemented and were repressed, Mau Mau strengthened monogamy both in the forest and in Nairobi, where couples married not because of Mau Mau's dictates, but to avoid detention and arrest. The conduct and repression of Mau Mau in Nairobi stifled malaya accumulation, however, although short-time prices increased somewhat. The women who fared best were invariably foreign-born prostitutes who were able to send their monies home almost as fast as they earned them. For Kenyan prostitutes the ability to survive the Emergency had to do with the urban values of the malaya form—neighborliness, friendship, quiet reciprocity—rather than with what form of prostitution they had practiced, or not practiced, during Mau Mau. The women who by 1963 were able to build houses in Mathare were generally women who had been malaya prostitutes before 1953. Private property did not transform African relationships and responsibilities within the city, as the East African Royal Commission had, in its innocence, imagined that it would. Indeed, private property, and the values of neighborliness, cooperation, and accumulation that had characterized African locations before 1939 and squatters' settlements between 1939 and 1953 sustained many prostitutes during the Emergency and reemerged after Mau Mau, articulated by fairly experienced practitioners of the malaya form. The women who left the communities of Pumwani and Bahati to build and live in Mathare carried their commitment to urban life and civic responsibility with them. By the early 1960s overcrowded slums provided the social life, the stability, and the welfare for the infirm and unemployed that the official housing estates failed to offer.

It was not just that urban geography was changing in the postwar years; men and women were changing as well. The attentiveness of colonial officials to the skilled work force they housed has given us a picture of men complaining about the dangers of criminal gangs. But these same men petitioned the state for control over their fellows and their fellows' lovers. African women did not passively accept this control; they either mediated its implementation or attempted to refine it by forming women's wings of African welfare associations. Much of the African activism of the postwar era was in part about a transformation of private life—the same goal the state attempted in the construction of Gorofani and Kaloleni—and this shaped the conduct of African public and private affairs in ways that this study only begins to explore. Perhaps future studies of Africa after World War II will historicize African conceptualizations and constructions of gender and move our understanding of the meaning of private life beyond the study of colonial social engineering and into the realm of African visions of African society.

9

Women, Wage Labor, and the Limits of Colonial Control

This book has been about a central contradiction of colonialism, characterized by the way it mobilized and utilized wage labor. Colonial states could create and recruit a wage labor force, but they could not maintain it. This meant that they had to create their work force again and again, to return to the countryside to find fresh workers for their enterprises, to construct the conditions of migrant labor. If we see this contradiction as a specific relationship between men—Africans, officials, and a few capitalists—we see that social reproduction took place in the African countryside, and this kept workers' wages low. We also see the disruption of African social life, the exploitation of African workers, the deliberate coercion of the colonial state. But for men to return to work, day after day and month after month and sometimes year after year, they had to eat, sleep, and have some companionship; otherwise they could not and quite possibly would not do their jobs. In the townships and the cities of the colonial world, wherever workers lived away from the actual workplace, maintenance and reproduction took place in illicit relationships between men and women and landlords and tenants. Therefore, if we see this central contradiction as a relationship that *included* women—as well as the other shadowy categories of the aged and the religious—we see that the situation of the maintenance and reproduction of the work force was beyond the reach of the state. If the creation and reproduction of a work force is seen as a relationship between men and women, we see the disruption of African social life, the exploitation of African workers, and the limits of colonial control.

Prostitution emerged from a similar contradiction: prostitution emerged out of crises in peasant and pastoral households; it flourished because of the

221

state's inability to dominate city life, which allowed prostitutes to replenish generations of male migrants. Teenage daughters of pastoralists came to Nairobi before 1910 because the state could penetrate the kraal but not the streets of the new city. The wazi-wazi form developed because the state could transform the social basis of agricultural production in Buhaya; it prospered in Nairobi because the state could not control the neighborhoods a few miles from State House.

It would be too simple, however, to say that colonialism brought a market economy to the countryside and a moral economy to the towns. Both city and countryside were burgeoning market economies. But the former was fully controlled by its service occupations, women and men who accommodated the needs of male migrants and tenants as completely and as reciprocally as the colonial state accommodated headmen and labor recruiters. This did not mean that colonial states firmly controlled the countryside; they did not: acts of rural resistance took place constantly. But colonial states were able to change relations in the countryside because they were able to have an impact on labor and production regimes.

It is sometimes suggested that colonial states did not control African cities because they did not wish to, or because doing so was considered unnecessary and prohibitively expensive. But the colonial experience in Kenya does not support these ideas. In the years before 1920, when officials had no pretensions about remaking Africans and had a strong faith in African self-reliance, workers were left to fend for themselves, to live wherever they could find accommodation. In this way, Ainsworth's dream that male migrants would build huts for themselves in the urban locations was not very different from officials' complaints about Africans residing in Nairobi goat pens: in both cases, workers' homes were workers' responsibilities. But it was the women who went to town because there was no one to help them at home, and the men the state had proclaimed to be too old and useless for waged work, who were able to house the labor force. Cities had been literally new ground since before the turn of the century: in townships women could violate the norms of their communities and own and sell huts.

After 1920, when Africans' ability to build houses wherever they could lost some of its charm, the state was able, after considerable prodding from the Indian community, to create legitimate urban spaces for Africans, as long as Africans built the housing there themselves. The state could provide space, not housing. In these legal spaces, not only did prostitutes and landlords—categories that overlapped—maintain Kenya's urban labor force, but they demanded an obedience to rules and codes of which the state had little or no knowledge. Malaya prostitutes of the 1920s scoffed at the police but adhered to the values of Pumwani and Pangani. This was not a contradiction or a disregard for civic orderliness; it was their loyalty to one community and disdain for another. The influences that shaped Nairobi had less to do with the sanitary standards of the colonial state than with coastal Islamic values of hierarchy and respect and how to manage space and diversity for profit. Men and women in the locations contested this as a specialized malaya form was developed in Danguroni and quite possibly in Quarry Road a few years earlier. But landlords stood their ground against unruly tenants and the state, refused to reduce rents in the early 1930s, and proved almost immoveable from Pangani later in the decade. Indeed, it is possible that the state's six-year assault on private landlords in the 1930s backfired. In the end, the demolition of Pangani did not just reformulate urban space, it made the option of illegal property ownership in the undemolished squatters' settlements very attractive, and undermined the state's notion of legal space and legal property. The state's rehousing scheme may have relocated 175 Pangani householders, but for the most part it was the hegemony of the Muslim elite that determined who went to live where: coastal dominance, and not the advantages of colonial-built stone houses and controlled rents, sent Kikuyu and Kamba Muslims into the rooms of Shauri Moyo. Ten years later, Muslim women became absentee landlords of the houses they had just built in squatter settlements because they did not want to leave a Muslim community to go live among their Christian tenants. The "old Muslims" who controlled prewar Pumwani shaped the subsequent pattern of African property ownership throughout the colonial city.

But it was in the postwar years, when colonial states wanted desperately to control the cities they had created, that they failed most noticeably. It did not seem to matter how much they spent or what they built in which materials. They failed precisely because they could build walls and drains, but no lasting bonds. The bedspaces designed to facilitate the circulation of unskilled labor left no room for community ties, let alone friends and visitors: a house was not a home. Their forays into landlordism brought colonial officials—by 1948 already committed to a vision of remaking Africans—into areas of African social life that they had studiously avoided for years. In order to confront the new realities of urban life, they would have had to grapple with issues of gender and sexuality at least as seriously as the African welfare associations were then doing. More to the point, the state's attempts at landlordism brought them into conflict with

African landlords, prostitutes, and brewers, the service occupations whose terrain the city had been for almost fifty years. The municipal estates that did develop strong community bonds did so in the culture of opposition that so worried Tom Askwith: Marurani and later Bahati were both united in the early 1950s, Marurani in protecting its brewers from the police, Bahati as the center for Mau Mau oathing. Postwar colonial attempts to control Nairobi also failed precisely because of the kind of city colonial rule had made Nairobi—a place where most of the work force lived illegally, squatters in illicit relations with landlords and neighbors, who lived outside the structures of colonial supervision.[1]

If colonialists could not control their cities, how could they control the illegal work that took place within them? In Nairobi this lack of jurisdiction did not come from ignorance of women's illicit work, it came from contact with it. The social reproduction prostitutes sold was not, by definition, undifferentiated. But the source of this differentiation was in the woman's labor form, not race or class: in places as public as Danguroni, white men acclimated themselves and paid dearly for the same services that the poorest of male migrants received for substantially less money. Such short-time sexual relations had a great deal to do with white male ambivalence about their visits to Pumwani, but they were the result of prostitutes' ability to control and direct sexual relations regardless of the amount of money they might earn from them. Illegal sexual relations were ungovernable: sexual access to prostitutes—whatever its cost—did not mean the ability to regulate their behavior.

The relations between European men and prostitutes, and to a lesser extent rickshaw drivers and taxi drivers, reveal less about the character of white settlers and officials than they did about the character of the individuated service occupations of the colonial city. The work of drivers and prostitutes brought them into close contact with, and gave them increased access to, all the accoutrements of respectability—associations with Europeans, secure accommodation, and legal documentation. But prostitutes used jobs, housing, and associations with European men not as a way to begin legitimate enterprises or enter the legal labor force, but as a way to make their prostitution more efficient and profitable. They incorporated legal documents and secure housing into their labor process; they did not change the nature of that labor. Prostitutes in Nairobi did not wish to abandon prostitution to join the ranks of respectable society—many did not make such a distinction—they wanted to become rich. Those who did not, "didn't want to be rich here, they wanted to be rich in Tanganyika."[2] The woman who slept on the veranda of a Pumwani house so she could save rent money to build a house in Mathare did not represent the desperate watembezi prostitution of a homeless woman; she represented careful planning, a belief in private property, and the manipulation of a form of prostitution: she represented capitalist labor discipline.

Men's labor had been contested in the early years of colonial rule as fathers and officials struggled over who could control it, or at least its product. But those struggles ended at the homestead's gate. Women's labor was largely uncontested; if a woman "wanted to sell her body no one bothered her."[3] Prostitutes' work was family labor. This was not just true for the young pastoralist girls who came to Nairobi before 1910, it was true for malaya women as well, working to create families with themselves as heads of households. For the most part, the extent to which women reproduced male labor power depended not on men's needs but on the woman's labor form. Women's labor forms emerged from transformations in the countryside, not from the vicissitudes of male wage labor in the city. The labor forms of prostitution reflected the degrees of differentiation within the countryside: the two labor forms that were most aggressively family labor, the watembezi and the wazi-wazi, emerged after rapid losses of disposable property—livestock and cash crops. The malaya form—in all its variety, including its rarified form of accumulation in mid-1930s Danguroni— emerged from all the complex differentiations within peasant households, and the wide variety of meanings that subsistence production had in central and eastern Kenya. The processes by which women went from their homes to East African towns did not reveal as much about the degree of colonial involvement in rural economies as they did about the abilities of families and individual women to solve their problems through the mobilization of their own labor. The monetization of the colonial economy did not always make Africans dependent on colonial enterprises; in the early years of the century, waged and domestic labor provided a breathing space for many pastoral Africans reconstructing their societies. Daughters' earnings, if used judiciously, could keep the market at a distance. Maasai askaris helped the British subdue the Nandi and Maasai women prostituted themselves in Nairobi until they had earned enough to retreat from the cash economy and its demands that they sell their labor power and their cattle. The difference between the watembezi and wazi-wazi forms and the malaya form was, for women's families, the difference between controlling a daughter's labor and being disinherited from the fruits of that labor. While we do not know enough about all the varieties of subsistence production in central and eastern Kenya—families planting European food crops for their own consumption but with an eye to selling the surplus—to identify the households that malaya women were likely to abandon, we can say that whatever happened in Buhaya and Buganda as cash crops were introduced to small holders did not take place in central and eastern Kenya. Where prostitution became part of rural accumulation, its study allows for a more nuanced picture of agrarian households than do studies of men and their herds and their crops. Just as the study of prostitution shows that we cannot separate rural Africa from urban Africa, it demonstrates the extent to which the notion of a captured peasantry is gender-specific and therefore incomplete. At least in the particular case of the wazi-wazi form in East Africa, the greater the degree of incorporation into the world economy, the more active was daughters' participation in prostitution. The degree to which 1930s Haya menfolk might have been captured by the market was equalled by the degree to which Haya daughters and ex-wives were beyond the control of the colonial state.

But why does one form of prostitution flourish, while another flounders? As my introduction shows, states were never able to control and regulate prostitution, although they could transform its conduct and put severe constraints on various forms' accumulation for a time. But prostitutes did not see the state as impenetrable, or even give it credit for what it had accomplished: life on Nairobi's streets was never so difficult that watembezi and even a few malaya women did not think they could outsmart the state, and dispossessed malaya landlords in Shauri Moyo were credited with owning property there by women in Pumwani forty years later. Indeed, the fact that no new forms of prostitution developed after 1939 or that the watembezi form lost its distinctive patterns of accumulation between 1946 and 1956—although these resurfaced in the 1970s, if not before—does not reflect the state's ability to deal with vice or the city's streets; it reflects a change in family solutions to family problems. These changes may be attributed to the ability of the colonial state to penetrate rural Africa after the late 1930s, but the integrity and the autonomy of prostitutes' labor forms emerged out of decisions women made about how best to reproduce a household.

Women's concerns about how to reproduce a household, in the long run or for a few minutes, determined how prostitution was conducted in Nairobi. Prostitutes stratified the work force far more meaningfully than the state's efforts did: poor men could purchase fleeting domesticity while skilled and self-employed men could afford night-long imitations of married life. Men nevertheless determined what these relationships would consist of. Bathwater, bread, cleanliness, respect—these were universally available in 1920s Pumwani prostitution: not only did these reproduce labor power but they did so in a gendered vision of service that working men could purchase. Malaya women suggested that much of what transpired between prostitutes and customers was negotiated: they had to persuade men to be generous. The twenty years in which malaya prostitutes developed specifically ethnic conceptions of service, appropriate behavior, and responsibility indicated that men were not passive objects in their own maintenance. The rise of Danguroni, the prostitution of malaya women outside KAR camps, the watembezi prostitution that flourished in Bahati in the early 1950s, revealed the extent to which even the shortest of short-time relations met the differing reproductive strategies of prostitutes and customers. During World War II, when many men in Nairobi were without a family presence even a day's walk from the city, men made specific demands for specific services from prostitutes. And what did soldiers and POWs want? They wanted loyalty, and personal attention, and greetings in their own language—they wanted the reproduction of intimacy.

Starting in the late 1930s but becoming most vocal in the late 1940s—the same years that labor protest rocked the continent—female labor was contested. The colonial state had commandeered Kikuyu women for the terracing programs of the late 1940s; the growing number of African welfare associations began to demand regulation and control over prostitutes' work and behavior. But the policing of runaway daughters and estranged wives was not just the work of respectable African men: it involved women, and it involved attempts to regulate male behavior as well. The Women's Section of the African Workers Federation, the Kikuyu General Union, Luo Union, Luo Union Women's Branch, and Mau Mau all created fora in which the nature and extent of sexual relations and race relations could be debated. The conditions of intimacy—who might provide it and who might have access to it—was a subject for public discussion in African politics of the postwar years. Most of these groups sought to control women's behavior with the aid of the colonial state; the state continually dismissed such requests, which suggests that it had not penetrated postwar urban life and how little it knew of African concerns. The group that did not seek state approval, Mau Mau, struggled separately in the forest to define gender, marriage, and women's and men's work. Indeed, in Mau Mau's armed citizenship of shared domesticity and warfare households were reproduced without—and this was yet another affront to the colonial state—any houses at all. It was only with Operation Anvil in 1954, facilitated by five British Army battalions, that the colonial state could control Nairobi.

My point is not that by the 1950s Nairobi had become a "concrete for-est" of official nightmares. The city had always been beyond official reg-ulation. This was not because of the character of Nairobi, but because control was already exerted in its wattle-and-daub huts, in the shambles of River Road, and its ethnic mosques. These were the spaces Africans estab-lished, negotiated, and controlled, with their own ideas about property, family, and loyalty, and their own relationships. Whenever the colonial state attempted, half-heartedly and unsuccessfully, to attack malaya accu-mulation, watembezi accumulation, or Muslim property owners, they usually did so in response to pressures from within their own administra-tion, because these groups, and their persistence, revealed the power and autonomy of African communities and the ineptitude of the state. The complex negotiations between prostitutes and their customers not only reproduced men's labor power when—and where—the state and private enterprises did not; in so doing they constrained colonial control.

Notes

Chapter One

1. Alexandre-Jean-Baptiste Parent-Duchatelet, *De la prostitution de la ville de Paris*, 2 vols. (Paris: J.-B. Bailliere, 1836); Jill Harsin, *Policing Prostitutes in Nineteenth-Century Paris* (Princeton: Princeton University Press, 1985), pp. 113–27; Sander L. Gilman, *Difference and Pathology: Stereotypes of Sexuality, Race, and Madness* (Ithaca: Cornell University Press, 1985), pp. 94–95; Charles Bernheimer, "Of Whores and Sewers: Parent-Duchatelet, Engineer of Abjection," *Raritan* 6, 3 (Winter 1987), pp. 72–90.

2. William Acton, *Prostitution*, ed. Peter Fryer (London, 1870), p. 26, quoted in Judith R. Walkowitz, *Prostitution and Victorian Society: Women, Class, and the State* (Cambridge: Cambridge University Press, 1980), p. 46.

3. Guglielmo Ferrero, Review of *La criminalité féminine* by Raymond de Rykere, *Archivo di Antropologia Criminale* 12 (1891), p. 572, quoted in Mary Gibson, *Prostitution and the State in Italy, 1860–1915* (New Brunswick, NJ, and London: Rutgers University Press, 1986), pp. 138–40.

4. *Standard and Diggers News*, 15 February 1897, quoted in Charles van Onselen, *Studies in the Social and Economic History of the Witwatersrand*, vol. 1, *New Babylon* (London: Longman, 1982), p. 105.

5. Judith R. Walkowitz, "Male Vice and Female Virtue: Feminism and the Politics of Prostitution in Nineteenth-Century Britain," in Ann Snitow, Christine Stansell, and Sharon Thompson, eds., *Desire: The Politics of Sexuality* (London, Virago, 1984), pp. 43–61.

6. Walkowitz, *Prostitution and Victorian Society*, pp. 192–213; Edward A. Alpers, "The Somali Community at Aden in the Nineteenth Century," *Northeast African Studies* 8, 2–3 (1986), p. 159.

7. Quoted in Walkowitz, *Prostitution and Victorian Society*, p. 212.

8. Mark Thomas Connelly, *The Response to Prostitution in the Progressive Era* (Chapel Hill: University of North Carolina Press, 1980), pp. 122–23.

9. *Downward Paths: An Inquiry into the Causes Which Contribute to the Making of the*

Prostitute, foreword by A. Maude Royden, (London, 1913), quoted in Walkowitz, *Prostitution and Victorian Society* p. 212; see also Connelly, pp. 122–28.

10. Janet M. Bujra, "Women 'Entrepreneurs' of Early Nairobi," *Canadian Journal of African Studies* 9, 2 (1975), pp. 213–34, and "Production, Property, Prostitution: 'Sexual Politics' in Atu," *Cahiers d'études africaines* 65, 17 (1977), pp. 13–39; Margaret Strobel, *Muslim Women in Mombasa, 1890–1975* (New Haven and London: Yale University Press, 1979), pp. 138–47; Richard Symanski, "Prostitution in Nevada," *Annals of the Association of American Geographers* 64, 3 (1974), pp. 357–77; Paula Petrik, "Capitalists with Rooms: Prostitution in Helena, Montana, 1865–1900," *Montana: The Magazine of Western History* 3 (1981), pp. 28–41.

11. Connelly, pp. 62–66, 120–27.

12. Ruth Rosen, *The Lost Sisterhood: Prostitution in America, 1900–1918,* Baltimore and London: Johns Hopkins University Press, 1982), p. 108.

13. Barbara Meil Hobson, *Uneasy Virtue: The Politics of Prostitution and the American Reform Tradition* (New York: Basic Books, 1987), pp. 143–44.

14. Joan Hori, "Japanese Prostitution in Hawaii during the Immigration Period," *Hawaiian Journal of History* 15 (1981), pp. 113–24.

15. Marion S. Goldman, *Gold Diggers and Silver Miners: Prostitution and Social Life on the Comstock Lode* (Ann Arbor: University of Michigan Press, 1981), pp. 102–4. Jennifer James's massive survey of five thousand Seattle prostitutes in 1970 revealed that most of the women who had pimps did so out of choice (Jennifer James et al., *The Politics of Prostitution* [Seattle: Social Research Associates, 1977], pp. 55–58).

16. Mwanisha Ahmed, Shauri Moyo, 17 January 1976.

17. Rosen, p. 114; see also Kathleen Barry, *Female Sexual Slavery* (Englewood Cliffs, NJ: Prentice Hall, 1979), pp. 45–70, 90–102.

18. Goldman, p. 57; Frances Finnegan, *Poverty and Prostitution: A Study of Victorian Prostitutes in York* (Cambridge and New York: Cambridge University Press, 1979), p. 135; Rosen, p. 83; Anne M. Butler, *Daughters of Joy, Sisters of Misery: Prostitutes in the American West, 1865–1890* (Urbana and Chicago: University of Illinois Press, 1987), p. 61; Hobson, p. 108.

19. Pauline Tarnowsky, *Etude anthropométrique sur les prostitutes* . . . (Paris, 1889), quoted in Gilman, *Difference and Pathology,* pp. 95–96.

20. Rosen, p. 100.

21. Joel Best, "Careers in Brothel Prostitution: St. Paul, 1865–1883," *Journal of Interdisciplinary History* 12, 4 (Spring 1982), p. 616.

22. Judith R. Walkowitz and Daniel J. Walkowitz, "'We Are Not Beasts of the Field': Prostitution and the Poor in Plymouth and Southampton under the Contagious Diseases Act," in Mary Hartman and Lois W. Banner, eds., *Clio's Consciousness Raised: New Perspectives on the History of Women* (New York: Harper and Row, 1974), pp. 192–225.

23. Edward J. Bristow, *Prostitution and Prejudice: The Jewish Fight against White Slavery, 1870–1939* (New York: Schocken, 1984), p. 179.

24. Hobson, p. 86.

25. Goldman, pp. 16, 25.

26. Rosen, pp. 137–47; Hobson, pp. 85–94.

27. Connelly, pp. 120–35.

28. Rosen, pp. 146–47; Hobson, pp. 88–94.

29. This was a category in many surveys of the causes of prostitution; see Rosen, p. 146.

30. See my "Colonial State and An African Petty Bourgeoisie," in Frederick Cooper, ed., *Struggle for the City: Migrant Labor, Capital, and the State in Urban Africa* (Beverly Hills and London: Sage, 1983), pp. 167–94.

31. Paul Greenough, *Prosperity and Misery in Modern Bengal: The Famine of 1943– 1944* (Oxford: Oxford University Press, 1982), pp. 55–58.

32. Sue Gronewold, "Beautiful Merchandise: Prostitution in China, 1860– 1936," *Women and History* 1 (Spring 1982), p. 19.

33. Lucie Cheng Hirata, "Free, Indentured, Enslaved: Chinese Prostitutes in Nineteenth-Century America," *Signs: Journal of Women in Culture and Society* 5, 1 (1979), p. 9.

34. Gronewald, pp. 46–49.

35. David McCreery, "'This Life of Misery and Shame': Female Prostitution in Guatemala City, 1880–1920," *Journal of Latin American Studies* 18 (1987), pp. 341– 42.

36. Gail Hershatter, "The Hierarchy of Shanghai Prostitution, 1870–1949," *Modern China* 15, 4 (October 1989), pp. 491–93.

37. Finnegan, pp. 85–87.

38. Best, p. 609.

39. Bujra, "Women 'Entrepreneurs,'" pp. 213–34; White, "Colonial State."

40. Van Onselen, pp. 120–23; Elizabeth B. van Heyningen, "The Social Evil in the Cape Colony, 1868–1902: Prostitution and the Contagious Diseases Acts," *Journal of Southern African Studies* 10, 2 (1984), pp. 185–87; Donna J. Guy, "White Slavery, Public Health, and The Socialist Position on Legalized Prostitution in Argentina, 1913–1936," *Latin American Research Review* 23, 3 (1988), pp. 61–62.

41. Bristow, pp. 102, 111–14.

42. Pasuk Phongpaichit, *From Peasant Girls to Bangkok Masseuses* (Geneva: International Labour Organization, 1982), pp. 46–47.

43. Richard J. Evans, "Prostitution, State, and Society in Imperial Germany," *Past and Present* 70 (1976), pp. 106–29; Walkowitz, *Prostitution and Victorian Society,* pp. 192–201.

44. See my "Women's Domestic Labor in a Colonial City: Prostitution in Nairobi, 1900–1950," in Jane Parpart and Sharon Stichter, eds., *Patriarchy and Class: African Women at Home and in the Workplace* (Boulder, CO: Westview Press, 1988), pp. 139–60.

45. Kenneth Ballhatchet, *Race, Sex, and Class under the Raj: Imperial Attitudes and Policies and Their Critics, 1793–1905* (New York: St. Martin's Press, 1980), p. 40; Rosen, pp. 1–2; Gronewald, p. 37; Truong Thanh-Dam, "The Dynamics of Sex Tourism: The Case of Southeast Asia," *Development and Change* 14 (1983), pp. 533– 53; Gerda Lerner, "The Origin of Prostitution in Ancient Mesopotamia," *Signs: Journal of Women in Culture and Society* 11, 2 (1986), pp. 236–54.

46. Laketch Dirasse, "The Socioeconomic Position of Women in Addis Ababa: The Case of Prostitution," Ph.D. thesis, Boston University, 1978, pp. 4–8.

47. Gilman, *Difference and Pathology*, pp. 99–101; Gibson, p. 139.

48. Ruth Mazo Karras, "The Regulation of Brothels in Later Medieval England," *Signs: Journal of Women in Culture and Society* 14, 2 (1989), pp. 399–425.

49. Leah L. Otis, *Prostitution in Medieval Society: The History of an Urban Institution in Languedoc* (Chicago: University of Chicago Press, 1985), pp. 65, 82–83.

50. Mark D. Meyerson, "Prostitution of Muslim Women in the Kingdom of Valencia: Religious and Sexual Discrimination in a Medieval Plural Society," in Marilyn J. Chiat and Kathryn L. Ryerson, eds., *The Medieval Mediterranean: Cross-Cultural Contacts* (St. Cloud, MN: North Star Press, 1988), pp. 87–95.

51. Dirasse, p. 55.

52. Goldman, p. 94.

53. Eleanor M. Miller, *Street Woman* (Philadelphia: Temple University Press, 1987), pp. 36–39; Best, pp. 607–8.

54. See my "Prostitution, Identity, and Class Consciousness during World War II," *Signs: Journal of Women in Culture and Society* 11, 2 (1986), pp. 255–73; Goldman, pp. 76–77.

55. Goldman, pp. 76–77; Rosen, p. 107; see also Finnegan, pp. 158–60.

56. Judith R. Walkowitz, "Jack the Ripper and the Myth of Male Violence," *Feminist Studies* 8, 3 (Fall 1982), pp. 543–74, and "Myths and Murderers," review of *The Age of Sex Crime* by Jane Caputi and *The Lust to Kill: A Feminist Investigation of Sexual Murder* by Deborah Cameron and Elizabeth Frazer, *Women's Review of Books* 5, 6 (March 1988), pp. 7–8.

57. Harsin, pp. 148–94; see also McCreery, p. 339.

58. Hershatter, p. 470.

59. Robert Prus and Styllianoss Irini, *Hookers, Rounders, and Desk Clerks: The Social Organization of a Hotel Community* (Toronto: Gage Publishing, 1980), pp. 16–20, 78–79.

60. Wambui Murithi, Pumwani, 14 December 1976; Nell Kimball, *Her Life as an American Madam* (New York: Macmillan, 1970), quoted in Rosen, p. 107; see also Ruth Rosen and Sue Davison, *The Mamie Papers* (Old Westbury, NY: Feminist Press, 1977), letter 27, p. 77.

61. Jennifer James, "Mobility as an Adaptive Strategy," *Urban Anthropology* 4 (1975), pp. 349–64.

62. See Neil Larry Shumsky and Larry M. Springer, "San Francisco's Zone of Prostitution, 1880–1934," *Journal of Historical Geography* 7, 1 (1981), pp. 75–76.

63. Dirasse, pp. 81–82; see also Walkowitz and Walkowitz, pp. 219–20; chapter 3 of this book.

64. Finnegan, pp. 114–18, 132–35; Prus and Irini, pp. 19–22.

65. Walkowitz, *Prostitution and Victorian Society*, pp. 15–21, 209–12; Bristow, pp. 156–79; Luise White, "Prostitution, Differentiation, and the World Economy: Nairobi, 1899–1939," in Marilyn J. Boxer and Jean H. Quataert, eds., *Connecting Spheres: Women in the Western World, 1500 to the Present* (Oxford and New York: Oxford University Press, 1986), pp. 223–31.

66. Otis, pp. 49–50.

67. George Chauncey, Jr., "The Locus of Reproduction: Women's Labour in the Zambian Copperbelt, 1927–1953," *Journal of Southern African Studies* 7, 2 (1981), pp. 148–49.

68. Goldman, p. 58.

69. Quoted in Hori, p. 119.

70. Gronewald, p. 51; Hershatter, pp. 467–68.

71. Connelly, p. 22.

72. Harsin, p. 37.

73. Goldman, p. 92.

74. Quoted in Dirasse, p. 80.

75. Petrik, p. 38; Renee Pitten, "Houses of Women: A Focus on Alternative Life-Styles in Katsina City," in Christine Oppong, ed., *Female and Male in West Africa* (London: George Allen and Unwin, 1983), p. 295.

76. See Curt Gentry, *The Madams of San Francisco* (Sausalito, CA: Comstock, 1964); James R. Gray, *Red Lights on the Prairie* (Toronto: Sphere, 1974); Douglas McDonald, *The Legend of Julia Bulette and the Red Light Ladies of Nevada* (Las Vegas: Nevada Publications, 1980; H. Gordon Frost, *The Gentlemen's Club: The Story of Prostitution in El Paso* (El Paso, TX: Mangan, 1983).

77. Walkowitz, *Prostitution in Victorian Society*, pp. 211–12.

78. Rosen, p. 43.

79. Hershatter, p. 488.

80. Katherine Arnold, "The Introduction of Poses to a Peruvian Brothel and Changing Images of Male and Female," in John Blacking, ed., *The Anthropology of the Body* (London and New York: Academic Press, 1977), pp. 179–96.

81. Rosen, p. 90.

82. Sally Stanford, *Lady of the House* (New York: Putnam, 1966), p. 9, quoted in Rosen, p. 91.

83. Gibson, pp. 153–54.

84. Frost, p. 73.

85. McCreery, p. 347, Harsin, pp. 288–90.

86. Best, p. 609.

87. Goldman, pp. 64, 77–78.

88. Phongpaichit, p. 52.

89. Frederick Cooper, "Urban Space, Industrial Time, and Wage Labor in Africa," in Frederick Cooper, ed., *Struggle for the City: Migrant Labor, Capital, and the State in Urban Africa* (Beverly Hills and London: Sage, 1983), p. 11.

90. Carol and Leonard and Isidor Walliman, "Prostitution and Changing Morality in the Frontier Cattle Towns of Kansas," *Kansas History* 11 (1979), pp. 34–53.

91. Thomas Colchester, London, 8 August 1977.

92. Abner Cohen, *Custom and Politics in Urban Africa: A Study of Hausa Migrants in Yoruba Towns* (Berkeley and Los Angeles: University of California Press, 1969), pp. 55–70; see also Hori.

93. Pitten, p. 293.

94. Bristow, p. 147; Rosen, p. 83.

95. Kenneth G. McVicar, "Twilight of an East African Slum: Pumwani and the Evolution of African Settlement in Nairobi," Ph.D. thesis, University of California, Los Angeles, 1968, p. 245.

96. Goldman, pp. 76, 93; Rosen, p. 94; Butler, pp. xviii, 60, 86.

97. Butler, p. 60.

98. B. G. M. Sundkler, "Marriage Problems in the Church in Tanganyika," *International Review of Missions* 34, 134 (1945), pp. 253–58.

99. Goldman, pp. 106–9; Luise White, "Colonial State," pp. 167–94, and "Vice and Vagrants: Prostitution, Housing, and Casual Labour in Nairobi in the Mid-1930s," in Francis Snyder and Douglas Hay, eds., *Labour,'Law, and Crime: An Historical Perspective* (London: Tavistock, 1987), pp. 202–27.

100. Strobel; Claire C. Robertson, *Sharing the Same Bowl: A Socioeconomic History of Women and Class in Accra, Ghana* (Bloomington: Indiana University Press, 1984); Kristin Mann, *Marrying Well: Marriage, Status, and Social Change among the Educated Elite in Colonial Lagos* (Cambridge: Cambridge University Press, 1985); Tabitha Kanogo, *Squatters and the Roots of Mau Mau* (London: James Currey, 1987); Susan Geiger, "Women in Nationalist Struggle: TANU Activists in Dar es Salaam," *International Journal of African Historical Studies* 20, 1 (1987), pp. 1–26.

101. See for example Leroy Vail and Landeg White, "Forms of Resistance: Songs and Perceptions of Power in Colonial Mozambique," in Donald Crummey, ed., *Banditry, Rebellion, and Social Protest in Africa* (London: James Currey, 1986), pp. 193–228; C. A. Hamilton, "Ideology and Oral Tradition: Listening to the Voices 'from Below,'" *History in Africa* 14 (1987), pp. 67–86; Marjorie Mbilinyi, "'I'd Have Been a Man': Politics and Labor Process in Producing Personal Narratives," in Personal Narratives Group, eds., *Interpreting Women's Lives* (Bloomington: Indiana University Press, 1989), pp. 204–27; Marjorie Shostak, "'What the Wind Won't Take Away': The Genesis of *Nisa—The Life and Words of a !Kung Woman*," in Personal Narratives Group, eds., *Interpreting Women's Lives*, pp. 228–40.

102. Jan Vansina, *Oral Tradition* (Chicago: Aldine, 1967), p. 160.

103. Jan Vansina, *Oral Tradition as History* (Madison: University of Wisconsin, 1985), p. 8.

104. Frederick Cooper, "The Treatment of Slaves on the Kenya Coast in the Nineteenth Century," *Kenya Historical Review* 1, 2 (1973), pp. 92–93, and *Plantation Slavery on the East Coast of Africa* (New Haven and London: Yale University Press, 1977), p. 171.

105. Vansina, *Oral Tradition as History*, p. 9.

Chapter Two

1. The East African Protectorate became the colony of Kenya in 1920.

2. Godfrey Muriuki, *A History of the Kikuyu, 1500–1900* (Nairobi: Oxford University Press, 1974), p. 87; Richard Waller, "The Maasai and the British, 1895–1905: The Origins of an Alliance," *Journal of African History* 17 (1976), pp. 533–34.

3. A. T. Matson, *Nandi Resistance to British Rule, 1890–1906* (Nairobi: East Africa Publishing House, 1972), pp. 156–58, 257, 260, 264; Nandi Operations, Intelligence Diary, Col. J. H. Sadler's Dispatch, 17 January 1906, CO 533/11/5070; Richard Meinertzhagen, *Kenya Diary, 1902–1906* (Edinburgh: Oliver and Boyd, 1957), pp. 187, 191, 239, 256, 282.

4. Gavin Kitching, *Class and Economic Change in Kenya: The Making of an African Petite-Bourgeoisie* (New Haven: Yale University Press, 1980), pp. 200–207; H. E. Lambert to P. Wyn Harris, "Limitation of Brideprice," 4 August 1948, Secretariat 1/12/12; Patricia Stamp, "Kikuyu Women's Self-Help Groups: Toward an Understanding of the Relations between Sex-Gender System and Mode of Production in

Africa," in Claire Robertson and Iris Berger, eds., *Women and Class in Africa* (New York: Holmes and Meier, 1986), pp. 27–46; see also Bridget O'Laughlin, "Mediation of Contradiction: Why Mbum Women Do Not Eat Chicken," in Michelle Zimbalist Rosaldo and Louise Lamphere, eds. *Women, Culture, and Society* (Stanford, CA: Stanford University Press, 1974), p. 315.

5. John Lonsdale and Bruce Berman, "Coping with the Contradictions: The Development of the Colonial State in Kenya, 1895–1914," *Journal of African History* 20 (1979), pp. 498, 501–2; Kitching, pp. 200–207; Carolyn M. Clark, "Land and Food, Women and Power, in Nineteenth Century Kikuyu," *Africa* 50, 4 (1980), pp. 360–63.

6. Robert L. Tignor, *The Colonial Transformation of Kenya: The Kamba, the Kikuyu, and the Maasai from 1900 to 1939* (Princeton: Princeton University Press, 1976), p. 313; Waller, p. 530; Cynthia Brantley, *The Giriama and Colonial Resistance in Kenya, 1800–1920* (Berkeley and Los Angeles: University of California Press, 1981), p. 35; Charles H. Ambler, *Kenyan Communities in the Age of Imperialism: The Central Region in the Late Nineteenth Century* (New Haven and London: Yale University Press, 1988), pp. 96–97; Charles van Onselen, "Reactions to Rinderpest in Southern Africa, 1896–1897," *Journal of African History* 13 (1972), pp. 473–74.

7. Marc H. Dawson, "Smallpox in Kenya, 1880–1920," *Social Science and Medicine* 13B, 4 (December 1979), pp. 245–47; Muriuki, p. 155; J. Forbes Munro, *Colonial Rule and the Kamba: Social Change in the Kenya Highlands, 1889–1939* (Oxford University Press, 1975), pp. 47–48. Mortality estimates over 50 percent seem to have been used to justify land alienation in the Kenya highlands; see John Boyes, *John Boyes, King of the Wakikuyu*, ed. G. W. C. Bulpett (London: Methuen and Company, 1911); Kenya Land Commission, *Evidence* (London: HMSO, 1934), 1:696 (Boedecker), 723 (Father Bernhard), 726 (Boyes), 746 (Patterson).

8. Ambler, p. 97.

9. Brantley, p. 35; see David Parkin, "Kind Bridewealth and Hard Cash: Eventing a Structure," in John L. Comaroff, *The Meaning of Marriage Payments* (London and New York: Academic Press, 1980), pp. 197–220.

10. This is based on limited data. Most of what we know about the pre-1898 epidemics comes from the accounts of individual officers of the Imperial British East Africa Company, which frequently reflected their own goals. John Ainsworth "liberated" forty-four pawned Maasai women purchased or captured by Kamba in 1893, and ninety-nine in 1894, suggesting an increase in both pawning and cattle raiding (John Ainsworth, "Kenya Reminiscences," n.d., covering 1890–1900, Rhodes House, RH MSS Afr. s. 380; History of Fort Hall, 1888–1944, DC/FH 1/6/1; Munro, pp. 38–39; Meinertzhagen, *Kenya Diary*, p. 291; "Native Affairs: Return of Akamba from Kenya," 1921–32, DC/NYI 3/6).

11. Elijah Kimani and Habili Kibui, in H. S. Kabeca Mwaniki, *Embu Historical Texts* (Nairobi: East African Literature Bureau, 1974), p. 304.

12. Tignor, p. 16; Francis George Hall, Letters, vol. 3, passim, RH MSS Afr. s. 57.

13. Miryamu Wageithiga, Pumwani, 11 August 1976; Hidaya Saidi, Pumwani, 2 March 1977.

14. These were the very men who had been extending their farms at the expense of grazing lands, often to the dismay of a generation of young men and war-

riors, shortly before rinderpest first appeared in East Africa. See Peter Rogers, "The British and the Kikuyu, 1890–1905: A Reassessment," *Journal of African History* 20 (1979), pp. 255–69. At the height of the famine in 1899, one pound of grain cost as much as one rupee and was rapidly purchased by caravan and IBEAC agents (p. 260).

15. Goats were not affected by rinderpest. The record from IBEAC punitive expeditions indicates how many cattle the agriculturalist Kikuyu had and how few cattle survived. In 1893 two expeditions led by Hall in the Fort Smith area netted 5 head of cattle and 992 sheep and goats, although, given that rinderpest was fatal for sheep, most of the small stock would have been goats; in ten raids against the Maasai during 1893–95 Hall captured 500 head of cattle and 1,800 goats. Similar figures obtained for central and western Kenya until the turn of the century (Muriuki, p. 154; Waller, p. 537; Military Intelligence, Nandi, November 1905, CO 628/1/41333; Nyeri District Cash Book, July 1903, DC/NYI 6/2).

16. Dawson, "Smallpox in Kenya," p. 246; Megan Vaughan, *The Story of an African Famine: Gender and Famine in Twentieth-Century Malawi* (Cambridge: Cambridge University Press, 1987), pp. 120–24.

17. Marcia Wright's study of the autobiographies of women in the late-nineteenth-century Tanganyika-Nyasaland corridor reveals that in times of duress brothers may refuse to take on the burden of a dead brother's wife; see "Women in Peril: A Commentary on the Life Stories of Captives in Nineteenth Century East-Central Africa," *African Social Research* 20 (December 1975), pp. 800–819.

18. Halima Hamisi, Kajiado, 8 November 1976; Hannah Mwikali, Kajiado, 8 November 1976; Nineta Lilande, Pumwani, 18 March 1977. Recent scholarship, however, strongly suggests that "ethnic identity" is a concept that only emerged at the start of the twentieth century; see Ambler.

19. Abdullah, a Maasai who came to Nairobi in 1904, interviewed by Richard Waller, n.d., MT/M/T11; see also Amina Hali, Pumwani, 4 August 1976; Hannah Mwikali; Halima Hamisi; Ambler, pp. 132–33.

20. Hannah Mwikali.

21. Wright, p. 819. Amber suggests that the rapid expansion of pawning "during the famine years encouraged men to view female labor as a commodity" (p. 133), but does acknowledge the ways women might have internalized and manipulated such a perception.

22. Munro, p. 47.

23. Frederick Jackson, *Early Days in East Africa* (London: Arnold and Company, 1930), pp. 325–26.

24. Ambler, p. 139.

25. Halford John Mackinder Papers, 20 July and 30 September 1899, RH MSS Afr. r29. A rupee was then valued at 1/4. Mackinder was the first in a long line of observers to profess a speedy demise of the Maasai because of the ravages of sexually transmitted disease. See also Marc H. Dawson, "The Many Minds of Sir Halford J. Mackinder: Dilemmas of Historical Editing," *History in Africa* 14 (1987), pp. 27–42.

26. Gerhard Lindblom, *Kamba Folklore*, (Uppsala: Appelbergs Boktryckeri Aktielog, 1934), 3:42, quoted in Ambler, p. 140.

27. Janet M. Bujra, "Pumwani: The Politics of Property," Social Science Research Council (U.K.), London, 1972, mimeo, pp. 51–52, and "Women 'Entrepreneurs,'" pp. 213–34.

28. Meinertzhagen, *Kenya Diary,* pp. 12–13.

29. Anthony Clayton and Donald C. Savage, *Government and Labour in Kenya, 1895–1963* (London: Frank Cass, 1974), pp. 21–22; Tignor cites a figure of three thousand whites in the protectorate in 1911, including settlers, missionaries, administrators, and merchants (p. 22).

30. Lonsdale and Berman describe "the ease with which Africans could earn a cash income from household production, free from all the terrors of unknown disease and irascible employers which disfigured the labor market" ("Contradictions," p. 501). See also Rogers, pp. 255–69; Clayton and Savage, p. 69n.

31. Clayton and Savage suggested that "the Africans themselves [were] becoming sufficiently familiar with coin to prefer it" (p. 28); Kitching, pp. 212–13.

32. East African Protectorate, Native Labour Commission 1912–13, *Evidence and Report* (Nairobi: Government Printer, 1913), passim (hereafter NLC); Kitching, p. 217.

33. See Norman Leys, *Last Chance in Kenya* (London: Hogarth Press, 1931), pp. 15–42; Clayton and Savage, chapter 2.

34. By the 1930s the Kipsigis (Lumbwa) used the same term to describe cattle raids and wage labor (I. Q. Orchardson, "Some Traits of the Kipsigis in Relation to Their contacts with Europeans," *Africa* 4, 1 [1931], p. 468).

35. Kitui Political Record Book, part 1, 1898–1912, PC/CP 1/2; Kyambu Political Record Book, 1912, PC/CP 1/4/2; Philip Mayer to P. Wyn Harris, "Bridewealth Limitation among the Gusii," 21 December 1948, Secretariat 1/12/12; Waller, p. 532; Rogers, p. 257; Ronald Hyam, "Concubinage and Colonial Service: The Crewe Circular (1909)," *Journal of Imperial and Commonwealth History* 14, 3 (May 1986), pp. 172–73; Clayton and Savage, p. 78n; Kikuyu District Political Record Book, 1908–12 PC/CP 1/4/1; Nyeri District Cash Book, July 1903–March 1907, DC/NYI 6/2; Eldama Ravine Cash Book, April 1902–March 1906, DC/ER 4/3; NLC, pp. 231–34. In 1936 the Digo District Officer, G. R. B. Brown, suggested that the higher the value of the livestock used for bridewealth the fewer choices a woman had in marriage (Digo District Annual Report, G. R. B. Brown Papers, RH MSS Afr. s. 545).

36. Nyeri District Cash Book, July 1903–March 1907; Eldama Ravine Cash Book, April 1902–March 1906; *Times of East Africa,* 23 December 1905; *Advertiser of East Africa,* 25 March, 15 April 1910.

37. Kitching, pp. 213, 216, 244–45.

38. Bujra, "Women 'Entrepreneurs,'" p. 215.

39. S. H. Fazan, *Memo on the Rate of Population Increase of the Kikuyu Tribe,* Nairobi, 1937, cyclostyled, DC/KBU 6/2. The higher bridewealth was in Kiambu and then in the settled areas of the Rift Valley; see Kanogo, *Squatters,* pp. 24–25.

40. G. Gordon Dennis, "Our First Marriage at Kenia," *Kikuyu News* 56 (August—September 1915), pp. 4–6; Dr. Phelp, "Character sketches: Jonathan and Jason," *Kikuyu News* 86 (December 1923), pp. 1–3.

41. G. H. Osborne refers to several cases in which disinherited, unmarried Muslim converts sued their fathers' estates for cows for bridewealth while their fathers

were still alive (Osborne, Acting [Ag.] DC Kitui, 8 June 1910, Ukamba Province File, Settlement of Swahilis, 1910, DC/MKS 10A/9/1).

42. Meinertzhagen, *Kenya Diary*, p. 296.

43. Marc H. Dawson, "Socio-economic and Epidemiological Change in Kenya, 1880–1925," Ph.D. thesis, University of Wisconsin, Madison, 1983, pp. 199–217.

44. Norman Leys, appendix to the Nakuru Annual Medical Report, 1909, "An Account of Venereal Disease in Naivasha District," Ainsworth miscellaneous papers, PC/NZA 2/3. I assume that the prices quoted are those prostitutes charged Europeans, and that Africans paid considerably less.

45. Quoted in Ronald Hardy, *The Iron Snake* (London: Collins, 1965), pp. 241–43.

46. Asst. District Superintendent of Police, Nairobi, to Ag. Provincial Commissioner (PC) Nairobi, 6 June 1907; Secretary of Native Affairs to the Principal Judge of the High Court of Mombasa, 28 October 1907, Judicial I/353.

47. W. Robert Foran, *A Cuckoo in Kenya: The Reminiscences of a Pioneer Police Officer in British East Africa* (London: Hutchinson, 1936), pp. 146–47.

48. C. H. Stigand, *The Land of Zinj* (London: Constable, 1913), pp. 229, 277. Bujra noted a large proportion of Nandi and Kipsigis prostitutes in Nairobi before World War I ("Women 'Entrepreneurs'").

49. Nandi District Annual Report, 1913, PC/NDI 1/2.

50. Mervyn W. H. Beech, Asst. District Commissioner (DC) Dagoretti, Memorandum on the Kikuyu point of view, 12 December 1912, Kiambu Political Record Book, PC/CP 1/4/2.

51. John Ainsworth, PC Nyanza, memo regarding the question of Swahilis, Sudanese, and other Africans at present residing in townships, 9 June 1911, CO 533/130/12081.

52. See N. Leys, "Venereal Disease": "The elaborate structure of native custom and belief falls when we touch it and yet we express an indignant surprise at the disorder of our own creation." See also Clayton and Savage, chapter 2, passim; Frank Furedi, "The African Crowd in Nairobi: Popular Movements and Elite Politics," *Journal of African History* 14 (1973), p. 276.

53. E. Boedecker, "The Early History of Nairobi," Kabete, 1936, typescript, MacMillan Library, Nairobi; G. H. Mungeam, *British Rule in Kenya, 1895–1912* (Oxford: Oxford University Press, 1966), p. 67; Bujra, "Pumwani," pp. 9–10, and "Women 'Entrepreneurs,'" p. 215; Andrew Hake, *African Metropolis: Nairobi's Self-Help City* (Sussex: Sussex University Press, 1977), pp. 35–36, 173–76; interviews, passim.

54. See for example Bujra, "Women 'Entrepreneurs'"; Kenneth Little, *Women in African Towns* (Cambridge: Cambridge University Press, 1973), pp. 76–77; van Onselen, 1:103–4.

55. Nairobi District Political Record Book, 1911, DC/NBI 1/1/11; Stigand, p. 229; Halima Hamisi; Amina Hali.

56. According to Ronald Hyam such liaisons made the turn-of-the-century conquest, administration, and exploitation of tropical territories possible, and were substantially more liberal—for white males—than the kinds of imperialism that were to come (pp. 170–86).

57. T. H. Cashmore, "Your Obedient Servant, 1895–1918," n.d., typescript, RH MSS Afr. s. 1034, p. 52; Meinertzhagen, *Kenya Diary*, pp. 9–13; Hyam, pp. 172–73; Miryamu Wageithiga.

58. Quoted in McVicar, pp. 240–41. I seriously doubt that any woman was given a cow in exchange for sexual intercourse.

59. Amina Hali; Halima Hamisi; Hannah Mwikali; Miryamu Wageithiga.

60. Bujra, "Women 'Entrepreneurs,'" p. 221.

61. Foran, pp. 146–47; Stigand also noted the Swahili robes of Maasai prostitutes (p. 277).

62. Miryamu Wageithiga; Amina Hali; Bujra, "Pumwani," pp. 53–54, and "Women 'Entrepreneurs,'"p. 223.

63. Clayton and Savage, pp. 82–85; Donald C. Savage and J. Forbes Munro, "Carrier Corps Recruitment in the British East African Protectorate, 1914–1918," *Journal of African History* (1966), pp. 313–42; Geoffrey W. T. Hodges, "Manpower Statistics for the British Forces in East Africa, 1914–1918," *Journal of African History* 19 (1978), pp. 101–16, and *The Carrier Corps: Military Labor in the East African Campaign, 1914–1918* (Westport, CT: Greenwood Press, 1986), pp. 93–106, 207–8; Marc H. Dawson, "Health, Nutrition, and Population in Central Kenya, 1890–1945," in Dennis D. Cordell and Joel W. Gregory, eds., *African Population and Capitalism* (Boulder, CO, and London: Westview Press, 1987), pp. 210–11; John Overton, "War and Economic Underdevelopment: State Exploitation and African Response in Kenya, 1914–1918," *International Journal of African Historical Studies* 22, 2 (1989), p. 204.

64. Hodges, *Carrier Corps*, p. 77, and "Manpower Statistics," pp. 112–13; Clayton and Savage, p. 83.

65. Mwana Harusi bint Oman, Calfonya, 5 February 1977; Walkowitz, *Prostitution and Victorian Society*, pp. 203–4.

66. Mwanisha Waligo, Pumwani, 20 May 1976; Muthoni wa Karanja, Mathare, 25 June 1976; Wangui Fatuma, Pumwani, 29 December 1976; Fatuma Ali, Pumwani, 21 June 1976; Chepkitai Mbwana, Pumwani, 1–2 February 1977.

67. Bujra, "Women 'Entrepreneurs,'" p. 224.

68. Mervyn W. H. Beech, DC Malindi, to PC Mombasa, 4 March 1915, quoted in Savage and Munro, pp. 316–17.

69. DC Kericho to PC Nyanza, 5 April 1916, quoted in Dawson, "Socioeconomic and Epidemiological Change in Kenya," p. 223.

70. Mwana Harusi bint Oman; Mwanisha Waligo; Muthoni was Karanja; Amina Hali; Wangui Fatuma; Bujra, "Pumwani," pp. 53, 57, and "Women 'Entrepreneurs,'" p. 224.

71. Amina Hali; Miryamu Wageithiga; Mwanisha Waligo; "Native Huts in Kileleshwa," 27 July 1917, MD 13/581/1.

72. Bujra, "Pumwani," pp. 51–57.

73. "Movement of Natives from Pangani, Mombasa, and Masikini Villages to Native Reserve and Location," 1921, MD 40/443/4.

74. David Clark, "Unregulated Housing, Vested Interest, and the Development of Community Identity in Nairobi," *African Urban Studies* 3 (Winter 1978–79), pp. 33–34.

75. Shamba Plots, Nairobi River, 1912, MD 40/438; see Gareth Stedman Jones, *Outcast London: A Study of the Relationship between Classes in Victorian Society* (Oxford: Oxford University Press, 1971), pp. 13–16, 167, 188–93.

76. W. J. Simpson, *Report on Sanitary Matters in the East African Protectorate, Uganda, and Zanzibar* (Nairobi: Government Printer, 1914), p. 53; first report of the subcommittee on the Simpson scheme, MNC, 10 April 1915.

77. MNC minutes, 5 November 1918, MacMillan Library, Nairobi.

78. For a fuller discussion of Contagious Diseases laws, see chapters 1 and 7; Walkowitz, *Prostitution and Victorian Society,* pp. 69–89; Mary Murname and Kay Daniels, "Prostitutes and 'Purveyors of Disease': Venereal Disease Legislation in Tasmania, 1886–1945," *Hecate* 5 (1979), pp. 5–21; Ballhatchet, pp. 10–14, 62–67; David J. Pivar, "The Military, Prostitution, and Colonized Peoples: India and the Philippines, 1885–1917," *Journal of Sex Research* 17 (August 1981), pp. 256–69; van Heyningen, pp. 170–91; Alpers, pp. 155–63.

79. Maynard W. Swanson, "The Sanitation Syndrome: Bubonic Plague and Urban Native Policy in the Cape Colony, 1900–1909," *Journal of African History* 18 (1977), pp. 408–10.

80. Native Location, Nairobi, Draft Rules, 7 October 1914, MD 40/443. The dangers of freehold were to become painfully obvious to workings of the colonial state, when during World War I the Town Clerk and the Medical Department tried to remove the Somali settlement from Nairobi East. While the site of their new location was being debated—the KAR objected to the proposed site, because of the risks of disease—Somali headmen bought thirty-eight plots in Nairobi East, outside of municipal control. See "Somali Village Nairobi: Removal of Nairobi East Township," 1916–18, MD 40/827.

81. See N. Leys, "Venereal Disease"; E. P. C. Girouard, memo to all PCs, 1911, DC/NVA 4/1; John Ainsworth, PC Kisumu, memo to all DCs, 10 October 1911, CO 533/130/12081.

82. Native Location Committee minutes, 22 January 1915; "Movement of Natives from Pangani, Mombasa, and Masikini Villages"; Bujra, "Pumwani," pp. 60–62.

83. W. McGregor Ross to Chief Secretary, Committee on Native Location, 10 February 1912, MD 40/443/1.

84. See "Somali Village Nairobi."

85. T. Jawatson, Town Clerk, to A. R. Paterson, 13 January 1921, MD 40/443/4; MNC minutes, 5 June 1922.

86. A. R. Paterson, "Housing in Nairobi," *Kenya Observer* 2 April 1923.

87. Norman Leys, *Kenya,* 4th ed. (London: Frank Cass, 1973), pp. 288–89.

88. "Movement of Natives from Pangani, Masikini, and Mombasa Villages"; Mwanisha Waligo; Mwana Harusi bint Oman; Miryamu Wageithiga; Bujra, "Pumwani," pp. 12–13, and "Women 'Entrepreneurs,'" pp. 213–34.

89. Dirasse, pp. 114–34, 168–70.

90. Scrounging, even at times of severe dislocation, was not random behavior. See Vaughan, pp. 119–47.

91. See Frederick Cooper, "Peasants, Capitalists, and Historians," *Journal of Southern African Studies* 7, 2 (1981), pp. 284–314.

Chapter Three

1. Clayton and Savage, p. 110; Kanogo, *Squatters*, pp. 37–39.

2. Labour Circular 1, 23 October 1919, quoted in Clayton and Savage, p. 110; chapter 4 contains a good summary of this legislation, as does R. M. A. van Zwanenberg, *Colonial Capitalism and Forced Labour in Kenya, 1919–1939* (Nairobi: East African Literature Bureau, 1975), chapters 4 and 7; N. Leys, *Kenya*, p. 416.

3. Frederick Cooper suggests that settlers could readily subvert the state because of "shared conceptions of work, land, and economic order that transcend the periodic diverge of imperial or settler interests" (*From Slaves to Squatters: Plantation Labor in Zanzibar and Coastal Kenya, 1890–1925* [New Haven and London: Yale University Press, 1980], p. 71).

4. Clayton and Savage, pp. 150–51; Sharon Srichter, *Migrant Labour in Kenya: Capitalism and the African Response* (London: Longman, 1982), pp. 73–74.

5. Michael P. Cowen, "Capital and Peasant Households," essay, Nairobi, 1976; Michael P. Cowen and J. R. Newman, "Real Wages in Central Kenya, 1924–1974," essay, Nairobi, 1975; Soko Kagawa, Pumwani, 10 December 1976; Ahmed Hussein, Pumwani, 1 April 1977; Timotheo Omondo, Goina, Yimbo, 22 August 1986.

6. Clayton and Savage, p. 140; Bildad Kaggia, *Roots of Freedom, 1921–1963* (Nairobi: East Africa Publishing House, 1975), p. 9; Ziro wa Bogosha, Pumwani, 18 March 1977; Salim Hamisi, Pumwani, 29 March 1977; Zebede Oyoyo, Goina, Yimbo, 16 and 23 August 1986.

7. Hake, p. 45.

8. Nairobi Annual Medical Report, 1929, quoted in Hake, p. 45.

9. E. B. Hosking, memorandum on the native locations of Nairobi, n.d., probably written 1923–25, Coryndon Papers, RH MSS Afr. s. 633, box 5/1; Hake, p. 45; Richard Stren, *Housing the Urban Poor in Africa: Politics, Policy, and Bureaucracy in Mombasa*, Research Series 34 (Berkeley: Institute of International Studies, 1978), pp. 187–88.

10. Nairobi Annual Medical Report, 1928.

11. Hosking, memorandum on the native locations; Amina Hali.

12. Amina Hali; Miryamu Wageithiga; Hidaya Saidi; Mwana Harusi bint Ramadhani, Pumwani, 4 June 1976.

13. The suspension of the gold standard raised the value of the silver rupee coin and note from 1/4 in 1919 to as high as 2/10, after which it was stabilized at 2/ until it was replaced by the shilling coin in 1921. The fluctuations in the value of the rupee appeared to raise the value of wages paid to Africans, and this may account for some of the very high wages reported in colonial documents, since employers had everything to gain in their demands for wage reductions by exaggerating existing wage rates. See Clayton and Savage, pp. 139–46.

14. Ibid., p. 151; Salim Hamisi; Ziro wa Bogosha; Farouk Mohammed, Calfonya, 13 March 1977.

15. Clayton and Savage, p. 148.

16. Prices derived from Cowen's and Newman's notes for "Real Wages in Central Kenya"; Stichter, *Migrant Labour*, pp. 45, 51, 71–74.

17. There is one vague archival reference in 1923 to what may have been malaya

prostitution, that there were women in Pumwani "who made their living cohabiting with various persons for periods of a month or longer" (Health Office, confidential memo 8/77/1, on prostitution, 11 October 1923, MD 28/854/1.

18. Amina Hali; Miryamu Wageithiga; Kayaya Thababu, Pumwani, 7 January 1977; Hidaya Saidi.

19. Fauzia Abdullah, Pumwani, 10 October 1976.

20. Odhiambo Okinyi, Shauri Moyo, 23 February 1977; Ziro wa Bogosha; Ahmed Hussein; Soko Kagawa; Farouk Mohammed; Salim Hamisi; Omolo Okumu, Pumwani, 2 March 1977; Mohammed Omari, Pumwani, 9 February 1977; Richard Mulembe, Pumwani, 18 February 1977; Samuel Kariuki, Shauri Moyo, 4 March 1977; John Mwakalili, Shauri Moyo, 6 March 1977; Thomas Mukama, Eastleigh, 10 March 1977; Peter Mwenyi, Pumwani, 15 March 1977; Mutiso Katumbe, Pumwani, 16 March 1977; Abdullah Kaviti, Pumwani, 23 March 1977; Daudi Wagulisa, Pumwani, 29 March 1977; Habib Hasan, Pumwani, 2 April 1977.

21. Miryamu Wageithiga; Fauzia Abdullah; Hidaya Saidi; Ahmed Hussein; Farouk Mohammed.

22. Fauzia Abdullah; Amina Hali; Kayaya Thababu; Wambui Murithi; Habib Hasan.

23. Hake, p. 46; R. M. A. van Zwanenberg, "History and Theory of Urban Poverty in Nairobi: The Case of Slum Development," *Journal of East African Research and Development* 2, 2 (1972), pp. 184–88; Furedi, p. 277.

24. Eric R. St. A. Davies, Municipal Native Affairs Officer (MNAO), "Some Problems Arising from the Conditions of Housing and Employment of Natives in Nairobi," Nairobi, August 1939, typescript, Housing of Africans in Nairobi, MD 40/1131 (hereafter Davies Report).

25. See van Zwanenberg, "Urban Poverty in Nairobi"; Furedi.

26. H. A. Carr's memorandum, in *Kenya Land Commission, Evidence* (London: HMSO, 1934), 1:1124–30.

27. Bujra, "Women 'Entrepreneurs,'" p. 217.

28. Amina Hali; Wambui Murithi; Wangui Fatuma; Nineta Lilande.

29. Hamis bin Athman, Pumwani, letter to the editor, *Habari*, translated by Department of Native Affairs, 20 November 1923, Housing of Africans in Nairobi, MD 40/1131/1.

30. Zaina Kachui, Pumwani, 14 June 1976; Chepkitai Mbwana; Mwanisha Waligo; Amina Hali; Kayaya Thababu; Miryamu Wageithiga; Mwana Himani bint Ramadhani, Pumwani, 4 June 1976; Fauzia Abdullah.

31. Asha binti Juma, Pumwani, 2 June 1976.

32. Habiba Maua, Eastleigh, 17 May 1976; Fatuma Ali; Mwana Harusi bint Oman.

33. Fauzia Abdullah.

34. Mwana Harusi bint Oman; Chepkitai Mbwana.

35. Kayaya Thababu.

36. Hadija Njeri, Eastleigh, 5 May 1976; Miriam Musale, Pumwani, 18 June 1976; Wangui Fatuma; Asha Mohammed, Pumwani, 1 March 1977; Habiba Maua.

37. C. M. Dobbs, PC Nyanza, memorandum on infanticide, 1–2 February 1933, RH MSS Afr. s. 665.

38. Bujra, "Women 'Entrepreneurs,'"p. 224.

39. Ibid., pp. 227–29.

40. PC Coast Province to Colonial Secretary, 23 June 1930, "Legal Ownership of Huts by Independent Women," PC/Coast 59/4; Strobel, pp. 58–64.

41. A. R. Paterson to Chief Secretary, "Cost of Native Housing," 12 April 1940, MD 40/1131/1; H. A. Carr's memorandum, p. 1124; Bujra, "Pumwani," pp. 9–13.

42. Bujra, "Women 'Entrepreneurs,'" pp. 225–29; Thomas Colchester, London, 8 August 1977; Kayaya Thababu.

43. Margaret Githeka, Mathare, 2 March 1976; Tabitha Waweru, Mathare, 13 July 1976.

44. Habiba Maua; Mwanisha Waligo; Miryamu Wageithiga; Kayaya Thababu; Wangui Fatuma; Hidaya Saidi; Bujra, "Pumwani," pp. 50–63.

45. Bujra, "Pumwani," pp. 40–42, 51–57; Ali Mohammed, Pumwani, 28 March 1977; Ahmed Hussein; Salim Hamisi; Ziro wa Bogosha; Odhiambo Okinyi; Omolo Okumu; Richard Mulembe; Thomas Mukama.

46. Salima binti Athmani, Pumwani, 18 June 1976.

47. Eric Stokes, *English Utilitarians and India* (Oxford: Oxford University Press, 1959), pp. 222–28; John Clive, *Macaulay: The Shaping of an Historian* (New York: Knopf, 1973), pp. 427–75. The Indian Evidence, Contract, and Post Office Acts were also applied to East Africa (J. S. Mangat, *The History of the Asians in East Africa, c. 1886 to 1945* [Oxford University Press, 1969], p. 63n).

48. Hill, Principal Health Officer, Nairobi, suggested revising the township rules so that sanitary issues could be prosecuted under their evidence requirements and not the IPC's (16 November 1906, Lodging Houses, Nairobi, MD 13/63).

49. Wambui Murithi.

50. Hadija Njeri.

51. Kayaya Thababu; Chepkitai Mbwana; Wambui Murithi; Mwana Harusi bint Oman; Hidaya Saidi.

52. Swanson, pp. 387–90; Stedman Jones, pp. 186–93.

53. East African Protectorate, Economic Commission, *Final Report,* part 1, 1919 (Nairobi: Government Printer, 1920), in G. W. McGregor Ross Papers, RH MSS Afr. s. 1178(1).

54. B. W. Cherwitt to Sanitation Officer, Nairobi, 3 October 1916, Lodging Houses, Amendments to Rules, 1914–17, MD 13/537.

55. Town Clerk to A. R. Paterson, 13 January 1921, New Native Location: Nairobi, MD 40/443/1; MNC minutes, June 1922, quoted in Bujra, "Pumwani," p. 11.

56. B. W. Cherwitt to Principal Sanitation Officer, Nairobi, 14 February 1917, Somali Village, Removal of Nairobi East Township, 1916–18, MD 40/827.

57. MNC, J. W. Radford, Report of the Subcommittee on the Native Location, 5 October 1918.

58. Ann Beck, *A History of the British Medical Administration of East Africa, 1900–1950* (Cambridge: Harvard University Press, 1970), pp. 138–39, 146–47.

59. William G. A. Ormsby-Gore to Henry Robert Brooke-Popham, 15 June 1937, RH MSS Afr. s. 1120.

60. See Stren, pp. 127–29, for Paterson's defeat in his attempt to sanitize Mombasa's Old Town.

61. *Official Gazette,* 22 December 1920, p. 1158, quoted in van Zwanenberg, "Urban Poverty in Nairobi," p. 196.

62. Kadir Ali, Abdulhussein Estate, River Road, letter to Nairobi Town Clerk, 30 September 1915, River Road, Insanitary Conditions, MD 13/505; Muthoni wa Karanja; Chepkitai Mbwana; Miryamu Wageithiga; Mwana Harusi bint Oman; Hadija Njeri; Hidaya Saidi; Margaret Githeka; Soko Kagawa; Ziro wa Bogosha; Ahmed Hussein.

63. Soko Kagawa; Ziro wa Bogosha; Ahmed Hussein.

64. Chepkitai Mbwana; Hidaya Saidi.

65. Miryamu Wageithiga; Chepkitai Mbwana; Habiba Maua; Hidaya Saidi.

66. P. P. L. H. Nyanzi and [illegible] to A. R. Paterson, PMO, 17 July 1923, re brothels in River Road, Venereal Disease in Kenya, MD 28/854/1.

67. Health Office, confidential memo 8/77/1.

68. P. P. L. H. Nyanzi and [illegible] to A. R. Paterson, 21 November 1923, "Incest in Nairobi," MD 28/854/1.

69. J. R. Tate, DC Nairobi, to PC Nairobi, 29 July 1914, Native Location, MD 40/443.

70. Health Office, confidential memo 8/77/1.

71. Hodges, *Carrier Corps,* pp. 59, 123–25; Richard Meinertzhagen, *Army Diary, 1899–1926* (Edinburgh: Oliver and Boyd, 1960), pp. 211–17.

72. See Bujra, "Women 'Entrepreneurs,'" pp. 219, 221, 230–32; Chepkitai Mbwana; Mwana Harusi bint Oman; Hidaya Saidi; Soko Kagawa; Ziro wa Bogosha; Ahmed Hussein.

73. A. R. Paterson to Chief Native Commissioner, 12 October 1923, re brothels and prostitutes in Nairobi, Venereal Disease in Kenya, MD 28/854/1.

74. Nyanzi and [illegible] to Paterson, 21 November 1923.

75. A. R. Paterson to Chief Native Affairs Commissioner, 30 November 1923, MD 28/854/1.

76. A. R. Paterson to Chief Native Commissioner, 30 November 1923, MD 28/854/1.

77. Chepkitai Mbwana; Miryamu Wageithiga; Wangui Fatuma.

78. A. R. Paterson to Chief Native Commissioner, 13 October 1923, MD 28/854/1.

79. Nyanzi and [illegible] to Paterson, 21 November 1923.

80. P. P. L. H. Nyanzi and [illegible] to Paterson, 3 May 1924, re prostitution in Nairobi, MD 28/854/1.

81. Hewitt to A. R. Paterson, 3 May 1924, re prostitution in Nairobi, MD 28/854/1.

82. Ziro wa Bogosha; Ahmed Hussein.

83. F. S. Joelson, ed., *East Africa Today* (London: 1928), quoted in Hake, p. 28.

84. Ziro wa Bogosha.

85. Kayaya Thababu.

86. Chepkitai Mbwana.

87. Wambui Murithi; see also Hadija Njeri; Kayaya Thababu.

88. Kayaya Thababu.

89. Wambui Murithi; see also Kayaya Thababu.

90. Mwana Harusi bint Ramadhani; see also Fauzia Abdullah.

91. Wanjiko Kamau, Mathare, 1 July 1976.

92. Local Native Council (LNC) minutes, 22–23 November 1928, KBU/LNC/1, 1928–31.

93. Robert H. Bates, "The Agrarian Origins of Mau Mau: A Structural Account," *Agricultural History* 61, 1 (1987), p. 21; Stichter, *Migrant Labour,* pp. 75–77; Kanogo, *Squatters,* pp. 47–49; Dawson, "Population," pp. 212–15.

94. E. B. Hosking, MNAO, report on the native locations and housing, MNC minutes, September 1929.

95. E. B. Hosking to Town Clerk, 29 January 1930, "Municipal Native Housing," MNC file "Native Housing."

96. Margaret Githeka; Miryamu Wageithiga; Hadija Njeri; Wambui Murithi.

Chapter Four

1. Mwana Harusi bint Ramadhani.

2. Davies Report, pp. 3–4.

3. E. B. Hosking, memorandum on the working of bylaw 557, Native Residents and Visitors Permits, circulated at meeting of Native Affairs Committee, MNC, 7 July 1930; E. G. Tisdall, DC, to Chief Native Commissioner, 11 August 1931, Pass Laws for Town Natives in Nairobi, Lab 9/1109.

4. The Davics Report estimated a shortage of fifty-seven hundred places in Pumwani for Africans already employed in Nairobi (p. 13); K. A. T. Martin and Thomas Colchester claimed that "18,000 or 19,000 Africans" "slept in highly overcrowded and unhealthy conditions" (memorandum for the Native Affairs Committee, prepared by the Principal Medical Officer and the Municipal Native Affairs Officer, on the housing of Africans in Nairobi, 30 April 1941, CO 533/528/38397/2, p. 5). Colchester later admitted to inflating this figure (Thomas Colchester, London, 12 August 1977).

5. Governor Henry Robert Brooke-Popham to Malcolm MacDonald, Secretary of State for the Colonies, 31 July 1939, CO 533/513.

6. Native Affairs Department Annual Report, 1933, quoted in Stichter, *Migrant Labour,* pp. 95; Cowen and Newman, p. 5; Kitching, pp. 59–62; Kanogo, *Squatters,* pp. 61–68.

7. MNC, Native Affairs Committee minutes, 9 June 1933.

8. Margaret Githeka.

9. Amina Hali; Mwanisha Waligo; Zaina binti Ali.

10. E. B. Hosking, report on the native locations and housing, 1929, Native Affairs Committee, quoted in van Zwanenberg, "Urban Poverty in Nairobi," p. 189; H. A. Carr's memorandum, p. 1124. In 1933 Pangani's population was said to have dropped to twenty-seven hundred (Hake, p. 56), but that may have been wishful thinking by those advocating its demolition.

11. Van Zwanenberg, "Urban Poverty in Nairobi," p. 189; Clayton and Savage, pp. 210–11; David Throup, *Social and Economic Origins of Mau Mau* (Athens: Ohio University Press, 1987), p. 171.

12. Mzee Ambari, interviewed by R. M. A. van Zwanenberg, Pumwani, 23 November 1971; Amina Hali.

13. E. B. Hosking to Town Clerk, 25 May 1932, Native Housing in Nairobi, Lab 9/1697/70.

14. MNC quoted in van Zwanenberg, "Urban Poverty in Nairobi," p. 189. Sleeping on the floor was not evidence of overcrowding in and of itself, since few laborers would have owned beds: men often slept on sacks or blankets on the floor (Clayton and Savage, p. 210). The question for early 1930s Nairobi is, how many men in Pumwani and Pangani slept in passageways while rooms remained vacant?

15. MNC, Native Affairs Committee minutes, 18 May 1934, 10 April 1935, 1 September 1936.

16. Amina Hali; Mzee Ambari; Ibrahima binti Musa, Pumwani, 1 December 1976; E. G. Tisdall, memorandum re native housing, 9 July 1937, MD 40/1131/1; H. A. Carr's memorandum, p. 1121; Zaina Kachui; Miriam Musale; Salima binti Athmani; Asha Wanjiru, Pumwani, 23 December 1976; Monica Nyazura, Pumwani, 13 January 1977; MNC, Native Affairs Committee minutes, 8 April 1938.

17. Ibrahima binti Musa; see also Frederick Cooper, *On the African Waterfront: Urban Disorder and the Transformation of Work in Colonial Mombasa* (New Haven and London: Yale University Press, 1987), pp. 182–85.

18. MNC minutes, 26 June 1933; MNC, Native Affairs Committee minutes, 4 June 1937.

19. E. B. Hosking to Labour Officer, Nairobi, 1 March 1932, Lab 9/1707/70/251.

20. Amina Hali.

21. Njoki wa Thiongo, Eastleigh, 21 July 1976; Hadija Njeri.

22. Salima binti Athmani.

23. Zaina Kachui; Wangui Fatuma; Digo District Annual Report, 1936.

24. C. M. Clark, p. 362; Bates, p. 21.

25. Zaina Kachui.

26. Miriam Musale.

27. Thomas Mukama; Ahmed Hussein; Mohammed Omari; Farouk Mohammed; Salim Hamisi; Odhiambo Okinyi; Mutiso Katumbe.

28. Rehema binti Hasan, Pumwani, 21 December 1976; Salima binti Athmani; Richard Mulembe; Thomas Mukama; Farouk Mohammed.

29. Inter-Territorial Committee for the East African Dependencies, *A Standard Swahili-English Dictionary* (Oxford: Oxford University Press, 1939), p. 70.

30. Zaina Kachui; Salima binti Athmani; Hadija Njeri.

31. Salima binti Athmani.

32. Ahmed Hussein; Mohammed Omari; Salim Hamisi; Richard Mulembe; Odhiambo Okinyi; Samuel Kariuki.

33. Salima binti Athmani.

34. Ibid.; Rehema binti Hasan.

35. Thomas Mukama; Odhiambo Okinyi.

36. Rosen, pp. 87–92.

37. Walkowitz, *Prostitution and Victorian Society*, p. 250.

38. Hyam, p. 182.

39. Hadija Njeri.

40. Salima binti Athmani.

41. Hadija Njeri.

42. Salima binti Athmani; see also Elizabeth Kamya, Pumwani, 17 August 1976.

43. Hadija Njeri; Pass Laws for Town Natives, 1931, Lab 9/1109.

44. Salima binti Athmani.

45. Ibid.

46. Many of these ideas first appeared in my "Vice and Vagrants," pp. 202–27.

47. Cowen and Newman, p. 7.

48. Municipal Native Affairs Department, Nairobi Annual Report, 1938, quoted in Stichter, *Migrant Labour*, p. 111.

49. MNC, Native Affairs Committee minutes, 4 June 1937; Thomas Mukama; Farouk Mohammed; Albert Mutsoke, Shauri Moyo, 14 March 1977; Opiyo Oyugi, Pumwani, 28 March 1977.

50. MNC, Native Affairs Committee minutes, 8 April 1938; Gathiro wa Chege, Mathare, 9 July 1976; Elizabeth Kamya; Hadija binti Nasolo, Pumwani, 3 and 8 March 1977; Zaina Kachui; Ibrahima binti Musa.

51. Clayton and Savage, pp. 209–10.

52. Miriam Musale.

53. Davies Report, pp. 3–4; see also Wambui Murithi.

54. Mwanisha Waligo; Zaina Kachui; Miriam Musale.

55. Jomo Kenyatta, *Facing Mount Kenya: The Tribal Life of the Gikuyu* (London: Secker and Warburg, 1953), pp. 131–34; Carl G. Rosberg, Jr., and John Nottingham, *The Myth of "Mau Mau": Nationalism in Kenya* (New York: Praeger 1966), pp. 106–31; Kanogo, *Squatters*, pp. 77–80; Odhiambo Okinyi; Omolo Okumu; Habib Hasan; Mwanisha Waligo; Ibrahima binti Musa. The gap between circumcised and uncircumcised was not as indissoluble or as culturally binding as scholars and nationalists might have us believe. In the 1950s, during the Mau Mau revolt, when being a Kikuyu was grounds for arrest, many Luo men were said to have become Muslims, been circumcised, and married Kikuyu Muslim women so they both could remain in town; see pp. 207–8.

56. Margaret Githeka.

57. Odhiambo Okinyi; Samuel Kariuki; Mwanisha Waligo; Margaret Githeka. Mwanisha Waligo said that if a Luo came to her door, "I might ask a shilling more, but I could not force him."

58. Asha Wanjiru; Wangui Fatuma; Ibrahima binti Musa; Monica Nyazura, Pumwani, 13 January 1977.

59. Monica Nyazura; Asha Wanjiru.

60. Asha Wanjiru.

61. Asha Mohammed; Margaret Githeka; Salim Hamisi; Mutiso Katumbe; Thomas Mukama; Mohammed Omari.

62. Margaret Githeka; Beatrice Nyambura, Mathare, 8 July 1976; Njoki wa Thiongo; Hadija Njeri.

63. Thomas Mukama; Farouk Mohammed; Omolo Okumu.

64. Asha Wanjiru.

65. Hadija Njeri; Habiba binti Mahmood, Eastleigh, 5 May 1976; Thomas Colchester, London, 12 August 1977.

66. Evans, pp. 106–10; Rosen, pp. 3–4.

67. Christine Stansell, *City of Women: Sex and Class in New York, 1789–1860* (Urbana and Chicago: University of Illinois Press, 1987), pp. 171–72.

68. Walkowitz, *Prostitution and Victorian Society,* pp. 196–97; Stansell, pp. 176–80.

69. Davies Report; Sharon Stichter, "Women and the Labor Force in Kenya, 1895–1964," *Rural Africana* 29 (Winter 1975–76), p. 56; Wanjira Ng'ang'a, Mathare, 8 July 1976; Hadija binti Nasolo.

70. Clayton and Savage, p. 209; Wanjira Ng'ang'a.

71. See Cooper, *Waterfront,* pp. 124–27; E. P. Thompson, "Time, Work-Discipline, and Industrial Capitalism" *Past and Present* 38 (1967), pp. 56–97.

Chapter Five

1. McVicar, p. 241; Soko Kagawa; Thomas Mukama; Richard Mulembe.

2. Miriam Musale.

3. Amina Hali; Kayaya Thababu; Salim Hamisi; Richard Mulembe.

4. Rehema binti Hasan; Monica Nyazura; Salim Hamisi; Ziro wa Bogosha; Richard Mulembe.

5. Sara Waigo, Mathare, 1 July 1976; Rehema binti Hasan; Monica Nyazura; Asha Mohammed.

6. Monica Nyazura.

7. Esther Akinyi, Pumwani, 8 October 1976; Margaret Githeka; Hidaya Saidi; Mwana Himani bint Ramadhani; Monica Nyazura; Wangui Fatuma.

8. Margaret Githeka; Monica Nyazura; Miriam Musale; Asha Mohammed; Wangui Fatuma; John Kioko, Shauri Moyo, 6 March 1977; Salim Hamisi; Richard Mulembe; Mutiso Katumbe; Thomas Mukama. None of the men I interviewed reported paying wazi-wazi women less than 1/.

9. Margaret Githeka.

10. Soko Kagawa; Abdullah Kaviti.

11. Margaret Githeka.

12. Quoted in McVicar, p. 241; see also Margaret Githeka.

13. See Jocelyn Margaret Murray, "The Kikuyu Female Circumcision Controversy, with Special Reference to the Church Missionary Society's 'Sphere of Influence,'" Ph.D. thesis, University of California, Los Angeles, 1974.

14. Miryamu binti Omari, Pumwani, 25 March 1977.

15. Ibrahima binti Musa.

16. Zaina binti Ali; Asha Mohammed.

17. Mwana Harusi bint Ramadhani.

18. Wangui Fatuma.

19. Karim K. Janmohammed, "Ethnicity in an Urban Setting: A Case Study of Mombasa," in Bethwell A. Ogot, ed., *Hadith 6: History and Social Change in East Africa* (Nairobi: East African Literature Bureau, 1976), pp. 199–202; Cooper, *Waterfront,* pp. 68–73; Stichter, *Migrant Labour,* pp. 109–10.

20. Zaina binti Ali. My data indicate that between 1936 and 1946 some working Luos paid about the same price for short-time with women who were not Haya as did wealthy Muslim property owners and merchants, although Luo men did not

visit prostitutes as often. See Omolo Okumu; Odhiambo Okinyi; Mohammed Omari; Soko Kagawa; Farouk Mohammed.

21. Jane Akumu, Shauri Moyo, 25 October 1976; Daniel Otieno, Pumwani, 25 February 1977; Habib Hasan; Salima binti Athmani; Margaret Githeka; Esther Akinyi.

22. Miriam Musale; Sara Waigo.

23. McVicar, p. 244. More inadvertent praise for the malaya form came from *The Mombasa Social Survey,* which interviewed 174 malaya women—there was no wazi-wazi form in Mombasa—in a working-class area and concluded, "It is a tribute to the police that prostitution is not more obvious" (G. M. Wilson, ed., Nairobi, 1959, typescript, p. 580).

24. Aiden W. Southall and Peter C. W. Gutkind, *Townsmen in the Making: Kampala and Its Suburbs* (Kampala: East African Institute of Social Research, 1957), pp. 79–83.

25. McVicar, p. 244; Southall and Gutkind, pp. 82–83; Wilson, pp. 561–80; J. A. K. Leslie, *A Social Survey of Dar es Salaam* (Oxford: Oxford University Press, 1963), pp. 226–33; Little, pp. 90–91.

26. Tabitha Waweru.

27. Southall and Gutkind, pp. 82–83. McVicar also contains a discussion of skin color and bridewealth among Kikuyu and Kamba in the 1960s, in which the author forgets that "black" and "brown" are descriptive terms among African peoples (pp. 242–44).

28. Odhiambo Okinyi; Salim Hamisi; Mahmood Silla, Pumwani, 3 March 1977.

29. Southall and Gutkind, pp. 82–83; Birgitta Larsson, personal communication, 15 June 1984; see also Bengt Sundkler, *Bara Bukoba: Church and Community in Tanzania* (London: C. Hurst and Company, 1980), pp. 61–69.

30. Southall and Gutkind, p. 82; H. Rehse, *Kiziba: Land und Leute* (Stuttgart, 1910), quoted in Brigit Storgaard, "Women in Ujamaa Villages," *Rural Africana* 29 (Winter 1975–76), pp. 145–47.

31. Southall and Gutkind, p. 82.

32. B. G. M. Sundkler, pp. 253–60.

33. Ibid., p. 253.

34. Many of these ideas first appeared in my "Colonial State," pp. 167–94.

35. Zaina Kachui; Sara Waigo; Salima binti Athmani; Miriam Musale; Wangui Fatuma.

36. Birgitta Larsson, "A Dying People? Women, Church, and Social Change in North-western Tanzania under British Rule," essay, March 1987, pp. 32–35.

37. Hans Cory and M. N. Hartnoll, *Customary Law of the Haya Tribe* (London: Lund Humphries, 1945), pp. 59, 228; Ralph A. Austen, *Northwest Tanganyika under German and British Rule: Colonial Policy and Tribal Politics, 1889–1939* (New Haven: Yale University Press, 1968), pp. 224–25; Goran Hyden, *Beyond Ujamaa in Tanzania: Underdevelopment and an Uncaptured Peasantry* (London: Heinemann, 1980), pp. 45–52; Rogers K. K. Molefi, "The Political Ecology of Agriculture and Health in Northwest Tanganyika, 1890–1960," Ph.D. thesis, Dalhousie University, Halifax, Nova Scotia, 1985, pp. 135–36; Marja-Liisa Swantz, *Women in Development: A Creative Role Denied?* (New York: St. Martin's Press, 1985), pp. 50–52, 70–76.

38. Swantz, pp. 73–76; Larsson, pp. 30–35.

39. Beatrice Nyambura; Njoki wa Thiongo; Wanjira Ng'ang'a.

40. Thomas Colchester, London, 8 August 1977; Wambui Murithi; Asha Wanjiru; Tabitha Waweru.

41. Asha Wanjiru; Elizabeth Kamya; Zaina Kachui; Wangui Fatuma.

42. Salima binti Athmani; Wangui Fatuma. In the 1960s a Haya wazi-wazi prostitute told McVicar that she preferred to stay in Pumwani rather than move to one of Nairobi's recently Africanized suburbs because "here there are a lot of girls from my home, and also many other people, all living close by. If I had any trouble—like a man tries to beat me—I can call for help and at least someone will hear me" (McVicar, p. 245).

43. Zaina Kachui; Salima binti Athmani; Miriam Musale; Bujra, "Women 'Entrepreneurs,'" p. 227.

44. Larsson, p. 33; see also Salima binti Athmani.

45. Margaret Githeka; see also Tabitha Waweru; Mwana Himani bint Ramadhani; Wangui Fatuma.

46. Butler, p. 42.

47. Tabitha Waweru.

48. Miriam Musale.

49. Mwanisha Waligo; Zaina Kachui; Miriam Musale; Tabitha Waweru; Wangui Fatuma; Esther Akinyi.

50. Asha Wanjiru; see also Zaina Kachui; Mwanisha Waligo.

51. Rehema binti Hasan; see also Mwana Himani bint Ramadhani; Miriam Musale.

52. Asha Wanjiru; Zaina Kachui.

53. In 1945 there as a total of 5,188 police in the colony (Anthony Clayton and David Killingray, *Khaki and Blue: Military and Police in British Colonial Africa* [Athens: Ohio University Press, 1989], p. 113). Throup claims that there was one policeman for every thousand inhabitants of Nairobi, and by 1947 they were too unpopular to enter the African areas safely (*Social and Economic Origins*, p. 172).

54. Jane Akumu; Asha Wanjiru.

55. Throup, *Social and Economic Origins*, pp. 67–68.

56. See also Habiba Maua; Zaina Kachui; Hadija Njeri.

57. Mwana Himani bint Ramadhani; Amina Hali; Miryamu Wageithiga; Wangui Fatuma. Bujra called this phenomenon "the adoption of psuedo-kin," a term that obscures the resistance and lineage foundation this process entails ("Women 'Entrepreneurs,'" pp. 230–32).

58. Musenga Kaseli, Pumwani, 21 December 1976; Zaina binti Ali; Tabitha Waweru; Mwanisha Waligo.

59. Sara Waigo; see also Thomas Colchester, London, 12 August 1977; Hidaya Saidi; Amina Hali.

60. Miryamu Wageithiga; Wangui Fatuma; Bujra, "Pumwani," p. 53, and "Women 'Entrepreneurs,'" pp. 231–32.

61. CNC minutes, African Advisory Committee, Nairobi, 2–3 July 1946, 6–7 August 1946, 20 January 1947, 1946–49, MAA 2/5/223.

62. Thomas Colchester, London, 12 August 1977.

63. Tamima binti Saidi, Pumwani, 15 March 1977.

64. Alisati binti Salim, Pumwani, 22 February 1977; Thomas Colchester, London, 12 August 1977; White "Colonial State," and chapter 6.

65. See Walkowitz, *Prostitution and Victorian Society,* p. 194; Stansell, pp. 176–77.

66. Kanogo, *Squatters,* pp. 46–47.

Chapter Six

1. Ainsworth, "Question of Swahilis," and PC Nyanza to Ag. Chief Secretary, Nairobi, reply on the subject of Swahilis and other Africans, 16 October 1911, CO 533/130/12081.

2. Settlement of Swahilis, Ukamba Province, 1910, DC/MKS 10A/9.

3. John Ainsworth, PC Nyanza, memo to all DCs, 10 October 1911, CO 533/130/12081.

4. Ainsworth, "Question of Swahilis."

5. Ibid.

6. NLC, pp. 130, 190–96.

7. Ainsworth, memo to all DCs.

8. See John Lonsdale, "The Politics of Conquest: The British in Western Kenya, 1894–1908," *Historical Journal* 20, 4 (1977), pp. 841–70; N. Leys, "Venereal Disease."

9. Ainsworth's third memo requested that the Railway Department provide reduced fares for the repatriation of convicted vagrants (reply of 16 October 1911).

10. Radford to Principal Medical Officer, 28 August 1916; Bowring, telegram, 19 September 1916, Somali Village, Nairobi, 1916–18, MD 40/827.

11. See Louis Chevalier, *Laboring Classes and Dangerous Classes in Paris during the First Half of the Nineteenth Century* (Princeton: Princeton University Press, 1973), pp. 257–93, 359–73; Frederick Cooper, "The Guerilla Army of the Unemployed: The Labor Process and Class Conflict in Post-War Africa," paper presented to the seminar on the Informal Sector in the Center and the Periphery, Johns Hopkins University, Baltimore, 8–10 June 1984.

12. Chepkitai Mbwana; Mwanisha Waligo; Zaina Kachui; Amina Hali; Tabitha Waweru; Kayaya Thababu. The "lack of proper supervision" was held responsible for the exceptionally insanitary conditions of the Railway Landhies and Starehe in the late 1920s and early 1930s. See A. R. Paterson to Ag. Chief Secretary, Nairobi, 10 March 1927, MD/SAN 713/1; A. P. Ling, Chief Sanitation Inspector, Medical Department (MD), to A. R. Paterson, Director, Medical and Sanitary Services, re Government Employees Location, Nairobi, 8 July 1932, MD 40/1131/1.

13. Asha binti Juma.

14. Hadija Njeri; Wangui Fatuma; Zaina Kachui; Kayaya Thababu.

15. Zaina Kachui; Wanjira Ng'ang'a; Wambui Murithi; Zaina binti Ali.

16. Brooke-Popham to Malcolm MacDonald, 31 July 1939.

17. Ibid.; Clayton and Savage, p. 215; Cowen and Newman, p. 9.

18. *East African Standard,* 25 May 1950, quoted in Throup, *Social and Economic Origins,* p. 195. For a more realistic view of how landlords protect their tenants' homes as well as their own sources of income, see Michael Chege, "A Tale of Two Slums: Electoral Politics in Mathare and Dagoretti," *Review of African Political Economy* 20 (January–April 1981), pp. 74–88.

19. E. B. Hosking to KLC, in KLC, *Evidence,* 1:1152.

20. See Colin Leys, *Underdevelopment in Kenya* (Berkeley: University of California Press, 1974), pp. 266–69; Cooper, "Guerilla Army."

21. Amina Hali; Chepkitai Mbwana; Miryamu binti Omari; Thomas Colchester, London, 12 August 1977.

22. H. A. Carr's memorandum, p. 1123; Shams-ud Deen, LegCo, telegram to William G. A. Ormsby-Gore, 11 August 1936, Clearance of Pangani Village, CO 533/462/13/0905; van Zwanenberg, "Urban Poverty in Nairobi," pp. 184–94; Hake, p. 50.

23. Van Zwanenberg, "Urban Poverty in Nairobi," pp. 191–94; Nairobi Medical Officer of Health Annual Report, 1941.

24. Sanitary segregation in the 1920s had moved many laborers too far from Nairobi employers. Indeed, "one of the reasons for wishing to abolish the native settlement at Kibera is . . . to effect a distribution so that those natives who can justify their presence in the town should go to Pumwani" (Kenya Land Commission, *Report*, cmd. 456 [London: HMSO, 1934], p. 173). The other reason was that Kibera was on Crown Land favored as the site of a golf course; see also van Zwanenberg, "Urban Poverty in Nairobi," pp. 190–92; Swanson, pp. 387–410.

25. E. B. Hosking, DC Nairobi, to Commissioner for Lands and Settlement, 13 May 1931, CP 9/15/3.

26. H. A. Carr's memorandum, p. 1123.

27. Van Zwanenberg, "Urban Poverty in Nairobi," pp. 192–95.

28. A Wade to William G. A. Ormsby-Gore, 20 August 1936, CP 533/462/38005/13.

29. H. A. Carr's memorandum, 1129–30; Monica Nyazura; Chepkitai Mbwana; Miryamu binti Omari; Ibrahima binti Musa.

30. Malim bin Hamis, on behalf of Kikuyu Muslims, in KLC, *Evidence,* 1:1167.

31. Omari bin Shareef and Mwalimu bin Haji, African Moslem representatives, KLC, *Evidence,* 1:1166.

32. Mzee Ambari.

33. Ibid.; Amina Hali; Ibrahima binti Musa; Thomas Colchester, London, 12 August 1977; Native Affairs Committee minutes, MNC, 8 April 1938, 13 May 1938, 3 November 1938; Finance Committee, MNC, 25 May 1938.

34. Asha binti Juma.

35. Alisati binti Salim.

36. Davies Report, pp. 8–9; Stren, p. 189; White, "Colonial State," pp. 179–84.

37. Hadija Njeri; Sara Waigo.

38. Native Affairs Committee minutes, MNC 8 April 1938; Finance Committee minutes, MNC, 25 May 1938.

39. Hidaya Saidi; see also Fatuma Ali; Sara Waigo; Asha Mohammed.

40. Miryamu binti Omari.

41. A. R. Paterson to Chief Secretary, Nairobi, 27 January 1925, Housing of Natives, Cost of Quarters, MD 40/1131/15. He also wrote that anyone "seriously considering" the recommendations for huts six feet high made of corrugated iron should try living in one first; "in a hot climate I can imagine nothing more uncomfortable."

42. A. R. Paterson, memorandum on native housing, 24 March 1930, MD 40/1131/1.

43. H. A. Carr's memorandum, p. 1126.

44. A. R. Paterson, reply to Financial Secretary, MNC, 16 September 1938, MD 40/1131/1.

45. E. B. Hosking, minute to Financial Secretary, MNC, 12 July 1936; Financial Secretary, MNC, to A. R. Paterson, 16 September 1938, MD 40/1131/63.

46. A. R. Paterson to Financial Secretary, MNC, 12 April 1939, MD 40/1131/63.

47. Thomas G. Askwith to E. M. Hyde-Clarke, 20 November 1947, African Housing: General 1946–51, Lab 9/1751; F. W. Carpenter, Labour Officer, 23 March 1950, Control of Rents, Lab 9/1759; Thomas G. Askwith to Superintendent, CID, Nairobi, 29 October 1947, City African Affairs Officer Correspondence, 1947–50, MAA 8/22.

48. Paterson to Ag. Chief Secretary, Nairobi, 10 March 1927; Ling to Paterson, 8 July 1932.

49. Thomas G. Askwith, MNAO, "The Nairobi African Advisory Council: A Study in Social Relationships," 1 September 1948, City African Affairs Officer Correspondence, MAA 8/22.

50. Martin and Colchester, memorandum for the Native Affairs Committee.

51. Salima binti Athmani.

52. Nairobi Medical Officer of Health Annual Report, 1948.

53. Henry Robert Brooke-Popham to Sir Henry Moore, CO, 24 October 1939, Brooke-Popham letters, RH MSS Afr. s. 1120/2, ff. 3/9.

54. Central Province Annual Report, 1939, MAA 2/3/1.

55. Hosking to Commissioner for Lands and Settlement, 13 May 1931.

56. Thomas Colchester, MNAO, Annual Report, 1941, quoted in Stichter, *Migrant Labour* p. 120.

57. Ernest A. Vasey, *The Housing of Africans in the Urban Areas of Kenya* (Nairobi: Kenya Information Office, 1946), pp. 11–12.

58. African Advisory Council minutes, 5–6 August 1947, Nairobi, MAA 2/5/223.

59. Lydia Nthenga, Pumwani, 7 March 1977.

60. Fatuma Ali.

61. Municipal Treasurer to Ag. Commissioner for Local Government, 23 March 1950, Control of Rent, Lab 9/1759.

62. Ernest Vasey, report on the housing of Africans in townships and trading centres, Nairobi, April 1950, pp. 9–10, K.728.

63. Thomas G. Askwith to C. Tomkinson, 22 August 1945, Administration Policy: Urban Areas, Nairobi, 1945–47, MAA 7/491; Throup, *Social and Economic Origins*, pp. 174–75.

64. Thomas G. Askwith, African Advisory Council minutes, 2–3 December 1946, Nairobi, MAA 2/5/223.

65. Tom Mbotela to Superintendent, CID, Nairobi, 28 October 1947, MAA 8/22; Thomas G. Askwith to Superintendent, CID, Nairobi, 20 October 1947, African Affairs Officer Correspondence, 1947–50, MAA 8/22.

66. Thomas G. Askwith, African Advisory Council minutes, 30–31 March 1948, Nairobi, MAA 2/5/223.

67. Vasey, report on housing, p. 8.

68. *Sunday Post* (Nairobi), 15 February 1953, quoted in Stren, p. 208.

69. Sir Wilfred Havelock, former Minister for Local Government, interview with Richard Stren, 1967, quoted in Stren, p. 208.

70. Member for Health, Lands, and Local Government in the Legislative Council, 6 May 1953, quoted in Stren, p. 208.

71. Carole Wilson Dickerman, "Africans in Nairobi during the Emergency: Social and Economic Changes: 1952–1960," M. A. thesis, University of Wisconsin, Madison, 1978, pp. 35–36.

Chapter Seven

1. E. M. Sigswoth and T. J. Wyke, "A Study of Victorian Prostitution and Venereal Disease," in Martha Vicinus, ed., *Suffer and Be Still: Women in the Victorian Age* (Bloomington and London: Indiana University Press, 1973), pp. 77–99; Pivar, pp. 256–69.

2. "In some ways this has been a 'good war' for the district" (C. A. Connell, DC Kitui, 1942, quoted in Clayton and Savage, p. 230).

3. Clayton and Savage, p. 244; Nairobi Medical Officer of Health Annual Reports, 1942, 1944.

4. A. Haywood and F. A. S. Clarke, *The History of the Royal West African Frontier Forces* (Aldershot, England: Gale and Polden, 1964), pp. 330–31; David Killingray, "Military and Labour Recruitment in the Gold Coast during the Second World War," *Journal of African History* 23 (1982), pp. 83–95; Ernest Christian Lanning, "The Role of British Forces in Africa," August 1981, RH MSS Afr. s. 1734, box 7, and personal communication, 13 June 1989.

5. *Mombasa Times,* 11, 12, and 26 September 1942, quoted in Clayton and Savage, p. 237.

6. Clayton and Savage, pp. 245, 261n. It is not clear how enforceable this ordinance was, or how easily it might be circumvented by hiring servants for visitors or children.

7. Ibid., p. 245; Stichter, *Migrant Labour,* pp. 112, 121.

8. See Gucu G. Gikoyo, *We Fought for Freedom* (Nairobi: East Africa Publishing House, 1979), p. 14.

9. Farouk Mohammed; Thomas Mukama; John Mwakalili; Joseph Njoroge, Pumwani, 26 March 1977. In 1940 it was observed that job switching was particularly frequent near military camps; see Cowen and Newman, pp. 11–12. Specific cooking skills, especially a knowledge of baking, were essential for cooks in European households and often could not be taught on the job by non-Swahili-speaking employers to illiterate staff. For an excellent account of domestic servants' networks in a less-suburban city than Nairobi, see Jeanne Penvenne, "The Streetcorner Press: Worker Intelligence Networks in Lourenço Marques, 1900–1962," Working Paper 26, African Studies Center, Boston University, 1980, esp. pp. 4–11.

10. Stichter, *Migrant Labour* p. 114; Clayton and Savage, p. 250. African wartime pay schedules for civil servants ranged from 20/ to 60/ (Learner), 63/ to 90/ (Grade 1), and 95/ to 150/ (Grade 2) (Henry Robert Brooke-Popham to Malcolm MacDonald, 8 August 1938, quoted in Clayton and Savage, p. 263n).

11. Patrick arap Titi, Pumwani, 1 March 1977; John Mwakalili; Joseph Njoroge; Clayton and Savage, pp. 230–31.

12. Thomas Colchester, London, 12 August 1977; Wanjira Ng'ang'a; Robin Murray, "The Chandarias: The Development of a Kenyan Multinational," in Raphael Kaplinsky, ed., *Readings on the Multinational Corporation in Kenya* (Nairobi: Oxford University Press, 1978), pp. 289–91; Clayton and Killingray, pp. 252–54; Lanning, personal communication, 13 June 1989.

13. Stichter, "Women in the Labor Force," p. 58. There was in 1944 a combined total of 42,308 Indians and Europeans in Nairobi.

14. Tabitha Waweru; Monica Nyazura; Jane Akumu; Wangui Fatuma; James Ndolonga, Pumwani, 23 March 1977.

15. Wanjira Ng'ang'a; Omolo Okumu; Samuel Kariuki.

16. Beatrice Nyambura; Asha Mohammed; Sara Waigo; Tabitha Waweru; Hadija Njeri; Wanjira Ng'ang'a; Thomas Mukama.

17. Cowen and Newman, pp. 31–33.

18. Thomas Colchester, London, 12 August 1977; Mahmood Silla; Cowen and Newman, p. 33. Complaints about adulterated milk were common in Kenya, especially in the 1920s; see Chief Native Commissioner to Harran, PMO, 3 September 1921, and Harran to Chief Native Commissioner, 10 September 1921, MD 38/1057/1. Under the 1940 bylaw the milk in Nairobi was purchased only from European farms, thus increasing the price somewhat.

19. Committee appointed to "Enquire into and report whether the essentials of life are beyond the economic capacity of officers of the Government and of the KUR&H in the lower grades," *Report* (Nairobi: Government Printer, 1942), quoted in Cowen and Newman, p. 8.

20. Cowen and Newman, p. 34.

21. Wambui Murithi; Zaina binti Ali; Mwanisha Waligo; Samuel Kariuki; Mahmood Silla; Thomas Colchester, MNAO, to G. M. Rennie, 8 November 1944, Trading by Africans 1946–50, C&I 6/782; David Anderson and David W. Throup, "Africans and Agricultural Production in Colonial Kenya: The Myth of the War as Watershed," *Journal of African History* 26 (1985), pp. 336–39; Clayton and Savage, p. 242; Throup, *Social and Economic Origins*, pp. 65–66.

22. Hadija Njeri; Njoki wa Thiongo; Margaret Githeka; Muthoni wa Karanja; Wanjira Ng'ang'a.

23. Farouk Mohammed; Omolo Okumu; Albert Mutsoke; Thomas Mukama; Mahmood Silla.

24. Wangui Fatuma; Salima binti Athmani; Thomas Mukama; Daniel Otieno; John Mwakalili; James Ndolongo; Patrick arap Titi; Habib Hasan.

25. Amina Hali; Gathiro wa Chege.

26. William W. Sanger, *The History of Prostitution: Its Extent, Causes, and Effects throughout the World* (1897; New York: Eugenics Publishing Co., 1937), pp. 453–54; Finnegan, pp. 85–87, 157; Goldman, pp. 64–65.

27. Connelly, pp. 124–27; Walkowitz, *Prostitution and Victorian Society*, pp. 246–49.

28. Walkowitz, "Male Vice and Female Virtue," pp. 43–61.

29. Dawson, "Population," pp. 212–14.

30. Zenabu Githera, Pumwani, 30 December 1976; Wanjira Ng'ang'a; Gathiro wa Chege; Sara Waigo; Asha Mohammed.

31. Margaret Githeka.

32. Dawson, "Population," p. 215.

33. Thomas Colchester, London, 12 August 1977.

34. David Throup is scathing about the agricultural version of this policy: "only romantically inclined Englishmen, escaping from the pressures of life in industrial Britain, could have failed to realise that this idealized image of African communalism was a delusion and have attempted to foist upon the Kikuyu a system of land law that bore little resemblance to their own traditions" (*Social and Economic Origins*, p. 75).

35. Stichter, *Migrant Labour*, p. 110.

36. Mwanisha Ahmed; Asha Mohammed; Zenabu Githera.

37. See Walkowitz and Walkowitz, pp. 219–20.

38. Edwina Kamau, Eastleigh, 20 September 1976; Thomas Colchester, London, 8 August 1977; Wangui Fatuma; Hadija Njeri; Beatrice Nyambura. The belief and the reality that prostitutes and policemen play out part of their romantic involvement in courts is prevalent in Nairobi today as well; see Nici Nelson, "'Women Must Help Each Other': The Operation of Personal Networks among *Buzaa* Brewers in Mathare Valley, Kenya," in Patricia Caplan and Janet M. Bujra, eds., *Women United, Women Divided* (Bloomington and London: Indiana University Press, 1979), pp. 77–98.

39. Tabitha Waweru; Edwina Kamau.

40. Tabitha Waweru; Beatrice Nyambura; Edwina Kamau; Faith Wangoi, Mathare, 12 April 1976; Rebecca Nyaggah, Eastleigh, 5 September 1976; Margaret Muthoni, Mathare, 15 September 1976; Farida Kamau, Pumwani, 10 August 1976.

41. Miriam Musale; Zaina Kachui; Sara Waigo; Elizabeth Kamya; Tabitha Waweru; Margaret Githeka; Gathiro wa Chege; Asha Mohammed; Omolo Okumu; Albert Mutsoke; Daniel Otieno; Samuel Kariuki; Patrick arap Titi; James Ndolonga; Mahmood Silla.

42. Asha Mohammed; Tabitha Waweru; Gathiro wa Chege; Margaret Githeka; Monica Nyazura; Zaina Kachui; Mwana Himani bint Ramadhani.

43. Beatrice Nyambura.

44. Wangui Fatuma; Elizabeth Kamya.

45. Zaina Kachui; Asha Wanjiru.

46. Ibrahima binti Musa.

47. Thomas Colchester, London, 12 August 1977; Hadija Njeri; Ibrahima binti Musa.

48. Stichter, *Migrant Labour*, p. 121.

49. Edwina Kamau; Faith Wangoi; Beatrice Nyambura.

50. Edwina Kamau; Beatrice Nyambura; Rebecca Nyaggah.

51. Ibrahima binti Musa; Rehema binti Hasan.

52. Njoki wa Thiongo; Hadija Njeri.

53. Edwina Kamau; Beatrice Nyambura.

54. Beatrice Nyambura; see also Alisati binti Salim; Tabitha Waweru.

55. A Welwisher [*sic*] of Nairobi to Chief Secretary and PMO, Nairobi, n.d., filed October 1942, Public Health and Sanitary Administration in Nairobi, MD/SAN 713/3.

56. Thomas Colchester, London, 8 August 1977.

57. Ibid.; Sara Waigo; Alisati binti Salim; Margaret Muthoni; Tabitha Waweru; Beatrice Nyambura. "A Welwisher" claimed that Dass sold the property to the Municipality while it was sublet to the African, but continued to collect the rent. Property owners in Nairobi were virtually immune from prosecution for their subtenants' actions, so the existence of a subtenant may have been a useful fiction for all concerned; see Lodging Houses, Amendments to Rules, 1914–17; Ag. Town Clerk vs. Jadavji Dhangi, Indian Bazaar, Criminal Case 817/14, MD 13/537.

58. Mwanisha Waligo.

59. Salima binti Athmani; Monica Nyazura; Mwana Himani bint Ramadhani.

60. Sara Waigo; Asha Mohammed.

61. Asha Wanjiru; see also Asha Mohammed; Mwana Himani bint Ramadhani.

62. Farouk Mohammed; Thomas Mukama; Albert Mutsoke.

63. Thomas Colchester, London, 8 August 1977; Asha Wanjiru; Killingray, p. 85; Clayton and Savage, p. 237.

64. Kachui herself parcelled out sexual relations. She asked a Kamba man working at the Kibera golf club, next to the KAR camp, to make appointments with soldiers for her, and she went to the club at night to meet soldiers there. She never paid the man for his help, but she did leave her considerable earnings in a strongbox at the club, which he broke into, leaving her with 60/.

65. Muthoni wa Karanja; Amina Hali; Elizabeth Kamya; Ibrahima binti Musa. Njoki wa Thiongo said they cut off women's breasts and ate them.

66. Waruhiu Itote [General China], "Mau Mau" General (Nairobi: East Africa Publishing House, 1967), pp. 9–15, 23–29; John Spencer, James Beauttah, Freedom Fighter (Nairobi: Stellascope Publishing Company, 1983), p. 55; Susan Jeffords, The Remasculinization of America: Gender and the Vietnam War (Bloomington and London: Indiana University Press, 1989), pp. 54–86.

67. See Myron J. Echenberg, "Tragedy at Thiaroye: The Senegalese Soldiers' Uprising of 1944," in Peter C. W. Gutkind, Robin Cohen, and Jean Copans, eds., African Labor History (Beverly Hills and London: Sage, 1978), pp. 109–28, and "'Morts pour la France': The African Soldier in France during the Second World War," Journal of African History 26 (1985), pp. 363–80.

68. Peter Musili, Machakos, 18 February 1987.

69. See Judith Fingard, Jack in Port: Sailortowns of Eastern Canada (Toronto and London: University of Toronto Press, 1982), pp. 88–95.

70. Killingray, p. 85; Ernest Christian Lanning, "Some Notes on the British Military Presence in West Africa," August 1981, Rhodes House, Oxford, typescript, RH MSS Afr. s. 1734, box 7, pp. 23–24.

71. See Davies Report; Kenya Government, Report . . . the Essentials of Life, 1942; Paterson to Chief Secretary, Nairobi, "Cost of Native Housing."

72. Kayaya Thababu; see also Amina Hali; Zaina Kachui, Mwana Himani bint Ramadhani.

73. Clayton and Savage, p. 232.

74. Asha Wanjiru; Salima binti Athmani; Zaina Kachui; Elizabeth Kamya.

75. Thomas, Colchester, London, 8 August 1977; Fatuma Ali; Richard Gethin, "An Old Settler Remembers," n.d., RH MSS Afr. s. 1277(1).

76. Thomas Colchester, London, 8 August 1977. Prostitutes in Moshi, Tanganyika, did the same during World War II, for reasons colonial officials thought

had to do with reinvesting in the industry that made them rich; see Nicholas J. Wescott, "The Impact of the Second World War on Tanganyika, 1939–1949," Ph.D. thesis, Cambridge University, 1982, p. 161.

77. Salima binti Athmani.

78. Zaina Kachui. Similar cases were reported in Kenya's Northern Frontier District, where "troops were know to go to the back door of the canteen to get native women from the 'boys'" (minutes of meeting of "A" Branch, East African Command, 11 September 1943, Venereal Disease in Kenya, MD 28/854/4).

79. Asha Wanjiru; Sara Waigo; Asha Mohammed; Farida Monteo.

80. See also Asha Wanjiru.

81. Asha Wanjiru.

82. Sara Waigo; see also Mwanisha Waligo; Monica Nyazura.

83. Asha Mohammed; Sara Waigo; Asha Wanjiru.

84. Sara Waigo; Asha Mohammed.

85. Asha Wanjiru; Wangui Fatuma; Sara Waigo.

86. Walter Elkan, "Is a Proletariat Emerging in Nairobi?" *Economic Development and Cultural Change* 24, 4 (July 1976), pp. 695–706; Janet M. Bujra, "Proletarianization and the 'Informal Economy': A Case Study from Nairobi," *African Urban Studies* 3 (Winter 1978–79), pp. 47–66.

87. Most of this material first appeared in my "Prostitution in Nairobi," pp. 255–73.

88. Walkowitz and Walkowitz, pp. 192–223; Walkowitz, *Prostitution and Victorian Society*, pp. 13–31, 69–112; Murname and Daniels, pp. 5–21; Pivar, pp. 256–69; van Heyningen, pp. 170–91; Alpers, pp. 156–60; Judith Fingard, *The Dark Side of Life in Victorian Halifax* (Halifax, N.S.: Pottersfield Press, 1989), pp. 95–113.

89. Ballhatchet, pp. 10–14, 62–67; Walkowitz, "Male Vice and Female Virtue," pp. 43–57; Ellen Carol DuBois and Linda Gordon, "Seeking Ecstasy on the Battlefield: Danger and Pleasure in Nineteenth-Century Feminist Sexual Thought," in Carole S. Vance, ed., *Pleasure and Danger* (London: Routledge and Kegan Paul, 1984), pp. 33–34; Bernheimer, pp. 77–90.

90. See George L. Mosse, *Nationalism and Sexuality* (Madison: University of Wisconsin Press, 1985), p. 27.

91. James Liston, Port Health Officer, Mombasa, to Director of Medical Services, Nairobi, 4 August 1943, Venereal Disease in Kenya, MD 28/854/4.

92. E. S. Hale, Medical Officer (MO), Meru, to CO, 5th KAR, Meru, and Ag. DMS, Nairobi, 22 September 1938, Venereal Disease in Kenya, MD 28/854/4.

93. A. R. Paterson to Hon. Chief Secretary, Nairobi, 2 February 1942, Venereal Disease in Kenya, MD 28/854/4.

94. A. R. Paterson, DMS, to Hon. Chief Secretary, Nairobi, 11 December 1939, Venereal Disease in Kenya, MD 28/854/4.

95. The lowest birthrates were just north of Mombasa; see Medical Department Annual Report, "Public Health," 1939, p. 8; A. R. Paterson to MO, Native Civil Hospital, Eldoret, 8 October 1945, Venereal Disease in Kenya, MD 28/854/4.

96. East African Command (KAR) suggested that officers give this speech to their troops (*Current Affairs* 9 [1944], Venereal Disease in Kenya, MD 28/854/4).

97. Thomas Colchester, London, 8 August 1977; Fatuma Ali; Hidaya Saidi.

98. Lanning, "British Military Presence," pp. 30–31; Clayton and Killingray, p. 188.

99. Amina Halı; Hidaya Saidi; Wambui Murithi; Fatuma Ali; Hadija Njeri; Wangui Fatuma; Faith Wangoi; Beatrice Nyambura; Chepkitai Mbwana; Monica Nyazura; Margaret Githeka; Hadija binti Nasolo; Elizabeth Kamya; Ibrahima binti Musa; Miriam Musale; Zaina Kachui; Njoki wa Thiongo; Gathiro wa Chege.

100. Lanning, "British Military Presence," p. 51.

101. Tabitha Waweru; see also Miryamu binti Omari.

102. Muthoni wa Karanja.

103. Lanning, personal communication, 13 June 1989; Clayton and Killingray, p. 160.

104. Hadija Njeri; Odhiambo Okinyi.

105. Abdullah Kaviti.

106. Elizabeth Kamya.

107. Naomi Kayengi, Pumwani, 3 August 1976.

108. Omolo Okumu; Samuel Kariuki; John Mwakalili; Albert Mutsoke; Opiyo Oyugi. Only one man, a Luo (Okumu), seems to have had any strong feelings about Ganda female sexuality before 1939.

109. Naomi Kayengi.

110. Margaret Githeka; see also Miryamu binti Omari. *Grunet* probably means grenade, referring to the shape of the orchitis.

111. Sander L. Gilman, *Disease and Representation: Images of Illness from Madness to AIDS* (Ithaca and London: Cornell University Press, 1988), p. 6.

112. O. Mannoni, *Prospero and Caliban: The Psychology of Colonization* (New York: Praeger, 1964), pp. 97–121.

113. Randall M. Packard and Paul Epstein, "Epidemiologists, Social Scientists, and the Structure of Medical Research on AIDS in Africa." essay, 1989.

Chapter Eight

1. Throup, *Social and Economic Origins*, pp. 171–96; John Iliffe, *The African Poor: A History* (Cambridge: Cambridge University Press, 1987), pp. 170–71, 176, 187.

2. Throup, *Social and Economic Origins*, p. 191.

3. Thomas G. Askwith to Superintendent, CID, Nairobi District, 29 October 1947, City African Affairs Officer Correspondence, 1947–50, MAA 8/22.

4. CNC minutes, African Advisory Council, Nairobi, 13–14 September 1948, MAA 2/5/223.

5. Ibrahima binti Musa; CNC minutes, African Advisory Council, 5–6 August 1947, MAA 2/5/223.

6. Naomi Kayengi.

7. Naomi Kayengi; see also Mary Masaba, Pumwani, 28 February 1977.

8. Salome Ogai, Shauri Moyo, 30 July 1986.

9. Ramadhan Faraj, who had been opposed to police raids in the locations, was stoned in his car after leaving the African Advisory Council meeting in February 1947 (CNC minutes, African Advisory Council, 3–4 March 1947, MAA 2/5/223).

10. David Goldsworthy, *Tom Mboya: The Man Kenya Wanted to Forget* (Nairobi: Heinemann, 1982), p. 13.

11. Zaina Kachui; Sara Waigo; Mwanisha Waligo; Asha Wanjiru.

12. Salima binti Athmani; see also Elizabeth Kamya; Zaina Kachui; Margaret Githeka.

13. See Estelle B. Freedman, "'Uncontrolled Desires': The Response to the Sexual Psychopath, 1920–1960," in Kathy Peiss and Christina Simmons, eds., *Passion and Power: Sexuality in History* (Philadelphia: Temple University Press, 1989), pp. 200–201; Walkowitz, "Jack the Ripper," pp. 543–74.

14. Throup, *Social and Economic Origins,* pp. 191–92.

15. Stichter, *Migrant Labour,* pp. 133–34; Cowen and Newman, pp. 13–15; John Mwakalili; Joseph Njoroge; see also Patrick arap Titi.

16. Albert Mutsoke; Mutiso Katumbe; John Musili, Pumwani, 20 March 1977; Daudi Wagulisa.

17. Odhiambo Okinyi; James Ndolonga; Opiyo Oyugi.

18. Juma Farid, Pumwani, 11 March 1977; Peter Mwenyi; Mutiso Katumbe; Salim Hamisi.

19. CNC minutes, African Advisory Council, Nairobi, 1–2 March, 1948, MAA 2/5/223.

20. CNC minutes, African Advisory Council, Nairobi, 5–6 August 1947, MAA 2/5/223.

21. Furedi, p. 282; John Spencer, "KAU and Mau Mau: Some Connections," *Kenya Historical Review* 5, 2 (1977), p. 212; Throup, *Social and Economic Origins,* pp. 175–76; Tom Mbotela to Superintendent, CID, Nairobi, 26 October 1947, MAA 8/22; Intelligence Reports: Radio Posta 1947–48, MAA 8/105; Gakaara wa Wanjau, *Mau Mau Author in Detention* (Nairobi: Heinemann, 1988), p. 163.

22. These were compiled from the notes from Cowen and Newman.

23. Municipal Treasurer to Ag. Commissioner for Local Government, 23 March 1950; Margaret Githeka; Sara Waigo; Beatrice Nyambura; Naomi Kayengi; Farida Monteo; Ibrahima binti Musa; Monica Nyazura; Alisati binti Salim; Asha Mohammed; Hadija binti Nasolo; Lydia Nthenga; Tamima binti Saidi; Louise Kaseem, Pumwani, 28 march 1977.

24. Kenya Government. *The Pattern of Income, Expenditure, and Consumption of African Labourers in Nairobi, October–December 1950* (Nairobi: Government Printer, 1951), Kenya National Archives, K331.LAB. In Nairobi in late 1950 the mean African cash wage was 44/ and the mean cash expenditure was 52/.

25. CNC minutes, African Advisory Council, Nairobi, 4–5 February 1946, 7–8 July 1947, MAA 2/5/223.

26. Monica Nyazura; Fatuma Ali; Farida Monteo.

27. David William Cohen and E. S. Atieno Odhiambo, *Siaya: The Historical Anthropology of an African Landscape* (Athens: Ohio University Press, 1989), p. 98.

28. Ayoo Were, Pumwani, 24 February 1977; Lydia Nthenga; Hadija binti Nasolo; Fatuma Ali; Mary Masaba.

29. Tomkinson to S. LaFontaine, 10 March 1938, Native Associations, PC/CP 8/5/4 ADM 25.

30. Thomas Colchester, London, 12 August 1977. Eric St. A. Davies, who had described the inevitability of teenage Kikuyu prostitution in 1938, refused to recognize Luo Union.

31. Kipsigis-Nandi Union to DC Nairobi, 29 April 1944, Native Associations, PC/CP.8/5/4 ADM 29/5.

32. Thomas G. Askwith, MNAO, report to Town Clerk, Nairobi, March 1947, in Elspeth Huxley Papers, RH MSS Afr. 782, box 2/2.

33. Larsson, p. 34.

34. C. F. Atkins, DC Nairobi, to A. Kabatia, President, KGU, April 1951, Native Associations, etc., 1938–50, PC/CP 8/5/4 ADM 29/5; DC Central Nyanza to Secretary, Luo Union, Kisumu Branch, re bylaws of the Luo Union, 6 May 1955, Registrar of Societies, 329, vol. 1/18.

35. Thomas G. Askwith, Annual Report on African Affairs in Nairobi, 1946 (Nairobi, March 1947), in Elspeth Huxley Papers, RH MSS Afr. 782, box 2/2; Intelligence and Security, African Workers' Federation, 29 April 1948, MAA 8/109.

36. P. Wyn Harris to Hon. Member for Law and Order, 14 October 1948, Law and Order, Legal Matters, etc, MAA 8/132.

37. John Spencer, *The Kenya African Union* (London: Routledge and Kegan Paul, 1985), pp. 205–8.

38. Andrew Gathea, KGU Headquarters, Nairobi, to DCs, Kiambu, Fort Hall, Nyeri, and Embu, 25 June 1950, Native Associations, 1938–50, PC/CP 8/5/4 ADM 29/5; A. Kabatia, President, KGU, Nairobi, to C. F. Atkins, DC Nairobi, April 1951, PC/CP 8/5/4 ADM 29/5; notes of a discussion between W. O. Townsend and S. Kipkoech, 3 August 1950, Pass Laws for Town Natives, Lab 9/1/09.

39. Cooper, *Waterfront*, pp. 115–24, 142–58, 175–93; Luise White, "Separating the Men from the Boys: Constructions of Gender, Sexuality, and Terrorism in Central Kenya, 1939–1959," *International Journal of African Historical Studies* 23, 1 (1990), pp. 1–26.

40. Andrew Gathea to DCs, Kiambu, Fort Hall, etc., 25 June 1950.

41. Dedan Githengi, "Immorality of Kikuyu Women," 28 January 1948, City African Affairs Officer Correspondence, MAA 8/22; Throup, *Social and Economic Origins*, p. 190.

42. Thomas Colchester, London, 12 August 1977.

43. Mugo Mwatha, Nairobi, 9 February 1977; see also Ibrahima binti Karim, Pumwani, 16 February 1977.

44. Kabatia to Atkins, April 1951; see also Ag. Labour Commissioner to Townsend, 3 August 1950, Pass Laws for Town Natives, Nairobi, Lab 9/1109.

45. Ayoo Were, Pumwani, 24 February 1977.

46. Mary Atieno, Pumwani, 23 February 1977.

47. DC Central Nyanza to Secretary, Luo Union, Kisumu.

48. Alice Margaret Abouji, interview, 11 January 1970, in Margaret Odhiambo, "Luo Union Nairobi Branch: An African Welfare Organization," B.A. dissertation, University of Nairobi, 1970, History Department Archives, D/7/2, p. 68.

49. Salome Ogai.

50. P. Wyn Harris, "Bride Price," 21 December 1948, ADM 40/1/113; Kitching, pp. 110–29, 144–55, 233–40; Throup, *Social and Economic Origins*, pp. 63–81.

51. Salima binti Athmani; Chepkitai Mbwana; Sara Waigo; Ibrahima binti Musa; Juliana Rugumisa, Pumwani, 17 March 1977.

52. Asha Mohammed; Sara Waigo; Salome Ogai.

53. Omolo Okumu; Richard Mulembe; John Mwakalili; Thomas Mukama; Patrick arap Titi; Habib Hasan.

54. Mahmood Silla; Juma Farid; Ahmed Hussein; Farouk Mohammed; Habib Hasan.

55. Hadija binti Karim, Pumwani, 16 February 1977; see also Mary Masaba; Mwanisha Waligo; Kayaya Thababu.

56. Louise Kaseem; see also Mary Masaba; Hidaya Saidi.

57. Elizabeth Kamya; Monica Nyazura; Naomi Kayengi.

58. Asha Mohammed.

59. Richard Mulembe; John Mwakalili; Thomas Mukama; Mutiso Katumbe; James Ndolonga; Habib Hasan; Peter Mwenyi; Juma Farid.

60. Tamima binti Saidi.

61. Asha Mohammed; Sara Waigo; James Ndolonga; Peter Mwenyi.

62. Ibrahima binti Musa.

63. Tabitha Waweru.

64. Naomi Kayengi.

65. Both officials and researchers shared a belief in the importance of clothing to women that in fact revealed its importance to themselves. In the early 1960s the District Officer in Dar es Salaam commiserated with African men "who reported that they had to supply 'a constant succession of new garments, ear-rings and plastic sandals' to keep their wives and female companions from the 'smooth operators' or from simply leaving" (Geiger, p. 11). In a 1961 study of teenage prostitutes in Nairobi, a British sociologist interviewed one hundred soldiers at the British Military Hospital about prostitutes' habits of dress and reported that girls tended to wear brassieres and not panties, to "give their breasts the type of uplift to which Europeans particularly would be attracted" and because they were easy to buy secondhand (Julius Carlebach, *Juvenile Prostitutes in Nairobi* [Kampala: East African Institute of Social Research, 1961], pp. 28–29).

66. Beatrice Nyambura.

67. Farouk Mohammed; Albert Mutsoke.

68. Omolo Okumu; Juma Farid; Mahmood Silla.

69. Rebecca Nyaggah; Edwina Kamau; Margaret Githeka; Alisati binti Salim.

70. Edwina Kamau; Rebecca Nyaggah; Alisati binti Salim.

71. Rebecca Nyaggah; Edwina Kamau; Beatrice Nyambura.

72. Muthoni wa Karanja.

73. Farida Monteo; Zenabu Githera; Chepkitai Mbwana.

74. Wanjira Ng'ang'a.

75. G. R. B. Brown, City African Affairs Officer, "Observations on the Nairobi Strike," 23 May 1950, MAA 8/22; Makhan Singh, *History of Kenya's Trade Union Movement to 1952* (Nairobi: East African Literature Bureau, 1969), pp. 277–86; Throup, *Social and Economic Origins,* pp. 172, 178–79, 193–95; Furedi, pp. 275–90.

76. Mutiso Katumbe; John Musili; John Ndolonga; Abdullah Kaviti.

77. A brief summary of the literature would include Josiah Mwangi Kariuki, *"Mau Mau" Detainee* (Harmondsworth, England: Penguin, 1963); Donald Barnett and Karari Njama, *Mau Mau from Within* (New York: Monthly Review Press, 1966); Rosberg, and Nottingham, *The Myth of "Mau Mau"; Itote, "Mau Mau" Gen-*

eral; Joram Wamweya, *Freedom Fighter* (Nairobi: East Africa Publishing House, 1971); Ngugi Kabiro, *The Men in the Middle* (Richmond, B.C.: Liberation Support Movement, 1973); Mohammed Mathu, *The Urban Guerilla* (Richmond, B.C.: Liberation Support Movement, 1974); Anthony Clayton, *Counter-Insurgency in Kenya: A Study of Military Operations against Mau Mau* (Nairobi: Transafrica Publishers, 1976); a special issue of *Kenya Historical Review* 5, 2 (1977); Maina wa Kinyatti, *Thunder from the Mountains: Mau Mau Patriotic Songs* (London: Zed, 1980), and *Kenya's Freedom Struggle: The Dedan Kimathi Papers* (London: Zed, 1987); Spencer, *The Kenya African Union;* John Lonsdale, "Explanations of the Mau Mau Revolt, Kenya, 1952–1956," in Tom Lodge, ed., *Resistance and Ideology in Settler Societies* (Johannesburg: Ravan, 1986), pp. 168–77; Bates, "The Agrarian Origins of Mau Mau," pp. 1–28; David W. Throup, "The Origins of Mau Mau," *African Affairs* 84 (July 1985), pp. 399–434, and *Social and Economic Origins of Mau Mau;* Kanogo, *Squatters and the Roots of Mau Mau;* Frederick Cooper, "Mau Mau and the Discourses of Decolonization," *Journal of African History* 29 (1988), pp. 313–20; White, "Separating the Men from the Boys"; John Lonsdale and Bruce Berman, *Unhappy Valley: Class, Clan, and State in Colonial Kenya* (Athens: Ohio University Press, forthcoming).

78. Itote, pp. 127–38; Barnett and Njama, p. 479; wa Kinyatti, *Kenya's Freedom Struggle,* p. 34.

79. J. M. Kariuki, pp. 60–61, 160–62; Tabitha Kanogo, "Kikuyu Women and the Politics of Protest: Mau Mau," in Sharon Macdonald, Pat Holden, and Shirley Ardner, eds., *Images of Women in Peace and War* (Madison: University of Wisconsin Press, 1987), pp. 85–87.

80. Intelligence and Security, "Mumenyereri," 1947–50, MAA 8/106; see also Throup, *Social and Economic Origins,* pp. 151–57.

81. Quoted in F. D. Corfield, *Historical Survey of the Origins and Growth of Mau Mau,* Cmd. 1030, (London: HMSO, 1960), p. 137.

82. J. T. Kamunchulah, "The Meru Participation in Mau Mau," *Kenya Historical Review* 3, 2 (1975), p. 193.

83. Cora Ann Presley, "The Mau Mau Rebellion, Kikuyu Women, and Social Change," *Canadian Journal of African Studies* 22, 3 (1988), pp. 502–27.

84. G. R. B. Brown, confidential memo, 23 May 1950, City African Affairs Officer Correspondence, MAA 8/22.

85. Salome Ogai; Mathu, p. 18; H. K. Wachanga, *The Swords of Kirinyaga: The Fight for Land and Freedom* (Nairobi: Kenya Literature Bureau, 1975), p. 49.

86. Salome Ogai; Kabiro, p. 55; Mathu, p. 14.

87. Salome Ogai.

88. Ibid.; Bujra, "Pumwani," pp. 66–70.

89. Kabiro, pp. 34, 54–55.

90. Tamima binti Saidi; Ibrahima binti Hussein, Pumwani, 3 August 1986; Margaret Nabudere, Pumwani, 3 August 1986.

91. Spencer, *Kenyan African Union,* p. 208; Asha Kamau, Pumwani, 20 October 1976; Ibrahima binti Hussein; Margaret Nabudere.

92. Asha Mohammed; Edwina Kamau; Asha Kamau; Ibrahima binti Hussein.

93. I owe these points to the pioneering work of Cora Ann Presley, in particular "The Transformation of Kikuyu Women and Their Nationalism," Ph.D. thesis,

Stanford University, Stanford, CA, 1986, pp. 201–29, "Kikuyu Women in the 'Mau Mau' Rebellion," in Gary Y. Okihiro, ed., *In Resistance: Studies in African, Caribbean, and Afro-American History* (Amherst: University of Massachusetts Press, 1986), p. 57, and "Social Change," pp. 502–27.

94. Presley, "Social Change" Rosberg and Nottingham, p. 338; Kenya Government, Community Affairs Department, Annual Report, 1953, p. 25.

95. Mathu, p. 14.

96. Policy for issue of passbooks in Nairobi, War Council minutes, 21 May 1954, Administration: Unrest, General, 1953–54, MAA 2/5/184I; Beatrice Nyambura; Muthoni wa Karanja; Njoki wa Thiongo.

97. Ibrahima binti Musa.

98. Mwana Himani bint Ramadhani; Hadija binti Nasolo.

99. Hadija binti Nasolo.

100. Asha Kamau.

101. Muthoni wa Karanja; Zaina Kachui; Furedi, p. 282; Wachanga, pp. xxvii–xxxix.

102. Dickerman, p. 18; Lonsdale, "Explanations," p. 174.

103. Hadija binti Nasolo.

104. Yosuf Mwangi, Pumwani, 3 August 1986.

105. Mathu, p. 27; Dickerman, p. 30.

106. Bujra, "Pumwani," pp. 66–68.

107. Dickerman, p. 19.

108. Bujra, "Pumwani," p. 69.

109. Yosuf Mwangi; Asha Ahmed, Pumwani, 3 August 1986.

110. Dickerman, p. 19; Wanjira Ng'ang'a.

111. Dickerman, pp. 35–36; Sara Waigo; Gathiro wa Chege.

112. Dickerman, pp. 41–44, 55–56.

113. Richard Mulembe; Odhiambo Okinyi; Daniel Otieno; Omolo Okumu; Samuel Kariuki; Juma Farid; Albert Mutsoke; James Ndolonga; Habib Hasan.

114. Elizabeth Gachika, quoted in Presley, "Transformation of Kikuyu Women," p. 255.

115. Odhiambo Okinyi; Daniel Otieno; Juma Farid; Albert Mutsoke; James Ndolonga; Habib Hasan.

116. Clayton, p. 25.

117. Clayton, pp. 25–26; Asha Kamau; Hadija binti Nasolo; Yosuf Mwangi; Margaret Nabudere; Juma Abdullah, Pumwani, 3 August 1986; Ibrahima binti Hussein.

118. Wamweya, pp. 129–30; Asha Mohammed; Wanjira Ng'ang'a.

119. Asha Kamau; Margaret Nabudere; Ibrahima binti Hussein; Fatuma Mutiso, Pumwani, 4 August 1986.

120. Mary Atieno; Tamima binti Saidi.

121. Hadija binti Nasolo; Margaret Nabudere; Hawa binti Hussein, Pumwani, 3 August 1986.

122. East African Royal Commission 1953–55, *Report* (London: HMSO, 1955), p. 214; see also Cooper, "Decolonization," pp. 313–20.

123. *Report of the Committee on African Wages* (Nairobi: Government Printer, 1954), pp. 32, 54–55.

124. F. T. Holden, minority report to the Commission on African Wages, quoted in Clayton and Savage, pp. 374–75.

125. East African Royal Commission, p. 183.

126. McVicar, p. 169.

127. African Affairs Department, Annual Report 1956, p. 160; Dickerman, pp. 55–57.

128. Cooper, *Waterfront,* p. 180; Kitching, pp. 397–98.

129. Dickerman, p. 55.

130. M. Chege, p. 79.

131. Bujra, "Proletarianization," pp. 47–66.

132. Ibid., pp. 57–62; Nelson, "'Women Must Help Each Other,'" pp. 77–98.

133. Bujra, "Proletarianization," p. 63.

134. East African Royal Commission, p. 212.

135. McVicar, p. 79; Hake, pp. 97, 104.

136. Hake, pp. 113–16.

137. D. Clark, pp. 33–37.

138. M. Chege, pp. 83–85.

139. Hake, p. 80.

140. Bujra, "Proletarianization," p. 51.

141. Nelson, "'Women Must Help Each Other,'" pp. 77–98; McVicar, pp. 79–81; Nici Nelson, "Female Centered Families: Changing Patterns of Marriage and Family among Buzaa Brewers of Mathare Valley," *African Urban Studies* 3 (Winter 1978–79), pp. 85–103; Sara Waigo; Margaret Githeka.

142. Hake, pp. 158–59; M. Chege, pp. 77–78.

143. Zenabu Githera; M. Chege, pp. 78–79.

144. Quoted in McVicar, p. 245.

145. See Carlebach.

146. Nelson, "Female Centered Families," p. 91.

147. Hadija Njeri; Nici Nelson, "'Selling Her Kiosk': Kikuyu Notions of Sexuality and Sex for Sale in Mathare Valley, Kenya," in Patricia Caplan, ed., *The Cultural Construction of Sexuality* (London and New York: Tavistock, 1987), pp. 217–39.

Chapter Nine

1. My thinking on these issues has been greatly influenced by the work of Frederick Cooper, especially "Urban Space, Industrial Time, and Wage Labor in Africa" and *On the African Waterfront,* especially chapter 6, "Work Disorder, and the Crisis of Colonialism in Africa," pp. 247–78.

2. Zaina Kachui.

3. Margaret Githeka.

References

Books, Articles, and Manuscripts

Alpers, Edward A. "The Somali Community at Aden in the Nineteenth Century." *Northeast African Studies* 8, 2–3 (1986), pp. 143–68.

Ambler, Charles H. *Kenyan Communities in the Age of Imperialism: The Central Region in the Late Nineteenth Century.* New Haven and London: Yale University Press, 1988.

Anderson, David M., and David W. Throup. "Africans and Agricultural Production in Colonial Kenya: The Myth of the War as Watershed." *Journal of African History* 26 (1985), pp. 327–45.

Arnold, Katherine. "The Introduction of Poses to a Peruvian Brothel and Changing Images of Male and Female." In John Blacking, ed., *The Anthropology of the Body*, pp. 179–96. London and New York: Academic Press, 1977.

Austen, Ralph A. *Northwest Tanganyika under German and British Rule: Colonial Policy and Tribal Politics, 1889–1939.* New Haven: Yale University Press, 1968.

Ballhatchet, Kenneth. *Race, Sex, and Class under the Raj: Imperial Attitudes and Policies and Their Critics, 1793–1905.* New York: St. Martin's Press, 1980.

Barnett, Donald, and Karari Njama. *Mau Mau from Within.* New York: Monthly Review Press, 1966.

Barry, Kathleen. *Female Sexual Slavery.* Englewood Cliffs, NJ: Prentice Hall, 1979.

Bates, Robert H. "The Agrarian Origins of Mau Mau: A Structural Account." *Agricultural History* 61, 1 (1987), pp. 1–28.

Beck, Ann. *A History of the British Medical Administration of East Africa, 1900–1950.* Cambridge: Harvard University Press, 1970.

Bernheimer, Charles. "Of Whores and Sewers: Parent-Duchatelet, Engineer of Abjection." *Raritan* 6, 3 (Winter 1987), pp. 72–90.

Best, Joel. "Careers in Brothel Prostitution: St. Paul, 1865–1883." *Journal of Interdisciplinary History* 12, 4 (Spring 1982), pp. 597–619.

Boedecker, E. "The Early History of Nairobi." Kabete, 1936. MacMillan Library, Nairobi. Typescript.

Boyes, John. *John Boyes, King of the Wakikuyu*. Ed. G. W. C. Bulpett. London: Methuen and Company, 1911.

Brantley, Cynthia. *The Giriama and Colonial Resistance in Kenya, 1800–1920*. Berkeley and Los Angeles: University of California Press, 1981.

Bristow, Edward J. *Prostitution and Prejudice: The Jewish Fight Against White Slavery, 1870–1939*. New York: Schocken, 1984.

Bujra, Janet M. "Production, Property, Prostitution: 'Sexual Politics' in Atu." *Cahiers d'études africaines* 65, 17 (1977), pp. 13–39.

———. "Proletarianization and the 'Informal Economy': A Case Study from Nairobi." *African Urban Studies* 3 (Winter 1978–79), pp. 47–66.

———. "Pumwani: The Politics of Property." Social Science Research Council (U.K.). London, 1972. Mimeo.

———. "Women 'Entrepreneurs' of Early Nairobi." *Canadian Journal of African Studies* 9, 2 (1975), pp. 213–34.

Butler, Anne M. *Daughters of Joy, Sisters of Misery: Prostitutes in the American West, 1865–90*. Urbana and Chicago: University of Illinois Press, 1987.

Carlebach, Julius. *Juvenile Prostitutes in Nairobi*. Kampala: East African Institute of Social Research, 1961.

Chauncey, George, Jr. "The Locus of Reproduction: Women's Labour in the Zambian Copperbelt, 1927–1953." *Journal of Southern African Studies* 7, 2 (1981), pp. 135–64.

Chege, Michael. "A Tale of Two Slums: Electoral Politics in Mathare and Dagoretti." *Review of African Political Economy* 20 (January–April 1981), pp. 74–88.

Chevalier, Louis. *Laboring Classes and Dangerous Classes in Paris during the First Half of the Nineteenth Century*. Princeton: Princeton University Press, 1973.

Clark, Carolyn M. "Land and Food, Women and Power, in Nineteenth Century Kikuyu." *Africa* 50, 4 (1980), pp. 357-71.

Clark, David. "Unregulated Housing, Vested Interest, and the Development of Community Identity in Nairobi." *African Urban Studies* 3 (Winter 1978–79), pp. 33–46.

Clayton, Anthony. *Counter-Insurgency in Kenya: A Study of Military Operations against Mau Mau*. Nairobi: Transafrica Publishers, 1976.

Clayton, Anthony, and David Killingray. *Khaki and Blue: Military and Police in British Colonial Africa*. Athens: Ohio University Press, 1989.

Clayton, Anthony, and Donald C. Savage. *Government and Labour in Kenya, 1895–1963*. London: Frank Cass, 1974.

Clive, John. *Macaulay: The Shaping of an Historian*. New York: Knopf, 1973.

Cohen, Abner. *Custom and Politics in Urban Africa: A Study of Hausa Migrants in Yoruba Towns*. Berkeley and Los Angeles: University of California Press, 1969.

Cohen, David William, and E. S. Atieno Odhiambo. *Siaya: The Historical Anthropology of an African Landscape*. Athens: Ohio University Press, 1989.

Connelly, Mark Thomas. *The Response to Prostitution in the Progressive Era*. Chapel Hill: University of North Carolina Press, 1980.

Cooper, Frederick. *From Slaves to Squatters: Plantation Labor in Zanzibar and Coastal Kenya, 1890–1925*. New Haven and London: Yale University Press, 1980.

———. "The Guerilla Army of the Unemployed: The Labor Process and Class

Conflict in Post-War Africa." Paper presented to the seminar on the Informal Sector in the Center and the Periphery, Johns Hopkins University, Baltimore, 8–10 June 1984.

_____. "Mau Mau and the Discourses of Decolonization." *Journal of African History* 29 (1988), pp. 313–20.

_____. *On the African Waterfront: Urban Disorder and the Transformation of Work in Colonial Mombasa.* New Haven and London: Yale University Press, 1987.

_____. "Peasants, Capitalists, and Historians." *Journal of Southern African Studies* 7, 2 (1981), pp. 284–314.

_____. *Plantation Slavery on the East Coast of Africa.* New Haven and London: Yale University Press, 1977.

_____. "The Treatment of Slaves on the Kenya Coast in the Nineteenth Century." *Kenya Historical Review* 1, 2 (1973), pp. 87–107.

_____. "Urban Space, Industrial Time, and Wage Labor in Africa," in Frederick Cooper, ed., *Struggle for the City: Migrant Labor, Capital, and the State in Urban Africa,* pp. 7–50. Beverly Hills and London: Sage, 1983.

Cory, Hans, and M. N. Hartnoll. *Customary Law of the Haya Tribe.* London: Lund Humphries, 1945.

Cowen, Michael P. "Capital and Peasant Households." Essay, Nairobi, 1976.

Cowen, Michael P., and J. R. Newman. "Real Wages in Central Kenya, 1924–1974." Essay, Nairobi, 1975.

Dawson, Marc H. "Health, Nutrition, and Population in Central Kenya, 1890–1945." In Dennis D. Cordell and Joel W. Gregory, eds., *African Population and Capitalism,* pp. 201–17. Boulder, CO, and London: Westview Press, 1987.

_____. "The Many Minds of Sir Halford J. Mackinder: Dilemmas of Historical Editing." *History in Africa* 14 (1987), pp. 27–42.

_____. "Smallpox in Kenya, 1880–1920." *Social Science and Medicine* 13B, 4 (December 1979), pp. 245–50.

_____. "Socio-economic and Epidemiological Change in Kenya, 1880–1925." Ph.D. thesis, University of Wisconsin, Madison, 1983.

Dennis, G. Gordon. "Our First Marriage at Kenia." *Kikuyu News* 56 (August–September 1915), pp. 4–6.

Dickerman, Carole Wilson. "Africans in Nairobi during the Emergency: Social and Economic Changes, 1952–1960." M.A. thesis, University of Wisconsin, Madison, 1978.

Dirasse, Laketch. "The Socioeconomic Position of Women in Addis Abada: The Case of Prostitution." Ph.D. thesis, Boston University, 1978.

DuBois, Ellen Carol, and Linda Gordon. "Seeking Ecstasy on the Battlefield: Danger and Pleasure in Nineteenth-Century Feminist Sexual Thought." In Carole S. Vance, ed., *Pleasure and Danger: Exploring Female Sexuality,* pp. 31–49. London: Routledge and Kegan Paul, 1984.

Echenberg, Myron J. "'Morts pour la France': The African Soldier in France during the Second World War." *Journal of African History* 26 (1985), pp. 363–80.

_____. "Tragedy at Thiaroye: The Senegalese Soldiers' Uprising of 1944." In Peter C. W. Gutkind, Robin Cohen, and Jean Copans, eds., *African Labor History,* pp. 109–28. Beverly Hills and London: Sage, 1978.

Elkan, Walter. "Is a Proletariat Emerging in Nairobi?" *Economic Development and Cultural Change* 24, 4 (July 1976), pp. 695–706.

Evans, Richard J. "Prostitution, State, and Society in Imperial Germany." *Past and Present* 70 (1976), pp. 106–29.

Fingard, Judith. *The Dark Side of Life in Victorian Halifax*. Halifax, N.S.: Pottersfield Press, 1989.

———. *Jack in Port: Sailortowns of Eastern Canada*. Toronto and London: University of Toronto Press, 1982.

Finnegan, Frances. *Poverty and Prostitution: A Study of Victorian Prostitutes in York*. Cambridge and New York: Cambridge University Press, 1979.

Foran, W. Robert. *A Cuckoo in Kenya: The Reminiscences of a Pioneer Police Officer in British East Africa*. London: Hutchinson, 1936.

Freedman, Estelle B. "'Uncontrolled Desires': The Response to the Sexual Psychopath, 1920–1960." In Kathy Peiss and Christina Simmons, eds., *Passion and Power: Sexuality in History*, pp. 199–225. Philadelphia: Temple University Press, 1989.

Frost, H. Gordon. *The Gentlemen's Club: The Story of Prostitution in El Paso*. El Paso, TX: Mangan, 1983.

Furedi, Frank. "The African Crowd in Nairobi: Popular Movements and Elite Politics." *Journal of African History* 14 (1973), pp. 275–90.

Geiger, Susan. "Women in Nationalist Struggle: TANU Activists in Dar es Salaam." *International Journal of African Historical Studies* 20, 1 (1987), pp. 1–26.

Gentry, Curt. *The Madams of San Francisco*. Sausalito, CA: Comstock, 1964.

Gibson, Mary. *Prostitution and the State in Italy, 1860–1915*. New Brunswick, NJ, and London: Rutgers University Press, 1986.

Gikoyo, Gucu G. *We Fought for Freedom*. Nairobi: East Africa Publishing House, 1979.

Gilman, Sander L. *Difference and Pathology: Stereotypes of Sexuality, Race, and Madness*. Ithaca: Cornell University Press, 1985.

———. *Disease and Representation: Images of Illness from Madness to AIDS*. Ithaca and London: Cornell University Press, 1988.

Goldman, Marion S. *Gold Diggers and Silver Miners: Prostitution and Social Life on the Comstock Lode*. Ann Arbor: University of Michigan Press, 1981.

Goldsworthy, David. *Tom Mboya: The Man Kenya Wanted to Forget*. Nairobi: Heinemann, 1982.

Gray, James R. *Red Lights on the Prairie*. Toronto: Sphere, 1974.

Greenough, Paul. *Prosperity and Misery in Modern Bengal: The Famine of 1943–1944*. Oxford: Oxford University Press, 1982.

Gronewald, Sue. "Beautiful Merchandise: Prostitution in China, 1860–1936." *Women and History* 1 (Spring 1982), pp. 1–114.

Guy, Donna J. "White Slavery, Public Health, and the Socialist Position on Legalized Prostitution in Argentina, 1913–1936." *Latin American Research Review* 23, 3 (1988), pp. 60–80.

Hake, Andrew. *African Metropolis: Nairobi's Self-Help City*. Sussex: Sussex University Press, 1977.

Hamilton, C. A. "Ideology and Oral Tradition: Listening to the Voices 'from Below.'" *History in Africa* 14 (1987), pp. 67–86.

Hardy, Ronald. *The Iron Snake.* London: Collins, 1965.

Harsin, Jill. *Policing Prostitution in Nineteenth-Century Paris.* Princeton: Princeton University Press, 1985.

Haywood, A., and F. A. S. Clarke. *The History of the Royal West African Frontier Forces.* Aldershot, England: Gale and Polden, 1964.

Hershatter, Gail. "The Hierarchy of Shanghai Prostitution, 1870–1949." *Modern China* 15, 4 (October 1989), pp. 463–98.

van Heyningen, Elizabeth B. "The Social Evil in the Cape Colony, 1868–1902: Prostitution and the Contagious Diseases Acts." *Journal of Southern African Studies* 10 2 (1984), pp. 170–91.

Hirata, Lucie Cheng. "Free, Indentured, Enslaved: Chinese Prostitutes in Nineteenth-Century America." *Signs: Journal of Women in Culture and Society* 5, 1 (1979), pp. 3–29.

Hobson, Barbara Meil. *Uneasy Virtue: The Politics of Prostitution and the American Reform Tradition.* New York: Basic Books, 1987.

Hodges, Geoffrey W. T. *The Carrier Corps: Military Labor in the East African Campaign, 1914–1918.* Westport, CT: Greenwood Press, 1986.

———. "Manpower Statistics for the British Forces in East Africa, 1914–1918." *Journal of African History* 19 (1978), pp. 101–16.

Hori, Joan. "Japanese Prostitution in Hawaii during the Immigration Period." *Hawaiian Journal of History* 15 (1981), pp. 113–24.

Hyam, Ronald. "Concubinage and Colonial Service: The Crewe Circular (1909)." *Journal of Imperial and Commonwealth History* 14, 3 (May 1986), pp. 170–86.

Hyden, Goran. *Beyond Ujamaa in Tanzania: Underdevelopment and an Uncaptured Peasantry.* London: Heinemann, 1980.

Iliffe, John. *The African Poor: A History.* Cambridge: Cambridge University Press, 1987.

Inter-Territorial Committee for the East African Dependencies. *A Standard Swahili-English Dictionary.* Oxford: Oxford University Press, 1939.

Itote, Waruhiu. *"Mau Mau" General.* Nairobi: East Africa Publishing House, 1967.

Jackson, Frederick. *Early Days in East Africa.* London: Arnold and Company, 1930.

James, Jennifer. "Mobility as an Adaptive Strategy." *Urban Anthropology* 4 (1975), pp. 349–64.

James, Jennifer, et al. *The Politics of Prostitution.* Seattle: Social Research Associates, 1977.

Janmohammed, Karim K. "Ethnicity in an Urban Setting: A Case Study of Mombasa." In Bethwell A. Ogot, ed., *Hadith 6: History and Social Change in East Africa,* pp. 186–206. Nairobi: East African Literature Bureau, 1976.

Jeffords, Susan. *The Remasculinization of America: Gender and the Vietnam War.* Bloomington and London: Indiana University Press, 1989.

Kabiro, Ngugi. *The Man in the Middle.* Richmond, B.C.: Liberation Support Movement, 1973.

Kaggia, Bildad. *Roots of Freedom, 1921–1963.* Nairobi: East Africa Publishing House, 1975.

Kamunchulah, J. T. "The Meru Participation in Mau Mau." *Kenya Historical Review* 3, 2 (1975), p. 193–216.

Kanogo, Tabitha. "Kikuyu Women and the Politics of Protest: Mau Mau." In

Sharon Macdonald, Pat Holden, and Shirley Ardner, eds., *Images of Women in Peace and War,* pp. 78–96. Madison: University of Wisconsin Press, 1987.

———. *Squatters and the Roots of Mau Mau.* London: James Currey, 1987.

Kariuki, Josiah Mwangi. *"Mau Mau" Detainee.* Harmondsworth, England: Penguin, 1963.

Karras, Ruth Mazo. "The Regulation of Brothels in Later Medieval England." *Signs: Journal of Women in Culture and Society* 14, 2 (1989), pp. 399–425.

Kenya Historical Review, special issue, 5, 2 (1977).

Kenyatta, Jomo. *Facing Mount Kenya: The Tribal Life of the Gikuyu.* London: Secker and Warburg, 1953.

Killingray, David. "Military and Labour Recruitment in the Gold Coast during the Second World War." *Journal of African History* 23 (1982), pp. 83–95.

Wa Kinyatti, Maina. *Kenya's Freedom Struggle: The Dedan Kimathi Papers.* London: Zed, 1987.

———. *Thunder from the Mountains: Mau Mau Patriotic Songs* London: Zed, 1980.

Kitching, Gavin. *Class and Economic Change in Kenya: The Making of an African Petite-Bourgeoisie.* New Haven: Yale University Press, 1980.

Larsson, Birgitta. "A Dying People? Women, Church, and Social Change in North-western Tanzania under British Rule." Essay, March 1987.

Leonard, Carol, and Isidor Walliman. "Prostitution and Changing Morality in the Frontier Cattle Towns of Kansas." *Kansas History* 11 (1979), pp. 34–53.

Lerner, Gerda. "The Origin of Prostitution in Ancient Mesopotamia." *Signs: Journal of Women in Culture and Society* 11, 2 (1986), pp. 236–54.

Leslie, J. A. K. *A Social Survey of Dar es Salaam.* Oxford: Oxford University Press, 1963.

Leys, Colin. *Underdevelopment in Kenya.* Berkeley: University of California Press, 1974.

Leys, Norman. *Kenya.* London: Frank Cass, 1973. Reprint of 1924 edition.

———. *Last Chance of Kenya.* London: Hogarth Press, 1931.

Little, Kenneth. *Women in African Towns.* Cambridge: Cambridge University Press, 1973.

Lonsdale, John. "Explanations of the Mau Mau Revolt, Kenya, 1952–1956." In Tom Lodge, ed., *Resistance and Ideology in Settler Societies* pp. 168–77. Johannesburg: Ravan, 1986.

———. "The Politics of Conquest: The British in Western Kenya, 1894–1908," *Historical Journal* 20, 4 (1977), pp. 841–70.

Lonsdale, John, and Bruce Berman. "Coping with the Contradictions: The Development of the Colonial State in Kenya, 1895–1914." *Journal of African History* 20 (1979), pp. 487–505.

———. *Unhappy Valley: Class, Clan, and State in Colonial Kenya.* Athens: Ohio University Press, forthcoming.

McCreery, David. "'This Life of Misery and Shame': Female Prostitution in Guatemala City, 1880–1920." *Journal of Latin American Studies* 18 (1987), pp. 333–53.

McDonald, Douglas. *The Legend of Julia Bulette and the Red Light Ladies of Nevada.* Las Vegas: Nevada Publications, 1980.

McVicar, Kenneth, G. "Twilight of an East African Slum: Pumwani and the Evolution of African Settlement in Nairobi." Ph.D. thesis, University of California, Los Angeles, 1968.

Mangat, J. S. *The History of the Asians in East Africa, c. 1886 to 1945*. Oxford: Oxford University Press, 1969.

Mann, Kristin. *Marrying Well: Marriage, Status, and Social Change among the Educated Elite in Colonial Lagos*. Cambridge: Cambridge University Press, 1985.

Mannoni, O. *Prospero and Caliban: The Psychology of Colonization*. New York: Praeger, 1964.

Mathu, Mohammed. *The Urban Guerilla*. Richmond, B.C.: Liberation Support Movement, 1974.

Matson, A. T. *Nandi Resistance to British Rule, 1890–1906*. Nairobi: East Africa Publishing House, 1972.

Mbilinyi, Marjorie. "'I'd Have Been a Man': Politics and Labor Process in Producing Personal Narratives." In Personal Narratives Group, eds., *Interpreting Women's Lives*, pp. 204–27. Bloomington: Indiana University Press, 1989.

Meinertzhagen, Richard. *Army Diary, 1899–1926*. Edinburgh: Oliver and Boyd, 1960.

———. *Kenya Diary, 1902–1906*. Edinburgh: Oliver and Boyd, 1957.

Meyerson, Mark D. "Prostitution of Muslim Women in the Kingdom of Valencia: Religious and Sexual Discrimination in a Medieval Plural Society." In Marilyn J. Chiat and Kathryn L. Ryerson, eds., *The Medieval Mediterranean: Cross-Cultural Contacts*, pp. 87–95. St. Cloud, MN: North Star Press, 1988.

Miller, Eleanor M. *Street Woman*. Philadelphia: Temple University Press, 1987.

Molefi, Rogers K. K. "The Political Ecology of Agriculture and Health in Northwest Tanganyika, 1890–1960." Ph.D. thesis, Dalhousie University, Halifax, Nova Scotia, 1985.

Mosse, George L. *Nationalism and Sexuality*. Madison: University of Wisconsin Press, 1985.

Mungeam, G. H. *British Rule in Kenya, 1895–1912*. Oxford: Oxford University Press, 1966.

Munro, J. Forbes. *Colonial Rule and the Kamba: Social Change in the Kenya Highlands, 1889–1939*. Oxford: Oxford University Press, 1975.

Muriuki, Godfrey. *A History of the Kikuyu, 1500–1900*. Nairobi: Oxford University Press, 1974.

Murname, Mary, and Kay Daniels. "Prostitutes and 'Purveyors of Disease': Venereal Disease Legislation in Tasmania, 1886–1945." *Hecate* 5 (1979), pp. 5–21.

Murray, Jocelyn Margaret. "The Kikuyu Female Circumcision Controversy, with Special Reference to the Church Missionary Society's 'Sphere of Influence.'" Ph.D. thesis, University of California, Los Angeles, 1974.

Murray, Robin. "The Chandarias: The Development of a Kenyan Multinational." In Raphael Kaplinsky, ed., *Readings on the Multinational Corporation in Kenya*, pp. 284–307. Nairobi: Oxford University Press, 1978.

Mwaniki, H. S. Kabeca. *Embu Historical Texts*. Nairobi: East African Literature Bureau, 1974.

Nelson, Nici. "Female Centered Families: Changing Patterns of Marriage and Family among Buzaa Brewers of Mathare Valley." *African Urban Studies* 3 (Winter 1978–79), pp. 85–103.

————. "'Selling Her Kiosk': Kikuyu Notions of Sexuality and Sex for Sale in Mathare Valley, Kenya." In Patricia Caplan, ed., *The Cultural Construction of Sexuality*, pp. 217–39. London and New York: Tavistock, 1987.

————. "'Women Must Help Each Other': The Operation of Personal Networks among *Buzaa* Brewers in Mathare Valley, Kenya." In Patricia Caplan and Janet M. Bujra, eds., *Women United, Women Divided*, pp. 77–98. Bloomington and London: Indiana University Press, 1979.

Odhiambo, Margaret. "Luo Union Nairobi Branch: An African Welfare Organization." B.A. dissertation, University of Nairobi, 1970, History Department Archives, D/7/2.

O'Laughlin, Bridget. "Mediation of Contradiction: Why Mbum Women Do Not Eat Chicken." In Michele Zimbalist Rosaldo and Louise Lamphere, eds., *Women, Culture, and Society*, pp. 301–18. Stanford, CA: Stanford University Press, 1974.

van Onselen, Charles. "Reactions to Rinderpest in Southern Africa, 1896–1897." *Journal of African History* 13 (1972), pp. 473–88.

————. *Studies in the Social and Economic History of the Witwatersrand.* Vol. 1, *New Babylon.* London: Longman, 1982.

Orchardson, I. Q. "Some Traits of the Kipsigis in Relation to Their Contracts with Europeans." *Africa* 4, 1 (1931), pp. 466–74.

Otis, Leah L. *Prostitution in Medieval Society: The History of an Urban Institution in Languedoc.* Chicago: University of Chicago Press, 1985.

Overton, John. "War and Economic Underdevelopment: State Exploitation and African Response in Kenya, 1914–1918." *International Journal of African Historical Studies* 22, 2 (1989), pp. 201–21.

Packard, Randall M., and Paul Epstein. "Epidemiologists, Social Scientists, and the Structure of Medical Research on AIDS in Africa." Essay, 1989.

Parent-Duchatelet, Alexandre-Jean-Baptiste. *De la prostitution de la ville de Paris.* 2 vols. Paris: J.-B. Bailliere, 1836.

Parkin, David. "Kind Bridewealth and Hard Cash: Eventing a Structure." In John L. Comaroff, *The Meaning of Marriage Payments*, pp. 197–220. London and New York: Academic Press, 1980.

Penvenne, Jeanne. "The Streetcorner Press: Worker Intelligence Networks in Lourenço Marques, 1900–1962." Working Paper 26, African Studies Center, Boston University, 1980.

Petrik, Paula. "Capitalists with Rooms: Prostitution in Helena, Montana, 1865–1900." *Montana: The Magazine of Western History* 3 (1981), pp. 28–41.

Phelp, Dr. "Character Sketches: Jonathan and Jason." *Kikuyu News* 86 (December 1923), pp. 1–3.

Phongpaichit, Pasuk. *From Peasant Girls to Bangkok Masseuses.* Geneva: International Labour Organization, 1982.

Pitten, Renee. "Houses of Women: A Focus on Alternative Life-Styles in Katsina City." In Christine Oppong, ed., *Female and Male in West Africa*, pp. 291–302. London: George Allen and Unwin, 1983.

Pivar, David J. "The Military, Prostitution, and Colonized Peoples: India and the Philippines, 1885–1917." *Journal of Sex Research* 17 (August 1981), pp. 256–69.

Presley, Cora Ann. "Kikuyu Women in the 'Mau Mau' Rebellion." In Gary Y. Okihiro, ed., In *Resistance: Studies in African, Caribbean, and Afro-American History*, pp. 54–67. Amherst: University of Massachusetts Press, 1986.

_____. "The Mau Mau Rebellion, Kikuyu Women, and Social Change." *Canadian Journal of African Studies* 22, 3 (1988), pp. 502–27.

_____. "The Transformation of Kikuyu Women and Their Nationalism." Ph.D. thesis, Stanford University, Stanford, CA, 1986.

Prus, Robert, and Styllianoss Irini. *Hookers, Rounders, and Desk Clerks: The Social Organization of a Hotel Community.* Toronto: Gage Publishing, 1980.

✝ Robertson, Claire C. *Sharing the Same Bowl: A Socioeconomic History of Women and Class in Accra, Ghana.* Bloomington: Indiana University Press, 1984.

Rogers, Peter. "The British and the Kikuyu, 1890–1905: A Reassessment." *Journal of African History* 20 (1979), pp. 255–69.

Rosberg, Carl G., Jr., and John Nottingham. *The Myth of "Mau Mau": Nationalism in Kenya.* New York: Praeger, 1966.

Rosen, Ruth. *The Lost Sisterhood: Prostitution in America, 1900–1918.* Baltimore and London: Johns Hopkins University Press, 1982.

Rosen, Ruth, and Sue Davidson. *The Mamie Papers.* Old Westbury, NY: Feminist Press, 1977.

Sanger, William W. *The History of Prostitution: Its Extent, Causes, and Effects throughout the World.* New York: Eugenics Publishing Co., 1937. First published 1897.

Savage, Donald C., and J. Forbes Munro. "Carrier Corps Recruitment in the British East African Protectorate, 1914–1918." *Journal of African History* 7 (1966), pp. 313–42.

Shostak, Marjorie. "'What the Wind Won't Take Away': The Genesis of *Nisa—The Life and Words of a !Kung Woman.*" In Personal Narratives Group, eds., *Interpreting Women's Lives*, pp. 228–40. Bloomington: Indiana University Press, 1989.

Shumsky, Neil Larry, and Larry M. Springer. "San Francisco's Zone of Prostitution, 1880–1934." *Journal of Historical Geography* 7, 1 (1981), pp. 71–89.

Sigsworth, E. M., and T. J. Wyke. "A Study of Victorian Prostitution and Venereal Disease." In Martha Vicinus, ed., *Suffer and Be Still: Women in the Victorian Age*, pp. 77–99. Bloomington and London: Indiana University Press, 1973.

Singh, Makhan. *History of Kenya's Trade Union Movement to 1952.* Nairobi: East African Literature Bureau, 1969.

Southall, Aiden W., and Peter C. W. Gutkind. *Townsmen in the Making: Kampala and Its Suburbs.* Kampala: East African Institute of Social Research, 1957.

Spencer, John. *James Beauttah, Freedom Fighter.* Nairobi: Stellascope Publishing Company, 1983.

_____. "KAU and Mau Mau: Some Connections." *Kenya Historical Review* 5, 2 (1977), pp. 201–24.

_____. *The Kenya African Union.* London: Routledge and Kegan Paul, 1985.

✝ Stamp, Patricia. "Kikuyu Women's Self-Help Groups: Toward an Understanding of the Relations between Sex-Gender Systems and Mode of Production in Africa." In Claire Robertson and Iris Berger, eds., *Women and Class in Africa*, pp. 27–46. New York: Holmes and Meier, 1986.

Stansell, Christine. *City of Women: Sex and Class in New York, 1789–1860*. Urbana and Chicago: University of Illinois Press, 1987.

Stedman Jones, Gareth. *Outcast London: A Study of the Relationship between Classes in Victorian Society*. Oxford: Oxford University Press, 1971.

Stichter, Sharon. *Migrant Labour in Kenya: Capitalism and the African Response*. London: Longman, 1982.

———. "Women and the Labor Force in Kenya, 1895–1964." *Rural Africana* 29 (Winter 1975–76), pp. 45–67.

Stigand, C. H. *The Land of Zini*. London: Constable, 1913.

Stokes, Eric. *English Utilitarians and India*. Oxford: Oxford University Press, 1959.

Storgaard, Brigit. "Women in Ujamaa Villages." *Rural Africana* 29 (Winter 1975–76), pp. 135–56.

Stren, Richard. *Housing the Urban Poor in Africa: Politics, Policy, and Bureaucracy in Mombasa*. Research Series 34. Berkeley: Institute of International Studies, 1978.

Strobel, Margaret. *Muslim Women in Mombasa, 1890–1975*. New Haven and London: Yale University Press, 1979.

Sundkler, B. G. M. "Marriage Problems in the Church in Tanganyika." *International Review of Missions* 34, 134 (1945), pp. 253–66.

Sundkler, Bengt. *Bara Bukoba: Church and Community in Tanzania*. London: C. Hurst and Company, 1980.

Swanson, Maynard W. "The Sanitation Syndrome: Bubonic Plague and Urban Native Policy in the Cape Colony, 1900–1909." *Journal of African History* 18 (1977), pp. 387–410.

Swantz, Marja-Liisa. *Women in Development: A Creative Role Denied?* New York: St. Martin's Press, 1985.

Symanski, Richard. "Prostitution in Nevada." *Annals of the Association of American Geographers* 64, 3 (1974), pp. 357–77.

Thanh-Dam, Truong. "The Dynamics of Sex Tourism: The Case of Southeast Asia." *Development and Change* 14 (1983), pp. 533–53.

Thompson, E. P. "Time, Work-Discipline, and Industrial Capitalism." *Past and Present* 38 (1967), pp. 56–97.

Throup, David W. "The Origins of Mau Mau." *African Affairs* 84 (July 1985), pp. 399–434.

———. *Social and Economic Origins of Mau Mau*. Athens: Ohio University Press, 1987.

Tignor, Robert L. *The Colonial Transformation of Kenya: The Kamba, the Kikuyu, and the Maasai from 1900 to 1939*. Princeton: Princeton University Press, 1976.

Vail, Leroy, and Landeg White. "Forms of Resistance: Songs and Perceptions of Power in Colonial Mozambique." In Donald Crummey, ed., *Banditry, Rebellion, and Social Protest in Africa*, pp. 193–228. London: James Currey, 1986.

Vansina, Jan. *Oral Tradition*. Chicago: Aldine, 1967.

———. *Oral Tradition as History*. Madison: University of Wisconsin, 1985.

Vaughan, Megan. *The Story of an African Famine: Gender and Famine in Twentieth-Century Malawi*. Cambridge: Cambridge University Press, 1987.

Wachanga, H. K. *The Swords of Kirinyaga: The Fight for Land and Freedom*. Nairobi: Kenya Literature Bureau, 1975.

Walkowitz, Judith R. "Jack the Ripper and the Myth of Male Violence." *Feminist Studies* 8, 3 (Fall 1982), pp. 543–74.

_____. "Male Vice and Female Virtue: Feminism and the Politics of Prostitution in Nineteenth-Century Britain." In Ann Snitow, Christine Stansell, and Sharon Thompson, eds., *Desire: The Politics of Sexuality,* pp. 43–61. London: Virago, 1984.

_____. "Myths and Murderers." Review of *The Age of Sex Crime* by Jane Caputi and *The Lust to Kill: A Feminist Investigation of Sexual Murder* by Deborah Cameron and Elizabeth Frazer. *Women's Review of Books* 5, 6 (March 1988), pp. 7–8.

_____. *Prostitution and Victorian Society: Women, Class, and the State.* Cambridge: Cambridge University Press, 1980.

Walkowitz, Judith R., and Daniel J. Walkowitz. "'We Are Not Beasts of the Field': Prostitution and the Poor in Plymouth and Southampton under the Contagious Diseases Act." In Mary Hartman and Lois W. Banner, eds., *Clio's Consciousness Raised: New Perspectives on the History of Women,* pp. 192–225. New York: Harper and Row, 1974.

Waller, Richard. "The Maasai and the British, 1895–1905: The Origins of an Alliance." *Journal of African History* 17 (1976), pp. 529–53.

Wamweya, Joram. *Freedom Fighter.* Nairobi: East Africa Publishing House, 1971.

wa Wanjau, Gakaara. *Mau Mau Author in Detention.* Nairobi: Heinemann, 1988.

Wescott, Nicholas J. "The Impact of the Second World War on Tanganyika, 1939–1949." Ph.D. thesis, Cambridge University, 1982.

White, Luise. "A Colonial State and an African Petty Bourgeoisie." In Frederick Cooper, ed., *Struggle for the City: Migrant Labor, Capital, and the State in Urban Africa,* pp. 167–94. Beverly Hills and London: Sage, 1983.

_____. "Prostitutes, Reformers, and Historians." *Criminal Justice History* 6 (1985), pp. 201–27.

_____. "Prostitution, Differentiation, and the World Economy: Nairobi, 1899–1939." In Marilyn J. Boxer and Jean H. Quataert, eds., *Connecting Spheres: Women in the Western World, 1500 to the Present,* pp. 223–31. Oxford and New York: Oxford University Press, 1986.

_____. "Prostitution, Identity, and Class Consciousness during World War II." *Signs: Journal of Women in Culture and Society* 11, 2 (1986), pp. 255–73.

_____. "Separating the Men from the Boys: Constructions of Sexuality, Gender, and Terrorism in Central Kenya, 1939–1959." *International Journal of African Historical Studies* 23, 1 (1990), pp. 1–26.

_____. "Vice and Vagrants: Prostitution, Housing, and Casual Labour in Nairobi in the Mid-1930s." In Francis Snyder and Douglas Hay, eds., *Labour, Law, and Crime: An Historical Perspective,* pp. 202–27. London: Tavistock, 1987.

_____. "Women's Domestic Labor in a Colonial City: Prostitution in Nairobi, 1900–1950." In Jane Parpart and Sharon Stichter, eds., *Patriarchy and Class: African Women at Home and in the Workplace,* pp. 139–60. Boulder, CO: Westview Press, 1988.

Wilson, G. M., ed. *The Mombasa Social Survey.* Nairobi, 1959. Typescript.

Wright, Marcia. "Women in Peril: A Commentary on the Life Stories of Captives in Nineteenth Century East-Central Africa." *African Social Research* 20 (December 1975), pp. 800–819.

van Zwanenberg, R. M. A. *Colonial Capitalism and Forced Labour in Kenya, 1919–1939*. Nairobi: East African Literature Bureau, 1975.

————. "History and Theory of Urban Poverty in Nairobi: The Case of Slum Development." *Journal of East African Research and Development* 2, 2 (1972), pp. 163–205.

Official Publications: Parliamentary Papers and Reports

Corfield, F. D. *Historical Survey of the Origins and Growth of Mau Mau*. Cmd. 1030. London: HMSO, 1960.

East African Royal Commission 1953–1955. *Report*. Cmd. 9475. London: HMSO, 1955.

Kenya Land Commission. *Evidence*. 2 vols. London: HMSO, 1934.

Kenya Land Commission. *Report*. Cmd. 456. London: HMSO, 1934.

Official Publications: East African Protectorate and Kenya Government

[F. W. Carpenter, chairman]. *Report of the Committee on African Wages*. Nairobi: Government Printer, 1954.

East African Protectorate. Economic Commission. *Final Report*, part 1. Nairobi: Government Printer, 1920.

East African Protectorate. Native Labour Commission 1912–13. *Evidence and Report*. Nairobi: Government Printer, 1913.

Kenya Government. *The Pattern of Income, Expenditure, and Consumption of African Labourers in Nairobi, October–December 1950*. Nairobi: Government Printer, 1951.

Kenya Government. *Report of the Committee Appointed to "Enquire into and Report Whether the Essentials of Life Are beyond the Economic Capacity of Officers of the Government and KUR&H in the Lower Grades."* Nairobi: Government Printer, 1942.

Simpson, W. J. *Report on Sanitary Matters in the East African Protectorate, Uganda, and Zanzibar*. Nairobi: Government Printer, 1914.

Vasey, Ernest A. *The Housing of Africans in the Urban Areas of Kenya*. Nairobi: Kenya Information Office, 1946.

Index